A History of
The Institution of Electrical Engineers
1871-1971

The Institution of Electrical Engineers, Savoy Place

Geoffrey Fletcher

A History of
The Institution of Electrical Engineers
1871–1971
by
W. J. Reader

Based on research by
Rachel Lawrence, Sheila Nemet and Geoffrey Tweedale

Peter Peregrinus Ltd. on behalf of
THE INSTITUTION OF ELECTRICAL ENGINEERS

Published by: Peter Peregrinus Ltd., London, United Kingdom,
on behalf of The Institution of Electrical Engineers.

British Library Cataloguing in Publication Data

Reader, W. J.
     History of the Institution of Electrical
     Engineers, 1871-1971.
     1. Institution of Electrical Engineers—
     History
     I. Title   II. Lawrence, Rachel   III. Nemet,
     Sheila   IV. Tweedale, Geoffrey
     621.3'06'041   TK1.I427
     ISBN 0 86341 103 7

The text for this book was prepared on IBM System 6 and BBC Micro
floppy discs by the author.
Millford Reprographics International Ltd converted the data from the
floppy discs using an Intermedia Multi-disc Reader on-line to a CCI
Europe CX2000 phototypesetting system. The text pages were produced
using the CCI "Bookbuilder" automatic pagination program and output on
a Linotype Ltd Linotron 202WL phototypesetter.
The book is typeset in 12/14 Bembo.

Printed in England by Short Run Press Ltd., Exeter

CONTENTS

Foreword

Rollo Appleyard's *History of the Institution of Electrical Engineers*, published in 1939, covered the years from 1871 to 1931. Towards the end of 1981 I was invited by Sir James Redmond and his colleagues on the IEE's Editorial Panel to produce a survey of the Institution's existence which would concentrate chiefly on the century following the foundation of the Society of Telegraph Engineers in 1871 and glance more briefly at events since then. Sir James and the members of the Panel have given me a free hand in carrying out the work and I am most grateful to them for their sustained and genial interest in its progress.

Mrs E D P Symons, the Institution's Archivist, has supported the project with professional skill, unfailing enthusiasm and the hospitality of her departmental coffee pot. I should like to thank her and to thank Miss Jean Robertson, her secretary, for shepherding my typescript through a long process of drafting.

I have had steady support, shrewd comment and active help both from Mr H H W Losty, the Secretary to the Institution, and from Mr M E Smythe, Director of Professional Services. Professor J M Meek, Past President, Dr G F Gainsborough, formerly Secretary, and the late Mr A T Crawford have been kind enough to give me the benefit of their knowledge of the Institution in commenting on the text, and Dr Brian Bowers of the Science Museum has allowed me to draw freely on his knowledge of the history of electrical engineering. I am grateful to them all and also to those who have given me interviews, often with hospitality as well. Their names are listed among my sources of information in Appendix 9.

I am deeply indebted to Mrs Rachel Lawrence for her research on the years up to 1939; to Mrs Sheila Nemet for hers on the years after that and for much painstaking work on the completed text; and to Dr Geoffrey Tweedale for his work on Victorian membership statistics: a most laborious task. The book is theirs as well as mine, and I hope they will derive some satisfaction from the use I have made of the effort they have put into it.

Cambridge   WJR
November 1986

List of Tables and Figures

Part One: The Telegraph Engineers

The Great Eastern during the 1865 Atlantic cable laying voyage. (IEE Archives)

Chapter 1

The Emergence of the Telegraph Engineer, 1837–1870

The Institution of Electrical Engineers came into existence, as the Society of Telegraph Engineers, in 1871. At that time middle-class Englishmen, for whose benefit, largely, the Society was founded and the Institution still exists, lived in a wide and hopeful world. At home, the world's first industrial economy supported the world's richest nation, and the wealth which industry created was flowing ever more widely through society: during the 1870s the standard of living, in so far as it is measurable by the consumption per head of sugar, tea and tobacco, rose by 39 per cent (sugar), 36 per cent (tea) and 11 per cent (tobacco),[1] and plenty of other evidence, numerical and literary, points the same way. There were problems – plenty of them – but in the widely admired political framework of Victorian England, in which individual liberty and respect for authority were balanced as nowhere else, solutions would surely be found. 'The Victorian era', said the President of the IEE in 1901, 'will ever shine forth as a lustrous jewel in the history of the world.'[2]

Abroad, the British Empire did not reach its largest extent until the 1920s, when it was not far from collapse, but in the early 1870s an engineer could find plenty of scope for his talents in India, while in 'the colonies' – those vast areas of white settlement in Canada, at the Cape and in Natal, in Australia and New Zealand – an Englishman could travel and earn his living as freely as at home. Americans had been so ill-advised as to leave the Empire. Nevertheless the United States remained, in the words of J R Seeley, Regius Professor of History at Cambridge in 1883, 'almost as good as a colony; our people can emigrate thither without sacrificing their language or chief institutions or habits'.[3] To the south of the United States the Latin American countries were rich with opportunity, though Seeley might have thought them less attractive for emigration.

On the Continent, no country in the 1870s yet presented any serious industrial competition to Great Britain except Germany. The power of Germany and its army, made apparent on the battlefields of France in 1870-1871, excited the admiration of one of the leading military members of the IEE, General Webber, who referred in 1894 to 'the army of the greatest nation in Europe'.[4] German industrial power was already causing uneasiness in the early 1870s, but not so acutely as later, though in the field of telegraph engineering, an English speciality, the firm of Siemens & Halske had been growing since 1847.[5]

On the furthest eastern horizon, Japan was thrusting into the circle, still small, of industrial nations. With great shrewdness and persistence, the Japanese were seeking the best practice in all fields – industrial, commercial, military, naval and administrative – and the best instruction. In 1873 a twenty-six-year-old Englishman, W E Ayrton, became Professor of Natural Philosophy and Telegraphy in the Imperial College of Engineering, Tokyo, and in 1875 John Perry joined him as Professor of Engineering. Each later became FRS and President of the IEE.[6]

This world was an engineer's world. In the 1860s and 1870s the Thames was being embanked and the London drainage system was being laid out; telegraph cables were being laid across continents and through oceans; transcontinental railways were being pushed across the USA; the St Gotthard and Severn Tunnels were under construction. 'At the head of all the new professions', wrote a well-known journalist and social commentator, 'must be placed that of the civil engineer... [His profession] is the pioneer of progress and civilisation, moral and material, all the world over; it gratifies that adventurous instinct which is the heritage of the English race. The civil engineer who spans rocky defiles, pierces mountains, unites continents, and by designing new schemes of railway and telegraphic extension annihilates space and time, is the modern representative of the navigator of the Elizabethan era... who sailed over remote seas in quest of new lands and fresh enemies to subjugate. The head master of a large public school recently observed to the present writer that three out of every four of his pupils would, if polled, declare for engineering.'[7]

'Civil engineer' was a wide-ranging term brought into use in the eighteenth century to distinguish the engineer whose works were peaceful – docks, harbours, canals, bridges, roads – from the 'Royal Engineer' whose business lay mainly with fortifications. By 1818, in the expanding economy of the early Industrial Revolution, civil engineers were sufficiently confident of their own identity to found the Institution of Civil Engineers. It was chiefly concerned, as it still is, with public works, but another branch of the engineering profession was coming into prominence: mechanical engineering. The civil engineers saw no reason why their Institution should not embrace it. In 1824 Thomas Tredgold, redefining the objects of the Institution of Civil Engineers, started with 'the general advancement of Mechanical Science' and went on to mention 'the art of directing the Great Sources of Power in Nature'.[8]

Then and much later the great constructors, and others, were inclined to look down on mechanical engineers. What, after all, were they, but upstart mechanics? 'The machine engineers', said H Byerley Thomson in 1857, 'are not strictly civil engineers, nor are they in the sense of our original definition, professional men.'[9] His 'original definition' defined a profession as an occupation in which 'a man for a reward places at the public service his intellectual labour, and the fruits of intellectual knowledge, and experience', so that the clear implication of Thomson's remarks was that, however good a 'machine engineer' might be with his hands, he had no great need for his brain.

Not surprisingly, perhaps, the Civils and the Mechanicals did not find each other's company congenial, and the Mechanicals thought the Civils paid too much attention to their members in London and too little to those in the provinces. In 1847 the Institution of Mechanical Engineers was set up – in Birmingham.

In the disharmony between the Civils and the Mechanicals various enduring problems of professional organisation presented themselves. How far could one institution look after the interests of a profession's various branches, especially new ones as they sprouted to meet the demands of new technology? Where should the dividing line be drawn between the professional man and the artisan, the technician and the craftsman? How could a fair balance be struck between London and the provinces?

These problems are not peculiar to engineering. If we consider some of their nineteenth-century manifestations we find that the Law Society was founded in 1825, within the general framework of the legal profession, to look after solicitors as distinct from (if necessary, in opposition to) barristers; that the Pharmaceutical Society came into existence in 1841 in response to the doctors' determination to keep apothecaries out of medical practice; that when the British Medical Association was formed in Worcester in 1832 (as the Provincial Medical and Surgical Association) one of its aims was 'Maintenance of the Honour and Respectability of the Profession generally in the Provinces'.[10]

By the time the Mechanicals set up house for themselves, in 1847, another branch of engineering was beginning to emerge, dedicated, in Tredgold's words (slightly paraphrased) to 'the art of directing [one of] the Great Sources of Power in Nature' – electricity. In 1843 an article on 'Recent Applications of Electricity to the Arts' appeared in *Companion to the Almanac*, a serious-minded annual publication put out with the *British Almanac* by the Society for the Diffusion of Useful Knowledge whose Chairman was Lord Brougham.

'There are periods in the history of all the sciences', says the author of the article, 'when truths, hitherto known and studied only by philosophers, become the property of the world at large, by being rendered applicable to directly useful purposes.' 'The useful applications of *electricity*', he goes on to say, 'have been so recent, and the strides now making so gigantic, that there has not been time to classify and illustrate them. One week's discoveries may greatly surpass those of the previous week, and the mind is almost bewildered by the various paths in which art is receiving contributions from science.'[11] The 'useful applications of *electricity*' were lightning conductors, copper sheathing (an unsuccessful attempt by Sir Humphry Davy to cure corrosion of ships' copper bottoms by electrolytic action), submarine operations (chiefly clearing wrecks and blasting rock with black powder), electric moving power and electro locomotive power (both very tentative), electrical telegraph, electro-metallurgy, electro-gilding and plating, electrotype and electrotint. Of all these applications, when the article was written, the most spectacular was the electrical telegraph, which represented by far the most advanced electrical technology of its day, comparable perhaps with the technology of data processing in the 1980s.

Electric telegraphy, so called to distinguish it from visual telegraphy which was already well known, was being developed, in the 1830s, in various forms in various countries. It was first brought to commercial success in Great Britain. There, in the congenial atmosphere of the most advanced industrial economy of the day, two unlikely, uneasy partners – W F Cooke, an Indian Army officer turned medical student, and Charles Wheatstone, a scientific investigator of great brilliance with a practical turn of mind – succeeded from 1837 onward in applying electric telegraphy to the purposes of another technical wonder of the age: the railways. About eight years later Cooke and Wheatstone sold their rights for £120,000 to the Electric Telegraph Company, incorporated by Act of Parliament on 18 June 1846 as the first large undertaking in the newest of all industries, the electrical industry.[12]

Twenty-two years later, in 1868, there were 4,119 telegraph offices in the United Kingdom and 22,036 miles of line.

In the Empire, India and the colonies were developing their own systems. Even more ambitious were the great oceanic cable routes, which in 1866 entered their greatest period with the layout of the first permanently successful Atlantic cable from Brunel's immense steamship *Great Eastern*. London, said Charles W Siemens in 1873, was 'the principal centre of the Telegraphic enterprise of the world', and he pointed out 'the remarkable fact that the manufacture of insulated wire and of submarine cables, is almost entirely confined to the banks of the Thames.'[13]

This was all good news for the middle classes, for in Samuel Smiles's England good jobs were not plentiful. Unless a boy had powerful 'interest' to get him into, say, an £80-a-year Government clerkship or sufficient ability to succeed in the ferociously competitive exams which were just coming into vogue, such as those for the fabulously well-paid Indian Civil Service; unless his father could place him in a family business or professional practice or provide him with training and capital to set up on his own, his prospects were bleak. A girl's were even bleaker, but then women who had to support themselves were not really fit for polite society, and of course no lady would dream of doing so if she did not have to. She could hardly remain a lady if she did.

In 1870 the telegraph companies in the United Kingdom were employing about 2,030 men and 470 women. Of the women it was said: 'They have quickness of eye and ear and delicacy of touch, they are more patient than men during long sitting in one spot and take more kindly to sedentary employment; they will willingly work for lower wages than men; the remuneration will tempt women of fairly good education, while men equally well educated would seek for … higher pay; and lastly, women are less disposed than men to "strike".' With that glance at the women telegraph operators of 1870, 'bringing with them the materials for their own dinners, but … provided gratuitously with cooking vessels, crockery, table-linen, firing and attendance',[14] we shall leave them. Telegraph operators they were and telegraph operators they would remain, in no way fit to become members of a professional institution.

The same would have been true of most of the 2,000 men, but not of all, for amongst the employees of the telegraph companies, ever since the companies had been formed, a new kind of engineer had been emerging, and an engineer's prospects were much brighter than a telegraph clerk's, but becoming a clerk might be a step on the road to becoming an engineer. The term 'electrical engineer', in 1870, had barely come into use, but the 'telegraph engineer' had to know a good deal about electricity, and that marked him off sharply from the Civils and the Mechanicals.

Civil and mechanical engineers worked largely by the light of experience and were sceptical, as a rule, of theory and 'book learning'. So were some telegraph engineers, but none could afford to ignore scientific principles entirely. They were the essential foundation of telegraph engineering, without which it could not exist. Moreover, knowledge of electricity, rightly regarded as a most mysterious phenomenon, bordering on the supernatural, could only be extended by experiment and calculation. The telegraph engineer was the first kind of engineer who, to do his job properly, had to share the outlook of the scientist as well as being a competent technologist. 'The engineer', said Sir William Preece at the turn of the century, 'must be a scientific man.'[15] He was speaking, by then, of engineers in general, but the telegraph engineers had led the way.

From the earliest days, therefore, becoming a telegraph engineer required a fairly high standard of education, preferably with a scientific bias to it. That would be expensive: so would a period of apprenticeship afterwards. The more eminent among the early telegraph engineers (probably the less eminent, too, but information is hard to come by) came from comfortably middle-class surroundings and moved in circles where scientific pursuits were cultivated and where many individuals knew one another, so that a promising young man could fairly easily get useful introductions.

All this is certainly true of Sir William Cooke. His father was a surgeon in Ealing, at a time (Sir William was born in 1806) when surgeons represented the most enterprising and scientifically minded branch of the medical profession. He went to Edinburgh University and thence into the Indian Army, which suggests influential patronage, since Indian cadetships in the 1820s were eagerly sought and were not offered in open competition. He was introduced to Wheatstone by Michael Faraday and P M Roget (1779-1869), 'physician and savant', who was one of the founders of the University of London and compiler of the *Thesaurus of English Words and Phrases*.[16] Wheatstone himself came from a provincial background, being the son of a music-shop proprietor in Gloucester, but from the age of twenty-one he was in business as a musical instrument maker in London, where his versatile brilliance carried him into the centre of the scientific world of the day.

A rather similar pattern of family circumstances, educational influences and personal connections can be traced among some of the pioneers of long-distance submarine cables. Sir Charles Tilston Bright (1832-1888), though born near Wanstead, Essex, belonged to a family of Yorkshire gentry. On the strength of 'family connections on the governing body', he was educated at Merchant Taylors' School and, with his brothers, was intended for Oxford, but 'heavy pecuniary losses on the part of their father' prevented that, and young Charles, being much interested in electricity and chemistry, answered an advertisement in *The Times* 'for gentlemen's sons with education' and became a telegraph clerk with the Electric Telegraph Company at Harrow Station on the London & North-Western Railway.[17]

Cromwell Varley (1828-1883), who claimed descent from the Lord Protector, was the son of Cornelius Varley (1781-1873) whose talents ran with equal success to water-colour painting and to the design of optical instruments. John Varley (1776-1842), an uncle, was a landscape painter, a highly successful and influential art teacher, and an astrologer. A cousin, Andrew Pritchard (1804-1882), was a microscopist. Cromwell Varley himself studied telegraphy after he left school, and in 1846, 'through the influence of William Fothergill Cooke', he was engaged by the Electric Telegraph Company, thus starting a career which was to lead him to the heights of his profession.[18] Two of his brothers also became telegraph engineers.

The brothers Edwin and Latimer Clark, responsible between them, according to Latimer's obituary, 'for the construction of much of the telegraphic system of this country', came to engineering by routes which show how fluid and undifferentiated technical occupations were in the first half of the nineteenth century. Edwin (1814-1894) was at first a mathematics master, Latimer (1822-1898) an industrial chemist, and both were railway surveyors. Edwin was superintending engineer, under Robert Stephenson, for the building of the Britannia Bridge across the Menai Straits and then, having attracted the attention of J L Ricardo, MP, Chairman of the Electric Telegraph Company, he became Chief Engineer to that company. Latimer accompanied him as his assistant in both appointments, and when Edwin retired, at forty, he succeeded him, in 1854. Further we will not, at present, follow him, except to remark that from about 1860 onward he was becoming more and more preoccupied with his own enterprises and that after he died his obituarist called him 'a civil engineer in the broadest sense'.[19]

In 1854 Latimer Clark married Margaret Helen Preece, which was fortunate for her brother, William Henry Preece (1834–1913). He had been intending to become an army officer (most unusual, at that time, for a middle-class boy) but by 1852 his father, a businessman who had done well in Caernarvon, where W H Preece was born, but badly after he moved to London, had lost so much money that he could no longer contemplate the expense of buying William a commission and subsidising his pay. Instead, in a manner much more suited to William's social position, Latimer Clark, presumably already in love with Margaret Helen, introduced him to Edwin, and he joined the Electric Telegraph Company in March 1853.[20] He was engaged as a clerk, but he did not long remain one: rumbustious and able, he went to the top of the postal telegraph service.

Such, then, were some of the ablest of the young men who came into the profession of telegraph engineering when it was new. Young men who rapidly began attaching a string of patents, papers and other publications to their names, demonstrating an enquiring, inventive and enterprising turn of mind. Opportunity opened before them, uncluttered by past experience, unblocked by seniors reluctant to give way, for telegraphy – like the railways a few years earlier, like some branches of electronic technology 140 years later – was on the crest of its earliest, freest wave of expansion.

They came from the same social level that was supplying the other expanding professions of mid-Victorian England, but in one important respect the telegraph engineer differed from the typical professional man of his day. To get a start, unless he had a place waiting for him in a family practice, the young doctor, lawyer, architect or civil engineer usually had to face the cost and risk of setting up on his own or in partnership. Not so the telegraph engineer. He could confidently hope for salaried employment, but at the same time, once he had established himself, there was no obstacle to going into business on his own, very profitably, like Latimer Clark, Cromwell Varley, Sir Charles Bright and many others.

The telegraph engineer's profession might seem essentially peaceful, but at the first Ordinary General Meeting of the Society of Telegraph Engineers (page 22), in February 1872, Captain Dawson, RN, suggested other possibilities. He rose and addressed the President: 'You have explained, Sir, very fully that the Society intends to discuss the application of electricity to civilised purposes. Do you propose to discuss its application to the uncivilised purposes of war?'

The President was evidently disconcerted. 'I think', he replied, 'I should ask for a little explanation of what you mean by "uncivilised purposes".'

Captain Dawson's reply was brief and brutal: 'The uncivilised purposes of civilised war.'[21]

Captain Dawson, as a sailor, may have been thinking chiefly of the electrically fired static 'torpedoes' ('mines' seems to be the appropriate modern word) which were widely used in harbour defences during the American Civil War and later, but from the time of the Crimean War (1854-1856) onward, field telegraphs were rising in military importance. 'It was clearly shown in the campaign of 1866 [the "Seven Weeks' War" between Prussia and Austria]', said a speaker before the Society of Telegraph Engineers in 1872, 'that modern warfare was almost an impossibility without the aid of the electric telegraph in the field.'[22] Some commanders, it may be added, did not like this new-fangled gadgetry very much. They thought it gave their superiors far too much opportunity to interfere with their freedom of action.

In the British Army responsibility for all things technical, except guns, lay with the Royal Engineers. Until 1871 'telegraphy' seems chiefly to have meant visual signalling, although short lines had been laid in the Crimea and in India during the Mutiny, and the Army Telegraph School, in 1872, was reported to have trained 350 men since 1857 and to have sent twenty-eight telegraphists to Persia. Then in 1871 a Field Telegraph Troop, RE, was set up, with an establishment of four officers, forty-one NCOs, and twenty signallers in a total strength of 249. Twelve wire wagons were provided, each carrying 3 miles of insulated wire.[23] The Royal Engineers were set to become large employers of telegraphists and telegraph engineers.

Victorian officers of the Royal Engineers and Royal Artillery had the advantage, denied to their civilian contemporaries, of being trained at the Royal Military Academy, Woolwich ('The Shop'), one of the very few establishments in the United Kingdom which concentrated on technical and scientific education. The course of study there was serious; the entrance examination, which replaced patronage in 1857, was stiff; competition for entry was severe, because success at Woolwich opened a gateway not only to military distinction but to opportunities in civil life as well. Sir Edward Sabine (1788-1883), after active service in the Royal Artillery at the end of the Napoleonic Wars, entered on a scientific career of the utmost distinction which culminated in ten years (1861-1871) as President of the Royal Society. Sir Vivian Majendie (1836-1898), another gunner, served in the Indian Mutiny and then became HM Chief Inspector of Explosives for nearly thirty years (1871-1898), from which post he exerted a decisive influence on the development of the British explosives industry. Inspecting officers of railways, who presided over enquiries into accidents, were always graduates of Woolwich, and they still are.

Officers of the Royal Engineers were numerous and prominent in the affairs of the Society of Telegraph Engineers, passing easily between military and civil applications of telegraphs, particularly after the inland telegraphs, under the Post Office, became another branch of the public service. Nor were the benefits of military technical training confined to officers. Other ranks also, on leaving the Army, transferred their skill to the expanding Post Office service.

Outside 'The Shop' scientific education, which the telegraph engineer badly needed, was very much on the outskirts of the educational establishment: engineering even more so, despite the establishment in 1827 of a course in 'mechanical philosophy' at University College, London; of a department of civil engineering, in 1838, at King's College, London, where Wheatstone was already Professor of Experimental Physics; and of a Chair of Civil Engineering and Mechanics at Glasgow in 1840. Durham University, founded in 1832, had an engineering department from the first, but it languished under the scepticism of engineering employers. Neither science nor engineering formed any necessary part of the much admired 'liberal education' – the education of a gentleman – which was dispensed in the public schools and in the universities of Oxford and Cambridge. That, especially at school, was directed at training character, not intellect, and at introducing a boy to the world of his social equals; but in so far as intellectual training entered into the matter at all, it was exclusively based on classical studies.

Professional education, whether for engineering or any other occupation, was something you went elsewhere for: to tutors and private establishments set up to meet an emerging demand. They had none of the prestige of the 'great schools', where they were looked down upon as 'crammers', but their teaching was adapted to a sense of purpose in their pupils which was lacking in most of the victims of the public schools' rigid classicism. They had also to reckon with their customers' determination to get value for money. There is no doubt that many of them taught very well. The names of most of them are lost, but from an obituary dealing with the very early years of telegraph engineering we get a glimpse of Kennington Technical College. There was a similar establishment in City Road, London, another in Chester, and there must have been many more, particularly as the demand for training in electrical theory grew in the latter part of the century. [24] As time went on, the problem of professional education became an enduring preoccupation of telegraph engineers and their successors, electrical engineers.

The supremacy of the classics did not go unchallenged, even close to the heart of the Establishment. F W Farrar (1831-1903), Dean of Canterbury, author of *Eric, or Little by Little*, and himself at one time a schoolmaster, argued in 1868 that a scientific education would be more useful than the Classics; 'And no sooner have I uttered the word "useful"', he went on, 'than I imagine the hideous noise which will environ me, and amid the hubbub I faintly distinguish the words vulgar, utilitarian, mechanical ... Well, before this storm of customary and traditional clamour I bow my head, and when it is over, I meekly repeat that it would be *more useful* . . . One would really think that it was a crime to aim at the material happiness of the human race.'[25]

The weight of educational orthodoxy, as Farrar said, was against him. Of 507 professors in the universities and other institutions in the United Kingdom in 1871, eighty-five dealt with scientific subjects other than medicine,[26] but although science at the professorial level was regarded as an acceptable, even admirable, pursuit for gifted individuals – Charles Wheatstone, William Thomson, James Clerk-Maxwell, all 'electricians', come to mind, and others later – yet scientific education for undergraduates was looked down upon in comparison with the humanities. But then undergraduates themselves were a rare species. Matthew Arnold, in 1866, said there were 6,362 in Prussia, with $18^{1}/_{2}$ million inhabitants, but in the United Kingdom, among a population of 30 million, 3,500. He thought there should have been 8,000.[27]

There were few Victorian undergraduates because, generally speaking, the Victorians considered that university education led to very few careers. Broadly, in descending order of indispensability of university education, they were: the Church and schoolmastering (*not* schoolteaching), which were closely intertwined; the higher branches of the Civil Service and the Indian Civil Service once competitive entry was established; politics and journalism, chiefly for the contacts which residence at Oxford or Cambridge would bring; medicine, but Oxford or Cambridge would be very much an optional extra and it was possible to qualify, as it still is, without taking a degree at all; finally, the law, although neither barristers nor solicitors needed to go to a university and it was most unusual for solicitors to do so. None of these careers, with the arguable exception of medicine, was a scientific career, and the list stops well short of telegraph engineering, or indeed of engineering of any sort, even though by 1871 there were twelve engineering professorships, none of them at Oxford or Cambridge.

The traditional English road to a professional career did not lie through a university but through apprenticeship: 'learning by doing'. For the solicitor, that meant an articled clerkship; for the doctor, 'walking the wards'; for the civil engineer, pupilage in the drawing office and on the site; for the mechanical engineer, 'going through the mill'. 'Premium apprentices', heading for a professional career, were marked off from apprentices on the way to becoming skilled tradesmen by the fees which their parents paid and by the expectation that they would study in their spare time. Engineering employers as a rule were apt to be scornful of academic achievements and young men who had them might find it politic to keep them hidden. The idea that engineers might qualify by examination was far, very far indeed, from the minds of most mid-century engineering employers, although Sir John Rennie, a most eminent civil engineer, said as early as 1867, speaking of his own profession, that qualification by examination was 'the only method by which it can take rank amongst the learned professions.'[28]

For the very early telegraph engineers, in the nature of the case, apprenticeships in factories directly concerned with telegraph supplies must have been difficult or impossible to find, and we have seen that several of the most eminent went directly into the employment of the telegraph companies. A little later, training as a mechanical engineer became an accepted route to telegraph engineering and then to electrical engineering. Sir James Douglas (1826–1898), who made his career in the building of lighthouses, was 'regularly apprenticed to a firm of mechanical engineers'. He became a member of the Institution of Civil Engineers and of the IEE, but he did not join the Mechanicals. R O G Drummond (1862–1898), a generation later, went through Mather & Platt's works and became an electrical engineer in South Africa after working as a mechanical engineer for the Cape Government Railways. Arthur Cecil, Lord Sackville (1848–1898), was sent by his father, the second Marquess of Salisbury, to live with his brothers and a tutor 'in the old half-ruined manor house at Cranborne' where 'much after the fashion of colonial life' the Marquess made his boys 'provide their comforts and luxuries by their own personal labour and exertion'. Then Lord Sackville went through two railway workshops, belonging to the Great Eastern and the Great Northern, before he became chief electrician under Sir Charles Bright for the laying of the submarine cable from Marseilles to Boma.[29]

Telegraph engineers had to make their way in a country where scientific education was undervalued. Nevertheless science itself – 'natural philosophy' – was highly regarded as a branch of knowledge, eminently suitable for the attention of gentlemen of independent means (there were not many salaried posts available for scientists) and intellectual curiosity. The foundation in 1660 of the Royal Society of London for the Promotion of Natural Knowledge conferred on scientific pursuits a cachet which they never afterwards lost, and the list of independent investigators in the eighteenth and nineteenth centuries – some, but not many, active in the universities, others in laboratories which they fitted out for themselves – is long and illustrious, including Henry Cavendish (1731–1810), Sir George Cayley (1773–1857), Sir George Lyell (1797–1875), W H Fox Talbot (1800–1877), Charles Darwin (1809–1882), James Joule (1818–1889), James Clerk-Maxwell (1831–1879) and Lord Rayleigh (1842–1919).[30]

The leading scientists of Victorian England, as these names suggest, were an influential group: men of substance with backing at the highest levels in society, especially while the Prince Consort was alive (he died in 1861). They were well aware of the value of publicity and of the need to communicate amongst themselves, and over many years they and their predecessors had built up a network of institutional arrangements, heavily concentrated in London but distributed also through Edinburgh, Dublin and the provinces, for lectures, demonstrations, publication of new work and, naturally, for thoroughly enjoyable controversy, professional politics and feuding.

At the head of all stood the Royal Society of London, drastically reorganised in 1846 when new Statutes were brought in which had the effect, over a generation, of changing the Society 'from a body of well-educated and cultivated men, of whom probably only one-third or rather more could be classed as men of science, to a scientific institution of the highest rank'.[31] The Royal Institution, founded in 1799, chartered in 1800, gave Sir Humphry Davy and Michael Faraday both research facilities and publicity, and from 1826 onward disseminated scientific information to a wide and fashionable audience in its Friday evening Discourses. The most ambitious venture in scientific publicity and public relations was the foundation of the British Association for the Advancement of Science in 1831. The founders took full advantage of the social standing of leading men of science, of their connections in every desirable direction and of the widespread interest in science generally. Moreover they avoided basing their new creation in London and took the risk of launching it, like a scientific Flying Dutchman, on a ceaseless peregrination round the cities of the British Isles and, later, of the British Empire.[32]

The *British Almanac* for 1871 lists eighty 'learned societies and institutions' in London. By no means were all scientific. The list includes the Royal Academy and the Society for Promoting the Employment of Additional Curates, besides the Historical Society and the Royal National Lifeboat Institution. There were sufficient, nevertheless, to cater for a wide range of scientific interests, for besides the Royal Society, the Royal Institution and the British Association there were half a dozen societies or so which specialised in various branches of science, as well as the Institution of Civil Engineers and numerous medical societies. Bernard Becker, in his book *Scientific London*, published in 1874,[33] listed sixteen 'great Scientific Institutions of which London ... is justly proud' including both the Institution of Civil Engineers and, by that time, the Society of Telegraph Engineers.

Outside London, the *Almanac* lists nine 'learned societies and institutions' in Edinburgh, including the Royal Society of Edinburgh, and in Dublin, five. In the provinces, the authors of *Gentlemen of Science* have identified over seventy scientific societies in 1850, and the number was on the increase. They were particularly strong, as might be expected, in Birmingham, Manchester and other great industrial towns, often going under the name of Literary and Philosophical Societies,[34] which commonly indicates the influence of Unitarians, well known for their predisposition towards science.

In London, societies met during a 'session' which lasted, roughly, from the beginning of November until the end of May or a little later. Meetings would be held fortnightly, with occasional special events such as conversaziones, dinners, exhibitions and so on, and the British Association would meet, outside London, in May or October; thus completing a pattern of activity which Dr Sophie Forgan has charted in all its complex detail.[35] There was a good deal of overlapping membership, especially among the more eminent savants and among able and ambitious men with their way to make, and during the season they would be bustling about, almost - sometimes quite – to the point of exhaustion, delivering a paper before one society, discussing someone else's before another, corresponding with each other, forming cliques, destroying reputations here, making them there, advancing their protégés' interests and their own, and generally participating in the advancement of science.

This was the world, the world of science, to which the telegraph engineers felt they belonged, but for many years there was no society catering specifically for them, nor, despite the great interest which electricity aroused, for 'electricians' generally. The Electrical Society of London, founded in 1837, just as electric telegraphy was beginning, had a brief, sad history. At one time it had ninety-six members who paid their subscriptions and an unspecified number who did not, but printing costs were heavy – the Society ambitiously undertook to print all papers presented – and expenses ruled high. The Society ran hopelessly short of money, its last meeting was held in 1843, and in 1845 it ceased to exist, having failed to survive the critical early period which many societies go through, when initial enthusiasm has faded, new members are not being attracted, and too many existing members fall behind with their subscriptions. During this dismal period the Secretary was C V Walker, who in 1876 became President of the Society of Telegraph Engineers.[36]

Telegraph engineers had the option of joining one or other of the existing engineering institutions. Several did, some joined both, and a few became prominent in the other institutions' affairs. The Civils, whose institution was felt to be the Great Mother of all engineers, were perfectly willing to receive the telegraph engineers, but the telegraph engineers, like the Mechanicals twenty or thirty years earlier, could hardly help feeling overshadowed.

The telegraph engineers of England, about 1870, were fully conscious of their standing as the leaders of their profession throughout the world, and their profession was growing. They never seem to have developed a sense of grievance towards the Civils as the Mechanicals did – quite the reverse, in fact – but, like the Mechanicals, they reached a point where they were no longer prepared to put up with a subordinate position within the Institution of Civil Engineers, which they always called, with great respect, the 'parent Institution'. They set about founding their own society: the Society of Telegraph Engineers.

References
1   Peter Mathias: *The First Industrial Nation*, 2nd Ed., 1983, p.419
2   W Langdon: 'Presidential Address', *J.IEE*, 1901, **31**, p.255
3   J R Seeley: *The Expansion of England*, 2nd Ed., 1911 Reprint, p.69

4   *J.IEE*, 1894, **23**, p.35

5   J D Scott: *Siemens Brothers 1858–1958*, 1958, p.24

6   Rollo Appleyard: *History of the Institution of Electrical Engineers (1871–1931)*, 1939, pp.291–292

7   T H S Escott: *England: its People, Polity and Pursuits*, 1885, pp.554–555

8   Sir R Wynne Edwards: 'A New Look at the Old' in T L Dennis (Ed): *Engineering Societies in the Life of a Country*, 1968, p.29

9   H Byerley Thomson: *The Choice of a Profession*, 1857, pp.300–301

10   Paul Vaughan: *Doctors' Commons*, 1959, p.8

11   *British Almanac and Companion 1843*: Companion, p.1

12   *DNB*, 1975: Articles on W F Cooke, Sir Charles Wheatstone; also Brian Bowers: *A History of Electric Light and Power*, 1982, pp.27–33

13   Sir W Siemens: Presidential Address, *J.STE*, 1872, **1**, p.27

14   *British Almanac and Companion, 1872*: Companion, p.88

15   Quoted by Prof. G F Fitzgerald: *J.IEE*, 1900, **29**, pp.399–400

16   *DNB*, Articles on Cooke, Roget

17   Charles Bright: *The Life Story of Sir Charles Tilston Bright, Civil Engineer*, 1908, pp.1–6

18   *DNB*, Article on Varley, C F. See also Varley, Cornelius; Varley, John; Pritchard, Andrew

19   *DNB*, Article on Clark, Joseph Latimer; Obituary, *J.IEE*, 1898, **27**, p.670

20   E C Baker: *Sir William Preece FRS, Victorian Engineer Extraordinary*, 1976, p.40

21   *J.STE*, 1872, **1**, p.35

22   *J.STE*, 1872, **1**, p.188

23   *J.STE*, 1872, **1**, p.173; Reference 6, p.40

24   *J.STE*, 1872–1873, **1**, p.139

25   F W Farrar: 'Public School Education', *Fortnightly Review*, 1868, **3** (new series), p.242

26   *British Almanac and Companion 1871*: Almanac, pp.58–67

27   Matthew Arnold: 'Report on Secondary Education' in Schools Enquiry Commission – *General Reports of Assistant Commissioners*, Vol.4, 1868, p.633

28   Sir John Rennie, *Autobiography*, 1875, p.431

29   Obituary notices, *J.IEE*, 1899, **28**, pp.672,673,666

30   Trevor I Williams (Ed): *A Biographical Dictionary of Scientists*, 1974, articles as listed

31   *The Record of the Royal Society of London for the Promotion of Natural Knowledge*, 1940, p.58

32   Jack Morrell and Arnold Thackray: *Gentlemen of Science*, 1981, *passim*

33   Bernard Becker and Henry S Cooke: *Scientific London*, 1874, p.v

34   Reference 31, p.12

35   Sophie Forgan: 'Science and the Metropolitan Map of Learning',
     unpublished conference paper presented at the Royal Institution Work-
     shop on 'Scientific London', 18 Feb. 1982. Copy in IEE Archives
36   IEE Archives SC Mss 42; *J.STE*, 1876, **5**, pp.13–19; Reference 6,
     pp. 19–22

Chapter 2

The Society of Telegraph Engineers: Foundation and Membership

In the summer of 1870 the Postal Telegraph Department had not long been formed to take over the telegraph system in the United Kingdom, and in June the 22nd Company of the Royal Engineers were working for the Department, putting in order a telegraph route alongside the Uxbridge–Oxford road which had been neglected by its former owners while they waited for nationalisation. One 'broiling afternoon' the men knocked off work for an hour and the officer in command, a thirty-two-year-old Captain called C E Webber, went to take his ease in the shade of a tree with the civilian engineer in charge of the route, Edward Graves (1834-1892).

It was under that tree, Webber claimed in 1892, that the idea of forming a Society of Telegraph Engineers was conceived.[1] He had been to a meeting of the Association of Gas Managers and Engineers, and he suggested to Graves 'that a somewhat similar society was wanted to bring telegraph engineers together'.

With due respect to Webber, we may doubt the literal truth of his pleasant pastoral idyll. For one thing, this casual conversation beneath a tree beside the Uxbridge Road seems to have made so little impression on Graves's mind that he did not join the Society until two years or more after it was formed. Moreover Webber himself, on another occasion, said that he made his suggestion – in May 1870, he thought – not to Graves but to Major Frank Bolton (1831-1887). 'Although', said Webber after Bolton's death, 'I have had the honour of being associated with him as one of the founders, I . . . have always said, that if it had not been for Frank Bolton the Society might not have come into existence at the early period that it did.'[2]

Bolton in 1870 was at the centre of a group who were trying to establish a telegraph engineers' society. His career had been unconventional, founded on joining the army as a private in spite of his middle-class background (his father was a surgeon). He had been given a commission from the ranks which might well have been his death warrant, for it consigned him to the White Man's Grave as an ensign in the Gold Coast Artillery. He survived three years' West African service, not all of it peaceful, returned to England, transferred to the 12th (East Suffolk) Foot as a Captain, and began to develop an interest in visual signalling.

In 1862 Bolton and a naval officer, Lieutenant P H Colomb, unknown to each other, each 'proposed to adapt to lights, the method so well known now to telegraphists, of the dot and dash' (Colomb is speaking in 1872) 'and to use it as a means of telegraphing by night in the army and navy'. When the two inventors found that they were duplicating each other's ideas they did not quarrel. Instead they collaborated and became friends, using, Colomb later told the Society, 'electric light and lime light'. What is even more remarkable is that the military and naval authorities encouraged them to collaborate, so that the signalling system they produced was taken up by both the Army and the Navy.

As a reward for his services to Army signalling, Bolton became an unattached Major in 1868 and then in 1871, while he was still nominally in the Army, the Board of Trade appointed him, under the Metropolis Water Act, to be water examiner to the Metropolis. In 1884 he published *London Water Supply*, but from the early sixties until his death there seems no doubt that this remarkable man's main interest lay in electricity and electric telegraphs.[3]

The Society of Telegraph Engineers came formally into existence on 17 May 1871 at a meeting held in 2 Westminster Chambers, Victoria Street, in the heart of what might be called the engineers' quarter of London. Only Bolton and seven others attended, but a great deal of preliminary work – letter-writing and discussion – had already been done, chiefly by Bolton, and presumably the meeting was called to ratify it. As early as August 1870 Bolton had circularised possible members with a letter inviting them to join and 'a copy of the proposed Rules and Regulations' for discussion and settlement at the first General Meeting. Altogether Bolton sent out about 150 letters and by the time the eight founders met on 17 May, seventy-three prospective members had applied to join. Rather high-handedly, it may be thought, the eight took it upon themselves to determine the original membership of the Society. They balloted for the first seventy-three and black-balled seven of them.[4]

At a second meeting, on 31 May 1871, there were eleven members present. Acting on the strength of provisional Rules and Regulations, they equipped the Society with a President, two Vice-Presidents, a Council of eleven members, a Treasurer and Librarian, an Honorary Secretary – Frank Bolton – and two Auditors. They also appointed a subcommittee of five 'to consider the Rules and Regulations of the Society'.[5]

The first President, Charles William Siemens, FRS, DCL (1823-1883), an engineer of the highest distinction, represented the first generation of electrical manufacturers. He had come from his native Prussia to England in 1843 and in 1859 he was naturalised. His family firm was interested in telegraphy from its earliest days and in electricity generally, and in England it was especially associated with the long-distance submarine cables which in the early seventies were England's pride and telegraphy's greatest glory.

Of the two Vice-Presidents, Lord Lindsay (1847-1913) was one of the wealthy and talented amateurs who were so important in Victorian science. He was heir to the 25th Earl of Crawford (whom he succeeded in 1880), he had wide scientific interests, connections in the highest circles, and his own private laboratory. From the point of view of the Society of Telegraph Engineers, he was a most desirable representative of a group whom the founders, or some of them, particularly wished to attract into the membership: 'that large and increasing body of Electricians', as Latimer Clark described them in 1879, 'who have no connection with telegraphic engineering or the practical applications of Electricity, but who pursue the subject from a pure love of science.'[6]

If William Siemens represented 'the practical applications of electricity' and Lord Lindsay 'a pure love of science', then the other Vice-President, Frank Ives Scudamore (1823-1884) represented what the founders probably thought of as the new Society's principal source of strength: the lively and expanding Postal Telegraph Department. Scudamore was a civil servant who had spent his whole career in the Post Office, where he had played a large part in setting up the Post Office Savings Bank in 1861. He had gone on to negotiate the transfer of the inland telegraphs to the state, and in 1872 he was at the head of the department which ran them, though not himself a telegraph engineer.[7]

The first Council had eleven (later twelve) members. Six (later seven) were telegraph engineers of greater or less eminence, including Sir Samuel Canning, Latimer Clark, Cromwell Varley, Willoughby Smith and R S Culley, Engineer-in-Chief of the Post Office. Sir Samuel Canning, a pioneer of submarine telegraphy, left the Council at the end of its first year and did not serve again, but the others, on or off the Council, continued active in the Society's affairs. After the civil engineers (four of the original six put 'CE' after their names) the next most numerous group on the first Council were serving officers: Captain P H Colomb, RN, and Captain E D Malcolm, Major R H Stotherd and Captain C E Webber, all of the Royal Engineers. 'Pure science' was represented, presumably, by G C Foster, FRS, Professor of Physics at University College, London. The Treasurer and Librarian, Robert Sabine, was an engineer: it is not clear whether he had a seat on the Council.

A great deal of thought and intelligence, supported by a great deal of letter-writing and discussion, was put into enlisting the services of the first officers and Council of the Society of Telegraph Engineers. Contemplating, perhaps, the ignominious end of the Electrical Society of London, the founders of the STE took care to see that the various groups from which they intended to draw their membership were represented by figures of acknowledged eminence. 'I am happy', said Siemens in his Presidential address to the first Ordinary General Meeting, 'to be able to point in our list of members to the historic names of Wheatstone, Cooke, and Morse, to the distinguished names [a nice distinction between 'historic' and 'distinguished'] of Thompson, Tyndall, and others scarcely less renowned.' If men of eminence were also men of substance, then so much the better, for an infant society might die, as the Electrical Society of London had died, of financial malnutrition.

The subcommittee on the Rules and Regulations consisted of Lord Lindsay, William Siemens, Captain Webber, Robert Sabine and EO Wildman Whitehouse. Siemens was on the Council of the Institution of Civil Engineers, and no doubt he offered guidance. The Society of Telegraph Engineers, said Latimer Clark in 1875, was 'modelled on the lines of the parent Society – the Institution of Civil Engineers; our rules, our constitution, and our proceedings, have all been closely copied from theirs'.[8]

'The Society of Telegraph Engineers', says the earliest statement of the Society's 'Objects', 'is established for the general advancement of Electrical and Telegraphic Science, and more particularly for facilitating the exchange of information and ideas among its Members.' There is nothing here about purely professional objects: about improving the profession's status, for example, or putting down malpractice, or enforcing standards of competence, yet these are all considerations which have often been taken into account in forming professional associations. Nor is there any sign of the kind of discontent which led the Mechanicals to break away from the Civils, or the kind of provincial jealousy of the capital which led to the formation of the British Medical Association.[9]

The STE's succinct statement reads far more like a statement of a learned society's aims than a statement of the aims of a professional association. It was as a learned society rather than a professional association that the STE came into existence: so much so that the formation of the Physical Society in 1874 was unwelcome to some of the leading members of the STE, though not to others, because it offered a challenge to them in the field of 'Electrical Science' which they intended to occupy. The telegraph engineers, it seems, felt secure enough in their claim to professional standing. What they were anxious to establish was their standing as 'scientific men' and 'electricians'.[10]

Following the example of the Civil Engineers, the Electricals established a hierarchy with two principal grades: Members and Associates, paying annual subscriptions, respectively, of 2 guineas (Foreign Members, £1) and 1 guinea. Admission to the Society was to be by proposal and seconding, supported by at least ten members, and by election. Qualifications for admission reflected the Society's dual nature as a professional association and a learned society.

The professional engineer's route to membership required him to have been 'regularly educated as a Telegraph Engineer according to the usual routine of pupilage, and to have had subsequent employment for at least five years in responsible situations'. Alternatively, he was required to 'have practised on his own account in the profession of a Telegraph Engineer for at least two years, and to have acquired a degree of eminence in the same'. Every Member had to be elected initially as an Associate and then he had to face another ordeal by ballot for transfer to the higher grade. An Associate had to be over twenty-one but his professional qualifications were left vague. Presumably they were covered by the requirement of 'regular education' for Members.

The modern reader will observe that the possibility that a telegraph engineer might qualify for admission to his professional association by getting a university degree evidently did not enter anyone's head, nor is there any mention of qualifying examinations, either to establish candidates' fitness for admission to the Society or to test their competence to practise their profession. Considerable emphasis, however, is placed on experience, on personal responsibility, and on 'a degree of eminence', and that emphasis has continued until the present day.

Those who were not telegraph engineers would be welcomed into the STE if they could show general proficiency in electrical science. 'This class', say the regulations for Associates, 'shall include persons whose pursuits constitute branches of Electrical Engineering [an early use of that term], who are not necessarily Telegraph Engineers by profession, but who are, by their connection with Science, qualified to concur with Telegraph Engineers in the advancement of professional knowledge.' The qualification on scientific grounds for the grade of Member was even more widely drawn. Such a member 'shall be so intimately associated with the science of Electricity or the progress of Telegraphy that the Council consider his admission to Member-ship would conduce to the interests of the Society'.

Besides Members, Foreign Members and Associates, there were two more grades in the hierarchy, one at each end of the scale of prestige, and in each case the duality of the Society's nature is observable. 'Students', say the Regulations, 'shall be persons not under eighteen and not over twenty-one years of age, who are serving pupilage to a Telegraph Engineer, or who are studying Natural Science, and are duly recommended by a Member.' Hon-orary Members were to be 'either distinguished individuals who from their position are enabled to render assistance in the prosecution of Telegraphic enterprises, or persons eminent for science and experience in pursuits con-nected with the profession of Telegraphy, but who are not engaged in the practice of that profession'.[11]

The Society held its first Ordinary General Meeting on the evening of Wednesday, 28 February 1872. The Telegraph Engineers had no suitable premises of their own so the 'parent Society' lent them the 'large hall' in the Institution of Civil Engineers' building at 25 Great George Street. The Civils made no charge, for which the Telegraph Engineers were properly grateful.[12] They and their successors continued without a meeting hall, dependent on

electrical theory as it was developing in his day. There is no doubt that he was frightened of mathematics, and fear drove him into a bullying arrogance towards opponents, especially Oliver Heaviside, against whom he was prepared to deploy all the influence his position gave him. 'I hate theory', said Preece in 1883. Ten years later, he made his second Presidential Address to the IEE a vehicle for his prejudices, referring to 'the phantasies of visionary mathematicians who monopolise the columns of our technical literature and fill the mind of the student with false conclusions. I have no sympathy', he went on, 'with the pure mathematician who scorns the practical man, scoffs at his experience, directs the universe from his couch, and invents laws to suit his fads.'[10]

Preece set out to annoy 'the professors', and he succeeded in annoying one of the more eminent of them: Silvanus P Thompson (1851–1916), Professor of Physics at Finsbury Technical College from 1885 until his death. Professional differences apart, Thompson and Preece were almost bound to dislike each other, for the fastidious Quaker principles of the one – and his teetotalism – would have grated on the rumbustiousness of the other. Preece enjoyed drinking. Thompson, on the other hand, would go out of his way to warn prospective dinner guests that they should not expect strong drink in his house.

Early in 1887 Thompson and Preece came into open collision before the STE when Thompson chose to advance into Preece's own professional field with his own solution to a troublesome technical problem: inductive interference with speech on long-distance telephone lines. 'For long I have maintained', said Thompson, 'the clue to long-range telephony is to use much more powerful transmitters and much less sensitive receivers.' In order to 'divide the current' which he required, Thompson proposed an apparatus with 108 microphones in parallel, though how it was to work commercially is not altogether clear.

'I utterly and totally dissent', said Preece, 'from nearly all his conclusions . . . the difficulty in speaking to long distances is not a question of apparatus at all . . . long-distance speaking can only be attained when a line is free from electrostatic and electromagnetic induction'. This was a straightforward technical disagreement, but personal animosity began to show when Preece accused Thompson of 'the perversion of history' in remarks he had made about the work of various innovators and inventors in telephony. Preece disagreed also, flatly and belligerently, with Thompson's use of technical terms: 'Every man in this room . . . knows that an induction coil is part and parcel of telephonic apparatus, and why on earth, then, does Professor Thompson call it a transformer?'[11]

The discussion ran on for two more meetings after the reading of the paper, and when Thompson came to reply to the discussion Preece had been 'detained by important engagements'. Thompson was not in the least inhibited. 'We all know', he said, 'how perfectly sure – in fact cocksure – Mr Preece is when he forms opinions or makes statements . . . He was cocksure . . . that my theory of long-range telephony was wrong. Now it may be admirable to be cocksure, but it is not scientific'. Thompson went on with a hostile survey of Preece's views over the preceding ten years, during which he accused him of executing 'two remarkable strategical movements: in the first place he buttered, and in the second place he hedged'. His reply to Preece stretches over fifteen pages of the *Journal*, and the President, perhaps somewhat overwhelmed, said he was sure that all would agree that Professor Thompson had 'favoured us with a very able reply to the very full discussion upon his paper. We wish him success with his telephones.'[12]

Fortnightly meetings, with or without acrimony, and the reports, acrimony included, which were published in the *Journal* were the main but not the only means by which the STE discharged its function as a learned society. The *Journal* also carried 'Original Communications'. One, in 1878, came from Lieutenant Savage, RE, writing from the Field Telegraph Office, Roorkee, India. 'I have been making splendid big telephones lately', he said, 'and they will do anything – almost talk of themselves.' His transmitters had magnets 18 inches long and a half inch in diameter; 'coils of very high resistance'; – diaphragms 6 inches across; mouthpieces 2 inches across. 'One I have just completed of this size', wrote Savage, 'is quite a startler; even at long distances it sounds as if the sender was shouting in one's ear. I am going to try about 400 miles tomorrow.'[13] As far as the *Journal* was concerned, unfortunately, tomorrow never came.

'This morning', wrote Professor H Macleod in 1882, 'I determined the resistance of my assistant, a boy of about 19.'[14] W C C Hawtayne, in 1890, carried vivisection further. He put alternating current at 2,000 volts from a 37-unit Mordey alternator through a 3-foot grass snake. 'There is not the least doubt that the snake got the whole current, as a spark was running from the end of the fuse wire all the time the current was on. At first the snake wriggled violently, but after a few seconds it became quite still, leading me to suppose it was dead; however, a couple of minutes after the circuit had been broken, its body began to heave and tremble, and in a minute or two more it became as lively as ever. I tried the experiment once more, with exactly the same result.' Unfortunately he omitted to take the snake's resistance before he killed it. Hawtayne's account reached the *Journal* by way of W H Preece.[15]

From the *Journal's* earliest days, in pursuance, no doubt, of the STE's broad international ambitions, abstracts of scientific papers from a wide range of publications appeared in it. In 1890 the IEE was receiving thirty-two English titles, fourteen American, thirteen French and eight German,[16] and abstracting from many more. The early international ambitions faded, but the abstracts became the foundation of one of the most important services provided by the Institution.

If the publication of papers is a necessary part of the activities of a learned society, so is the provision of a library, and a library of some sort seems to have come into existence as soon as the STE was founded. It was put on a regular basis, in the Society's rooms at 4 Broad Sanctuary, in 1880, with J A Frost as Librarian – they paid him 50 guineas a year – and, a little later, an assistant, so that from 1 January 1881 the library could stay open during the day and in the evening, not for the benefit of members of the STE only, but for members of other scientific bodies and, on application, members of the public generally. The librarian collected all electrical patent specifications – 430 electrical patents were taken out between 1 January and 15 December 1881 – but only £50 was allowed for the librarian's assistant and for the purchase and binding of new books and other publications.[17] 'The limited sum placed at the disposal of the Library Committee', said Frost, '. . . will not permit very much to be done towards perfecting the Library.'[18]

Before Frost became Librarian, he had been working on a catalogue of the collection of books and pamphlets relating to electricity, of various periods and in various languages, formed during fifty years or so by Sir Francis Ronalds (1788-1873). He was an independent scientist of the kind much sought after by the STE and he was among the earliest members. His scientific interests were various, and in 1816 he had offered a primitive but practical electric telegraph to the Admiralty who, without looking at it, told him 'that telegraphs of any kind are now wholly unnecessary'.[19] After that his library and the catalogue, which was intended also as a kind of electrical bibliography, became one of the main interests of his life. He left it to his brother-in-law, Samuel Carter, with instructions to preserve it 'so as to be of as much use as possible to persons engaged in the pursuit of electricity'. Carter, urged by Latimer Clark, a bibliophile as well as an engineer, handed it over on trust in 1875 to the STE.[20]

This was no doubt a compliment to the infant Society, but there were about 2,000 books and 4,000 pamphlets which needed binding,[21] and the Society was not rich. Moreover, although the Ronalds Library was undoubtedly of antiquarian and historical value, its practical value was limited. Nevertheless, in November 1880 Preece, as President, received members in the STE's Library, thrown open for the first time since the catalogue and binding of Sir Francis's collection had been completed.[22]

In June 1872 the STE held the first of a long line of conversaziones. It was held in a laboratory in Greek Street which belonged to Lord Lindsay, who probably bore the cost. His large electro-magnet was shown, as well as a collection of electrical and telegraphic apparatus, and above everything shone an illuminated motto perpetrated by Schütz Wilson:

'The Lords of Lightning we; by land or wave

The mystic agent serves us as our slave'.[23]

Every conversazione had an exhibition. It was the necessary scientific fig-leaf for a light-weight entertainment suitable for ladies, with refreshments and music, often provided by the string band of the Royal Engineers. A good deal of the cost, it seems, fell on the reigning President, but a 'Soirée/Conversazione' held at the South Kensington Museum in July 1879 was paid for by subscription. It was organised to coincide with the International Telegraph Congress and it was a sizeable affair. The sum of £638 19s 6d was raised 'and a further amount of £20 would be paid'; 1,087 invitation cards were issued and about 500 people came. Of £438 13s 9d paid out, £219 6s 0d went for refreshments and the rest, in sums of £50 downwards, for tents, lamps, band (£37 10s 0d), museum attendants, printing, stationery and postage, 'Siemens Bros Exp in connection with Electric Light' (£19 13s 3d) and minor items.[24] The string band of twenty-five, with six boy sopranos, was found by the Royal Artillery.

The Great Exhibition of 1851 had set a fashion for large international exhibitions. As the years went on the spread and improvement of railways and steam navigation, to say nothing of telegraph systems, opened the way for enterprising firms to send large and weighty exhibits to cities which formerly would have been impossibly remote: even as far as Australia and South America. During the eighties, with the rapid growth in Europe and America of the electrical industry, there were several specifically electrical exhibitions. Some had government backing and in all of them Great Britain, still generally seen as the world's leading industrial nation, stood to gain or lose prestige.

There was an opening here for an organisation to coordinate the response of British electrical engineers to these opportunities for British electrical manufacturers to show off their prowess before an international audience. The STE strove to fill the vacancy. It was new, financially weak and without influence in circles where official policy towards these exhibitions was decided, but it acted more or less as a trade association for the British electrical industry. Indeed since most of the leading electrical manufacturers of the day – R E B Crompton, Sir William and Alex Siemens, S Z de Ferranti and others – were also leading members of the STE, it might be said that the STE, as well as being a learned society, was also at this time a trade association, though not overtly. It was a role which Crompton and others were very willing to see it play.

For the Paris Exhibition of 1881, after confused and leisurely deliberations, Gladstone's Government appointed Lord Crawford (formerly Lord Lindsay), Sir Charles Bright and Professor D E Hughes, all members of the STE, as Commissioners, but the Treasury refused Lord Crawford's application for £500 for expenses.[25] Crawford, 'with yellow hair and blue spectacles', was to be seen, according to a contemporary, 'opening packing cases, cracking jokes, and helping to haul dynamos and set up instruments'.[26]

Crompton, an exhibitor, reported 'hard-working scientific men of the eminence of Lord Crawford, Professor Hughes, and others, hurrying about in their shirt-sleeves, in fact, doing our work for us, and assisting us in every way to get our exhibits in order . . . we should never have been ready in time but for them'.[27] The organisers of the Exhibition gave the STE a *diplôme d'honneur*, and the exhibitors gave the surplus of the Guarantee Fund – over £100 – to the society 'to whose exertions and co-operation much of the Success attending the British Section is due'.[28]

In its capacity as a learned society, the STE held two meetings in Paris, on 22 and 24 September 1881, 'attended by the Minister and by nearly all the eminent scientific men then in Paris'. They were chiefly there to attend deliberations on the definition of electrical units at a Congress of Electricians which 'consisted of some two hundred of the most distinguished savants of Europe, all nominated by their respective Governments'. The President of the STE, Lieutenant-Colonel C E Webber, described the Congress to the Society in January 1882, but it is clear that members of the STE who attended it were there not by virtue of their membership but as eminent 'savants' in their own right.[29]

Two exhibitions in 1882, one at Munich and one at the Crystal Palace, were local rather than international in scale. Preece, visiting Munich on behalf of the STE after an invitation had been received at three days' notice, devoted a good deal of his time to research into what he called 'the beerostatic capacity of the average Bavarian'. He succeeded, he said, in consuming in four days more beer than he had consumed in the previous four years of his existence. The small number of exhibits at Munich, mostly from South Germany, 'were quite on an equality', he reported, 'with the more numerous things . . . at Paris'.[30] The German electrical industry was going ahead fast.

News of the next big international electrical exhibition, at Vienna in 1883, was greeted at first with enthusiasm and energy. Then the Government snubbed the STE by appointing commissioners over the head of Sir Charles Bright, and within the STE W H Preece and Alex Siemens quarrelled with Sir Charles and his brother Edward.[31] Perhaps it is not surprising that the Vienna Exhibition has left far less of a mark on the STE's records than the Paris Exhibition two years earlier.

After Vienna British enthusiasm for exhibitions declined. Even before it, in 1882, Webber, as President, had shown some scepticism about international exhibitions and about the decisions of juries, and Preece had applauded the organisers of the Munich exhibition for awarding none of 'those absurd gold, silver and bronze medals'.[32] Exhibitors whom juries favour and exhibitors who win medals, however 'absurd' they may be, do not usually complain. Crompton, whose firm sent to the Paris exhibition 'a fine exhibit of . . . all the generating apparatus necessary for working Swan lamps', recorded with great satisfaction in his memoirs 'that "Cromptons" were awarded the first gold medal ever given for electric lighting plant'.[33] Other British manufacturers may not have done so well. Is it possible to detect, in Webber's and Preece's remarks, a faint flavour of sour grapes?

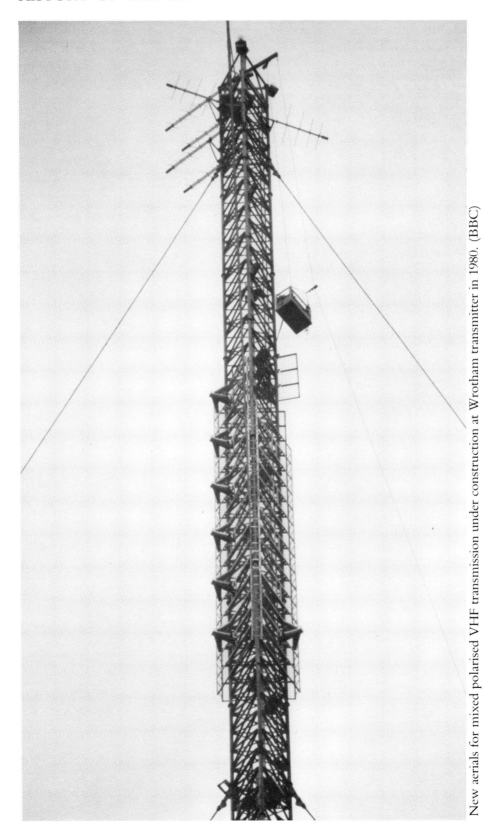

New aerials for mixed polarised VHF transmission under construction at Wrotham transmitter in 1980. (BBC)

References:
1   *J.STE*, 1873, **6**, pp.385–421; 1881, **9**, pp.278–307, pp.339–362
2   *J.STE*, 1887, **16**, pp.42, 81, 107
3   *J.STE*, 1880, **9**, p.159
4   *J.STE*, 1877, **6**, p.24
5   *J.STEE*, 1882, **10**, Reference 9, p.53; *J.IEE*, 1890, **19**, p.199
6   *J.STEE*, 1885, **14**, p.5
7   E C Baker: *Sir William Preece FRS, Victorian Engineer Extraordinary*, 1976, pp.356–359
8   Reference 9, p.79; R E Crompton: *Reminiscences*, 1928, pp.110–111, and MS of 1922, IEE Archives I/6.2; The Dynamicables: *Rules and List of Members*, 1905; The Dynamicables: *Report of the Electric Lighting Act Committee 1884*, p.1, Science Museum Archives CRO Misc.
9   Rollo Appleyard: *History of the Institution of Electrical Engineers (1871–1931)*, 1939, pp.96–97
10 *J.STEE*, 1883, **12**, p.139; *J.IEE*, 1893, **22**, p.67
11 *J.STEE*, 1887, **16**, pp.42, 72–73, 74, 75
12 *Ibid*, pp.132–147
13 *J.STE*, 1878, **7**, p.267
14 *J.STEE*, 1882, **11**, p.118
15 *J.IEE*, 1890, **19**, p.411
16 *Ibid*, pp.720–721
17 *J.STEE*, 1882, **10**, pp.435–436; CM 7 Dec. 1880
18 *Ibid*, pp.436–437
19 P Dunsheath: *A History of Electrical Engineering*, 1962, p.73
20 *DNB*, Article on Ronalds, Sir Francis
21 Reference 9, p.254
22 OGM, 10 Nov. 1880
23 *J.STE*, 1872, **1**, pp.226–227
24 Minutes of Conference Reception Committee, OCM Vol.1, 16 July 1879
25 Minutes of Paris Exhibition Committee, OCM Vol.1, 28 June and 22 July 1881
26 A P Trotter: *Reminiscences*, IEE Archives Mss 1, SC Mss 66
27 *J.STEE*, 1881, **10**, p.428
28 OGM, 23 March 1882
29 *J.STEE*, 1881, **10**, p.433; *J.STEE*, 1882, **11**, p.18
30 *J.STEE*, 1882, **11**, pp.518,521
31 Minutes of Vienna Exhibition Committee, OCM Vol.1, 25 May and 15 June 1883; CM 19 June 1883
32 *J.STEE*, 1882, **11**, p.520
33 R E Crompton: *Reminiscences*, 1928, pp.98,99

Part Two: The Power Engineers

44

10,000 V alternator in Deptford Central Electric Light Station during construction, 1889. (The Archives Department, Ferranti plc)

Chapter 4

The Rise of the Power Engineer, 1880–1895

I Telephones and Electric Light

The Society of Telegraph Engineers was very nearly founded too late. This was what the founders of the Society meant, whether they realised it or not, when they complained that the proposed scope of the Society's activities was too narrow. For over thirty years, from the commercial launch of electric telegraphy in the late 1830s until the laying of the first great oceanic cable routes, the telegraph engineers had the profession of electrical engineering to themselves, for no other practical application of electricity came anywhere near telegraphy in importance. By the time the telegraph engineers founded their Society, however, their lonely professional eminence was nearly at an end: so too, though they did not realise it, was British pre-eminence in electrical engineering, which had been founded on British pre-eminence in telegraphy, especially the submarine cables.

Electrical engineering in the early 1870s was on the verge of enormous and varied expansion: expansion which is still going on, well over a century later. It was at this period that electrical engineering passed through a phase, common in industrial development – industries as varied as railways, blasting explosives, motor cars, plastics, convenience foods come to mind – when barriers are broken, difficulties are overcome, and what had formerly, perhaps for many years, been experimental, tentative, premature, is enabled to roll forward into practicality and growth. Not only are technical problems solved but other conditions, financial, cultural and economic, are also right. Capital can be raised; demand exists; there is purchasing power in the market. In the case of electrical engineering during the 1870s, two possibilities became practicalities: telephones and electric lighting. They were both developments of major importance, but with very different implications in matters of technology, finance and marketing.[1]

Telephones could fairly easily be grafted on to existing telegraph systems with little in the way of capital expenditure or civil engineering, and they required virtually no power. On the other hand, for commercial success they relied on a demand for instantaneous communication by speech which developed quickly in the United States and very slowly in the United Kingdom where people did not – indeed, still do not – seem to feel the same urge to talk to each other, either on business or privately, over long distances. 'I do not hesitate to say', remarked a member in 1879, 'that there are not anything like as many as 500 telephones in actual daily use [in the United Kingdom], as compared with the 26,000 on the other side of the Atlantic.' In Chicago, he said, there were 700 subscribers, and 'as I learn by the last advices, the "calls" through the telephone upon the central office number over 8,000 daily'.[2]

Electric lighting was another matter altogether. It raised the prospect of generating power on a scale previously undreamt-of and of transmitting it over distances which might eventually reach hundreds of miles.[3] Moreover, if power could be generated and transmitted for lighting it could be generated and transmitted for other purposes also. Electrically operated factory plant and electric traction began in the eighties to come over the horizon of practicality. All this implied a capacity for massive mechanical and civil engineering, backed by proportionate capital investment organised through the financial institutions of the day. Electric lighting, moreover, was not cheap. Consumers, corporate or private, had to be affluent to contemplate installing it. Gas, which in the United Kingdom was efficient and widely available, was a formidable competitor.

By the mid-eighties a feeling of uneasiness was developing about British progress in the new branches of electrical engineering: telephones and electric light, and it shows in the records of the STE. In 1885 C E Spagnoletti, in his Presidential Address, discussed the lack of enthusiasm for telephones in Great Britain as compared with the USA which had already been deplored in 1879. 'This probably is due', he said, 'to some extent to our excess of boy labour and the facility with which a messenger or commissionaire can be obtained, our rapid means of transit, and moderate cab fares, together with a temperate climate, which during the summer is not so hot as to nearly melt the vitality out of us, and to make exercise really a subject of serious consideration'.

The picture of Americans fainting in their summer heat while British messenger boys and retired sergeant-majors rode comfortably in their cheap and rapid cabs – followed, at a discreet distance, by Dr Watson – is appealing, but there may have been a harder economic reason, too. Having said that in London there were about 7,000 instruments and twenty exchanges, Spagnoletti went on: 'Most of the subscribers are business men or commercial firms, and it is scarcely used here at all for domestic purposes and individual requirements, as it is in America. I fear the present price will prohibit its use for such purposes.'[4] The STE itself was put on the phone in 1883, without having to pay for it, by the United Telephone Company, whose Directors presumably calculated that what they lost in revenue they would gain in public relations.[5]

Electric lighting created a sensation in the late seventies and early eighties, attracting engineers, businessmen, financiers, and sufficient amateur investors to pump up a Stock Exchange boom with ignorant optimism. One of the professionals sold out near the top of the boom, made £100,000, and left others, as he says in his memoirs, to 'hold the baby'.[6] By 1885 all was gloom. 'All who are interested in its advancement', said Spagnoletti, referring to electric light, '. . . cannot but regret its present state of comparative stagnation.'[7]

This particular phase of 'stagnation' was passing away by the beginning of 1890 when Sir William Thomson, later Lord Kelvin, inaugurating his second term as President, spoke of 'The magnificent spring of energy which within the last six years has been imminent, and . . . which has been active during the past year.' It 'makes us', he said, 'for the time being almost forget everything but electric lighting.'[8] Nevertheless uneasiness remained about the disappointing progress, after a promising start, of electric lighting in England, and it found expression in various ways in the proceedings of the STE and its successor, the IEE.

One cause of uneasiness was the way in which electric light companies were financed. The company promoter, always a popular hate-figure, was never more so than in the eighties and nineties of the last century, when the law allowed greater scope for his imagination than it does now. Engineers, perhaps, have a particular distaste for those who deal only in money, and financiers had been very prominent during the early period of excitement over electric light. They became interested again as soon as 'stagnation' began to pass, and opinion did not distinguish readily between those who were reputable and those who were not. 'Its rapid development', said Preece in his Presidential Address in 1893, referring to electric light, 'has been seriously retarded in England by the operations of a monster called into existence by the limited liability legislation of recent years – the rapacious financial promoter – whose plunder in one year of our period far exceeds in amount the sum of all the thefts of all the highwaymen and burglars that were ever hanged.'[9]

That was good, colourful Welsh rhetoric and it went unanswered. Not so an attack delivered in the following year (1894) by Webber, now a Major-General, on the method by which capital had been raised in 1890 for the City of London Electric Light Company. What the General objected to was the formation of a 'pioneer company' to take certain preliminary steps before selling out, at a handsome profit, to the substantive company. 'Of course', said the General, 'there is no engineering justification for it, but the financial physician has prescribed it.'

The 'financial physician' was sitting in front of him, in the shape of Joseph Bevan Braithwaite (1855-1934), a Quaker stockbroker and company promoter with a particular interest in electric lighting who was a member of the IEE and Chairman of the City of London Company. Everyone, including

Webber, agreed that the Company was sound and efficient. Braithwaite reminded Webber that the pioneer company had been launched in November 1890 in the shadow of the Baring crisis (when the house of Baring had been rescued from collapse by the intervention of the Bank of England). Confidence had been so badly shaken that 'it was the common saying in the City that you could not borrow 15s on the security of a sovereign', but unless work started before the end of February 1891 two provisional orders authorising it would lapse. 'Under those circumstances', said Braithwaite, 'it seems to me it was a matter of great interest to electrical engineers that there should be men found sufficiently plucky to come forward and put down the hard cash to save those orders to provide the fees for General Webber and other consulting engineers, and also to give the electrical industry probably the greatest opportunity it ever had of showing what can be done in the way of electric lighting on a large scale.'[10] The General would not withdraw, but Braithwaite, it may be thought, won the battle.

The 'rapacious financial promoter' or 'financial physician' was a satisfying flesh-and-blood villain who could be blamed for holding up the devoted labours of honest engineers to provide the British public with electric light. In the years after 1882 another villain appeared: the Right Honourable Joseph Chamberlain, President of the Board of Trade, who carried the Electric Lighting Act 1882 through Parliament. The development of electric lighting was going ahead so fast in the early eighties that the need for general legislation to regulate it was urgent, and when the Act was passed it seems at first to have been pretty generally welcomed by engineers, manufacturers and others who would have to work within its framework.[11] Then, when the first electric light boom collapsed and 'stagnation' set in, in the mid-eighties, one provision in particular in the Act was discovered to be a serious obstacle to progress.

Clause 27 of the Act gave local authorities the power to buy out electricity undertakings within their area, after twenty-one years, at a price fixed solely by the value, at that date, of plant, materials and buildings. The clause, Dr Bowers has suggested, may reflect Joseph Chamberlain's bias in favour of municipal trading. It certainly made electricity supply unattractive to private investors, both because of the short period of unchallenged ownership that they were offered and because privately-owned undertakings, to make anything of their investment in so short a term, would have to charge so highly for supplies that they would be put at a hopeless disadvantage against gas.

By 1884 proposals for new electricity undertakings were tailing off. The Council of the STE, confident as businessmen (and others) often are in making economic judgments, decided that it was all the fault of the Act. First they appointed a committee to consider what steps should be taken by the STE to get the Act altered and then they resolved 'that the Society . . . have seen with regret that since the passing of the Electric Lighting Act of 1882 public lighting by Electricity has not made that advance in this country which was confidently expected and hence there has not been that stimulus to progress in many of the branches of Electrical Science which might have been expected, judging from the history of Submarine Telegraphs'. They went on to 'venture to request the President of the Board of Trade to consider whether the said restrictions may not be modified or removed'.[12]

In this way the STE took its place in a movement, already afoot, to get the Act of 1882 altered. It did not take the lead – its position in public affairs, as we have seen, was not strong enough for that – but in the elaborate committee work and lobbying which went on between 1884 and 1888 a number of individuals who were incidentally members of the STE, were prominent and so was the STE.

In 1886 Lord Bury presented to the House of Lords a petition drawn up by the STE because they did not think that a petition presented by the Civils was 'comprehensive' enough. The STE wanted to ensure that no amendment to the 1882 Act passed into law which did not place electricity undertakings on the same basis as other industrial enterprises.[13] That they did not get, but when a new Electric Lighting Act was passed in 1888 it extended to forty-two years the period after which a local authority would have a right to purchase an undertaking. Perhaps more important, if a local authority chose to buy, it would have to pay for the undertaking at its value as a going concern.[14]

The Electric Lighting Act of 1882, like the 'rapacious promoter', became part of the folklore of the electricity industry. In the early twentieth century it was frequently mentioned within the IEE, and as late as 1962 a Past President quoted it as a 'serious deterrent' to progress.[15] 'Serious' it was certainly thought to be at the time, but steps were taken to get rid of it and it was only in force for six years.

The most important obstacle, probably, to the rapid development of electric lighting in England was efficient, cheap and ubiquitous gas: a commodity far less readily available in the USA and other countries where electric lighting went ahead faster than in England. Moreover, much gas production was in the hands of local authorities who might not display overmuch enthusiasm for the new industry even though the Act of 1888, like the Act of 1882, was tilted in their favour.[16]

If, in the 1880s, the prospects for telephones and electric light looked cloudy, British engineers could still take comfort from a glance in the direction of telegraphy. 'The development of electrical science in which the British section was in advance of all other nations', said Sir Charles Bright and Professor Hughes, reporting on the Paris Exhibition of 1881, 'was ... Submarine Telegraphy.' Preece, ebullient as ever, reported on Munich almost a year later. 'I say it, who ought not to say it, perhaps' – but of course he did – 'but I think that we possess in England the finest working telegraph in the world.' Eleven years later, as President, he was in the same happy mood: 'Telegraphy has been advanced in this country more rapidly by the British Post Office than by any private undertaking, and we have certainly shot ahead of our smart cousins on the other side of the Atlantic. . ... Their engineers are looking to us to develop their inventions, and we have done so. They cannot always get them taken up in the States.'[17]

The confidence of these eminent telegraph engineers was no doubt justified. British enterprise led the way into telegraphy in the 1840s, and in the 1890s the great cable routes of the world were still mainly British in engineering, manufacture and management.[18] Telegraphs, like railways, were among the greatest nineteenth-century achievements, and British eminence in both was unquestionable. During the 1880s, however, as we have observed, the electrical industry of the twentieth century was beginning to emerge, and in that there were already signs, by 1890, that American and German firms might take the lead: a matter which British electrical engineers would find more and more disturbing as time went on.

II Society into Institution

If the uses of electricity were changing, the society which claimed to represent the electrical engineer's profession would have to change too. This was emphatically the view of Latimer Clark, a most distinguished engineer of broad interests and high culture. He considered from the first that the STE rested on too narrow a base, running the risk of alienating those whom it ought to attract, namely the 'electricians'. He did not mean craftsmen but scientists, including those of the greatest distinction, whose main interest was in electricity. He aired his views in his inaugural address as President, in 1875, and in 1876 suggested adding the words 'and of Electricians' to the Society's title.[19]

Nobody took much interest. Most of the members (see Table 3) were telegraph engineers and most of them, including Edward Graves, Engineer-in-Chief of the Post Office, were happy enough with the Society as it stood, although Latimer Clark warned them that if it did not broaden its appeal it would dwindle into insignificance. In 1880 he pushed matters to a head, and in a long letter to Edward Graves he set out his case. Graves evidently wished to run a society purely for 'telegraphists' (a word, like 'electrician', which has been devalued), 'leaving more scientific questions to be dealt with outside the Society by those who have a taste for them'. If they followed that course, said Clark, 'We must be prepared to see others take up the position we leave vacant, but which we could so easily occupy' – that is, the position of a learned society concentrating on electricity.

'There are two large bodies of electrical workers', Clark warned Graves, with an eye to the future, 'who remain practically outside our pale viz: those practical men who are daily introducing new applications of electricity of vast importance; and those students of electricity & scientific authors who work in private or in the great physical laboratories & who are the real pioneers of the science.' In this class Clark included not only the holders of recognised academic positions like Sir William Thomson, S P Thompson, John Hopkinson and others, but also those wealthy amateurs of science, such as Lord Crawford, who carried on a much earlier tradition – 'that large body of private scientific workers', as he had described them in his Presidential address, 'who love and pursue the science of Electricity without any thought of regarding it as a profession'.

'These men', Clark said, 'cannot afford to stand still merely because we prefer to remain a Society of Telegraphers & do not care to invite them into our ranks. An electrical society must be formed or else existing societies must supply the need ... there are many among us who think we have bestirred ourselves too late and that our chance is gone.' Then he took the brake off his imagination:

> Every scientific & technical Journal whether English or Foreign teems with papers on Electricity and Magnetism ... Electricity & Magnetism are if we may say so more in their infancy than ever, and are evidently only just about to take their real place in the world as perhaps the most powerful agents at the service of mankind. They are going to be employed in every branch of art & manufacture. They are just beginning to place themselves at the service of the million and a revolution is about to take place only comparable to that which took place at the introduction of steam. Electric lighting, electric heating, electric storage, electric transmission of force, electric locomotion, electric extraction of metals, electro-deposition, electro-chemistry, electric power and a thousand other applications of electric science great and small are going to make electricity one of the greatest features of the age, and ought we to stand by & see all this go on and be content to confine ourselves almost exclusively to one branch of the great subject?[20]

Slightly less than fourteen years before this letter was written the greatest electrical triumph of the age, up to that date, had been achieved: the laying from the *Great Eastern* of the first commercially successful Atlantic cable. In 1880 the pioneering giants of the early submarine cables, Latimer Clark among them, were still active, still conducting vast operations under the oceans of the world. Yet Clark dared to warn the 'telegraphists' that their occupation was merely 'one branch of the great subject' – electrical science – and in the next line he added an even deadlier insult, 'I consider that electric telegraphy has to a great extent had its day,' so fast was electrical technology moving in the early eighties.

At a General Meeting of the STE on 22 December 1880, the membership decided to alter the Society's title to The Society of Telegraph Engineers and of Electricians.[21] Thus Latimer Clark achieved his objective of signalling to the scientific world that the Society was not just a band of narrow-minded technicians intent only on their own professional affairs but a learned society anxious, as he put it in a letter to the President and Council in 1879, to attract 'a large number of amateur Electricians and men of Science, who have not hitherto joined us because they do not feel desirous or qualified to enrol themselves as members of a professional Society, and who are by no means assured that electrical researches of a purely scientific character would be appreciated by us'.[22]

The Society of Telegraph Engineers, under that title, was never a body corporate. Incorporation by Royal Charter was refused by the Privy Council in 1880, and the Society then took another route, much simpler and less expensive. In May 1883 the Society of Telegraph Engineers and Electricians was registered with the Board of Trade under Section 23 of the Companies Act 1867 and so became, within the meaning of that Act, a corporation: a legal person which could sue, be sued, and protect its name at law.

The new name of the Society, as well as indicating the breadth of its intentions, also expressed a conception of its nature, held by Latimer Clark and some of his contemporaries, in which the function of a professional association was kept strictly subordinate to that of a learned society. Latimer Clark himself even went so far as to commit the heresy of criticising the Civil Engineers. When the Society was formed, and afterwards, he said, he 'endeavoured to point out the danger and disadvantages that would arise if our Society, following too closely in the steps of our parent Institution, were to assume too professional and technical a character'.[23]

That was not a view that commended itself, in the middle and late eighties, to the growing body of electrical engineers, increasingly conscious of the separate identity of their branch of the engineering profession. As Latimer Clark himself said, there were other societies which could occupy the purely scientific ground which he coveted for the STEE. The Physical Society, founded in 1874 – to the great alarm of Francis Bolton – was one which several of the 'professors', and Latimer Clark himself, joined.[24] On the other hand, there was no organisation apart from the STEE which could act as an electrical engineers' professional association, and a professional association, as well as a learned society, was what the electrical engineers were determined to have, either within or outside the STEE.

Once again, discontent found expression in a proposal to change the Society's name, and to change it much more radically than before. At a meeting of the Council on 10 November 1887, W H Preece gave notice of a motion to alter the title of the Society to 'The Institution of Electrical Engineers'.[25] Crompton, at about the same time, was drafting another motion to indicate the strength of feeling among the membership:

> That as there is at present a widespread opinion prevalent that the Society of Telegraph Engineers and Electricians does not adequately represent the present body of Electrical Engineers in England and that this feeling may lead to the

formation of a new and rival Society – it is desirable that the Council should at once take steps to appoint a Committee to confer with two or more heads of the leading firms of Electrical Engineers not already represented on the Council, as to the best mode of making the Society more representative'. [26]

The change of name was thus an outward sign of inner turmoil. Technical change was altering the nature of the electrical engineer's profession. The passage of time was bringing a new generation towards the top of the STEE, and what they saw they did not unreservedly admire. In these uneasy circumstances preparations for the change of name went ahead under the presidency, ironically, of Edward Graves, who would have preferred to block Latimer Clark's less thorough-going proposal seven or eight years earlier. On 1 January 1889 the Registrar of Joint Stock Companies issued his Certificate of Incorporation to the Institution of Electrical Engineers.

III The Revolution of the Nineties

The engineers who were coming to the top of the IEE in the early nineties were professionally distinct from the founders of the STE in the early seventies. Men like R E B Crompton (1845–1940), J S Raworth (1846–1917), John Hopkinson (1849–1898), James Swinburne (1858–1958), A A Campbell Swinton (1863–1930), S Z de Ferranti (1864–1930), and their contemporaries were not concerned, generally speaking, with telegraphs or with telephones but with power and its applications in lighting, traction and factory plant, giving them stronger affinities with mechanical engineers than with 'men of science'. Raworth, for instance, was professionally interested in power, lighting and tramways, and he 'approached the designing of electrical machinery from the point of view of the mechanical engineer rather than from that of the electrician'.[27]

The new wave of electrical engineers were much more consciously engineers than electricians, in the old sense of that word, meaning an electrical scientist, and Sir William Preece, in the latter part of his career, showed his age by the value he attached to the title Electrician to the Post Office. The new men were disinclined to adulate 'professors' and had none of their elders' respect for wealthy amateurs. On the contrary, they were determined to create an exclusive, highly qualified body of professional men who could face – if necessary, outface – the lawyers and the doctors. One of their complaints about the IEE was that amateurs were admitted too easily, and if they had been compelled to make a choice between a learned society concerned with the advancement of electrical science and a qualifying body devoted to raising the standards demanded of candidates for membership, combined with a protective association to look after their material interests, there was not much doubt where their preference would lie, as the change of name indicated.

Members' discontent, in the early nineties, was concentrated on the Council. The way it was composed and chosen dated back to the very beginning of the STE, and members felt it was out of touch with them. 'At the head of the Institution', said Raworth at the Annual General Meeting of 1895, 'they had a great and noble Council . . . which did honour both to the Institution and to the profession. . . . But . . . the Institution and the Council were two separate entities, and each was pursuing its own existence without knowing what were the desires and aspirations of the other. . . . There had been a very slight influx of new blood or of members of Council derived actually from the initiative members of the Institution.'[28]

The Council of the IEE, in 1895, had thirty-three members. Vacancies, nominally, were filled by election at each AGM, but candidates were nominated by the sitting members only seven days in advance, so there was never time for opposition to develop and the Council was self-perpetuating. Moreover, the system was reinforced in 1888–1889 by Preece, who worked hard and successfully to reinstate an abandoned rule by which the number of nominations never exceeded the number of vacancies, so that voting by members became merely devout ritual, divorced as much from reality as from democracy. Of the Council's members one – in 1895, R E B Crompton – was President, four were Vice-Presidents, thirteen were Past Presidents, and fifteen, including three of the Associate grade, were 'ordinary members'.

The Past Presidents were a body of immense scientific distinction, including among their number the President of the Royal Society, Lord Kelvin, and nine other Fellows. They could sit and vote on the Council for life if they chose – they mostly did choose – and the Vice Presidents were also unassailable. The Past Presidents' average age was sixty and their turn of mind was conservative. Raworth was very rude about them, and about the Vice Presidents also. 'There were 17 permanent stuck-fast members . . . who not only had a voice but could also vote on the Council', he said, 'and only 15 active, movable members who had any communication with the members at large and who were drawn from the members within a reasonable time.'[29] The President was Raworth's contemporary and among the 'active, movable members' Raworth had sympathisers, but evidently he was not mollified.

A deputation representing the malcontent members waited on the Council in November 1895. At the AGM Raworth made it clear that they were offended by their reception. 'Members', he said, 'would scarcely believe him when he said that they found it extremely difficult to get the ear of the Council at all.' By the time he spoke to the AGM, members' discontent had found a focus: the Council's intention to nominate Sir David Salomons for the Presidency in 1896.

Sir David was a wealthy and talented amateur scientist precisely of the kind sought after by the founders of the STE and scorned by the rising professional engineers. He was also a Jew, which in Victorian England would have been widely, if furtively, held against him. He was born in 1852, took second class honours in the Natural Sciences Tripos at Cambridge in 1873, was called to the Bar in 1874 and in the same year joined the STE, then courting the amateur. His title came from his uncle, also David Salomons, who died in 1873 after having been Lord Mayor of London and a Liberal MP.

At Broomhill, his house near Tunbridge Wells, Sir David set up an elaborate workshop and laboratory. In 1874 he lit his house with incandescent electric lamps, claiming to be the first householder in England to do so, and all the switches and other accessories were home-made. Amateur though he was held to be, he published *Electric Light Installations and the Management of Accumulators*, a work in three volumes which ran to eleven editions during his lifetime and was translated into several languages. He was Chairman of the City of London Electric Lighting Company and in *Who's Who* described himself as an engineer.[30]

In the affairs of the STE and the IEE Sir David became very active, showing evidence of a good head for money matters and a tidy mind. The STE stood in need of both. He was generous to the Society and to the Institution not only with time but with hospitality and money, including the endowment of a scholarship. He joined the Council in 1887, became a Vice President in 1891 and in 1893 succeeded Edward Graves, who had died, as Treasurer. By 1894 he was senior Vice President, and since 1881 there had only been two years – 1889 and 1893 – when the senior Vice President of the preceding year had not become President. In each of those years a Past President – Sir William Thomson in 1889, W H Preece in 1893 – had been elected for a second term, and each had been followed as President by the Vice President whom for a year he had replaced. By well-established custom, therefore, Sir David Salomons could rely on being President of the IEE either in 1896 or 1897. His claim was recognised, though far from universally approved of, throughout the IEE and outside it.

When the Council came to choose the President for 1896, discontented members indicated plainly and publicly (they had the trade press on their side) that they would be seriously displeased if tradition were followed and Sir David Salomons were nominated. 'There is undoubtedly a widespread and exceedingly strong latent opposition to the proposed President', commented a leader in *The Electrician* on 15 November 1895, 'which the Council must be sadly out of touch with their constituents not to be aware of . . . no institution that wishes to be taken seriously ought to allow itself to be represented by mere amateurs'.[31] *The Electrician*, blaming the Council for 'a singular lack of foresight' and 'a policy of drift', concluded, 'it is perhaps too much to expect that one to whom they have rendered such a disservice will rescue them by gracefully retiring from the untenable position to which they have permitted him to aspire'.

This broad hint was reinforced by A E Mavor, who in a letter published in *The Electrician* said that if the Council insisted on nominating 'a most worthy and benevolent dilettante' its action would be 'opposed by a large part of the youth and energy of the profession'.[32] A week later A A Campbell Swinton, also in a letter to *The Electrician*, urged Sir David to rescue the Council by a 'sacrifice . . . not inconsiderable in itself'. On the following day, the Council heard Sir David do as Campbell Swinton suggested: he asked them not to put his name forward for the Presidency.[33] Preece praised Sir David's 'self-sacrificing course' and proposed John Hopkinson. Sir David seconded the motion. Hopkinson, who had been President in 1890, accepted 'with extreme reluctance' and was elected.

Having thus resoundingly defeated the Council, deeply humiliating Sir David Salomons in the process, Raworth, Swinton and their associates pressed on towards their main objective: to break the power of the Past Presidents and reconstruct the Council. After a temporary reverse at the AGM of 1895, they had induced the Council to set up a committee, with Hopkinson as Chairman, to consider members' suggestions for altering the IEE's Articles of Association. While this committee was sitting Raworth, at an Ordinary General Meeting on 26 March 1896, proposed a motion, much to Hopkinson's irritation, to refer the IEE's annual accounts back to the Council for amendment.[34] The motion was carried, striking another blow at the Council's dignity and Sir David's self respect, for he was Treasurer and took pride in his skill in such matters. It was also a blow at F H Webb, the ageing Secretary, another of the discontented members' targets.

Meanwhile the Committee on the Articles had reported on 10 March 1896. In June, with confirmation in July, the Articles were amended. Under the Articles in their new form the number of Members elected to the Council was raised from twelve to fifteen, plus three Associates, and over the succeeding two or three years Raworth and Campbell Swinton, as well as other Members of a reforming tendency, were elected. Other articles were altered so as to weaken various entrenched positions. First, no President, Vice President, Member or Associate was to hold office in the same capacity on the Council for more than three years in succession. Second, the Council was required, in making nominations to fill vacancies, to give at least twenty-eight days' notice before the AGM, so as to allow time for nominations from the body of the membership – a right which members in time to come did not neglect. Third, power was taken to allow Members or Associates to serve on committees of Council without themselves being Council members. Finally, although Past Presidents were all permitted to remain members of the Council, their voting power was cut, following a precedent set by the Civil Engineers, by allowing votes only to the immediate Past President and to the four senior Past Presidents present at a meeting.[35]

The reformers thus won an important battle, but not yet the war. Sir David Salomons was still Treasurer and the senior Vice President. In the autumn of 1896 his name was again put forward for the Presidency. This time he let it go forward, and on 15 October it came to the Council. Sir David left the room and his case was put by Professor D E Hughes, FRS (1830-1900), President in 1886 and celebrated for his development of the microphone and other devices. The opposition was led by another eminent professor, W E Ayrton, FRS, also a Past President (1892), who put up Sir Henry Mance, CIE (1840-1926), a telegraph engineer of the highest distinction whom Ayrton had probably known when he was Sir Henry's junior in the service of the Government of India in the 1860s. It is ironic that the candidate of the reforming party, who claimed to represent the younger members, should have been twelve years older than Sir David. Sir Henry won.

Hopkinson, as President, had to write to Sir David officially, Hughes having refused to do it for him. 'The conclusion at which the Council arrived', said Hopkinson, '. . . was that Sir Henry Mance should be nominated . . . for the reason that a movement is on foot to specially associate the year with Submarine Telegraphy and that therefore a man representative of that Department should be chosen as our President.'[36]

Hughes took a different view. 'This has been a Political election', he wrote unofficially to Sir David a few days afterwards. 'The real qualities and merits of the candidates have never been taken into consideration – there has been a rebellion against the Past Presidents – against the candidates proposed by the Council. Against all their Committees – and finally against their Secretary – for they decided to accept Mr Webb's resignation as Secretary as soon as a new one could be found.' 'The Council', he added, 'seem to hate the sight or presence of Past Presidents who they think interfere too much and are too often present at their meetings.' 'The present cry of the Council', Hughes went on with growing bitterness, 'is that as President we ought to be represented by a Professional and not by an Amateur. . . . I think they are wrong – as a vast number of our members are Amateurs . . . we ought to have honoured our society by electing you – our greatest and most prominent amateur – but a miserable clique of so-called Professionals (I call them Gas Mongers) has prevented the desire of those who can appreciate true merit.'[37]

Salomons announced his intention of resigning as Treasurer. Hopkinson was gravely embarrassed. Imploring him not to, Hopkinson wrote: 'We should agree that the office of President of the Instn of Elecl Engineers is hardly an office to be desired but you have reason for annoyance at the decision of this Council. It is as though you had been sounded as to rendering a person a service and after you had expressed your willingness that person asked someone else to render that service instead.'[38]

Sir David Salomons was deeply offended and no doubt distressed as well. Having resigned the treasurership, he withdrew from the IEE's affairs. He lived almost thirty years longer, until 1925, but he channelled his talent and his energy, both considerable, in other directions altogether, and there is no evidence that he and the Institution were ever reconciled, though he never resigned his membership and the Salomons Scholarship perpetuated his memory.

Raworth, Swinton and their allies were no doubt right in their main aim of trying to bring the Council into harmony with the membership which in theory elected it and to concentrate the Council's attention on the electrical engineering of the future rather than the telegraph engineering of the past. They may also have been right to insist on developing the IEE predominantly as a professional association rather than a learned society, even if by doing so they departed from the original aims of the founders of the STE. They were certainly right in carrying out a thorough reform of a constitution which, for a self-governing institution serving a fast-changing profession, had become indefensible. Need they, however, have been so clumsy and brutal in their methods? To have allowed Sir David his term as President, with a clear indication of their intentions for the future, would surely have done less harm than to stir up so much public and private bitterness, and it would have been a graceful gesture to one of the IEE's most generous benefactors. Graceful behaviour, it seems, did not come easily to the young or youngish lions, and perhaps Sir David had been too generous for his own good.

Their revolution accomplished, the new masters of the IEE faced the opportunities and the problems of electrical engineering in Great Britain in the early twentieth century. They had a very different prospect before them from that which had opened before the telegraph engineers in the mid-years of the nineteenth century, and they were developing a different kind of institution to deal with it.

References:

1   P Dunsheath: *A History of Electrical Engineering*, 1962, chap.14; Brian Bowers: *A History of Electric Light and Power*, 1982, Section 2
2   *J.STE*, 1879, **8**, p.328
3   Evidence of Sir William Thomson to Select Committee on Lighting, 1879, p.177; W Siemens: *The Electrician*, 1883, **10**, p.447
4   *J.STEE*, 1885, **14**, pp.16–18
5   Rollo Appleyard: *The History of the Institution of Electrical Engineers (1871–1931)*, 1939, p.77
6   H Osborne O'Hagan: *Leaves from my Life*, 1929, Vol.1, p.121
7   *J.STEE*, 1885, **14**, p.8
8   *J.IEE*, 1890, **19**, p.2
9   *J.IEE*, 1893, **22**, p.54

10 *J.IEE*, 1894, **23**, pp.126, 133, 187–188, 197; see also W J Reader: *A House in the City*, 1979, pp.100–104

11 Brian Bowers: 'Joseph Chamberlain and the First Electricity Act', presented at the 11th IEE Weekend Meeting on the History of Electrical Engineering, Birmingham, 15–17 July 1983. Brian Bowers: Reference 1, pp.155–158

12 CM, 12 Feb. 1885

13 OGM and CM, 13 May 1886

14 Brian Bowers: Reference 1, p.158

15 P Dunsheath: Reference 1, p.145

16 L Hannah: *Electricity before Nationalisation* , 1979, pp.5–10

17 *J.STEE*, 1882, **10**, p.405; 1882, **11**, p.528; *J.IEE*, 1893, **22**, p.39

18 Bernard S Finn: *Submarine Telegraphy – The Grand Victorian Technology*, 1973, p.31

19 *J.STE*, 1875, **4**, p.21; Letter, Latimer Clark to Edward Graves, 20 Feb. 1880, IEE Archives I/6.5 no. 16

20 Reference 19, Letter

21 Reference 5, p.65

22 Latimer Clark to President and Council, 22 March 1879, with CM, Nov. 1879

23 Reference 22, Letter

24 Reference 5, p.47; *J.STE*, 1875, **4**, p.22

25 Reference 5, p.106

26 *Ibid*

27 *The Electrician*, 1895, **36**, pp.294–296

28 *The Electrician*, 1895, **36**, p.243

29 *Ibid*

30 Obituary, *J.IEE*, 1925, **63**, p.1158; *Who was Who*, Vol.2, p.926

31 *The Electrician*, 1895, **36**, p.69

32 *The Electrician*, 1895, **36**, p.134

33 *The Electrician*, 1895, **36**, p.160

34 *The Electrician*, 1896, **36**, p.747

35 Report of the Committee on Amendments to the Articles of Association OCM Vol.2, 10 March 1896; Extract from 'Memorandum and Articles of Association of the IEE' 1892, with 1896 alterations in front

36 Letter, John Hopkinson to Sir David Salomons, 16 Oct. 1896, IEE Archives 550/9(b)

37 Letter, D E Hughes to Sir David Salomons, 21 Oct. 1896, IEE Archives 550/9(c)

38 Letter, John Hopkinson to Sir David Salomons, 22 Oct. 1896, IEE Archives 550/9(d)

Chapter 5

The Institution, the Profession and the Industry, 1895–1914

I Misgivings

The growth of electrical activity in Great Britain between 1895 and 1914 carried the membership of the IEE upwards by 170 per cent, from 2,604 members to 7,045. During the same period, so far as it is possible to judge from information given in membership lists, the ascendancy of the power engineers became overwhelming. In the early 1890s perhaps as many as 40 per cent of members may still have been telegraph engineers, plus a few more working on telephones, but by 1911 it seems likely that 80 per cent of the members were in electricity supply and traction or in electrical manufacturing: that is to say, they were power engineers concerned with 'heavy current' and heavy machinery – mechanical engineers specialising in electrical plant.

The growing size, solidity and financial strength of the Institution were displayed to the world when at last, on 1 June 1909, it took possession of a building of its own. For £50,000 the Institution bought the remaining seventy-six years of a ninety-nine-year lease, held from the Duchy of Lancaster by the Royal College of Physicians of London and the Royal College of Surgeons of England, of a building near Waterloo Bridge, on the Victoria Embankment in London. It stood on part of the site of the medieval Palace of the Savoy once occupied by John of Gaunt. The ground rent was to be £2,201 a year. The lease was later extended to the year 2058.

The building, designed to impress the onlooker with the dignity of the Royal Colleges, had been put up in the 1880s and Queen Victoria had laid the foundation stone. It housed examination halls, research laboratories and lecture rooms. It was twice as large – 20,500 square feet against 10,000 square feet – as the Civils' building and four times as large as the Mechanicals'. It had a lofty room of about 3,000 square feet on the first floor of the river front which, said the Institution's President, 'will be one of the handsomest libraries possessed by any scientific or engineering institution in London. The theatre, when completed' – the IEE altered the building considerably – 'will be about 30 per cent larger than that of the Civil Engineers.' Members of the IEE held an Ordinary General Meeting in the new building on 10 November

1910. They had provided themselves with a headquarters of style and capabilities.[1]

During the years leading up to the Institution's move into Savoy Place proportionately fewer members came to be employed in telegraphs and more in the manufacture of heavy plant and in electricity supply, so the proportion of members living in the provinces, particularly in the manufacturing areas of the North and the Midlands, increased, and the provincial members began to feel that the Institution's activities were too heavily concentrated in London. An indication of the way provincial members' minds were moving was given in 1893 when the Northern Society of Electrical Engineers was formed in Manchester.

It was largely the creation of George Preece, who had ceased to be Secretary of the STE somewhat abruptly (see page 25) in 1877. The Northern Society, said a press release, 'was not founded with any view of rivalry or opposition to the existing Institution of Electrical Engineers, but simply to enable members of the profession who are unable to attend meetings in London to do so in the provinces and at the same time to become acquainted with each other.'[2] John Hopkinson became President and George Preece a Vice President. Of eighteen members of the new Society's Council, ten were Members or Associates of the IEE. George Preece was neither.

Notwithstanding the Northern Society's protestations of friendliness towards the IEE, the suspicion remains that its formation may have been a lightly camouflaged declaration of independence. Certainly the Council of the IEE, not always very tolerant of potential rivals, behaved towards the newcomer very courteously, and when the Society was amalgamated with the IEE in 1900, after alterations in the IEE's Articles, it became the IEE's Manchester District Local Section on very favourable terms: all its members were accepted in the IEE without scrutiny. Members in other districts, meanwhile, no doubt encouraged by Manchester's example, had been working for autonomy, and on 14 December 1899 the Council of the IEE agreed to the formation of Local Sections in Dublin, Glasgow, Newcastle-upon-Tyne and Cape Town.

The IEE, while remaining a learned society based in London, became also an association representing British electrical engineers wherever they were in practice. Opinion outside London, always jealous of London's pre-eminence, became more than ever a matter of concern to the Council. The Council's composition was altered from time to time to take account of provincial affairs, and any suspicion in the provinces, justified or not, of neglect or metropolitan arrogance at Savoy Place was liable to send tremors of disunity through the fabric of the Institution.

The acquisition of a stately home and the establishment of local sections was all very impressive, but the state of electrical manufacturing in Great Britain, the essential background to the progress of the electrical engineering profession, was by no means so healthy as the prosperity of the Institution might suggest. The relative failure of British electrical manufacturing in the twenty years or so before the Great War was an early and conspicuous symptom of British industrial decline, and members of the IEE were uncomfortably aware of it.

In 1909 the President of the IEE chose to examine the situation in his inaugural Address.[3] He gave figures (see Table 4) to show that between 1899 and 1909 capital employed in Great Britain in telephones grew by 175 per cent, in electricity supply undertakings by 448 per cent, and in electric traction by 781 per cent. That might look like impressive growth, but 'electrical engineering', he said, 'was not as prosperous as it might be.' He might have emphasised his point, from his own figures, by showing that the growth of capital employed in electrical manufacturing, at 147 per cent, was by no means as great as the growth of capital employed in electricity-using activities, strongly suggesting what was in fact the case: that a good deal of plant was not being made in Great Britain but was being brought in from abroad.

Table 4: Capital Employed in Electrical Undertakings, 1899 and 1909

Undertaking	Capital employed	(£m)	Increase (%)
	1899	1909	
Telegraphs (a)	34.3	36.3	6
Telephones	7.7	22.1	175
Electricity supply	17.8	97.5	448
Electric traction	20.8	185.2	781
Miscellaneous	8.5	12.2	50
Manufacture	16.8	42.5	147

Note: (a) Exclusive of Government telegraphs
Source: *JIEE*, (1910) (adapted)

Electrical manufacturing in Great Britain, and in France also, after an encouraging start in the eighties, was decisively overtaken in the nineties, particularly at the 'heavy' end, both in Germany and in the USA. By 1914, not only were the largest British electrical manufacturing firms a great deal smaller than their largest German competitors – Siemens-Schuckertwerke were employing 80,000 men, with AEG close behind, against a maximum of 10,000 men employed by any British firm in the same industry – but several of the largest 'British' firms in electrical manufacturing were foreign-owned, such as British Westinghouse and British Thomson-Houston (both American) and Siemens Brothers (German).[4] British electrical engineering, before 1914, was suffering badly from foreign competition, and in saying so in 1909 the President was echoing alarm notes which had been sounded at the Institution's meetings since the turn of the century and before.

G F Fitzgerald, FRS, Erasmus Smith Professor of Natural and Experimental Philosophy in the University of Dublin and a leading member of the IEE, had been gloomy in 1900: 'We have not been pioneers in any great advance in the application of electricity', he said, 'since the development of submarine telegraphy. . . . No doubt there are some advantages in not being pioneers; we … can often enjoy learning by the mistakes of others. On the other hand, we lose such industries as electric tramway construction and polyphase transmission of power, and can never expect to be in the forefront of progress.'[5] He neglected the development of the turbo–alternator by C A Parsons – surely a 'great advance', even if not strictly in the *application* of electricity – but there was no doubt about the general truth of what he said.

The President of the IEE in 1909 was Gisbert Kapp (1852–1922), appointed in 1905 to the newly founded Chair of Electrical Engineering at Birmingham University. His own career gives a hint of one reason for the success of foreign electrical firms in competition with firms in Great Britain: the superiority of foreign systems of technical education. Kapp had been born an Austrian. He had a Scottish mother, and as a young man he emigrated to England, having been trained in mechanical engineering at the Federal Polytechnic in Zurich. After working somewhat uneasily for Crompton in the early eighties he built up a lucrative practice as a consulting engineer before going to Germany for ten years (1894–1904) as General Secretary to the newly formed German Association of Electrical Engineers.[6]

Like other successful incomers from continental Europe, such as Sir William Siemens in an earlier generation, Emile Garcke in his own, and Hugo Hirst (1863–1940) a little later, Kapp used an excellent Germanic technical education to make himself a formidable competitor to British engineers on their own ground. The danger of relying so heavily on talented foreigners was indicated by the President of the IEE in 1900. 'Must we, Boer-like', said John Perry, identifying himself with the wartime mood of the moment, 'always depend upon our Uitlander population, Fleming and German, Hollander, Huguenot and Hebrew, for the development of our natural resources?'[7]

The power of technical education in Germany, and also in America, was described to members of the IEE by their President, W E Ayrton, in 1892. He was Professor of Electrical Engineering at the Central Technical Institution, South Kensington, and for nineteen years, he said, he had 'taken some part' in 'an experiment which of all others has been the one I have had most at heart … how best to train the young electrical engineer'.[8] Those nineteen years included five (1873-1878) at the Imperial College of Engineering, Japan, which was then the largest establishment of its kind in the world, and Ayrton also knew German and American systems of technical education very well.

He showed his audience slides of the Technical High School at Charlotten-burg (Berlin), which, he said, covered an area five times as large as the South Kensington Institution, cost four times as much to put up, and had more than four times as much spent on its yearly maintenance. He showed photographs of other institutions on the Continent, including the Polytechnic at Zurich where Kapp had been educated, and of MIT and Cornell in the USA, describing lavish buildings, equipment, staffing and expenditure in each of them, and he concluded: 'my choice of magnificent Continental and American laboratories has been so great that I have hardly known which to select…. But there is one thing I cannot show you – and it must remain for the exercise of your influence as representatives of the electrical profession to make that possible – the British electrotechnical laboratories for education and research which are truly worthy of London, the capital of the world.' The eventual British answer to the German and American challenge in technical education was the Imperial College of Science and Technology, formed by amalgamating existing institutions, but it did not come into existence, even formally, until its Charter passed the Great Seal on 8 July 1907.[9]

Related to the deficiencies of British technical education was the wider question of British educational priorities as a whole. Ayrton quoted the opinion expressed in December 1891 by J B Bury, a classical scholar and historian, that 'the true function of a University is the teaching of useless learning' and Ayrton's friend John Perry, in 1900, deplored 'the fault of our methods of education that all our great men, our most important, most brilliant, best educated men … should remain so ignorant of physical science'.[10] Perry, Oliver Lodge and others were particularly hot against the traditional teaching of mathematics in schools, based almost entirely on Euclid, and Perry went so far as to say 'mathematics ought to be the natural language of the engineer, and at present it is a foreign language; we cannot read or write or think in it'.[11]

No doubt Perry would have deprecated the parody of the Mikado's song, 'I've got a little list', addressed by Crompton to Kapp in 1886:

> … whenever I require to design a dynamo
> > I've got a little eye!
> > I've got a little eye!
> > For whatever you may tell me,
> > I assure you it's 'no go'
> > With mathematics high!
> > With mathematics high!
> I'm not one of those people who have
> > got Clerk Maxwell pat,
> Those people who when 'talking shop',
> > talk shop to you like that $\int\int$
> I'm not like those who always like
> > to zero integrate
> The number of lines of force (or do I
> > mean 'equate'?)
> Nor can I work the calculus, nor do I
> > mean to try.

It's all my little eye,
It's all my little eye.[12]

Crompton's tongue was no doubt fairly near his cheek, but he was giving expression nevertheless to an English scepticism about theoretical knowledge and mathematical skill, inculcated by traditional English education and training (Crompton had been at Harrow and in various engineering works, but at no university), which the 'professors' in the IEE found deeply disturbing. In contrast to such attitudes Perry, Fitzgerald and others praised foreigners' faith in applied science and their educated knowledge of the principles underlying the advanced technology of the day, which went far to explain foreign pre-eminence, at the end of the century, in electrical engineering.

'What a revelation it was to almost all of us,' said Perry in 1900,

> that visit of a year ago to Switzerland! ... We were very much like what engineers of 1870 would have been if suddenly brought into a generating station. Is it not a fact that some of us, said to be eminent and thought to be practical, asked questions and made remarks which showed that we did not know the most elementary principles of three-phase working? Is it then any wonder that the traction schemes now being developed in England ... are altogether dependent on the use of foreign electrical machinery and employ foreign electrical engineers?[13]

These were serious insinuations for the President of the IEE to make in his Inaugural Address. That he had plenty of support is evident from the number of other addresses delivered at about the same time in much the same tone of voice: so much the same, indeed, that it is difficult to avoid the conclusion that they were all part of a concerted plan to put forward strongly held and controversial opinions. Much of this verbal firepower was directed at Sir William Preece.

Fitzgerald attacked Preece directly and at length in his Inaugural Address as Chairman of the Dublin Local Section of the IEE on 22 February 1900, and from an even loftier platform, in November, Perry delivered himself of what must surely be one of the fiercest assaults ever made by a President of the IEE upon a Past President: 'I feel a sort of degradation every time that I hear a successful, clever old member of the Institution sneering at mathematics ... his sneer is doing a great deal of harm to the younger members who admire his success, who forget that he has succeeded in spite of, and not because of, his neglect of mathematics'.[14] About three months later, speaking in Birmingham, Perry said 'he deprecated the tendency in the parent Institution to array professors and engineers against one another'.[15] Well he might!

If engineering education was to blame for British backwardness in electrical manufacturing, so also, it was frequently said, was British technical conservatism and unwillingness to scrap out-of-date plant. 'We here all know', said Perry in 1900, 'that the District and Metropolitan Railways might have been worked electrically years ago ... but of course the scrapping of a lot of steam locomotives was a serious thing. The loss of experience to English electrical engineers, because of this hatred of scrapping, is leading to incalculable losses.'[16]

Foreigners, Perry pointed out, had no such inhibitions. Kapp, in 1909, took a similar point. 'Their great staple industries', he said, referring to British manufacturers, '... had been fairly prosperous for generations; those on the Continent ... had to struggle into existence against English competition. To become successful they had to adopt every improvement which science put at their disposal. With them the application of electricity was almost a vital matter; with England only a desirable improvement.'[17] Kapp did not make himself popular by saying such things, but he was not alone in saying them, either within or outside the electrical industries.

Perhaps the banks were to blame, too. Crompton, in his memoirs, complained that English bankers' principles of business would not let them support his continental ventures in the eighties in the same way as German bankers supported his competitors, so that he lost contracts he might otherwise have gained.[18] James Swinburne, in 1899, wanted to see German banking practices transplanted to England, and in the same year S P Thompson, complaining that in England it was very difficult to raise moderate sums – £10,000 to £25,000 – to launch an invention, went on: 'We have ... in this country no organisation corresponding to the Industrial Banks of Germany, to the enlightened management of which the financing of sound schemes on a moderate scale can be entrusted.'[19] Finally there was the long-standing conviction, widely held within the industry and the profession, that the development of electricity supply in Great Britain had been gravely hindered by the electrical legislation of the eighties. So strongly was this view held, and so grave was the anxiety about foreign competition, that in 1901 the Council of the IEE set up a Committee on Electrical Legislation. The evidence which the Committee heard led them to resolve 'that, notwithstanding that our Countrymen have been among the first in inventive genius in electrical science, its development in the United Kingdom is in a backward condition', and they blamed especially 'the restrictive character of the legislation governing the initiation and development of electric power and traction undertakings, and the powers of obstruction granted to Local Authorities'.[20] The appointment of the Committee on Electrical Legislation was part of a campaign by a party within the IEE to influence public policy in a certain direction on electrical matters, and to that we shall return (page 78).

Whatever the faults of the Institution may have been in the years before the Great War, complacency was not one of them. On the contrary, in so far as the Institution represented the profession, then the profession, through the mouths of successive presidents, was critical both of itself and of the industry on which it relied for its livelihood. The Institution was accordingly attempting, in various ways and with varying degrees of unanimity among its members, to deal with some of the matters which were causing the profession so much uneasiness.

II 'Membership should be a real ... distinction.'

Prominent among these matters was the establishment of recognised standards of professional qualification. The founders of the STE, concerned chiefly to set up a learned society, had not conceived of it as a qualifying body. The fact that they admitted non-commissioned officers of the Royal Engineers (page 28) as Associates suggests that they were prepared to accept applicants who would probably in later years be classed as technicians, and the regulations for admission to the Associate grade were deliberately drawn wide in order to admit 'men of science' who were not professional engineers. The telegraph engineers' profession was small and they could no doubt rely on personal knowledge, brought to bear through the ballot box, to block unsuitable candidates for election.

This was by no means the attitude of the electrical engineers of the 1890s and later, nervous of foreign competition, aware of the excellence of foreign technical education, and anxious, as newcomers, to establish an impregnable position in the English professional class. In this determination to raise standards they were not alone among engineers. The Civils set up their first examinations for the grade of Associate Member in 1897, 'following a general movement towards more systematic investigation of candidates, which began in the late 1880s'.[21]

What the Civils did one day the Electricals, at this period, were very apt to do the next, and the younger and keener Electricals regarded their seniors in the Institution as deplorably casual in these matters. 'The standard of qualification required for full membership should be raised', wrote Campbell Swinton to the editor of *The Electrician* while the rebellion of the mid-nineties was at its height, 'so that such membership should be a real, and not as at present a practically nominal distinction.' Swinton mentioned 'full membership' but the reformers aimed principally at the Associate grade. That was logical, since the road to full membership lay inescapably through it and it also contained a large non-professional element, attracted deliberately by the founders of the STE and abhorrent to their successors.

Sir David Salomons, 'amateur' though he was, twice attempted to improve matters. In 1894, backed as usual by Professor Hughes, he suggested separating members' 'scientific attainments' from their 'asociation in an industrial point of view with Electrical or Telegraphic Sciences' by setting up a class of 'Industrial Members', and in 1895 he tried to create a grade of Associate Members, no doubt based on the model provided by the Civils, which would have been reserved for professional telegraph engineers and electricians. Both proposals were blocked in Council, by whom or why the minutes do not reveal.[22]

This left the road clear for the reforming party, and when new Articles of Association were adopted in 1899 they provided, much in the manner proposed by Sir David Salomons, for the grade of Associate Membership. The regulations governing it required, as the regulations governing the Associate grade had required, evidence from professional candidates of adequate technical education and of the exercise of professional responsibility, and every Associate Member was explicitly required to be 'either an Electrical Engineer or Electrician'. This was the origin of the grade of membership which, so far as the Institution was concerned, marked the attainment of full professional standing as an electrical engineer.

For individuals who were neither electrical engineers nor electricians (in the older and more elevated sense of the term) but who were 'interested in or connected with Electrical Science or Engineering, or who are so associated with the application of Electricity that the Council consider their admission as Associates would conduce to the interests of the Institution' the Associate grade was preserved. The intention evidently was to separate professionals from amateurs within the Institution by setting up a non-professional grade. Nevertheless Associates, equally with Associate Members, had voting powers and were eligible for membership of the Council. It is hardly surprising that at first many professionally qualified Associates, elected under the old regulations, took no steps towards the new grade created for their benefit.[23]

In 1911 a committee considering the Articles of Association once again came to the problem of providing both for professional electrical engineers and for others: as the committee put it, 'for "electrical persons" and "non-electrical persons".[24] 'Non-electrical persons' were to be 'persons of good education ... who are not electrical engineers but who are connectd with the applications of electricity', as for example:

Directors, managers, secretaries &c. of electrical undertakings.
Barristers and solicitors.
Tramway managers.
Scientists.
Engineers (non-electrical).
Patent agents.
Parliamentary agents.
Contractors.
Electrical surveyors.
Medical men &c., &c.

These they proposed to group together as 'Associates', remarking: 'For many years past, with the exception only of the last few months, no electrical engineers have been elected to this class', and as a consequence 'the Associate Class has distinctly increased its dignity.'

To maintain the dignity of the Associate Class 'and to emphasise its non-electrical character', they proposed a class of Licentiates, into which they suggested electing 'Electrical Persons', defined as 'persons of good education' who were '(a) electrical engineers ... not qualified by age, experience, or knowledge to become AMIEE, or (b) [persons] employed in a scientific or engineering capacity in the applications of electricity'. As examples they cited:

Junior electrical engineers.
Trained electrical engineers unable to pass the AMIEE examination [to be set up].
Engineers (e.g. with BOT certificates &c) in charge of electrical machinery and with good practical knowledge of electrical engineering.
Junior lecturers, and teachers of electrical engineering.

The Council was urged to give 'every encouragement . . . for the transfer of electrical persons from the present Associate Class to that of Licentiate', and the committee proposed for the purpose a new Article permitting Associates registered before the end of 1911 to apply for transfer to the new class without the signatures ordinarily required.

New Articles of Association were adopted by Special Resolution on 30 May 1912, and the committee's recommendations became the basis of Articles governing the various classes of membership. The title 'Licentiate' was rejected in favour of 'Graduate'. The term had been used by the Civils from 1837 to 1867 when it was replaced by 'Student', and the Mechanicals used it, from 1850 onward, 'for engineers who had not yet reached a position fitting them for full membership.'[25] 'Graduate', as the engineering institutions used the title, without reference to a university degree, covered the middle ground between those who were unquestionably qualified for some grade of professional standing and those who unquestionably were not. This intractable problem of discrimination between those who are not quite equal, faced by all the engineering institutions, has become steadily more acute as engineering has become more diverse and complex.

These elaborate regulations left in limbo the Institution's central difficulty as a qualifying body. How should it determine who was fit to be admitted to the class of Associate Member, giving him the right to put the letters AMIEE after his name and thus to announce to the world at large his acknowledged competence to practise electrical engineering as a profession? In 1905, on the motion of a Vice President, W H Patchell, instructions went out from the Council 'that in view of the large number of applications for admission to the Institution and for transfers within it ... it is desirable that the Elections and Transfers Committee should investigate the general education and standing of the applicants even more strictly than in the past. In the case of a candidate for example who may be a Shift Engineer or Wiring Contractor it must not be concluded that by his position alone he is sufficiently qualified for election or transfer'.[26] One way out of the difficulty was to set qualifying examinations. They were not popular among engineers, and the IEE resisted them until 1911. Then the Council adopted the recommendations of an Examinations Committee set up in November 1908.[27]

Intending students they refused to examine, preferring to require them, after 1 January 1913, 'to have passed either the Matriculation Examination of one of the British Universities, or the Studentship Examination of the Institution of Civil Engineers, or some school leaving or other equivalent examination'. In the years to come, notwithstanding their willingness to recognise the Civils' examination, the Electricals took a stand on the principle of not examining intending students, saying that they did not wish to deter any reasonably well-educated applicant so early in his career. This impeccably liberal view was not entirely to the liking either of the Civils or the Mechanicals.

The committee's most important recommendations proposed a system for examining candidates 'for direct admission as well as for transfer to Associate Membership.' The scheme was to come into force on 1 January 1913; candidates were to be at least 21 years old, and those who had obtained 'certain University Degrees or certain Diplomas in Electrical Engineering' were to be wholly or in part exempt. There was to be a 'general knowledge examination common to all branches of the profession' and an examination on one special subject chosen from Power, Lighting and Traction; Telegraphy; Telephony; Electro-chemistry and Electro-metallurgy. Alternatively, candidates might submit 'a thesis, paper or other contribution to electrical knowledge' on which they might be orally examined.

It seems to have been a sad day for the Council when they adopted these recommendations. They made clear how little faith they had in the system they were setting up. 'The standard of the examination', they recorded in the minutes, 'not to be too high. Easy questions to be set, the object being to show that candidates possess (a) general education, (b) a reasonable amount of fundamental knowledge in one of the branches of the profession.'

They went further. 'The candidate's admission or rejection not to depend solely on his answers to the papers set, but these to be considered in conjunction with the candidate's practical experience, which must be in accordance with the requirements of the Articles of Association.' British engineers' suspicion of 'book learning' ran deep. A P Trotter, coming down from Cambridge in 1878, was warned by 'more than one experienced engineer' to conceal the fact that he had a degree, and for many years that advice would have been sound.[28] The Mechanicals, traditionally even more suspicious of 'theory' than the Electricals, set up an examination system at about the same time: 1913. The Society of Apothecaries, by contrast, had been examining candidates for their licence to practise since 1817.

The Institution, remodelled by the new Articles, had six grades of membership. Honorary Members, Members and Associate Members were 'corporate members'. The 'non-corporate members' were the Associates, Graduates and Students. The distinction between 'corporate' and 'non-corporate' members, very important in years to come, appears for the first time in the Articles of 1912. It is not defined, but it is clear that the only members considered to be fully qualfied professional engineers were those in the three corporate grades.

With the Articles of 1912 the Institution at last acquired the structure desired by the rebels of the mid-nineties. Strictly defined qualifications, tested by examination, were required for the professional grades, and the only untidiness was round the boundaries of the Graduates' territory. Members of other professions might be welcome, in appropriate circumstances, in the IEE, but their 'non-electrical' standing was made plain by the redefinition of the Associate grade. For amateurs, contrary to the wishes of the founders of the STE, there was no place at all.

It is ironic that the chairman of the committee which so carefully defined the grades of membership had some of the wicked glamour of the buccaneer about him. Robert Hammond (1850-1915) made his reputation in the early days of electric lighting. It was as well that his own qualifications, like those of some other pioneers, were not put to the tests required by the IEE's new regulations. 'A big, breezy, red-headed man', A P Trotter called him, 'whose chief business had been the importation of iron ore from Spain ... Hammond professed to be an engineer, and was clever enough to grasp general ideas and to use technical jargon.'[29] Hammond's opinion of Trotter is not on record.

III 'A mere trades union …'?

Acting as a qualifying body is generally considered to be one of the main functions of a professional association, and when the reformed Council of the IEE began to take the matter seriously, from the mid-nineties onward, it caused no great controversy within the membership. Setting standards of professional competence fitted very well with the members' conception of a learned society, which the STE and the IEE had always claimed to be.

There was another line of action open to a professional association, strongly urged by some members but far less acceptable to others. John Perry, in his inaugural address as President in 1900, raised the matter in a characteristically provocative manner: 'Is electrical engineering', he asked, 'to remain a profession or is it to become a trade? Is this Institution to continue to be a society for the advancement of knowledge in the application of scientific principles to electrical industries, or is it to become a mere trades union?'[30]

By 'trades union', it is unlikely that he meant a trade *union* designed for collective bargaining on behalf of the members as individuals but rather a trade *association* which would bring pressure to bear in the common interest – if a common interest could be found – of firms in the electrical industries as a whole. The question whether this kind of activity was desirable had been asked in one way or another since the very beginning of the STE, and the membership had always been split between those who felt that anything but the advancement of knowledge was beneath the dignity of a society representing a learned profession and those who considered it to be a duty of their professional association to protect and advance their commercial and industrial interests.

Speaking at the end of his presidency in 1902, W E Langdon (1832–1905), an elderly telegraph engineer, summed the matter up:

> It is quite true that this Institution is a scientific Institution, but, gentlemen, I cannot see why a scientific institution should not also be representative of that profession which springs out of the science which is the basis of the Institution. We all of us have to remember that the position of the electrical engineering industry … is … very different to what it was some twenty or twenty-five years back. The birth of the dynamo has made possible a very large industry, and that industry demands some representation; it must have some one to fight its battles; and it appears to me there is no body and no institution in the kingdom which … stands in a more sound position for dealing with matters which affect its interest than this Institution.[31]

When Langdon spoke of fighting the electrical industry's battles, what he chiefly meant was dealing with the Government and Government departments, especially the Board of Trade, for as soon as public supplies of electricity became a practical possibility, round about 1880, they became a matter for public regulation and for legislation, for which the Board of Trade was responsible. The subjects covered ranged from the definition and standardisation of electrical units on the one hand to the powers of local authorities on the other, with such matters as the safety of domestic wiring and the use of bare overhead conductors in between. The representation of electrical engineers' interests required a combination, in varying proportions, of technical knowledge, financial acumen and political astuteness, backed up by general acceptance, especially in official circles, of the Institution's claim to be an authoritative source of technical advice.

A measure of the rise in stature of the Institution is provided by the progressively wider acceptance, over thirty years or so, of the Wiring Regulations first drawn up by a committee of the STE in 1882 when electric lighting was new and its potential dangers were imperfectly understood either by the enterprising householders who went in for it or by the technicians and craftsmen who installed it for them. These regulations had no force in law. They were simply suggestions for good practice, and any effect they might have would depend entirely on the public reputation of the body which issued them.

Fire insurance offices, consulting engineers and others were at first ill-disposed to accept the STE's authority in these matters, preferring instead to rely on rules of their own devising. By 1899 there were at least twenty-six sets of rules in existence. The Society and the Institution nevertheless persisted, continually revising and reissuing their Regulations as electricity supply developed. At the same time respect for the Institution grew. By 1916, when the seventh edition of the Wiring Regulations was published, they had been adopted by fifty insurers, including one of the most important, the Phoenix, which had long held out against them.[32]

One of the most enthusiastic advocates of using the IEE to bring influence to bear on public affairs was R E B Crompton. As far back as the eighties he had taken a hand in forming the Electrical and Allied Trades Section of the London Chamber of Commerce and in 1888 he was Chairman. Largely through the Section's good offices, in June 1889, a strong delegation, led by Sir William Thomson and Lord Rayleigh, met the President of the Board of Trade (the Prime Minister, Lord Salisbury, excused himself) to press for the establishment of a National Standardising Laboratory for Electrical Instruments.

This delegation represented the IEE as well as the Chamber of Commerce, but A P Trotter, who as 'electrical secretary' to the Electrical and Allied Trades Section attended the meeting, thought the Institution was a reluctant partner. 'It has always', he said in his reminiscences, written in 1941, 'taken the position of a scientific body uncontaminated by commerce', and that was one of the complaints of the discontented members in 1895-1896.

Certainly progress in the establishment of a National Physical Laboratory and in related developments such as the standardisation of electrical units was very slow. This, in Trotter's opinion, was partly because technical and scientific knowledge was not widespread in the classically educated Civil Service. He was a well-placed observer. From 1899 to 1917 he was Electrical Adviser to the Board of Trade, and in his reminiscences he assures us that the Treasury asked the President to submit an ampère and a volt for inspection and to show how they became a watt when one was multiplied by the other. A minute laboratory was set up at the headquarters of the Board of Trade in 1890, but it was not until 1894 that an Order in Council officially defined the ohm, the ampère and the volt, and another eight years passed before the National Physical Laboratory was set up in 1902.[33]

During the nineties the Board of Trade was concerned with regulations for overhead conductors and for the supply of electrical energy generally, including regulations drawn up under the provisions of the Tramways Act, and with the Electric Traction Regulations (Railways). The Institution, Crompton being very prominent, cooperated closely with the Board, where the Electrical Adviser from 1888 to 1899 was Major Philip Cardew, RE (1851–1910), a Member of the Institution and a member of Council between

1886 and 1891, and the Institution's advice on technical matters was taken very seriously.[34]

Efforts by the Institution in 1898–1899, independently of the Board of Trade, to establish much-needed uniformity in electrical engineering practice, especially in supply voltage and the frequency of alternating current, were ineffective. Varying practice, especially in voltage, frequency and type of current – direct or alternating – plagued electricity supply in Great Britain until long after nationalisation in the 1940s.[35]

In technical matters related to electrical engineering, at the cost of a great deal of voluntary work by some of its members, the Institution by the turn of the century established a unique position. There was a growing number of specialised associations (see Table 5) catering for electrical interests of various kinds, but only one body could claim to represent electrical engineering as a united profession, and that was the IEE.

Table 5: Formation of Organisations in and related to Electrical Engineering, 1837-1913

1837	London Electrical Society
1871	Society of Telegraph Engineers
1884	Junior Institution of Engineers
1886	Electro-Harmonic Society
1888	Electrical and Allied Trades Section of London Chamber of Commerce
1893	Northern Society of Electrical Engineers
1895	Incorporated Municipal Electrical Association
1897	Tramways and Light Railways Association
	Röntgen Society
1901	Electrical Contractors Association
1902	Municipal Tramways Association
1903	British Electrical and Allied Manufacturers' Association
	Rugby Engineering Society
1904	Metropolitan Association of Electric Tramways Managers
1905	Incorporated Association of Electric Power Companies
1906	Institution of Post Office Engineers
	Association of Municipal Engineers (Greater London)
1907	Institution of Automobile Engineers
1908	Institution of Municipal Engineers
1909	Illuminating Engineering Society
1910	Association of Consulting Engineers
1912	British Engineers' Association
1913	Wireless Society of London

The interests of those who were represented by these various bodies were not always in harmony. In 1913 the Municipal Electrical Association and the Electrical Contractors' Association asked the Institution to mediate between them. The mediation was not very successful, but the mere fact that it was requested shows how high the Institution's prestige by then stood.[36]

The Institution was also well placed for dealing with other professional bodies. In 1902, in an early episode of cooperation between engineering institutions, Crompton and Sir William Preece, fortified with a grant by the Council of £250, were nominated to represent the IEE on the Engineering Standards Committee set up in 1901 by the Civils on the initiative of Sir John Wolfe Barry. They had the support of the Mechanicals, the Iron and Steel

Institute and other bodies.[37] The Committee was the ancestor of the British Standards Institution.

Abroad, in the years just before and after the turn of the century, the Institution was active in paying and receiving foreign visits. Sometimes the results were disconcerting, as Perry revealed (page 65) after a visit to Switzerland in 1899, but for the most part the Institution seems to have been held in high regard, as when it was asked to nominate members of the jury at the International Electrical Congress held in Paris in 1900. At that Congress the IEE and the American Institute of Electrical Engineers held a joint meeting in the US pavilion, and in 1904 the IEE sent a strong delegation, subsidised with £600, to an International Congress at St Louis. It was made up of the President, R K Gray; a Past President, John Perry; two future Presidents – William Duddell and R T Glazebrook – a past and future President (Crompton); and Hugh Erat Harrison (the 'Huge Rat'), principal of the Hammond Company Electrical Engineering College, later Faraday House, founded by Robert Hammond.

At this Congress the American Government convened a Chamber of Delegates from Foreign Governments in which Crompton, Perry and Glazebrook were delegated to represent the British Government. From the Chamber's deliberations arose the International Electro-Technical Commission, devoted chiefly to standardisation, which had its headquarters in London and formed National Committees, eventually, in more than twenty countries, usually in association with any 'electro-technical society' which might exist. Much of the early work in establishing the Commission, between 1904 and 1906, was done by the IEE, an indication of its high international standing.

Lord Kelvin became President of the Commission, Colonel Crompton its Honorary Secretary, and when the British National Committee was formed it was designed to represent Pure Science, Designers of Electrical Machinery, Government Technical Departments, and Electrical Engineering generally. The IEE had a monopoly of these appointments and of the ceremonial appointments also, for the President of the Committee was the reigning IEE President, (Sir) John Gavey (1842-1923), Engineer-in-Chief of the Post Office, and the Vice Presidents were Sir William Preece and Alexander Siemens.[38]

At home, as the nineteenth century ran out, members of the Institution found themselves more and more concerned with municipal trading. In late Victorian England it was a live political issue, drawing on widely separated sources of support. It attracted businessmen like Joseph Chamberlain from motives of pride in their cities in spite of their almost religious faith in private enterprise in other fields of industry and commerce. Fabian socialists like Sidney and Beatrice Webb also supported it, seeking the triumph of collectivism.

Municipal trading was applied particularly to natural monopolies – gas, water, tramways, electricity supply – and in none of these, perhaps, were the supporters of municipal and private undertakings more bitterly opposed to each other than in electricity. There were members of the IEE on both sides of the line, though the greater weight of influence and sentiment lay on the private side, and during the last twenty years or so before the Great War the politics of electricity supply came to dominate the politics of the Institution.

References:

1 Rollo Appleyard: *A History of the Institution of Electrical Engineers (1871–1931)*, 1939, pp.187–192

2 Lawrence H A Carr: *The History of the North Western Centre of the IEE*, 1968, p.1.

3 Gisbert Kapp: 'Inaugural Address', *J.IEE*, 1909, **44**, pp.8–55

4 L Hannah: *Entrepreneurs and the Social Sciences*, LSE, 1983, pp.27–28.

5 *J.IEE*, 1899–1900, **29**, pp.401–402

6 D G Tucker: *Gisbert Kapp 1852–1922*, 1973

7 *J.IEE*, 1900–1901, **30**, p.53

8 *J.IEE*, 1892, **21**, p.5

9 *J.IEE*, 1892, **21**, p.32; see also A Rupert Hall: *Science for Industry*, 1982, p.30.

10 J Perry: Presidential Address, *J.IEE*, 1900–1901, **30**, p.64; J B Bury: 'Compulsory Greek', *Fortnightly Review*, 1891, **50**(new series), p.813

11 *J.IEE*, 1900–1901, **30**, p.63; J T Nicolson: *J.IEE*, 1901, 30, p.778; O Lodge: **30**, p.799

12 Letter, R E B Crompton to G Kapp, 18 Nov. 1886, Science Museum Crompton Historical Collection CRO A21-3

13 *J.IEE*, 1900–1901, **30**, pp.55–56

14 *J.IEE*, 1900–1901, **30**, pp.56–59

15 *J.IEE*, 1900–1901, **30**, p.802

16 *J.IEE*, 1900–1901, **30**, pp.57–58

17 *J.IEE*, 1910, **44**, p.36

18 R E Crompton: *Reminiscences*, 1928, p.132

19 J Swinburne: *J.IEE*, 1899–1900, **29**, p.237; S P Thompson: *J.IEE*, 1900, **29**, pp.30–31

20 Minutes of Committee on Electrical Legislation, OCM Vol.4, 25 March 1902

21 G Millerson: *Qualifying Associations*, 1964, pp.57–58.

22 CM, 25 Jan. 1894, 4 April 1895, 14 June 1896

23 Report of the Articles of Association Committee, OCM Vol.3, 14 June 1898; see also Articles of Association of 1899

24 Revision of Articles Committee, OCM Vol.7, 2 Oct. 1911

25 Reference 21, pp.57,68

26 CM, 13 April 1905
27 CM, 14 May 1911; Reference 1, pp.196–197
28 A P Trotter: *Reminiscences*, IEE Archives SC Mss 6.
29 Reference 28
30 *J.IEE*, 1900–1901, **30**, p.45
31 *J.IEE*, 1901–1902, **31**, p.1362
32 Brian Bowers: Lecture for IEE Wiring Regulations Centenary, 21 June 1982, p.19; IEE Archives(Special Series) III/9.1
33 Reference 28; 'The Board of Education Standards Laboratory', *Engineering*, 1906, **81**, p.683
34 CM, various, 1889–1896
35 Minutes of Committee on Uniformity, OCM Vol.3, 13 Dec. 1898, 13 June 1899; CM, 22 Dec. 1898, 16 Feb. 1899; Hannah: *Electricity before Nationalisation*, 1979, pp.38–41, 88–89
36 CM, 30 April 1913; *The Electrician*, 1914, **73**, p.321
37 CM, 23 Jan. 1902
38 Annual Report of Council, *J.IEE*, 1905, **35**, p.552; CM, 7 Dec. 1905, 26 July 1906; Reference 18, pp.205–206

Chapter 6

The Institution in Politics

In May 1899 Parliament was preparing to appoint a joint Committee to consider municipal trading. Campbell Swinton, who had considerable interests in electricity supply and was no doubt mindful of the growth of municipal entrprise, proposed a Committee of the Institution to report to the Council on the connection between municipal trading and electrical engineering. Long discussions followed, and members of the Council who had business interests in electricity supply went out of their way to swing the Council into open opposition, on principle, to municipal trading in electricity. Sydney Morse (1854-1929), a solicitor who acted for supply companies, tramway companies and light railway companies, proposed a motion, seconded by Crompton, which, in spite of efforts by Evershed and Cardew to get it neutralised, was carried in the form:

> that the Principle of Municipal Trading in competition with private enterprise in matters electrical is, in the opinion of the Council, prejudicial to Electrical progress.[1]

It was a plain statement – none could be plainer – and it is safe to say that over the following fifteen years, whatever position the Council might take up on particular matters, the opinion of most of its members on the general principle did not alter.

During the parliamentary session of 1900 four private Acts were passed to provide electric power over about 250 square miles in County Durham, 325 square miles in the suburbs of north London, 1,000 square miles in Lancashire, and 1,050 square miles in South Wales. These Acts covered the territory of numerous local authorities, and they provided the material for a paper by W L Madgen, 'The Electrical Power Bills of 1900: Before and After', delivered on 21 February 1901. In it Madgen attacked the whole system of electrical legislation in the United Kingdom, blaming it comprehensively for British backwardness in electrical development, which was then getting unwelcome publicity in what were not yet called 'the media', and completely exonerating the members of his own profession.[2]

'The electrical engineers of the United Kingdom', said Madgen, 'are not to blame, and there is no occasion for any apology on their behalf.' In support of this forthright assertion he quoted work on electric tramways by Lord Kelvin, on dynamo construction by Hopkinson, on the incandescent lamp

by Swan, and on AC transmission by Ferranti. 'What is the reason, then', he
asked, 'that our electrical industry is behind that of nearly every important
country in the world?'

To that question he supplied an unhesitating answer:

> It is due in the first place to silly legislation by Parliament and to obstruction by the
> numerous local authorities entrusted with arbitrary powers. In the second place it is
> due to a class of quasi-officials and their associates to whose direct monetary
> advantage it is that an opposition should be entered to every project in which they
> are not employed.

He went on to attack the Board of Trade – 'a body curiously constituted
and still more curiously named' – and he elaborated on the iniquities of local
authorities. 'The Acts of 1882-88 and their administration', he said, 'have
proved entirely congenial to the narrow exclusiveness of these bodies, who
are endeavouring even now in their opposition to the Power Bills, to insure
themselves against the developments of science and a cheap supply rather
than impair the prospect of their being able to have an isolated municipal
plant all to themselves some day or other.'

Madgen's simple-minded tirade was much to the taste of his audience.
Dissentients were few but formidable. Robert Hammond made himself
unpopular by asserting, first: 'The real factor in the backwardness of electric
light in this country is not the factor mentioned by Mr Madgen but the cheap
price of gas,' and then: 'We owe as an Institution a great debt of gratitude to
the local authorities in this country, for the customer who comes and puts
fourteen out of twenty-five millions into an industry is a desirable customer
and we, as electrical engineers, owe him a debt of gratitude.' This damnable
heresy was too much for Sidney Morse. 'It is perhaps as well', he said, 'that
some one should at once get up to suggest to the last speaker that his speech
was one which it would have been better to have left undelivered.' Professor
Ayrton, another heretic, suggested that the reason why Metropolitan Railway trains were not being run by electricity was not the fault of Parliament or
local authorities but of 'the lethargy of the chairman and directors of a private
company, the sort of company that we were assured ... would rejuvenate
Great Britain.'

This accusation incurred the scorn of Madgen himself: 'It [the Company] is
in itself a monument to private enterprise, but the net earnings are very
moderate ... and it is a grave question of finance whether the additional capital
cost ... would be an advantage to the proprietors.' Hugo Hirst, German by
origin, suggested 'that a great portion of the wrong of which we complain
lies with the electrical engineers themselves'. He pointed out that large
schemes of the type authorised in the four Acts 'can only be carried out with
some measure of success if electricity is generated and transmitted on principles that only a few years ago were pooh-poohed in this country by many of

the leading electrical men'. Hirst thus flatly contradicted Madgen, but no one contradicted Hirst, perhaps because his communication arrived late in the discussion, which ran over two meetings.

Most of those who joined in the discussion laid about them heartily at popular targets such as the Tramway Act 1870, the Electric Lighting Acts of 1882 and 1888, the Board of Trade (Campbell Swinton expressed surprise that the Archbishop of Canterbury sat on it *ex officio*), local authorities and municipal trading, which Vesey-Knox, a Dublin member, called 'socialistic experiment'. Crompton blamed 'certain members of this Institution who speak at these meetings' for the widespread impression among the public 'that we English electrical engineers are woefully behindhand in electrical knowledge'. Could he have had Hugo Hirst in mind? Ebenezer Howard took the opportunity to publicise the Garden City Association and Madgen wound up on a suitably public-spirited note:

> ... if the greatest evil of our time, the overcowding and the unhappy condition in which the working classes are living, can be alleviated by means of electrical power distribution and traction on a comprehensive scale, clearly then it is our duty to see that the path is cleared for us to carry out our mission.

Madgen's main aim in presenting his paper, as this peroration makes clear, was to propel the IEE into action 'to convince the Legislature as to the means it should take to enable us to carry on the service assigned to us', which would entail a wholesale attack on the prevailing state of the law governing electricity supply, and especially on the privileged position of the municipalities. For this bold and controversial suggestion he had a good deal of support, as the subsequent discussion showed. In case 'some technical objection', as he put it, 'might possibly be raised to any action we may take in this direction', he quoted various extracts from the Memorandum and Articles of Association of the Institution to show that the action he was pressing for was within the Institution's powers and he went on to suggest appointing a special committee 'to consider what steps should be taken to remove the restrictions upon us.'

The upshot of Madgen's paper, in May 1901, was that a committee of the IEE met to consider electrical legislation. A 'Note of Points for the Consideration of Witnesses' was drafted by Madgen, who acted as Reporter of the Committee and also sat as a member.[3] The members of the committee were numerous, and all except Madgen seem to have belonged to the Council. Voluminous evidence was recorded in full and printed, very much after the manner of a Royal Commission or Select Committee, and in March 1902 the Committee recorded its findings in a series of resolutions.[4]

The Committee resolved 'that, notwithstanding that our countrymen have been among the first in inventive genius in electrical science, its development in the United Kingdom is in a backward condition', and they blamed 'the restrictive character of the legislation governing the initiation and development of electric power and traction undertakings, and the powers of obstruction granted to local Authorities'. Since local boundaries usually had no reference whatever to the needs of the community in regard to electric supply and traction, the Committee wanted areas chosen, as gas, water and 'sanitary' areas were chosen, on the basis of economic principles and industrial demand. Legislation should be altered, the Committee suggested, to take away the blocking powers of local authorities. They underlined their suggestion by remarking 'that excessive time is occupied and expense incurred in obtaining authority to carry out electrical undertakings, and that important and growing industries are thereby checked'.

Finally, they made a thinly veiled attack on the administrative procedure of the Board of Trade: 'while this Committee recognises the ability of the technical officials of the Government Departments concerned, it feels very strongly that the period of adjustment of departmental regulations to engineering development should no longer be delayed until the industrial interests concerned are seriously hampered.' They then made the audacious suggestion 'that this Institution is a competent body to take part in revising the regulations from time to time, and to share the responsibility as in the case of the federal Government of Switzerland, and the Swiss Institution of Electrical Engineers'.

This proposal had been put forward by Colonel Crompton in his evidence to the Committee[5] and bears every sign of his brisk, not to say arrogant, self-assurance which led him, in giving evidence, to a cheerful disregard for inconvenient matters of fact. It was followed by a recommendation that the Institution should memorialise the Prime Minister – Lord Salisbury, at the very end of his career – to receive a deputation 'for the purpose of urging the removal of the present disabilities and restrictions which prevent Electrical Engineering from making the progress that the National interests demand and attaining at least the same level as in America, Germany and other industrial countries.'[6] The Prime Minister was duly approached, a date was fixed for the deputation, and in a somewhat belated access of caution, at a Committee meeting on 10 June 1902, the President was recommended to make clear that 'the Institution as a body did not express any views on the subject of municipal trading.'[7]

Salisbury deputed his nephew Gerald Balfour (1853-1945) to receive the representatives of the IEE. He was a Cambridge intellectual, a Fellow of Trinity with a taste for psychical research, who after five years as Chief Secretary for Ireland had been President of the Board of Trade since 1900. The officials of the Board of Trade, it may be supposed, did not greatly care for Colonel Crompton's recommendation, which they had been made aware of, that they should share their responsibilities with the IEE.

The IEE's deputation, twenty-five strong, waited on Balfour on 18 June 1902, being introduced by Lord Kelvin. It was led by the reigning President, James Swinburne, and accompanied by the Secretary of the Royal Society. It included half-a-dozen Past Presidents, various members of Council, and one of the last aristocratic amateurs of science: the 4th Earl of Rosse, elder brother of C A Parsons. Swinburne, supported by Crompton and five other speakers, put the Institution's case to Balfour.[8]

Swinburne asked for reform of the 'parochial legislation' of the eighties, for prevention of 'unreasoning obstruction' to electrical schemes by local authorities, for the abolition of compulsory purchase by local authorities of privately owned undertakings. He also criticised the organisation of the Board of Trade. A larger electrical staff was needed, he said, and he mentioned that 'the electric light even of inland towns comes under Fisheries and Harbours, perhaps because it was originally used in lighthouses'. 'As to whether municipal trading is good or bad in itself', he asserted disingenuously, 'we say nothing', but he asked for 'a Royal Commission to consider the whole question of electrical legislation.'

Balfour politely refused to accept the IEE's main contention. He thought it was undeniable, he said, that electrical industry in this country was backward as compared with America and Germany, but doubted whether that backwardness 'was due altogether to defects in legislation, or to regulations of an oppressive character, or to the abuse of power by local authorities'. Nevertheless, 'he did not for a moment contend that changes in the direction indicated by the Deputation might not be of a very beneficial character'. He hinted at two reforming Bills, though he 'could not hold out much hope that either Bill would be passed during the present Session, which was well occupied with important measures' (did this phrase indicate Gerald Balfour's view of the relative importance of electrical engineering?). As to a Royal Commission, he would consult his Cabinet colleagues 'but he must not be understood to pledge himself to recommend that a Commission should be appointed'. He promised to consider the question of strengthening the Board of Trade staff.

This was the meagre result of the IEE's ambitious venture into national politics. It was an anti-climax, no doubt because of the IEE's political innocence in challenging two powerful interests: the municipalities and the Board of Trade. Moreover, the Institution was a house divided. Crompton, Emil Garcke and others, because of the nature of their business, were enemies of the whole principle of municipal trading.

Other members, of whom Robert Hammond was evidently one, looked to municipal authorities for business and, in the words of the *Electrical Review*, were 'by no means opposed to the socialistic principles which are being so industriously introduced into municipal action'. Still others relied directly on municipal electricity undertakings for their livelihood. Of them the *Review* was scornful: 'We question if by coquetting with this pernicious interference with legitimate business the career of the electrical engineers embarked in it will be improved; there is a tendency on the part of the best men gradually to leave the ranks of the municipalities. ... The end will be a residue of case-hardened municipal servants of the calibre of the average municipal surveyor earning the same poor remuneration.'[9] Whether Sir John Snell (1869-1938) saw his portrait in that sentence is not on record, but on becoming President of the IEE in 1914 he said that the greater part of his professional life had been 'amongst municipal undertakings'.[10]

The internal politics of the Institution faithfully reflected the politics of the electrical industries, and particularly of electricity supply, which for twenty years or more before Sir John spoke had been complex and acrimonious. As Professor Hannah points out, the problem of developing large-scale inter-connected operations from the chaos of small undertakings inevitable in the early days of public supply seemed especially intractable in England. It existed in Germany and America also, but it was more quickly put tidy. It was especially bad in London, where in 1914 there were still seventy generating stations with a wide variety of systems and controlling authorities, municipal and private, against four stations in New York and four in Chicago.[11]

After the fiasco of the deputation to Balfour it became steadily more obvious that the British situation, with large undertakings set against small, and municipalities against companies, made it impossible for the IEE to act politically for a united profession, because a united profession did not exist. A Parliamentary and Industrial Committee, set up within the Institution in 1903 and still active in 1909, emasculated itself as soon as it was formed by resolving that 'no question involving Municipal Trading is a fit subject for consideration' and 'that the Committee should not initiate any action in any matter in which there is a conflict of interest between different members of the Institution.'[12]

Even in such an apparently uncontroversial matter as setting up a code of conduct for consulting engineers – surely a legitimate matter for a profes-sional institution to concern itself with – the politics of municipal trading made themselves felt, for what was at issue was the employment by munici-palities of consulting engineers rather than engineers on the staff of electrical manufacturers. Crompton complained of this custom in 1901, and much effort was directed towards checking methods of soliciting business which he and others considered unbecoming.[13]

The matter was settled in 1910 by adapting for the Electricals' purposes Regulations relating to Professional Conduct recently incorporated into the Civils' by-laws[14], but in enforcing its rules of professional conduct the IEE, like the other engineering institutions, could invoke no stronger sanction than expulsion. That did not in itself prevent the expelled member from practis-ing, unprofessional though his methods of practice might be.

The demand for action by the IEE on behalf of the commercial interests of the electrical industry as a whole persisted throughout the pre-war period, against the opposition of those – General Webber was one – who thought the Institution should confine itself strictly to matters of engineering technology, eschewing especially all matters of pricing and finance. In 1907, for instance, A Bergtheil, a consulting engineer, said he had several times mentioned to members of Council his belief that the Institution should do more for the industry commercially, but that he had always been met with the reply 'that the Institution was purely for the furtherance of technical matters, and that it was not within their province to interfere in commercial matters'. He failed, he said, to see why this should be 'in face of the fact that all other professional societies, such as the Law Society, Society of British Architects and the like are great safeguards to their various professions'.[15] In 1911, following the line of thought pursued by Bergtheil, the Committee for the Protection of Electrical Interests – not an IEE committee – suggested that the IEE should form an Industrial Section or Committee.[16]

The upshot was the last and most elaborate attempt, before the Great War, to bring the IEE's influence to bear on public policy. An Industrial Committee was formed, under the chairmanship of Hugo Hirst, with eighteen members drawn from the Institution and six, 'if so desired by the Council', from outside.[17] Government Departments and public bodies were expressly informed 'that the Committee is representative of the whole of the electrical industry and that its membership is not confined to Members of Council or of the Institution'.[18]

The history of the Industrial Committee was brief and unhappy. One of its earliest recommendations was that no report should be published in the Journal of the discussion at three meetings in March, April and May 1912 of 'The Causes preventing the more General Use of Electricity for Domestic Purposes'.[19] No report was published, and therefore we do not know what acrimony this apparently harmless topic stirred up, but it is a fair guess that municipal trading would have been one of the ingredients.

To approach the subject at all, during these years, especially in connection with London, was to tread on very sensitive ground indeed. When Dr Klingenberg of Berlin was invited in 1913 to present a paper, and proposed as his title 'Electricity Supply in large Cities with special reference to London Conditions', the Committee asked him to delete the reference to London.[20] A few months later, *The Electrician* referred to a statement that the Council 'stifled the discussion on Dr Klingenberg's Paper'. 'So far as we are aware', *The Electrician* went on, 'there is no justification for this statement', but it did recognise that 'very little discussion took place'.[21]

In March 1914 the Council of the IEE considered a report from the Industrial Committee on their own future. Their remarks were short, bleak and pointed. They started with a unanimous declaration 'that an organization should exist which is capable of protecting and promoting the legislative and industrial interests of the industry', and they went on to say 'that the present constitution and powers of the Industrial Committee are not such as to enable it to perform useful work'. Then they asked the Council whether it was advisable to enlarge the Industrial Committee's powers 'and give it the necessary authority to carry out the work referred to' or 'whether the Council be of the opinion that the consideration of these industrial questions is properly within the province of the Institution'. The Council responded emphatically. By fifteen votes to one, it got rid of the Industrial Committee.[22]

On 21 May 1914 the IEE held its Annual Meeting. 'The Council', reported *The Electrician*, 'were present in full force, but not more than 12 ordinary members took sufficient interest in the proceedings to attend.'[23] Before this derisively small audience Hugo Hirst discussed, in terms remarkable for their moderation, the reasons for the death of the Industrial Committee.

'It did not seem to be generally known', he said, 'that the Council considered it essential that the Industrial Committee should not deal with matters which might be considered to have a political bearing.' Since parliamentary powers had been granted to some 400 municipalities in regard to electricity supply stations, 'it was very difficult to find subjects connected with municipal electricity supply that did not touch politics'. He referred to Dr Klingenberg's paper, saying that when it was read 'the Council had some fears that the Paper might lead to a political discussion'.

The Council, said Hirst, had other wishes too which did not appear in the Committee's constitution, such as the view 'that questions which were to the detriment of a certain section of its' – presumably the IEE's – 'members should not be dealt with'. Some members of the Committee, said Hirst, were anxious to respect that wish, but others – and it is difficult not to believe that Hirst was one of them – 'felt that if a proposition that was for the benefit of the whole industry was brought forward some section might have to give way or suffer slightly'. Once again, 'it was difficult for the Industrial Committee to choose suitable subjects which were likely to meet with the approval of the Council'.

Then he passed to a fundamental division of opinion within the Council and, no doubt, within the membership generally: 'Well-known members of the Council who were respected by everybody thought that the high standard of the Institution might suffer if it lent its name to discussions dealing with money matters, such as finance or trade discounts, that were likely to enter into the discussion of industrial questions.' With calculated understatement, Hirst expressed his frustration with the Council's restrictions on the Committee's freedom of action, saying that 'he thought it was due to himself as chairman and to some of the members [of the Committee] ... to say that ... some of the limitations of the constitution ... acted against the possibility of the Industrial Committee doing such work as it was hoped could have been done'.

Three speakers on the topic of the Committee followed Hirst. Hugh Seabrook and Kenelm Edgcumbe both regretted 'the disinclination of the Council to take up the industrial side of electrical work'. W M Mordey, a Past President (1908) and a most distinguished electrical engineer, 'said he was one of those people who thought that the influence, dignity and usefulness of the Institution would be best maintained and increased by following the example that they had always had before them, of giving their attention to the scientific and engineering foundations of the electrical engineering industry, rather than by attempting in any way to make it a trade association'.

The short career of the Industrial Committee thus exposed once again irreconcilable differences of view on the true functions of the IEE. Hugo Hirst, there can be no doubt, was bitterly disappointed and he never again took so prominent a part in the Institution's affairs, nor, in spite of his eminence, was he ever President. In the embittered state of electrical politics before 1914, however, it is hard to see how the Industrial Committee could have been made to work as he desired or, if the attempt had been made, how it could have been prevented from splitting the Institution into fragments.

In 1914, the situation established in 1895 was reversed. Those who had been victorious then, and who wished to see the Institution, in Mordey's words, as a 'trade association', or in Perry's even more pejorative phrase (page 71), as 'a mere trades union', were decisively defeated. Those who wished to see it principally, again in Perry's words, as 'a society for the advancement of knowledge' were masters of the field.

References:

1   CM, 18 May, 31 May, 6 July 1899
2   *J.IEE*, 1900–1901, **30**, pp.475–508,514–39.
3   *Minutes of Proceedings of the Committee on Electrical Legislation of the Institution of Electrical Engineers* 1901 pp.1–2 Science Museum Crompton Historical Collection CRO–B–99
4   Minutes of Committee on Electrical Legislation, OCM Vol.4, 25 March 1902
5   Reference 3, pp.34–35
6   Reference 4, pp.138–139
7   Reference 4, 10 June 1902
8   'Report of Deputation to the Board of Trade' *J.IEE*, 1901–1902, **31**, p.1323
9   *Electrical Review*, 1902, **51**, pp.42–43
10 *J.IEE*, 1914–1915, **53**, p.1
11 L Hannah: *Electricity before Nationalisation*, 1979, pp.43–53
12 Minutes of Parliamentary and Industrial Committee, OCM Vol.4

13   Reference 3, pp.33–34; Circular of 17 Oct. 1902 setting out 'professional
     etiquette' for consulting engineers, The *Times Engineering Supplement* 6
     Feb 1907 covering letter from Bergtheil and Young to Secretary IEE, –
     IEE Archives I/6.1; Council Resolution 9, May 1907 appointing Com-
     mittee on Etiquette
14   'Annual Report of the Council', *JIEE*, 1910, **45**, p.734
15   Letter, Bergtheil and Young, Reference 13
16   CM, 14 Dec. 1911
17   CM, 28 March 1912
18   CM, 14 Nov. 1912
19   Industrial Committee Minutes, OCM Vol.8, 4 Nov. 1912
20   Industrial Committee Minutes, OCM Vol.9, 28 Oct. 1912
21   *The Electrician*, 1914, **73**, p.321
22   CM, 19 March 1914
23   *The Electrician*, 1914, **73**, p.302

Chapter 7

Towards the Charter, 1914–1922

I War and the Institution

In 1914 no one had ever seen a war between the major industrial countries of the world and no one could imagine what it would be like. The general impression was that it could not last long and that it would be a war of rapid, dramatic movement, rather after the pattern of the Franco-Prussian war of 1870-1871. Trench warfare on a front from Switzerland to the North Sea – siege warfare on a gigantic scale – was not foreseen on either side, nor was the total commitment of national resources, nor, above all, the scale of the slaughter. War could still be thought of as romantic adventure, or as the best of all outdoor games for nasty rough boys. Hence the enthusiasm displayed in all the belligerent countries when the Great War broke out.

The IEE had a strong military tradition. Its association with the Regular Army ran back to the founders of the Society of Telegraph Engineers, and in the general patriotic excitement of the late nineties the Council, led by John Hopkinson until he died and by R E B Crompton, but against the quakerly opposition of S P Thompson, took part in forming a Corps of Electrical Engineers, RE (Volunteers). The Corps had sent seven officers and forty-eight men, under Crompton's command, to South Africa in March 1900. In December of the same year, when it was generally thought that the war had been won, the survivors (four were dead) were welcomed back to England by John Perry, the Institution's President.[1] Crompton stayed on in South Africa, performing remarkable manoeuvres with traction engines, including hauling guns into action, much to Kitchener's displeasure.[2]

With this record of active military service behind them, the Council of the IEE fully shared in the mood of eager improvisation which seized the nation in 1914. In particular, they responded to an invitation issued to the three major engineering institutions from the Admiralty, presided over by Winston Churchill, to find men for the engineer units and the signal company of the Royal Naval Division, formed for land service from men who, before the war, had joined the RNVR under the impression that they would serve at sea, but for whom no ships could be found.[3]

From the IEE, 123 members, of whom nine were killed, joined the RND's Engineers. Long before the end of the war they had been dispersed to other units, which they considered a breach of the understanding on which they had been engaged. More serious, perhaps, their technical skill had largely been ignored and wasted. They were bitterly disappointed. 'If there had been less enthusiasm', said the report of a post-war IEE committee, 'and if they had waited, most of these men would have done better for themselves.'[4] It is a melancholy story. It summarises the initial enthusiasm, the muddle and waste, and the final disillusionment of the Great War.

In 1919 the Council reported that 181 Members, 930 Associate Members, 88 Associates, 170 Graduates and 652 Students had served in the war: 2,021 of all grades, representing about 30 per cent of the total membership in 1918. Of them 162 lost their lives, of whom sixty-eight were Students and sixty-nine, Associate Members.[5] As in other professions and skilled occupations, far too many electrical engineers were allowed to join the armed services in the early days of the war, regardless of whether they might have been more usefully employed elsewhere. Once a man was in the Army or Navy it was very difficult to claw him back, and there was no guarantee – as the members who served in the RND discovered – that he would be employed on technical duties. Efforts were made, as the war went on, to put matters right, but the waste of skill was very serious, and the initial mistake was not repeated next time war broke out.

The Institution's corporate life was severely disrupted. The membership fell from 7,084 in 1913 to 6,613 in 1917.[6] In 1915, only nine candidates entered for the Associate Membership examination, one failed to present himself on the day, and five passed. In 1918 the examination system was suspended.[7] Very early in the war, Government Departments began taking over rooms in the Institution's building, until in March 1917 the IEE, entirely dispossessed, moved its offices to Albemarle Street and once again found itself beholden to the Civils for the use of their meeting rooms and library. The Institution did not get possession in Savoy Place again until January 1921, and the building was not ready for ordinary use until the early summer.[8]

Despite these discouraging circumstances, throughout the war the Institution brought its influence widely and variously to bear. One of its less successful ventures was a long and energetic campaign for a National Electrical Proving House, which never came into existence in the form which the Institution sought, but the struggle was not abandoned until 1925.[9] On the other hand, in the summer of 1918 the IEE was seeking support from other organisations for the formation of 'a body corresponding to the British Commercial Gas Association ... in order to promote the extension of electric cooking and heating',[10] and that was soon set up. It became the British Electrical Development Association and lasted until 1968. In spite of having refused, earlier in the Institution's history, to meddle with patent law, the

Council in January 1918 appointed a Patent Law Committee which co-oper-
ated with the Civils and Mechanicals and with the Federation of British
Industries.[11]

Just before the war, in 1913, the Council of the IEE appointed a Research
Committee with S P Thompson, FRS, as Chairman and R T Glazebrook,
FRS (1854–1935), an ex-President and Director of the National Physical
Laboratory, as a member. By September 1915, with money which the war
had jolted the Government into providing, the IEE had nine projects in hand,
though the scale of them, if it can be measured by the financial support two of
them were receiving, can hardly have been impressive: £840 for a year's work
on the heating of buried cables; £250, also for a year's work, for investigating
the properties of insulating oils. The total sum provided by the Government
for the promotion of scientific and industrial research, in the Annual Estimates, was £25,000. The IEE received 4.36 per cent of it: no doubt they did
well.[12]

By 1918 Government grants were a little less exiguous, but it is clear that
nothing ambitious could ever be undertaken. An attempt to work jointly
with BEAMA (British Electrical and Allied Manufacturers' Association) did
not prosper – the manufacturers may have been nervous of giving their
secrets away – and in 1918 all the IEE's research work was handed over to the
Electrical Research Committee, set up with Government backing in 1917. It
was enlarged and in 1920 transformed into the British Electrical and Allied
Industries Research Association with a strong IEE presence and C H Wordingham, President in 1917–1918, as Chairman.[13]

In purely technical matters, where some members thought the Institu-
tion's true vocation lay, a great deal of work was done during the war on the
Wiring Regulations, on regulations for electrical equipment in ships, and on
Model General Conditions for Contracts. The war itself generated activity.
'We did a good deal last Session', said Wordingham in November 1918, 'in
connection with Coal Rationing and Diesel Fuel.'[14] Looking beyond the end
of the war, the IEE in July 1918 held an Overseas Engineering Trade
Conference with representatives from the British Electrical and Allied Manufacturers' Association (the main organisation on the manufacturing side of the
industry), the Cable Makers' Association and other organisations.[15]

From June 1915 onward, under Lloyd George as Minister of Munitions,
British industry began to pass under Government control: something which,
before the war, would have been inconceivable, especially under a Liberal
administration. Lloyd George's method, so far as possible, was to have the
ministry which controlled business run by businessmen, engaged as temporary civil servants. For the first time British businessmen, habitually secretive,
began to talk to one another, to find out how other people's firms were run,
to see advantages in rationalisation, to form schemes for merger and takeover

after the war – or even, in the case of the explosives industry, while it was still going on.

In this atmosphere pressure, heavy pressure, even heavier than before the war, was applied to strengthen the electrical manufacturing industry against foreign competition and to reorganise the supply side. The Government had a direct interest in improving the efficiency of supply in order to save coal and to make sure that manufacturing industry of all kinds got the power it needed for wartime output. The upshot was the establishment in June 1916 of a Department of Electric Supply and a great deal of investigation by official committees.

The IEE was bound to be consulted. It was thus placed in a situation congenial to those members who wished to see it bringing the influence of electrical engineers to bear on public policy, but beset by the kind of dangers to the unity of the Institution which had emerged before 1914. The problems which were being brought under review, though thrust into prominence by wartime urgencies, predated the war and would outlast it. They were also of great national importance. They demand separate consideration.

II 'An umbrella' – The Institution and the Industry

In March 1916, before the Department of Electric Supply was set up, the Board of Trade announced in *The Times* the appointment of committees to consider the post-war position of important British industries, especially in relation to foreign competition. On 23 March the Council of the IEE met, and two of its leading members – the President, C P Sparks, and Sir John Snell – forthwith wrote to suggest a committee on electrical engineering.[16]

The Board of Trade responded remarkably fast. By May the suggestion had been accepted and by 8 June Sparks had given evidence on behalf of the Council (not the Institution as a whole) before a committee appointed by the Board of Trade 'to consider the Position of the Electrical Trades after the War'. The Chairman was Sir Charles Parsons, inventor of the turbine and a Member of the Institution. There were five other members, of whom three – T Octavius Callender, Managing Director of Callender's Cable and Construction Company, James Devonshire and Sir John Snell – belonged to the IEE, so that the influence of members of the Institution was strong.[17]

From Sparks's evidence to the committee, as authorised by and reported to the Council,[18] a picture emerges of the state of the British electrical industry and of the fears and hopes of some of the most prominent men in it. Conscious, no doubt, of the size of the larger German and American electrical businesses, and of the Germans' cartel methods of attacking foreign markets, the Council asked for 'some combination of British Electrical Firms, especially with regard to overseas trade'. At home, they proposed 'a Government Tribunal ... to control the electricity supply industry of the country, and also to prevent indiscriminate addition or extension of Power Stations or Systems undesirable either in point of view of size, locality, or system'. The reaction to this suggestion, within the Institution, showed how delicate was the ground on which the Council was treading, and why it could not claim to present the views of the Institution as a whole. Several supply companies, mainly in London, protested against it and so did a group of twelve individual members.[19]

In a suggestion repugnant to Victorian free trade orthodoxy, still upheld with almost religious fervour in both political parties, the Council asked for a tariff to protect the home market, and in rather the same spirit they recommended setting up 'a permanent Advisory Committee to ensure that as far as possible raw materials and parts, as well as whole apparatus, necessary to the trade of the British Empire should be produced within the Empire' and they hoped that British Engineering Standards – which the IEE was doing a great deal to promote – would be adopted imperially. Bearing in mind, no doubt, the complaints frequently made of British diplomats' lofty attitude towards commerce, the Council asked for 'British-born Electrical Attachés to help in the Consular Service' and for 'Trade Commissioners'. The metric system, they urged, 'should be made compulsory after a reasonable period', and until then all trade catalogues should use both metric and British systems.

Parsons' committee was concerned with electrical manufacturing and overseas trade. The most important customers for electrical manufacturers in the United Kingdom were the supply undertakings. The organisation of supply, therefore, was of capital importance to the manufacturers. For many years, as we have seen, the organisation of supply had been a matter of bitter controversy which before 1914 had threatened to split the IEE into squabbling factions. Nevertheless the urgencies of war emphasised the necessity of dealing with it, and Sir Charles Parsons, at an early stage in his own enquiries, suggested setting up a committee to look into the problem.[20]

The committee came into being, in 1917, under the chairmanship of Sir Archibald Williamson (1860-1931), a Liberal MP who in 1922 became Lord Forres. He was a Scottish businessman – Scottish influence was for many years powerful on the borderland between business and politics – who served on numerous committees enquiring into subjects as various as Derelicts, Short Weight and the Telegraph Service.[21] There had already been an interim report on electric power supply by a committee under the chairmanship of Charles Merz, but before his committee's final report was issued, in 1918, Merz seems to have been overtaken by Williamson. Merz himself joined Williamson's Committee. So did Sir Charles Parsons, Sir John Snell and two other Members of the IEE – James Devonshire and George Hume, both of whom were later knighted.[22]

Of the twenty-three men who served on these three committees five, who all served on the Williamson Committee, also served on one of the other two, and at least four of them belonged to the IEE. There was thus a good deal of overlap between the membership of the three committees, and of the overlap, surely not by chance, prominent members of the IEE had almost a monopoly. The Council of the Institution was in fact diligent in preparing the ground not only for Sir Charles Parsons' committee, which they suggested, but for Sir Archibald Williamson's also. What seems to have been their first move, early in 1916, was to arrange for a thorough discussion of the whole problem of power supply in Great Britain.

'The present position of Electricity Supply in the United Kingdom and the steps to be taken to improve and strengthen it' was the title of a paper presented by Ernest T Williams in April 1916 and discussed, at the next meeting, by Charles Merz and other distinguished electrical engineers. Important differences of opinion emerged, particularly over the part to be played by the Government in the future organisation of the supply industry, and some speakers – J S Highfield, for instance, who became President in 1921, and C H Wordingham, President in 1917 and 1918 – thought Merz too critical of the existing state of electricity supply in Great Britain, but there was a general consensus that the way ahead ought to lie through much larger power stations and much more interconnection between them.[23]

Leaving on one side, therefore, the question of the part to be played by Government and the legislation which would be necessary – essentially political matters – the Institution was well placed to perform what many members regarded as its natural and proper function. It could offer professional advice on matters of electrical engineering without danger of tearing itself apart: a much more comfortable situation than the one which had destroyed the Industrial Committee in 1914.

At the meeting which heard Sparks's report of his evidence to Parsons, the Council set up an Electricity Supply Committee 'to report to the Council on the best means of co-ordinating and improving Electricity Supply in the United Kingdom'.[24] The Chairman was R A Chattock (1865-1936), who in 1925 became President. He was a power engineer who, after early experience with the Metropolitan Electric Supply Company, spent the major part of his career with Bradford Corporation, and he served as President of the Incorporated Municipal Electrical Association (IMEA). Nevertheless Charles Merz, whose sympathies scarcely lay with municipal enterprise, was also a member, and so was W B Woodhouse (1873-1940), another power company man, who became President of the IEE a year earlier than Chattock.[25]

There was evidently a real effort to draw the municipal and company undertakings together. The Committee was instructed to consult with the IMEA 'and other similar bodies', and at its first meeting members heard that the IMEA and the Incorporated Association of Electric Power Companies had together formed the National Electric Power Supply Joint Committee to consider linking supply undertakings in various districts. The IEE Committee seized the opportunity to arrange a conference with the Joint Committee, which was held on 27 July 1916.

This conference concluded that the Electricity Supply Committee of the IEE should 'devote its attention to the question of electricity supply from the point of view of the requirements of the country as a whole, and will deal with the engineering aspect of the matter'. The Joint Committee was to 'go into more immediate questions of organization and linking-up of existing undertakings, etc.'[26] Thus the Institution stood firmly on ground which was indisputably its own, as a professional engineering body, without attempting to trespass into the political swamps and quagmires which surrounded 'questions of organization and linking-up'. Perhaps a lesson had been learnt, and there was quite enough scope for debate and disagreement without straying outside the technical ring-fence.

With the appointment and, still more, the Report of the Williamson Committee, the affairs of the electricity industry were brought to the forefront of national politics. Everybody agreed that the industry needed reorganisation, and there was pretty general agreement that some central authority would have to be set up. Some of the businessmen, notably Sir Eric Geddes, who had been engaged with the organisation of industry for war, though they abominated socialism, were prepared for something not far short of nationalisation, but the general mood of Parliament, after the 'coupon election' at the end of 1918, was to get rid of Government control over business, so that opposition to any electricity measure which relied on compulsion rather than persuasion was not difficult to organise.[27]

The IEE manoeuvred cautiously. The Electricity Supply Committee, in their report suggesting the President's evidence for the Williamson Committee, recommended the setting-up of a Central Electricity Board but did not elaborate its powers. It asserted three unexceptionable 'considerations governing the generation of electricity' – reliability of supply, conservation of coal, furnishing the cheapest possible supply for all purposes – and confined its detailed recommendations to purely technical matters: frequencies, voltages for distribution and transmission, and wayleaves.

The President, C P Sparks, proposed to put before the Williamson Committee the recommendations which had been made to Sir Charles Parsons' Committee, the Electricity Supply Committee's Report, and the Interim Report of Merz's Committee, of which he was a member. He made it clear that he spoke on behalf of the Council, not the Institution. Even so, the committee of the Manchester Local Section resolved that 'as the President is a signatory to one of the Reports now before the Board of Trade Committee on Electricity Supply ... it is impossible for him to impartially represent the Institution as a whole'. When the Council disagreed with the resolution, the

Manchester Chairman withdrew it, but the incident shows how slippery a path the President had to tread.[28]

The Electricity (Supply) Bill of 1919 provided for Electricity Commissioners at the centre and for District Electricity Boards with compulsory powers to take over generation and establish interconnection, but when the Bill became law it had been seriously weakened by its opponents, who succeeded in replacing the Boards with Joint Electricity Authorities which, in spite of their title, were voluntary bodies. In 1922 a new Electricity Supply Act strengthened the JEAs by granting them financial powers, but the battle against Government control, in which, generally speaking, the power companies and the municipalities were on opposite sides, had for the time being gone against those who wished to see effective central control of electricity supply.[29] In this warfare the IEE did not take part. Instead, the Council did its best to discover and coordinate the views of IEE members and of the various representative bodies in the electrical industry. A committee consisting of the President, the four Vice Presidents, and the seven Chairmen of territorial centres was set up to plan the canvassing of members' views and a Special General Meeting, of which no details survive, was held on 29 May 1919.[30]

In the wider field, conferences were held on both Bills with representative associations in order to put together a joint report of their views. The Incorporated Municipal Electrical Association and the Association of Municipal Corporations, outnumbered heavily by associations representing the private undertakings, put in their own reports, but even then unanimity was elusive. The joint report on the 1919 Bill embodied the familiar criticisms of earlier electrical legislation and, although it accepted the idea of a Board of Electricity Commissioners, insisted that its functions 'should be exclusively judicial and advisory'. The preparation of district schemes 'should be left as a matter of free and natural development to the initiative of Undertakers'.[31]

In May 1921, when the second Bill was considered by a conference of nineteen organisations, the result was meagre: merely a resolution 'that in view of the divergence of opinion among the different interests represented ... the only recommendation they can make is that the Council should be asked to support the proposals for making the use of multipart tariff systems compulsory on application by undertakers'.[32]

During the years between 1914 and 1922 those in charge of the various branches of the electrical industry were forced to concentrate their minds on the resolution of problems which had been with them for the better part of forty years. Their interests conflicted, and the problem for the IEE was to be useful to its members without being partisan, for partisanship, as the events of the years before 1914 had shown, might be fatal. The situation, it may be thought, was handled with much greater skill and sophistication than on the previous occasion, and by its painstaking consultation with all the interests involved the IEE made out a good case for its claim to serve, as Wordingham put it in 1918, 'as an umbrella under which other Associations can meet'.[33] For the results of such meetings, profitable or otherwise, the IEE was not responsible.

III 'A very bitter pill' – the Institution and the Unions

During the years immediately before war broke out, the membership of the IEE had been rising strongly: from 6,327 in 1911 to 7,084 in 1913, an increase of about 12 per cent. Then for four successive years, from 1914 to 1917, the membership of the IEE dropped, from 7,084 in 1913 to 6,613 in 1917, a fall of nearly 7 per cent. Moreover the drop was more serious in the non-corporate grades – Graduates and Students – than among the corporate members, suggesting that young electrical engineers were not coming into the Institution. It was easy, and no doubt true enough, to say that they were going to the war instead. Nevertheless, such a sustained fall in the membership had never happened before (nor has such a fall happened since) and the Council, uneasy, appointed an optimistically named Committee on Increase of Membership.

'We are satisfied', the committee reported in July 1918, 'that there are many qualified Electrical Engineers in the Country who are not Members, and that the inflow of new members from the Student class is not commensurate with the inflow of young Electrical Engineers into the profession.'[34] Wordingham, probably one of the most active presidents the Institution has had, was much disturbed. 'Everyone must admit I think', he said late in 1918, 'that the industry has outgrown the present Institution and unless the latter be developed on much bolder and broader lines it will run serious danger of wilting and decaying.'[35]

One bolder line, of which Wordingham emphatically did not approve, ran towards membership of a trade union, for in the latter years of the war there was a good deal of discontent, particularly in the electricity supply industry and, as at any time when labour is scarce, unions were strong, growing stronger, and hungry for new members.[36] This militancy was brought rudely to the notice of the Council towards the end of 1917 when they were informed, as Wordingham put it, 'that very strenuous efforts were being made by the Electrical Trades Union to bring within its membership not only workmen, but engineers of all ranks up to and including Chief Engineers of Central Stations'.

Wordingham was outraged, but he knew that the IEE was in danger of being out-manoeuvred by the ETU. 'Obviously', he said, referring to the union's membership drive, 'that was an intolerable position, and it was incumbent upon the Institution to do something for its members', and 'something', with remarkable ineptitude, the Institution proceeded to do.

Taking a view from London, the Council observed that there were already half a dozen 'protective associations' in the supply industry, prepared to do for members in various branches of it the kind of work that a union would do, but to do it in a more gentlemanly way. The Council's solution to the problem presented by the ETU was to establish under the IEE's auspices one protective association for the whole industry 'which the members of these other Associations can join without any loss of dignity and without allowing one Association to think it had got the pull over the others.' The Council arranged for mass meetings at local centres where their proposals, detailed and authoritative, appointing Wordingham as first President of the new association, were explained and discussed.[37]

Nobody had told the Council, who seem to have been out of touch with provincial affairs (as discontented provincials had often said they were) that one of these protective associations was far more powerful than the rest and had no intention of being condescended to by the gentlemen from Savoy Place. 'When these Mass Meetings came to be held', said Wordingham, '... very violent opposition was experienced from one of these half dozen bodies, namely, the Electrical Power Engineers' Association.'

The Council could only retreat, and without much grace they did so. A single protective association for the industry was indeed formed, but it was formed by accepting inevitability and letting the Electrical Power Engineers' Association eat up all its smaller rivals. The EPEA thus triumphed, and the reason was that only the EPEA was constituted as a trade union.

'Now the Trades Union idea', said Wordingham,

> was a very bitter pill to most of us to swallow. I do not pretend for a moment that any one of the Council, nor in fact many members of the Association itself, wished to promote or to join a Trades Union, but that is practically put upon you by the Government. Unless you are one you are no better than a Mutual Admiration Society. In order to act effectually you must be a Trades Union, whether you like it or not. Some of us have gulped at this pill and some of us have more or less choked over it; but it has had to be swallowed.[38]

Wordingham's view of trade unions was heavily coloured by the recent establishment of 'Whitley Councils'. They were National Joint Industrial Councils, set up industry by industry on the advice of a committee under J H Whitley (1866–1935), later Speaker of the House of Commons, on which employers and employed were both represented. Wordingham was deeply offended. 'The Whitley Report', he said, 'most unfortunately recognises only two classes: workmen and employers. The brains of manufacturing Works and of all Technical Industries are left out altogether. ... It is a gross injustice and a most extraordinary oversight.'[39] It was also an unspoken, probably unconscious, recognition that in British business there was a growing hybrid class of which the members were more likely to be allied in sentiment with

the 'employers' than with the 'workmen' but who were themselves
employees with interests which differed from the interests of employers and
might conflict with them. This class consisted of professional managers, and
since the Institution's earliest days many electrical engineers and their predecessors, the telegraph engineers, had been professional managers. If they
felt that their profession, as well as engineering, was management, then
union membership – if they could find the right union – had much to offer.

The EPEA, as it was constituted after consultation with the IEE and others
in the summer of 1918, represented professional managers. Chief Engineers
were eligible for membership 'provided they are not employers or employers' representatives on an Industrial Council'. All new members of the
EPEA, after December 1921, would be required to have passed the AMIEE
examination or its equivalent. The result would be that eventually almost all
the members of the EPEA would be members of the IEE. The EPEA, so far
as power engineers were concerned, would in effect become the protective
department of the IEE. This would be very convenient, because it would
obviate the necessity for the Council of the IEE to soil its hands with
protective activities which, in spite of persistent demand from members, it
had always been loath to do. These considerations perhaps made the 'bitter
pill' of trade unionism easier to swallow, and in October 1918 'the Council
decided to recognize officially the Electrical Power Engineers' Association as
the protective Association for Engineers qualified to hold a responsible
position directly concerned with the production, transmission, distribution,
or utilization of electrical energy'.[40]

If the Council thought they had thus got rid of the problems presented by
trade unions, they were mistaken. These matters were never far below the
surface of the Institution's life, and from time to time they came into the
open, most conspicuously in the late 1960s (see pages 209–213). For the time
being, nevertheless, the agreement with the EPEA left the way clear for the
attainment of a long-desired objective: the grant of a Royal Charter to the
Institution of Electrical Engineers.

IV 'I am ambitious for the Institution': the Charter achieved

That Wordingham and his colleagues on the Council of the IEE, being
professional engineers, should find 'the Trades Union idea ... a very bitter pill
... to swallow' is in no way surprising. They took their professional standing
very seriously, and the principles of professionalism and trade unionism do
not sit easily together. 'So long as the ETU endeavour to force engineers into
their ranks', said Wordingham, 'so long must they be regarded in a hostile
spirit by the engineers, who never can possibly in any numbers I should hope
enter that Union ... because there is an essential difference between manual
work and technical and scientific work'.[41]

The difference would be formally recognised, and the claim of engineers (in Wordingham's sense of the term) to professional standing would be greatly strengthened by the grant of a Royal Charter. In this matter, when Wordingham spoke, engineering did not compare very well with other professions. Of the numerous engineering institutions only one – the Civils – had been granted a charter in the nineteenth century (1828), and only two had received charters later: the Naval Architects (1910) and the Mining Engineers (1915). Against this, taking two professions with which the engineers often compared themselves, the doctors could show the charters of the Royal College of Physicians of London (1518) and of the Royal College of Surgeons of England (1800); the solicitors, the charter of the Law Society (1831). Amongst other professionals and aspiring professionals, architects had been chartered in 1837, pharmacists in 1843, veterinary surgeons in 1844, accountants (for whom many engineers had a profound contempt) in 1880, surveyors in 1881, actuaries in 1884, chemists in 1885, patent agents in 1891, librarians in 1898, company secretaries in 1902, the Insurance Institute in 1912, the Institute of Metallurgy and Mining in 1915, and physiotherapists in 1920.[42]

If engineers felt slighted, who could blame them? The Electricals, perhaps, were particularly hard done by, since in 1880 a petition by the Society of Telegraph Engineers, nine years old, was opposed by the Civils and rejected by the Privy Council, although the Pharmaceutical Society, the Royal College of Veterinary Surgeons, and several other professional organisations had been chartered very much sooner after their foundation. After that rebuff, the matter of getting a charter for the IEE was not seriously raised again until 1912. The Mechanicals remained charterless until 1930.

When C P Sparks gave evidence to Sir Charles Parsons' committee in 1916 he recommended that the IEE should be granted a charter 'so as to improve the status and training of the Electrical Engineer', and his next recommendation was 'the establishment of a General Engineering Board consisting of representatives nominated by all the important Institutions, whom all Engineers (other than Mechanics) would be required to satisfy ... before they can be recognised as proficient, so as to ensure that every engineer shall qualify for his profession in the same manner as a doctor or solicitor'.[43] He thus emphasised the very great importance which the Institution attached to its concern for professional education and its function as a qualifying body.

Sparks might also have mentioned that without a charter the Institution could not protect itself in the courts from misuse of the initials MIEE and AMIEE, nor could a member distance himself from mechanics and others without professional qualifications by using the title 'chartered engineer'. All these matters were bound up with the question, which concerned the Civils and the Mechanicals as well as the Electricals, whether engineering (again, like the law and medicine) should be constituted by statute a closed profession, and they were all brought into focus by the IEE's pursuit of a charter, stirred into activity again after wartime torpor by C H Wordingham.

'I feel most strongly', said Wordingham in his Inaugural Address as President in November 1917, 'that it [the Institution] is seriously and unnecessarily handicapped by being constituted under the Companies' Acts. I am ambitious for the Institution; I want to see it occupying its proper place in the life of the nation and in the enjoyment of a Royal Charter which shall confer on it those powers which alone can enable it to take effectual action for the good of its members and ... of the general public whom they serve.'[44]

A Charter Committee was appointed, no doubt at Wordingham's instigation, which met once and reported. The members of the committee, according to Wordingham, were under the impression that they were expected to draw up a scheme for a charter which would have much the same effect as the Articles of Association which it was to replace, and that was what they did, not at all to the President's satisfaction. 'I ventured', Wordingham said, 'to unfold to the Committee something of what was in my mind ... and they were rather taken aback.'[45] They might well be. Wordingham's ideas, which he had foreshadowed in his Inaugural Address, were so ambitious that when he had worked them out in detail he felt bound to put them personally before the membership. In the late autumn and winter of 1918 he undertook a missionary tour round six of the greater Territorial Centres.[46]

If Wordingham had had his way, the IEE would have become the Royal Institution of British Electrical Engineers, governed by a Grand Council 'before which all important matters affecting the Industry would naturally come'. Below the Grand Council there would have been a Professional Council and seven Councils with members representing the major electrical industries, drawn from their own associations. There would have been a Manufacturers' Council, based on BEAMA and the Cable Makers' Association; a Company Power Supply Council, based on the Incorporated Association of Electric Power Companies, the Power Supply Companies of Great Britain, and the Conference of Chief Officials of the London Supply Companies; a Municipal Power Supply Council – 'this would naturally be furnished by the IMEA' – and four others, as well as a Research Council, a Commercial Development Council and a Protective Associations Council. These councils would have been represented on the Grand Council in proportion to their importance – 'I will not enter into details as to how their importance is to be gauged' – but for day-to-day purposes they would have acted independently of each other.

This elaborate machinery was intended to solve the problem which had so often presented itself to the IEE: how was one Institution to satisfy all branches of electrical industry, especially when their interests conflicted? Wordingham's scheme, as he pointed out, was intended to formalise the procedure already devised empirically by which the IEE operated as an 'umbrella' for all other associations. The RIBEE, for this purpose, would have been very much a corporate state. There was no place in this part of Wordingham's plan for the representation of individuals, even consulting engineers.

Individuals would have been the responsibility of the Professional Council which would have included representatives of all the main professional specialisms of electrical engineering and of the territorial centres, including those overseas. 'The Professional Council', Wordingham suggested, 'represents the whole of the members of the Electrical Industry in their individual capacity of Electrical Engineers irrespective of the branch to which they belong and for this reason the Professional Council should have a preponderating representation on the Grand Council.'

The Professional Council would have had two groups of functions. One would have covered the activities of the IEE as a learned society: papers, publications, library, bibliographies and digests. The other, more startling, 'would confer the right to practise in the different branches of Electrical Engineering'. As a necessary consequence 'it would deal with educational questions affecting electrical engineers and would hold examinations'. How the right to practise would be conferred Wordingham did not explain. He must have had the General Medical Council in his mind, and his proposal would have required not merely a charter, which would be a comparatively private matter, but a public Act of Parliament, about which the other engineering institutions would have had a great deal to say.

A year or so after Wordingham spoke, the kind of difficulties which would have arisen if his scheme had been carried forward were illustrated. Sir John Purser Griffiths, addressing the Civils as their President in November 1919, announced that the Institution of Civil Engineers would be seeking 'statutory powers to prescribe the qualifications and to conduct examinations for admission to the profession of civil engineering, to keep a register of civil engineers, and to prevent persons who are not fully qualified from holding themselves out as members of that profession'.[47]

Instantly, all other engineers became defensive and suspicious. Most of them favoured the principle of registration, but they were not prepared to have the machinery of registration dominated by the Institution of Civil Engineers, especially since it was not at all clear how a 'civil engineer' would be defined. Much consultation followed, between the President of the Electricals and the President of the Civils, and between various institutions, culminating in a conference at the Institute of Mining and Metallurgy on 24 February 1920 between representatives of the Mechanicals, the Electricals, the Naval Architects, the Mining Engineers, and of the Institute of Metals, the Iron and Steel Institute, the Society of Engineers, the Society of Chemical Industry and the Institution of Mining and Metallurgy. The conference asked the Civils not to proceed with their Bill and to convene a meeting of all the institutions concerned 'to consider the position'.[48]

The Civils agreed to the first part of the request but not to the second. Their senior Vice President, W B Worthington, privately told the President of the IEE, L B Atkinson, 'that it was perfectly clear that it would not have been possible to carry through either a private or public agreed Bill owing to the number of bodies, quite apart from the three principal Institutions, which claim to have representation on any Council of Registration practically as great as that of the three principal Institutions'. He added that the Civils were 'not dissatisfied' with not being able to carry their Bill through, because 'it might have involved control and interference both from other engineering and scientific bodies and also probably from Government officials, which would not have left to the Institution of Civil Engineers full control of the matter'.[49]

The implication of Worthington's two pronouncements is clear: that engineering should be presided over by a trinity and that the first person of the trinity should be the Institution of Civil Engineers. With the first claim the Electricals might have been willing to agree, but not with the second. Nor would other institutions, and thus the Civils ran into one of the problems which between 1840 and 1858 had delayed medical registration for eighteen years and wrecked sixteen Bills: namely the difficulty of placating interests within the profession which were just as unwilling as the Civils to give up their independence.[50] It was also a problem which, in a different form, the engineering institutions would run into between forty and fifty years later when they came to set up the Engineering Institutions Joint Council and then the Council of Engineering Institutions (pages 213–218).

The Civils, having failed in their attempt to establish and control the statutory registration of engineers, decided to settle for much less: simply a Supplementary Royal Charter to give their corporate members an exclusive right to the appellation 'Chartered Civil Engineer'. Before they went very far they enquired privately and possibly somewhat apprehensively whether their proposal 'would in any way interfere with the position of the Institution of Electrical Engineers, and whether the latter would agree to the necessity for a change in the Charter of the Civils'. The Electricals seized their opportunity. 'It was clear', Atkinson told Worthington, 'that any possible understanding as to non-opposition to a change in the Charter of the Civil Engineers must carry some understanding as to non-opposition by the Civils to the Electricals obtaining a Charter'. Worthington 'did not think a difficulty would arise in this direction'.[51] Nor did it. The Electricals' application for their belated charter was piloted expertly by Sir James Devonshire, and the charter was granted in September 1921. At the same time King George V became Patron of the Institution, and in their letter seeking His Majesty's patronage the Council took the opportunity to claim that the Institution had the largest membership – between nine and ten thousand – of any engineering or scientific society in Great Britain.[52]

The Charter as it was granted had none of Wordingham's proposed magnificence. It defined the 'objects and purposes' of the Institution in traditional terms: 'to promote the general advancement of Electrical Science and Engineering and their applications and to facilitate the exchange of information and ideas on those subjects among the Members ... and otherwise'. It forbade the Institution to 'carry on any trade or business or engage in any transaction with a view to the pecuniary gain or profit of the Members thereof', a clause which was later held to inhibit it from acting in any way as a 'protective association' for individuals or as a trade association for firms in the electrical industries. It made general provisions for the constitution and administration of the Institution which were elaborated in by-laws.[53]

Perhaps most important of all, in the contemporary view, was Clause 14, which entrenched the members' exclusive right to put appropriate initials after their names, especially MIEE and AMIEE, to indicate their professional qualifications. In 1924, following the Civils' example, the Electricals obtained from the Privy Council the right for corporate members to describe themselves as Chartered Electrical Engineers: a title which, in 1960, was said to have 'no legal standing'.[54] These measures carried electrical engineers as far as they could go, without elaborate and controversial legislation, towards a closed profession.

The grant of the charter to the Institution of Electrical Engineers, fifty years after the foundation of the Society of Telegraph Engineers, established it in the fullest sense as the representative organisation of a learned profession, extending its power – or perhaps it would be more correct to say its influence – in the direction of members' education, qualifications and public standing, but limiting narrowly the measures it might take, if occasion should arise, to fight for its members' material interests. In the terms which have been used previously in this history, it set the Institution's centre of gravity firmly in its function as a learned society and made no attempt to shift it, as many members, including apparently Wordingham, would have wished, towards a wider role in industrial politics.

References:
1 Rollo Appleyard: *The History of the Institution of Electrical Engineers (1871–1931)*, 1939, pp.152–153
2 R E Crompton: *Reminiscences*, 1928, pp.179–185
3 W S Churchill: *The World Crisis*, 1911–1918, 1938, Vol.1, p.192
4 Reference 1, pp.215–216; Report of the Engineer Units (RND) Committee, OCM Vol.9, 13 March 1919
5 'Annual Report of Council, *J.IEE*, 1919, **57** p.327
6 Appendix 5

7   CM, 27 May 1915; Reference 1, p.218

8   Reference 1, pp.218–219, 246–247

9   'Annual Report of Council', *J.IEE*, 1925–1926 **64**, p.661

10 Minutes of the Electrical Cooking and Heating Association Committee, OCM Vol.8, 5 July 1981

11 Annual Minutes of Patent Law Committee, OCM Vol.9, 27 June 1918

12 'Report of Council', *J.IEE*, 1915–1916, **54**, p.554

13 Minutes of Conference of the Research Committee and the BEAMA, OCM Vol.9, 1 Sept. 1918; Minutes of Research Committee OCM Vol.9, 18 Nov. 1918; Minutes of Committee of Vice Presidents, OCM Vol.8, 18 May 1918; 7 Nov. 1918; 'Annual Report of Council', *J.IEE*, 1920–1921, **59**, p.350

14 *J.IEE*, 1919, **57**, p.344

15 Minutes of Overseas Engineering Trade Conference, OCM Vol.8, 5 July 1918; CM, 17 Oct. 1918

16 CM, 23 March 1916

17 Report of the Departmental Committee appointed by the Board of Trade to consider the Position of the Electrical Trades after the War, Cmd 9072/1918 BPP (1918) Vol.13, p.355

18 CM, 11 May, 8 June 1916

19 CM, 8 June 1916: Committee of Vice Presidents, OCM Vol.8, 26 Oct. 1916

20 L Hannah: *Electricity before Nationalisation*, 1979, p.65

21 CM, 8 July 1916; *J.IEE*, 1916–1917, **55**, p.314; *Who was Who*, Vol.3

22 Interim Report on Electric Power Supply in Great Britain (Merz's Report), Cmd 8880/1917, BPP (1917–18) Vol.18, p.385; Report of the Committee appointed by the Board of Trade to consider the Question of Electric Power Supply (Williamson's Report) Cmd 9602/1918 BPP1918 Vol.8, p.611

23 *J.IEE*, 1915–1916, **54**, pp.581–588

24 'Annual Report of Council', *J.IEE*, 1916–1917, **55**, pp.314–315

25 CM, 8 June 1916

26 Reference 24

27 Reference 20, pp.67–74

28 Minutes of the Electricity Supply Committee, OCM Vol.8, 7 June 1917; CM 19 July 1917

29 Reference 20, pp.72, 80

30 CM, 15 April, 29 April 1919

31 'Institution Notes', *J.IEE*, 1919, **57**, pp.11–13

32 Minutes of Electricity Supply Bill (No 2) Conference, 6 May 1921, OCM Vol.11, pp.177–178, IEE Archives I/4.1

33 *J.IEE*, 1919, **57**, p.344

34 Minutes of Increase of Membership Committee, OCM Vol.8, 15 July 1918
35 *J.IEE*, 1919, **57**, p.348
36 Reference 20, pp.261–265
37 Committee of Vice Presidents, OCM Vol.8, 4 Apr. 1918, IEE Archives I/4.1
38 *J.IEE*, 1919, **57**, pp.340–341
39 *Ibid*, p.341
40 'Annual Report of Council', *J.IEE*, 1919, **57**, p330
41 *J.IEE*, 1919, **57**, p.342
42 Geoffrey Millerson: *The Qualifying Associations*, 1964, pp.221–245
43 CM, 11 May, 8 June 1916; *J.IEE*, 1915–1916, **54**, pp.673–674
44 *J.IEE*, 1918, **56** p.4
45 *J.IEE*, 1919, **57**, p.344
46 C E Wordington: 'The Institution': Address to the Territorial Centres, *J.IEE*, 1919, **57**, pp.344–348
47 *The Engineer*, 1919, **128**, p.458
48 CM, 26 Feb. 1920
49 'Memorandum of Proceedings at a Meeting on 23 Dec 1920', IEE Archives I/6.2
50 W J Reader: *Professional Men*, 1966, p.66
51 Reference 49
52 Reference 1, pp.245–246; Correspondence in IEE Archives I/6.2
53 For the full text of the IEE Charter, see Appendix 2
54 'An Institute of Engineers', developed from proposals made by Sir Willis Jackson at a Presidents' Meeting on 13 Jan. 1960, PM300 of 2 March 1960

Chapter 8

Wireless

I 'The growing edge of electrical science'

Between the mid-1890s and 1914 'wireless telegraphy' advanced from the laboratory to become a means of world-wide communication. It first came to the notice of the IEE in 1893 when W H Preece reported on experiments in communication by 'electro-magnetic disturbances' between Lavernock in South Wales and the island of Flat Holm 3.1 miles away in the Bristol Channel.[1] In 1896 G F Fitzgerald wrote to Oliver Heaviside about events at a meeting of the British Association. 'On the last day but one', he said, 'Preece surprised us all by saying that he had taken up an Italian adventurer who had done no more than Lodge and others had done in observing Hertzian rays at a distance. Many of us were very indignant at this overlooking of British work for an Italian manufacture. Science "made in Germany" we are accustomed to but "made in Italy" by an unknown firm was too bad.'[2] In November 1898 the twenty-four-year-old 'Italian adventurer' – not an altogether outrageous description – became a Member of the IEE and in March 1899 he addressed a crowded meeting on the spark transmitter. 'British work' was not neglected, for Oliver Lodge had spoken on 'Magnetic Space Telegraphy' in December 1898 and Sydney Evershed, an Associate, on 'Telegraphy by Magnetic Induction'.[3] Neither, however, had Marconi's genius for gaining publicity.

Over the years that followed the development of wireless telegraphy was dramatic. Some of the leading members of the IEE – Oliver Lodge, Ambrose Fleming and others – were closely and often litigiously concerned with it. The Institution, in 1912, lent its premises for an International Radio-Telegraphic Congress. Herbert Samuel, Postmaster-General, addressing the Congress about six weeks after the loss of the *Titanic*, spoke of 'measures relating to the compulsory installation of wireless telegraphy on board ships'.[4] In October 1913 the Council set up a national committee to serve a proposed international association for scientific experiments in wireless telegraphy.[5] The Institution's interest in the matter was shown by appointing as chairman of the committee the reigning President, W du B Duddell, FRS, a scientist and inventor of great brilliance in the field of high frequencies, who died in 1917 at the age of forty-four. He was President of the Institution in 1912-1913 and 1913-1914.

Although by 1914 wireless – or 'radio', as it was already being called – was rightly admired as a most wonderful example of applied science, yet its full impact was scarcely yet imaginable. It was regarded for practical purposes in the same way as the line and cable systems which since the 1840s had been carrying messages from point to point throughout the world and it was seen as chiefly useful between ships and shore or, in emergency, between ships at sea. For the first time since navigation began, it was possible to communicate with a ship below the horizon, and that in itself was wonder enough.

Wireless telephony, as distinct from telegraphy, was in its earliest stages. No one seriously considered it as a medium of mass communication or entertainment, though as early as 1906 one of Marconi's men, Captain H J Round, transmitted speech and music, in New York, to a distance of 4 miles. Experiments were going on in England for several years before 1914.[6]

The development of wireless was surrounded by popular interest. Just before the war there was a great deal of activity in setting up wireless clubs and wireless societies. Seven are listed in the *Electrical Trades Directory* for 1914, of which one, in Liverpool, was rather remarkably open to 'persons … of either sex', and no doubt there were many more. They were chiefly for the benefit of amateurs, including P F Rowell, the Institution's Secretary (page 122). At this stage in its development wireless was a subject which an amateur could readily pursue with a genuine feeling of being close to the frontiers of scientific knowledge.

The grandest of these societies, set up in July 1913 'to enable experimenters in wireless telegraphy to meet and exchange ideas and experiences,' was the Wireless Society of London. This was more than a purely amateur foundation, but in the person of Sir David Salomons, one of its Vice Presidents, it included a representative of an old and honourable tradition of amateur scientific investigation, and also a living reminder of the IEE's aggressive devotion to professionalism (pages 53–58). The Society's President, A A Campbell Swinton, had been one of the leaders of the movement within the IEE which had shut Sir David out of the Institution's Presidency. Among the eighteen Vice Presidents there were eleven, including Sir David, who put MIEE after their names, so that although the IEE was in no way officially connected with the Society, its influence was nevertheless likely to be strong, and perhaps also the influence of the Society would be strong in the Institution.

Wireless at this stage was still very much a matter for scientists rather than technologists. There is no evidence that anyone regarded it as a branch of electrical engineering as that term had come to be understood since the rise of 'heavy current' and the supply industry, though it was something in which an electrical engineer might legitimately take an interest. In 1914, accordingly, the Sectional Committee of the IEE responsible for Telegraphs and Telephones was directed to take account of Radio-Telephony. The power engineers at the head of the Institution, however, would still require a wireless expert, no matter how comprehensive his theoretical knowledge and his practical ability, to go through a regular course of engineering training before they would consider him qualified for membership of the IEE.

As matters stood in 1914, this might have been a justifiable view, though the telegraph engineers who were the IEE's founding fathers could scarcely have been expected to agree with it. Wartime development carried wireless rapidly towards the centre of the electrical scene, and it brought many members of the IEE, and many non-members also, into wireless work ranging from research and development at the highest level down to the simplest manual tasks. Many of the non-members saw no reason why they should not be admitted to the IEE, while those who were already members looked to the IEE, once peace returned, to cater for their interests more amply than before the war. Wireless engineers, that is to say, were developing professional self-consciousness, and by 1916 there was a movement on foot to found a Society or Institution of Wireless Engineers, altogether indepen-dent of the IEE. The model for it lay across the Atlantic, where in 1913 an Institute of Radio Engineers had been founded. By 1916, said W H Eccles, Professor of Electrical Engineering in the City and Guilds College and a member of the IEE's Council, it 'had already scored a great success in the valuable work of bringing together many of the best minds in America for the oral or written debate of wireless problems, and had established an admirable *Journal*'.[7] British radio engineers could plan to do likewise, and meanwhile they could join the American Institute. Many did.

Faced with a threat of competition in the Institution's professional field, the Council's instinctive reaction was one of alarm and hostility. There were good reasons. A new professional institution might set lower standards for qualification. A single institution, speaking on behalf of a united profession, might be expected to carry more weight than a number of institutions, possibly mutually hostile, representing professional splinter groups. There-fore the Council would always try to contain any new activity within the bounds of the IEE, and before the war it had been moving towards the idea of sectional meetings to provide for specialised interests.

As soon as the war ended the idea was revived. The General Purposes Committee of the Council, no doubt with the wireless engineers' proposed new society or institution in mind, suggested making a start with Wireless Telegraphy.[8] A Wireless Sectional Meetings Committee met for the first time on 17 February 1919. Wordingham, then President, suggested setting up a Wireless Section 'for obtaining, reading, and discussing papers which might afterwards be printed in the Institution *Journal*'. It came into being in the spring of 1919.[9]

The moment was propitious. The promoters of the new professional institution were 'confronted', in Eccles's words, 'by an array of financial difficulties' which hindered their plans. Members of the Institution, who had been baffled as long as the war lasted by a veil of official secrecy, were eager to hear of the development of wireless from those who had taken part in it. The new Section, accordingly, was instantly successful. In its first eighteen months 1,297 persons signed the Attendance Book, flocking to hear two lectures and eight papers of such merit that the Council were greatly embarrassed in distributing prizes and premiums. The outstanding feature of wartime development, according to Eccles, was the triode valve.

Dr Eccles's inaugural lecture as first Chairman of the Wireless Section took place after the session just described. Dr Graham Bell, aged seventy-three, also addressed the gathering. The Wireless Section, he told them, represented to him 'the advance guard of the British electrical world'. Eccles, commenting, said that wider public interest attached to wireless telegraphy than to any other branch of electrical engineering. 'Whatever the fascination is due to', he added, 'it seems to me to be the expression of a true instinct that in our subject we live nearer to the growing edge of electrical science than in other branches of engineering.'[10]

Eccles ended his address by calling up a vision of the future when 'strange engines of giant strength ... will be fed with electrons urged by millions of volts along vacuous conduits, and will be presided over by matterless switches. And the people of that age will look back and wonder why we in the twilight of the age of steam were so long content to urge slow floods of electricity through the crowded atoms of copper cables.' His prophecy was remarkably accurate in details and he was right also in his general implication: that wireless was much the most portentous innovation in electrical science since the development of large-scale, long-distance power supply. It was difficult, however, for the power engineers of the 1920s to see wireless in quite that way.

II Broadcasting: 'a concern for neutrality'

By the time the war ended, progress in radio telephony had been so great that in America broadcasting had already started. In Great Britain the complicated interplay of various interests – the Post Office, the Services, amateur wireless enthusiasts, electrical manufacturers – led tortuously to the foundation, in October 1922, of the British Broadcasting Company and to the launch of a national broadcasting service.

In the process of creating a new medium of mass communication – 'the wireless' – members of the IEE were prominently, professionally and controversially engaged. The Post Office's negotiators and spokesmen included the Engineer-in-Chief, Sir William Noble (1861-1943); the Inspector of Wireless Telegraphy, Commander (later Captain) F G Loring, RN (1869-1951); and E H Shaughnessy of the Engineering Department. In the companies there were

amongst others H J Round, Head of Research at Marconi, who had already
been concerned with broadcasting in America (page 107); A P M Fleming,
Head of Research at Metropolitan-Vickers; Basil Binyon, Managing Director of the Radio Communication Company; and Frank Gill, European Chief
Engineer for Western Electric, who became President of the IEE in 1922.
Among the numerous members who were influential in the Wireless Society
of London, which campaigned on behalf of amateurs, was the veteran
firebrand Campbell Swinton. Had he forgotten his hostility to amateurs in
the IEE in the nineties?

The Council did not involve the IEE in its corporate capacity with the
politics of broadcasting: nor indeed with the politics of wireless generally,
except for a brief – and successful – foray, under Swinton's leadership, into
opposition to the Wireless Telegraphy and Signalling Bill of 1925. It was
intended simply to confirm the Postmaster-General's right to collect licence
fees, but its provisions were held by the IEE and others to be tyrannical, and it
was dropped.[11]

Before 1914 the Council would almost certainly have taken a much more
active political line with such an important matter as broadcasting, as it had
done with electric supply, but in the early twenties it was content simply to
allow the Institution to act in its 'umbrella' role, first of all by providing
neutral ground – the building at Savoy Place – for negotiations.[12] During
1922 representatives of the manufacturing companies met several times at the
Institution's headquarters to work out a scheme, including arrangements for
patent-pooling, for setting up a broadcasting company. It seems likely that
the suggestion for using the IEE building may have come from Frank Gill
who, as chairman of what came to be known as the Manufacturers' Committee, presided over much of the hard bargaining which took place.

When the broadcasting company was founded, it needed offices and
studios. There was a transmitter at Marconi House in the Strand, and studios
were at first there as well, but it was hardly suitable as a permanent or even
semi-permanent home. On the other hand, the engineers did not want the
studios more than a mile from the transmitter for fear of trouble with the
land-line connection.[13] Where better than Savoy Place, since the company
already had close and amicable relations with the Institution?

In March 1923 the IEE leased seven rooms on their second floor and one on
their third to the company for £1,200, and by the end of the year more space
had been let for a further £1,000. Eventually the company occupied the first,
second and third floors of the west wing and, for an engineers' workshop,
part of the basement. In the summer of 1924 the company's managing
director, J C W Reith, enquired informally whether the Institution would
consider selling the whole building, and the idea was fully considered before
the General Purposes Committee turned it down.[14]

The BBC, first as a company, then as a public corporation, stayed in the IEE building, and in another building next door, until Broadcasting House was opened in Portland Place in 1932. 'Savoy Hill', encrusted with nostalgia, passed into the language and into legend. 'What began with a concern for neutrality', says Lord Briggs rather acidly, 'was to end in a wave of sentiment.'[15]

III The Institute of Wireless Technology: 'The virile progeny of a reluctant parent'

The typical electrical engineer of the early wireless age was a mechanical engineer who specialised in the manufacture or use of heavy, steam-driven electrical plant. He might have served his apprenticeship with a firm of electrical engineers, such as Cromptons or Anglo-American Brush, but he might equally have gone to Vickers, Sons & Maxim, Dennys the Dumbarton shipbuilders, or one of the great railway workshops. He would have studied, part-time, at a technical college, but full-time university education was still unusual for an engineer. He would probably have made his career either in manufacturing or power supply – perhaps in tramways or railways – or, for a few, in consultancy associated with power engineering.

Not much of this training or experience had any relevance to wireless, which needed neither generating sets of the kind erected in municipal power stations nor motors such as would drive railway locomotives, trams or factory plant. What wireless did need, on the other hand, was an understanding of certain branches of electrical theory such as education for a degree in physics might provide. Wireless engineers were also building up their own technology, for instance, in the construction and use of thermionic valves and in the design of aerials, which had very little indeed in common with the technology of electrical engineering as it was understood in Savoy Place.

As for the household 'wireless set', a prominent member of the IEE – Basil Binyon, speaking in 1925 as Chairman of the Wireless Section – said 'I must confess that I have noticed among the radio engineers of pre-broadcasting days a tendency to regard with some contempt those now engaged upon the design of broadcast receiving apparatus, and it is perhaps significant that with one or two exceptions this subject has hitherto been very largely ignored in papers read before this Section.'[16] If radio engineers in the IEE felt like that, it is hardly likely that orthodox electrical engineers were any more enlightened.

The Wireless Section of the IEE, nevertheless, was a success from the start, and in the early twenties it was the liveliest growing point in the Institution. Moreover, the members of its committee knew well how to blackmail the Council, in furtherance of the Section's interests, with hints of the threat of a separate wireless institution being formed. The Section flourished, and not only could any member of the IEE with a professional interest in wireless join it, but the door to its meetings was open to any member of the Institution who cared to enter.[17]

Discontent nevertheless remained. Many wireless engineers within and outside the IEE felt that their technology could not be adequately covered without setting up an institution of their own. More important, non-members of the IEE observed bitterly that any member had access to the Wireless Section regardless of the nature of his professional qualifications, whereas a non-member, however impressive his credentials, had to take the IEE's Associateship examination, which was designed mainly for the needs of power engineering, and to submit to the judgment of the IEE's Council, most of whom were not wireless engineers, before he could be admitted to membership of the Institution.

By the summer of 1925 the formation of an independent institution was in hand under the leadership of James Nelson, MIEE. He had the backing of Lord Gainford of Headlam (1860–1943), Chairman of the BBC, but a coal-owner, not an electrical engineer, and of Sir William Noble who, as Engin-eer-in-Chief of the Post Office, had pressed his staff to join the IEE.[18]

Nelson, in a letter published on 19 June 1925 in *The Electrician*, said 'a really technical society is wanted in Britain ... which would correspond to the Institute of Radio Engineers of America'. The subject, he said, had been 'talked over between a number of professional men and advanced amateurs' and 'a sufficient number of keen wireless men' had agreed to raise capital and to see the matter through. The rules and regulations of the new institution would, as far as possible, be taken from the constitution of the IEE or a similar body, much as the Society of Telegraph Engineers had once taken their constitution from that of the Institution of Civil Engineers.

The IEE was not flattered, and senior members were testy. 'The multi-plication of societies becomes a nuisance,' said Sir Oliver Lodge, and Pro-fessor G W O Howe trusted Mr Nelson to 'hesitate before giving way to the prevalent weakness for founding new societies'. J F Stanley advanced the orthodox Institution view that 'a fully-qualified wireless engineer must of necessity be also an electrical engineer' and, taking up another accepted attitude, scolded Nelson for talking to amateurs, pointing out that there was already a technical society for them, the Radio Society of Great Britain.

Nelson replied that an amateur might be 'more skilled and even better trained than his professional brother'. He complained that the IEE did not cover wireless matters adequately, for they only formed a very small propor-tion of the papers presented either at Savoy Place or in its local centres. 'My whole contention', he said, 'is that ... the radio man ... requires, say, 90 per cent of the papers, etc., to be radio matters and the balance kindred electrical subjects.'

'Radio matters', Nelson added, 'are quickly becoming so important that they cannot simply be attached as a side line to general electrical engineering.'

Here he came to the heart of the whole wrangle, and close to it was the wireless engineer's complaint that his technical competence should be judged by members, however eminent, of what he felt to be another profession. 'My question is this', wrote Y W P Evans, Secretary-designate of the new organisation, 'why should an applicant for the Wireless Section have to get into the IEE by his electrical qualifications?'[19]

Evans's question had been posed, in different words, by the editor of *Experimental Wireless*. The IEE was sufficiently worried by it to state, in a press notice drafted by P F Rowell, the Institution's Secretary, and issued by the Wireless Section, 'that it is possible for an engineer to become a member of the Institution with qualifications of a purely wireless nature'. He could do it by gaining 'adequate professional experience for a period of two years' and by passing the AMIEE examination in five subjects: English Essay or Translation from a foreign language; Applied Mechanics; Heat Light and Sound or Inorganic Chemistry; Electricity and Magnetism; Wireless and High Frequency Engineering.[20]

In the same notice, which was published in three electrical papers, the Wireless Section Committee acknowledged that 'some valuable suggestions have emerged from the recent correspondence' and promised 'careful consideration ... more particularly as regards the type and number of papers read and as to increasing the activities of the Wireless Section outside London'. The notice concluded with a pronouncement nicely calculated to infuriate wireless engineers who were not members of the IEE. 'As regards the suggested formation of a new Society', it ran, 'the Wireless Section Committee consider there is no need for it, because ... Wireless Engineers can obtain membership of the Institution and amateurs are already catered for by the Radio Society of Great Britain.'

Doubtless exasperated, the temporary secretary of the 'Proposed Radio Institute' commented on the Institution's statement in a letter to *The Electrical Times*: 'There are one or two points', he remarked acidly, 'which appear to have been omitted.' The most telling omission was that as well as passing the AMIEE examination and gaining the necessary experience, a candidate for admission to the IEE needed the support, based on personal knowledge, of five corporate members of the Institution. 'As the prospective candidate for admittance to the Wireless Section', said Evans, '... will not, in the majority of cases, have been connected with power engineers his chance of being intimately acquainted with members of the Institute [sic] is very remote.' He ended with the point that Nelson had taken: 'The IEE could sponsor wireless as it appeared in 1914, but now that wireless is almost as important an industry as electrical engineering it should be governed by its own body.'[21] The Editor of *The Electrical Times* published Evans's letter, but he did not agree with it. 'We consider', he wrote in a footnote, 'that the IEE is

incomparably better qualified than any other present or proposed organisation to safeguard and promote the interests of the wireless section of the
electrical profession.'

In this atmosphere, charged with a mixture of nervousness and contempt
on the side of the IEE and with bitterness on the side of the wireless engineers,
the new society – 'the virile progeny of a reluctant parent', as the historian of
the British Institution of Radio Engineers much later described it [22] – came
into existence, to the regret of *The Electrician*,[23] at a meeting held in the Hotel
Russell in London on 30 October 1925. It was intended from the first to call it
by its later title, which it assumed in 1940, but to avoid confusion with the
American society of the same name a rather awkward alternative was at first
chosen: the Institute of Wireless Technology. The Chairman for 1926 – there
was as yet no President – was James Nelson, and among the fifty-six
members on the roll one, Nelson, was a Member of the IEE, four were
Associate Members and one was an Associate.[24] By 1940 the membership
had risen to 1,425.

'One of the difficulties of the Institution of Electrical Engineers', said Evans
at the Hotel Russell, 'was that it obviously could not reduce the status which
it had already established for those desiring to become members, and the
result was that although the IEE catered for the advanced wireless engineer it
did not encourage the junior or regularly employed wireless engineer. There
was a gap between the work which the Radio Society of Great Britain was
doing and that which the Institution of Electrical Engineers did through its
wireless section.' That was a frank enough admission that the entry standards
of the new Institute, as the Council of the IEE had all along feared, would not
be as high as those of the IEE, though there was no reason why, with
vigilance and hard work among the educational establishments, they should
not rise with the passage of time, as the IEE's own standards had risen.
Moreover, those standards should be appropriate to the profession of wireless engineering, not to electrical engineering as the IEE, quite properly,
defined it.

There was a gap here, as Evans pointed out, and if the IEE would not fill it,
some other institution would. Failing a native British candidate for the post,
there was no doubt who the other institution would be. It would be the
American Institute of Radio Engineers. With that Institute the IEE was on the
best of terms, but that did not inhibit the Americans from accepting British
members. Why should it? Already, according to Nelson, also speaking at the
Hotel Russell, 'there were something like 500 members of the American
Institute of Radio Engineers in this country', and it was moving towards
setting up a local committee.[25]

It was useless, therefore, for the Council of the IEE or the Committee of its
Wireless Section to keep on asserting that the Institution provided all that
wireless engineers needed. A demand for more and different existed and it

would be met. If the IEE, quite properly devoted to the preservation of professional standards, could not or would not meet it, then an attitude of stubborn hostility to the Radio Engineers, doggedly maintained as it was to be through more than thirty years, was scarcely constructive. Moreover, the problem presented by the Radio Engineers – how to deal with new electrical technology – was not one that would go away. It would come back again with ever increasing frequency as the stream of change, over the years, accelerated into a torrent.

References:

1   *J.IEE*, 1893, **23**, p.65
2   Letter, G F Fitzgerald to Oliver Heaviside, 28 Sept. 1896, IEE Archives SC Mss 5
3   *J.IEE*, 1898, **27**, pp.738, 799, 852; *J.IEE*, 1899, **28**, p.273
4   *Daily Chronicle*, 5 June 1912
5   CM, 16 Oct. 1913
6   Asa Briggs: *The Birth of Broadcasting*, 1961, pp.32–33
7   *J.IEE*, 1920–1921, **59**, p.77
8   CM, 23 Jan. 1919; Annual Report of Council, *J.IEE*, 1919, **57**, p.326
9   Reference 7; 'Annual Report of Council', *J.IEE*, 1919–1920, **58**, p.312
10 *J.IEE*, 1920–1921, **59**, 77, 78, 84
11 CM, 19 Feb. 1925; Reference 6, pp.193–194
12 Reference 6, p.107
13 Rollo Appleyard: *The History of the Institution of Electrical Engineers (1871–1931)*, 1939, p.258
14 CM, 5 March, 31 May 1923; Reference 13, pp.258, 260; GPC, 28 July 1924
15 Reference 6, p.107
16 *J.IEE*, 1925–1926, **64**, p.83
17 Press Notice in Wireless Section Minute Book, 31 July 1925, IEE Archives I 4.13
18 *A Twentieth Century Professional Institution: Story of the IERE since 1925*, 1960, p.2
19 *The Electrician*, 1925, **94**, pp.728, 757; 1926, **95**, pp.41–42
20 Reference 17
21 *Electrical Times*, 1925, **68**, p.170
22 Reference 18, p.3
23 *The Electrician*, 1925, **95**, p.553
24 *J.Inst.W.Tel.*, 1926, **11**, p.39
25 Reference 18, p.2

Chapter 9

The Chartered Institution

I The Twenties, the Thirties and the National Grid

In 1920-1921 the British economy suffered the equivalent of a severe heart attack. The post-war boom collapsed, and in a few months the number of people out of work shot up from under half a million to about five times as many. The force of the depression was concentrated on the industries which had pre-eminently supported the prosperity and power of late Victorian England – cotton textiles, coal-mining, engineering and shipbuilding – and it spread economic ruin and social devastation across the manufacturing and mining areas of Scotland, Northern Ireland, Northern England and South Wales. The depressed 'basic industries' and the districts heavily dependent on them have remained permanently enfeebled ever since, and the effects of the depression of 1921 were reinforced ten years later by the onset of the depression of the thirties. The IEE's much-desired charter, granted in August 1921, therefore came into force during the bleakest economic weather of the century, when the symptoms of what has since been recognised as a deep-seated malady in the British economy were presenting themselves at their starkest. The number of people out of work never fell lower than a million between the wars, and in 1932 it reached almost three million. Such figures were not seen again for fifty years, and the thirties had scarcely passed into history before they passed also into folklore as a period of universal gloom, distress and misgovernment.[1]

This interpretation of events is as misleading as most folklore. Gloom was far from universal. Unemployment was severe in certain industries and in the older industrial areas, but motor manufacturing, chemicals, paper, some branches of light engineering, service trades such as motor transport and retailing and electrical engineering were buoyant, bringing widespread prosperity over large areas of the country, particularly in the Midlands and the South-east. Prices fell, standards of living rose, consumer goods multiplied and car-ownership became commonplace among the middle classes. In the thirties, with cheap money and in many occupations rising real wages there was a boom in house-building and all that went with it, such as furniture and household equipment, especially electrical equipment, including wireless sets, which by the time war broke out were in nine households out of ten.

'Shopping parades' in dormitory suburbs, new or rebuilt pubs beside the motor roads, and Marks & Spencer survive to tell an alternative tale of the years of depression. Moreover, in contrast to the country's experience after the disaster of 1921, the British economy as a whole recovered from the worst effects of the depression faster than the economy of the United States.

Nevertheless in too many important British industries between the wars the management seemed to suffer from chronic inability to improve organisation and technology so as to compete effectively in world markets. There was no mystery about what should be done: simply, it seems, an absence of the will to do it. Not least among the obstacles that stood in the way was obstinate conservatism among both management and men, finding expression particularly in restrictive practices, over-manning, and general resistance to change.

This is not a charge, generally speaking, which can justifiably be brought against those in charge of British electrical enterprises. On the manufacturing side they were uncomfortably aware that they had been overtaken, before the turn of the century, by the Germans and the Americans and during the Great War there was a great deal of debate on how to put matters right (pages 91–96). The debate covered a wide field, but it always came back to the necessity of radical reform of the whole national system of electricity supply aimed at standardisation of practice and at interconnection between areas, so that ultimately the whole country could be served by a relatively small number of large generating stations.

From 1926 onward, after many years of investigation and argument, the 'National Grid' began to take shape under the direction of the Central Electricity Board..Pylons marched across the countryside, to the accompaniment of outraged protest from conservationists. The scheme was completed in the mid-thirties, and at a time of difficulty in the winter of 1938 'it proved possible', as Professor Hannah says, 'to run the whole system in parallel for lengthy periods, providing much needed relief to southern power stations by exporting electricity from the northern areas in the peak periods'.[2]

That so large and controversial a project as the National Grid could be put in hand and carried out in the 1920s and 1930s does not suggest that the engineers then in charge of electricity supply were either timid or unjustifiably conservative in the conduct of their industry, whatever may have been the case among managers in other sectors of the economy. Nor, it would seem, were electrical engineers in manufacturing industry any less enterprising.

W H Eccles, reviewing 'the main lines of present-day electrical development' in his Presidential Address to members of the IEE in October 1926, pointed out that in many ways the output and use of electrical energy in Great Britain did not compare well with similar activities in other countries. Nevertheless, he also observed that in 1925 25 per cent of the turnover of the

British electrical industry was in exports, against comparable figures from Germany and the USA of 15.7 per cent and 5.5 per cent. Moreover, in the export both of heavy electrical machinery and of telegraphic apparatus British firms, in 1913 a long way behind German and American competitors, were ahead of them by 1925.[3]

It was unfortunate, no doubt, that 'in the new wireless industry America leads easily and Britain is last', but the general impression of the electrical industry conveyed by Eccles is very different from the impression that would be gained by studying the state of the steel industry, shipbuilding or coal-mining (when he spoke, the miners were staging their six-month-long and immensely damaging strike of 1926) in the mid-twenties. Those industries were prisoners of their past, whereas electrical engineering, like chemical manufacturing and some other industries, was being redesigned for the future. Evidently the investigation and argument which had gone on during the war, particularly in matters of electricity supply and foreign trade, had taken practical effect.

II Membership

With the granting of the Charter the IEE, about fifty years old, may be said to have come to maturity. Founded as the Society of Telegraph Engineers, a not very important offshoot of the Institution of Civil Engineers, it had grown, at first precariously, from a society of a few hundred members devoted to 'the general advancement of Electrical and Telegraphic Science' into the largest professional association in British engineering, nearly 10,000 strong in 1921 and continuing to grow at a yearly rate which, after a post-war burst of 16 per cent in 1920 and 1921, settled down during the 1920s and 1930s to about 3–4 per cent, except during the depression years of 1932 and 1933 when it fell below 2 per cent. By 1939 the total membership of the IEE had reached nearly 20,000.[4]

The membership was divided into two broad categories, corporate and non-corporate. The phrase 'corporate members', which came into use after the alteration of the by-laws in 1912, covered Honorary Members, Members and Associate Members. They formed the Body Corporate established by the Charter. Only the corporate members had full rights in the government of the Institution and in the Institution's view only Members and Associate Members (and Honorary Members who had belonged to one of these classes before elevation to Honorary status) were fully qualified electrical engineers, having satisfied the Institution's requirements both educationally and in carrying professional responsibility. They were the Chartered Electrical Engineers whose position, principally, the Charter had been designed (page 103) to protect. Between 1922 and 1939 the number of corporate members rose from 6,471 to 9,462, but as a proportion of the total it fell from 62 per cent to 50.

Over the same period, 1922 to 1939, the number of Students went up by 35 per cent, from 2,455 to 3,326, but as a proportion of the total it fell from 24 per cent to 17 per cent. At the same time the number of Graduates multiplied more than five-fold, from 934 to 4,780, and rose from 9 to 25 per cent of the total membership of the Institution. A Graduate was required, by By-law 15 of 1922, to be 'a person of good education, who is either an electrical engineer by profession or is employed in an engineering or scientific capacity in the applications of electricity'. In 1929 that by-law was altered to require 'every candidate for election or transfer to the class of Graduates' to 'have passed an examination or [possess] an educational qualification approved by the Council [not necessarily a degree]', and a note explained that the effect of the alteration was 'to ensure that only those who have satisfied the Institution's educational requirements shall be in the class of Graduates'.

Those who had the experience but not the educational qualification for Associate Membership were a class for whom, it is evident, Members of Council felt a special sympathy, as representing a vanishing breed of British engineer. They were transferred in 1929 from the class of Graduates to the class of Associates. That class had been reserved in 1912 (page 69) for 'members of some distinction who ... are not electrical engineers'. Members answering to that description, in 1929, became Companions, a title already used by the Mechanicals for a similar class.[5]

The meaning of this laborious and elaborate classification and reclassification, which took at least two years to bring into practical effect, was that in the Institution between the wars there was a large and rapidly growing class of electrical engineers who had passed or gained exemption from the Institution's examination for Associate Membership but who were barred from transfer to that class because they were held to be deficient in what the by-laws called 'Responsible Experience in Electrical Engineering.' They could not, therefore, lay claim to the designation 'Chartered Electrical Engineer'.

Graduates, in the IEE hierarchy, were classed with but above Students, and the assumption seems to have been that they would mostly be young or youngish men who only needed time and opportunity to pass across the Great Divide into the ranks of corporate membership. The fact that the class grew so much faster than the corporate classes of membership suggests, however, that opportunities were not plentiful. There were difficulties, too, in the way of a Graduate or Student who, in order to gain the experience necessary to become an Associate Member, needed a particular appointment. 'A young engineer', said the Committee of the North-Western Local Centre in 1935, in a memorandum to the Council, 'is unable to obtain the necessary responsible experience because he is not an Associate Member, whilst on the other hand he is refused admission as an Associate Member because he has not had the requisite experience.'[6] Such frustrations, said the Committee, were driving many Students and Graduates out of the Institution and engendering in those who remained a sense of grievance. By 1939, then, there must have been a good many disillusioned Graduates who were not over-young, and a letter written to the Secretary in 1944 complained that before the war the supply of qualified engineers exceeded the demand.[7] Concrete evidence is lacking, but it seems probable that in looking at the inter-war rise of the IEE Graduate class we are looking at one more stage in the rise of the technician engineer, for it was this kind of post which a Graduate might be educationally well-qualified to fill, but it might not provide him with the experience he needed for Associate Membership.

III The Scope of the Charter

The 'objects and purposes' for which the Institution was constituted were concisely defined in Clause 4 of the Charter:

> to promote the general advancement of Electrical Science and Engineering and their applications and to facilitate the exchange of information and ideas on those subjects amongst the Members of the Institution and otherwise.

For those purposes the Institution was empowered to hold meetings and exhibitions, to engage in printing and publishing, to take charge of the Ronalds Library and 'any supplemental or additional library', and 'to make grants of money, books, apparatus or otherwise for the purpose of promoting invention and research in Electrical Science and engineering'.

To the objects and purposes of the Institution thus narrowly defined there was added, in Clause 5, a specific prohibition:

> The Institution shall not carry on any trade or business or engage in any transaction with a view to the pecuniary gain or profit of the Members thereof.

By these clauses the Institution gained charitable status which exempted it from the payment of income tax. They thereby encouraged a cautious attitude to the whole conduct of the Institution's affairs which may not have been unwelcome to Presidents and members of Council who remembered the excitements of times gone by. Such cases as *Institution of Civil Engineers v. Commissioners of Inland Revenue*, 8 June 1931, which the Civils, who had been assessed to tax, won on appeal, were carefully watched, and on suitable occasions, no doubt, the result was discreetly applauded. The IEE itself was warned in 1929 that the authorities would in future disallow exemption from tax, but after lengthy proceedings the matter was dropped. 'The Institution', says the Council's Annual Report for 1930–1931, soberly triumphant, 'there-fore continues to be exempt from Income Tax'.[8]

The Institution was held to be debarred especially from any activity that might be related, however distantly, to matters of pay and conditions of employment: that is, from the normal activities of a trade union and of some professional associations. This had been a live issue (page 96) in the years around the end of the Great War, and evidently it continued to rankle in some members' minds, for at a dinner in Liverpool in November 1933 P V Hunter, President, saw fit to address the members of the Mersey and North Wales Centre on it.

'He wished', he is reported to have said,

> there were a more general appreciation of the difficulties which hedged the Council around in their endeavour to please everyone. For instance, members should not expect that the IEE could operate along the same lines as the British Medical Association or the Law Society. Then, too, there were societies which were to all intents and purposes trade unions. Now the IEE with its Royal Charter [but the Law Society had a Charter, too, and a much older one] existed for the advancement of electrical science as a whole, it was not empowered to promote the individual interests of members or to provide them with services of a nature which at once would bring headquarters face to face with a big claim from the Inland Revenue authorities.[9]

In 1931 the Council left the President, J M Donaldson, to decide what subscription the IEE should make to a body called the British Science Guild. The advice of the Secretary was firmly against any subscription at all. 'Although the Guild's activities', he said, 'are in some cases strictly scientific, they have also, I believe, taken up such questions as the salaries of scientific workers, which activity would be fatal to exemption from income tax.' In 1933 the Council decided against support for the Guild altogether because 'the matters to be dealt with by the Guild are outside the scope of the Institution's Charter'. At the same meeting the Council dealt in the same way with a suggestion from W T Townend, a member, that an Electricity Supply Bill then before Parliament was detrimental to householders – 'it would be outside the scope of the Institution's Charter to take action in connection with the Bill'.[10]

Some years later, in the autumn of 1937, the Institution was invited to join the British Management Council, organised 'to ascertain and represent both nationally and internationally the views of those concerned in management in Great Britain'. After a good deal of inquiry and discussion the General Purposes Committee reported against joining the Council 'as they are of the opinion that its objects are not sufficiently related to the objects of the Institution as set out in its Charter'. Early in 1938, after being asked by the Council to reconsider, the GPC relented so far as to feel that there would be no objection to appointing an 'observer', leaving the question of support to be considered later 'by which time it may be possible to judge whether its [the British Management Council's] activities come sufficiently within the scope of the Institution's Charter to ensure that support would not be likely to prejudice the Institution's exemption from income tax'.[11] It does not appear that 'support' was ever granted.

In matters like this the influence of the Secretary, P F Rowell (1874–1940), must have been very strong. Although born in London, he had been educated at the Royal College of Mauritius (Gold Medal for Mathematics and Leaving Scholarship, 1893), at Wren & Gurney's cramming establishment (though he did not call it that) and at King's College London, where he read Mathematics and Physics. After several years with engineering firms, including British Thomson-Houston, he joined the Secretary's staff in 1901. He became Accountant Clerk and Chief Assistant to W G McMillan, who died in January 1904 after six years in office.

The Secretary's post was advertised and ninety-five candidates applied for the job, illustrating the shortage of good middle-class employment in Edwardian England. G C Lloyd, Chief Assistant to his uncle, the Secretary of the Iron and Steel Institute, was appointed, but in 1908, after only four years with the IEE, he was offered his uncle's job and accepted it. The consequent vacancy at the IEE, once again advertised, drew eighty-one applicants, of whom the successful one was Lloyd's Chief Assistant, P F Rowell.

Rowell may have hoped to succeed Lloyd when he retired, but he can hardly have expected his opportunity to come so soon. As a consequence, like Webb in the very early days and like two of his successors, W K Brasher and G F Gainsborough, he was in office amply long enough to make his mark, as his advice to Donaldson on the British Science Guild illustrates. Indeed, he spent almost his entire career with the Institution. Like F H Webb, he had engineering experience but he was essentially an administrator.

After Rowell retired, in the late summer of 1939, the President expressed the Institution's gratitude for his part in the negotiations for the Charter and for the redrafting of the by-laws, for his care of the Institution's finances, for the development of local Centres and Sub-Centres, for liaison with French electrical engineers – he became a Chevalier of the Légion d'Honneur in 1936 – and for the exemption of the IEE from tax. He died in April 1940, a few months after he retired, which perhaps testifies to his single-mindedness in the service of the Institution.[12]

Rowell's conception of the Institution was shared during the latter part of his term of office by most of those responsible, as Council members and Presidents, for the running of the Institution's affairs and the formation of its policy. He and they saw it both as a learned society and as a professional association, but in no sense as a fighting body. Any kind of political or near-political controversy they were determined to avoid, in marked contrast to the behaviour of their predecessors before 1914. In the 1920s and 1930s, therefore, the Institution as a corporate body kept resolutely clear of all issues of public policy in which electrical engineers were professionally concerned and over which they would inevitably hold conflicting views. The biggest and bitterest of these issues was the controversy in the 1930s over the organisation of the distribution of electricity supplies.[13] The quarrel, like earlier quarrels over the generation of electricity, centred on the clash of interests between large undertakings and small, and between private and municipal ownership. Considerations of technology, political principle, profit and loss, and simple self-interest were intertwined, as they had been in the earlier disagreements (pages 78–86).

Some of the most distinguished figures in English electrical engineering were involved on one side or the other of the controversy. Many of them, notwithstanding the neutrality of the IEE as a body corporate, expressed their views freely in reading papers and taking part in discussions at meetings of the Institution. J M Donaldson, President in 1931, was less convinced than J M Kennedy, President four years later, of the virtues of size in distribution authorities. Their conflicting opinions emerged during a discussion in 1933 of a paper by Kennedy and Noakes on the costs of electricity supply and distribution in Great Britain.[14] There was no repetition, however, of the uninhibited acrimony which had occasionally erupted in Victorian meetings and in Perry's Presidential Address of 1900 (see page 65). Disagreements in the thirties were much more mildly expressed.

A curious result of the Institution's policy of neutrality was that when an attempt was made to bring engineers together in a Convention to discuss the reorganisation of distribution, it was not made by the IEE, which might have been expected to be the obvious convening body, but by one of the interested parties, the Incorporated Municipal Electrical Association.[15] The President and Secretary of the IEE met representatives of the IMEA and other organisations in 1934 and agreed that a convention should be held. They declined, however, to allow the IEE to take part as a body corporate, although the convention was held, in 1935, under the Institution's patronage and the GPC decided to issue a circular about it in the *Journal*.[16] The Council probably had no wish to repeat the Institution's disappointing experience as an opinion broker in 1921 (see page 95).

In 1933, when the controversy over distribution was becoming heated, the North-Western Centre proposed to set up a group to study economic and financial questions affecting the electrical industry and the employment of engineers. They asked, perhaps unwisely, whether their proposal would be outside the powers of the IEE's constitution. The Council, advised by the GPC, 'felt that any such scheme must inevitably introduce matters of a political character and thus fall outside the scope of the Institution'. If these topics were discussed at the Centre, the discussion must be held apart from IEE activities and the name of the IEE must not be associated with them.[17]

Such studied avoidance of the least breath of controversy, combined with determination to run no risk of having to pay income tax, severely restricted the range of subjects which the Council felt able to deal with. Even in the matter of electrical wiring regulations, long regarded as falling squarely within the IEE's field of action, great nervousness was shown in the face of demands for compulsion, bringing with them the possibility of legislation. In 1937, after the failure of repeated requests to the IEE to call a conference on compulsory wiring rules and compulsory registration, the Association of Supervising Electrical Engineers went ahead and called one, but the IEE turned down an invitation to be represented on a committee 'to investigate the question of compulsory methods'.[18]

This is not to say that the IEE withdrew from all public activity. It supplied three representatives to the Council of the Engineering Division of the British Engineering Standards Association, renamed the British Standards Institution in 1931, which it had been instrumental in founding, and it made the BESA and the BSI a grant of £1,000 a year, cut to £750 in 1939. On the other hand in 1923 the GPC recommended against a grant to the Electrical Development Association, also very largely a creation of the IEE, because 'there is some doubt whether the objects of the Association come within those of the Institution'.[19] Why hadn't they thought of that before?

Provided there was no possibility either of controversy or of a tax demand, leading members of the Institution were prepared to put a great deal of steady, unpaid effort into activities influencing the general legal and technical conditions under which electrical engineers practised their profession. Work on Model General Conditions for Contracts, on Regulations for Electrical Equipment in Ships and on the Wiring Regulations went on steadily between the wars. Certain other activities – the Power Lines Committee and the British Electrical Research Association are examples – disappear from the Council's Annual Reports between 1921 and 1939, and are not replaced by an equivalent number of new activities of a similar kind. Presumably it was difficult to find many which did not fall foul of 'the scope of the Charter'.

The readiness with which the Council had formerly approached controversy had been replaced, after hard experience, by a caution which, in retrospect, appears almost stifling, and the Council of the mature Institution was almost paralysingly concerned with preserving charitable status and exemption from tax. Nevertheless, it was deeply and increasingly concerned with the standing of engineers, especially electrical engineers, in the community, with cooperation with the other two 'senior Institutions', and with technical education and professional qualifications. It was in these fields, and in its care for the Institution's standing as a learned society, that the Council between the wars chiefly found constructive work to do.

References

1. Unemployment figures from Table E in *The British Economy – Key Statistics 1900–1966*. For a general survey see Peter Pagnamenta and Richard Overy: *All our working Lives*, 1984. See also H W Richardson: *Economic Recovery in Britain 1932–39*, 1967

2. L Hannah: *Electricity before Nationalisation*, 1979, p.142

3. *J.IEE*, 1926–1927, **65**, pp.1–12

4. 'Annual Reports of Council', *J.IEE*, Vols as appropriate

5. Report of the General Purposes and Membership Committees Joint Committee on Membership Qualifications, 31 March 1927, Ref 163/72 IEE Archives II/1.1.1, Secretary's marked copies of Council documents

6. Election to Associate Member. Memo from Committee of North-Western local Centre, 25 April 1925, Ref. 499/6. IEE Archives II/1.1.1, Secretary's marked copies of Council documents

7. Letter, W E Beale to Secretary, 15 Jan. 1944

8. *The Times Law Reports*, 21 June 1931, pp.466–468. *J.IEE*, 1930–1931, **69**, p.857

9. *Electrical Times*, 1933, **83**, p.736

10. Letter, Secretary IEE to J M Donaldson, 7 Dec. 1931, IEE Archives I/6.6; CM, 22 June 1933

11. CM, 5 Nov., 17 Dec. 1936, 11 Feb. 1937; GPCM, 12 Oct. 1937; CM, 8 Feb. 1938

12. *Who was Who* Vol.3; Rollo Appleyard: *The History of The Institution of Electrical Engineers (1871–1931)*, 1939, pp.182–183;'Annual Report of Council', *J.IEE*, 1934, **75**, p.807; 'Annual Report of Council', *J.IEE*, 1940, **86**, pp.575–576

13. Reference 2, pp.237–256

14. J M Kennedy and D M Noakes: 'Analysis of the costs of electricity supply and distribution in Great Britain', *J.IEE*, 1933, **73**, pp.112–114

15. Reference 2, p.249

16. CM, 25 Oct. 1934; GPCM, 13 Nov. 1934

17. CM, 26 Oct, 21 Dec. 1933

18. CM, 11 April, 24 Oct. 1935; 7 Jan., 16 Dec. 1937

19. GPCM, 26 Feb. 1923

Chapter 10

The Unestablished Profession

I 'The status of the engineer is still a dubious one.'

During the nineteenth century English engineers in general were full of self-confidence. Electrical engineers in particular knew they were at the leading edge of technology and could bask in the warm glow of Victorian approval of those who conferred upon their fellow men the benefits of applied science. Moreover, their profession paid very well. During the first twenty years or so of the new century, however, this happy state of affairs was changing. Was it, in the Electricals' case, because the British electrical industry had been overtaken by the Germans and the Americans, and the fact was publicly, prominently and frequently discussed? Was it because Continental and American engineers were better educated, better paid, and more highly esteemed in society? For whatever reason a mood of gloomy introspection began to develop among English engineers, including electrical engineers, which had not previously afflicted them.

It showed in the introduction to a paper given early in 1919, and repeated several times at various local centres, by Lieutenant-Colonel W A J O'Meara (1863–1939), a distinguished officer of the Royal Engineers who had been Chief Engineer at the Post Office from 1907 to 1912. 'Few are there', he said, 'who can be oblivious of the fact that the material prosperity and comfort, in modern times, of the dwellers in practically every quarter of the globe are essentially due to the activities of the engineering profession. ... Nevertheless, the status of the engineer is still a dubious one; at least it is so in this country, and there continue to exist in some quarters considerable misunderstandings as to his true functions and responsibilities.'[1]

The engineers' plight, as engineers frequently pointed out and continue to the present day to point out, is complicated by English usage, which applies the term 'engineer' equally to the designer of the Severn Bridge and to the craftsman – but he may not be a craftsman – who puts the Hoover right when it goes wrong. In the electrical engineers' case in the years between the wars there was further confusion over the word 'electrician', which had fallen from the high estate it held when Sir William Preece delighted in the title 'Chief Electrician' at the Post Office. In 1933 *The Electrical Times* assigned the electrician 'a rung on the ladder ... below that of the plumber'.

The professional engineer, being confused with the craftsman, stood lower in public esteem than those in other professions whom he regarded as his equals. 'Although', said *The Electrical Times*, 'the great British public is becoming "electrically minded" ... they have no particular notion as to what constitutes an engineer, an electrical engineer or an electrician, although they have well defined mental pictures of the doctor, the clergyman and the auctioneer and are often able to distinguish between a solicitor and a barrister.'[2] In 1925-1926 Thomas Carter addressed himself to the question of status in a paper to the IEE on 'The Engineer: his Due and his Duty in Life'.[3] Members were very sensitive to the issues which the paper raised. It was read and discussed not only in London but at Centres and Sub-Centres in Liverpool, Newcastle, Leeds, Manchester, Dundee and Cardiff. Carter and speakers in the discussion took a high philosophical and moral line, with quotations from the Bible, Humbert Wolfe and Hans Andersen, but when they descended to practical matters it soon became apparent that they perceived a close connection between the regard in which engineers were held and their pay, and between both of these matters and the level of engineering qualifications, leading in turn to consideration of engineering training and education.

These points were all made or implied in a contribution by J Conway to the discussion at Dundee on 11 February 1926:

> A properly trained engineer is of as good a mental calibre as, say, a doctor. He therefore deserves the same status, and one of the reasons why he does not get the same recognition is because he is poorly paid. The engineer will never attain to that status until the qualifications required to practise in the profession are as rigid as those for medicine.[4]

The attitude which Conway complained of, that engineers were not automatically considered equal to other professional men, was exemplified in the Royal Navy by Fleet Order 3241 of November 1925, which deprived engineer officers of executive rank; in the Civil Service by the low standing, and correspondingly low pay, of technical experts, complained of in *The Electrical Times* in 1929; and in business by the constitution of Winnington Hall Club at Brunner, Mond's, later ICI's, alkali works in Cheshire.

This was a management club to which university graduates and certain professional men – solicitors and accountants – were elected without question, but to which commercial men and engineers, unless they were graduates, which very few were, might not be elected for years, if at all, with the curious result that a young chemist freshly down from Oxford might find himself a member of the club whereas his superior in the office or the works, a sales manager or an engineer without a degree, might not be. ICI's first graduate engineer came to Winnington in 1926. He was Christopher Hinton, later Lord Hinton of Bankside and an Honorary Member of the IEE, and what he saw of the relative standing accorded to engineers and chemists did not please him in the least.[5]

'At present', Conway went on, still trying to account for the low standing of engineers, 'the return is far too poor for the training and ability required.' Quite what the 'return' was likely to be Conway did not say. In 1919 A S E Ackermann had quoted the salary of the Chief Engineer in 'a works of fair size' at £1,250 a year against £2,250 for the General Manager, remarking, 'That is a good illustration to a student of the relative market prices of the commercial side' (represented by the General Manager) 'and the purely technical side.'[6] In the Civil Service, according to *The Electrical Times*, 'the highest posts on the administrative side rise to £3,000 a year whereas ... the highest salary paid to any scientific head of a department is £1,500.'

The relationship, in business, between the 'commercial side' and the 'purely technical side' was a delicate point. Many engineers and other technical specialists – chemists, for instance, in ICI – scorned commercial activities and commercial men, and paid as little attention to them as they could, not always with the happiest results. Nevertheless, some of the most powerful figures in British business – Sir Harry McGowan, later Lord McGowan, of ICI, for example – were commercial men without technical or professional qualifications of any sort. Unless an engineer had some commercial training he could not expect a position in general management, with the standing, salary and influence on policy that would go with it.

O'Meara's paper in 1919 (page 125) had been largely a plea for a reversal of this attitude and for a proper commercial education, along American lines, for British engineers. In 1926 the point arose again in the shape of a demand, accepted by Carter and supported by R E B Crompton, eighty and aristocratic though he was, for professional recognition of 'sales engineers'. Their importance was growing rapidly as electricity moved more and more strongly into the household market, but salesmanship has always been a suspect activity in England.

In the early twenties senior members criticised the Institution 'for admitting to Associate Membership Sales Engineers who had little or no practical responsible experience in electrical engineering'. The question of experience was crucial, and the matter was still rumbling uneasily on in 1931 when the Membership Committee felt 'that non-insistence on the required period of responsibility ... would lower the status of membership, which has steadily improved during the last few years'. The Committee knew that 'in certain cases' sales engineers were responsible 'for drawing up and carrying out schemes in particular branches of electrical engineering', and that kind of work would generally be accepted for Associate Membership, but their uneasiness about salesmanship itself is evident.[7]

Whether an engineer's qualifications were to be commercial and technical, or technical only, discussion of them raised the question of a closed profession. Carter himself, pointing to the examples of the General Medical Council and the General Council of the Bar, proposed registration and a General Engineering Council 'endowed with power to deal with and take action on all matters affecting engineers'.[8] He suggested, clearly with the assent of most of those who listened to him, that 'it is largely because of ... the unestablished position of the profession that engineers have been too feeble a force in shaping the course of public life; their possibilities of individual and corporate usefulness do not come naturally to the public mind'. Nevertheless during the 1920s and 1930s the various branches of the engineering profession could never bring themselves to unite behind any proposal for compulsory registration, such as the Engineers' Registration Bill promoted by the Society of Technical Engineers in 1926, and the only register which existed was a voluntary register of wiring contractors.

The problem of status, linked as it was with pay and prospects, was common to all branches of engineering. Possibly it was less serious for the Civils, more serious for the Mechanicals, than for the Electricals, but they were all bedevilled by it and they thought it affected, among other things, recruiting. An engineering employer in 1926 complained 'that he had great difficulty in obtaining apprentice mechanical engineers, and that the quality of such as he did obtain was the poorest he had ever known'. 'The Electricals' case', Conway commented, was not so bad, 'yet it appears to me that we must just accept the best material that offers', which does not imply that he thought it would be very good.[9]

The common problems of the various branches of the engineering profession led to proposals for common action, or at least consultation. In 1922 the first common professional body, the Engineering Joint Council, was set up by the Civils, the Mechanicals, the Electricals and the Naval Architects. The IEE was by now the largest of the Institutions, but the conference which led to the founding of the EJC was organised by the Civils. This was considered fitting because their Institution, in the words of the Naval Architects' Secretary in 1921, was 'the parent of all other similar bodies'.[10]

'The Joint Council', said Clause 4 of its Constitution, 'shall consider matters referred to it by the Council of any one of the constituent Institutions, and shall be an advisory body without executive powers.'[11] It was designed, that is to say, to be nothing more than a discussion centre at a high level. Two past presidents – Roger T Smith and J S Highfield – represented the IEE on the Council during its first five years, and the first Chairman was W B Worthington, President of the Civils in 1921-1922.

'The Council', said the EJC'S report on its first five years, 'has in all held 36 meetings, and, although the actual amount of work accomplished appears slender, the Council has no doubt that the friendly discussions between its members have ... opened up the way to a closer cooperation between the important bodies of engineers they represent'.[12] The 'important bodies', however, were reluctant to let their cooperation get much beyond the stage of 'friendly discussions'. An elaborate proposal in 1932 by Loughnan St Lawrence Pendred, Editor of *The Engineer*, for a British Federation of Engineering Institutions, modelled on existing bodies in America, France and Germany, came to nothing, and a suggestion by the IEE, in 1937, aimed at giving the EJC some power to initiate proposals, was blocked by the Civils.[13] In 1962 Sir Kenneth Hague, who was then President of the Civils, said the EJC 'failed largely because of ... frustration ... Its constitution was too rigid', leading to 'mere talk without action'.[14] Nevertheless, it lasted for thirty years, from 1922 to 1952.

The Civils, though determined not to let the EJC or any other body impede their freedom of action, were nevertheless eager, in 1936, to get the support of the IEE and other engineering institutions in 'placing before the general public information concerning the status and functions of engineers of all kinds'.[15] A meeting of seventeen institutions in January 1937, at which J M Kennedy represented the IEE, led to proposals for the formation of an Engineering Public Relations Committee. The Civils already had a public relations officer of their own – they must have been amongst the earliest bodies to appoint one – and he, evidently an enterprising individual, pre-sented the Council of the IEE, in the spring of 1937, with rules for an Engineering Public Relations Fund. Its object was defined as providing money for the Engineering Public Relations Committee 'to assist them in the work of disseminating knowledge for the general advancement of Engineer-ing Science'. That was held by counsel to be within the powers conferred by the IEE's Charter, and so the Council agreed to make a grant to the Committee at the rate of 2d per member: £145 in total.[16]

The setting up of the Engineering Public Relations Committee was the most positive move made by the engineering profession as a whole, before the Second World War, to improve its public standing. The idea came from the Civils. The Electricals at first supported it, though with how much enthusiasm is uncertain. Then in 1939 there was a proposal to double the rate of grant to the Committee from 2d to 4d per member. The Civils were agreeable and also offered an extra £300 and the loan of staff. Other institu-tions, including the IEE, demurred. Denied adequate funds, the Committee was reduced in July 1939 to the status of an advisory body and the subscrip-tion from each of the bodies represented became 2 guineas only, with 1 guinea for bodies affiliated to it.[17]

The IEE's Council was extremely nervous of doing anything in connec-tion with the Public Relations Committee which might have been construed as lying outside the powers of the Charter. In April 1939, for instance, they advised against the Committee considering the advisability of the registration of engineers. The reason was that it did not come within the Committee's terms of reference, which provided for the dissemination of knowledge 'for the general advancement of engineering science'.[18] This, no doubt intentionally, was a very close paraphrase of the Charter's central definition of the IEE's 'objects and purposes' (page 241), and the Council were determined to hold closely to it. In this frame of mind, it is hardly surprising that they refused extra support to the Committee and concurred in reducing its level of activity to the point of extinction. It is only surprising that for a while they consented to give as much support as they did. Somebody at the Institution of Civil Engineers must have been very persuasive.

The Council's very strict interpretation of the powers conferred on the Institution by the Charter severely limited any action they might take aimed at improving engineers' status. The Charter prevented direct action to improve their members' pay and conditions, which were generally agreed to bear very closely on the problem of status. Pay and conditions, however, were closely linked with standards of qualification and hence with technical education. Both these matters, during the years between the wars, occupied a great deal of the IEE's attention.

II Technical Education: HNC ... HND

'The status of any profession', said E W Marchant (1876–1962), delivering his Inaugural Address as President of the IEE on 20 October 1932, 'depends to a very large extent on the character of the education which its members must receive'.[19] As Professor of Electrical Engineering at Liverpool University, Marchant had a vested interest in education, but the truth of what he said was not in doubt and he emphasised it by a reference to a profession with which electrical engineers frequently and somewhat enviously compared with their own. 'It is not many generations', Marchant went on, 'since the profession of the surgeon was looked on askance', and the reason he gave was that surgeons used to operate 'in the spare time ... available ... after fulfilling their ordinary duties as barbers.'

The barber-surgeons had not undergone long and arduous training, intellectual as well as practical, which would set them above the general run of skilled craftsmen and gain them, as professional men, both a comfortable livelihood and the respect of society. Both could be secured by improving their education and raising the level of their qualifications. The barber-surgeons secured them, losing the trade of a barber and gaining the profession of a surgeon in the process. The IEE, as we have seen in previous chapters, pursued the same means to the same ends, and after the grant of the Charter it pursued them even more energetically than before.

By the time the Great War ended there was a good deal of uneasiness about the education and training of English engineers. O'Meara, in 1919, complained that a traditional engineering apprenticeship, even when combined with attendance at a technical college, did not give any instruction in what would later be called 'business studies' – 'accountancy and book-keeping, banking, mercantile law, political economy, repairs and depreciation, sociology etc.' – which placed English engineers at an international disadvantage by neglecting to prepare them for general management.[20] In America particularly, O'Meara said, commercial subjects were taught as a normal part of an engineer's education, and he voiced a familiar complaint: 'The American engineer occupies, as a rule, a far stronger and much more important position . . . than that accorded to his confrère in this country. The same is true . . . in many of the countries on the continent of Europe, where the engineer's knowledge and skill are appreciated practically at the same value and to the same extent as in the United States of America.'[21] O'Meara's listeners, including three future Presidents – A P M Fleming, W H Eccles and E W Marchant, all closely concerned with professional education – agreed wholeheartedly with him. O'Meara, in replying to the discussion, said that in his opinion 'the drawing up of the curricula of engineering studies is not a matter that should be left entirely in the hands of the teaching profession'. He suggested setting up a committee of employers, engineers and teachers.[22]

This suggestion was not taken up in precisely the form suggested, but it is probably not entirely a chance coincidence that a little more than two years after the discussion of O'Meara's paper a committee appointed by the Council of the IEE was advising the Council to commit itself to cooperation with the Board of Education in the practical administration of an ambitious scheme for setting up and running a national system of courses of instruction in engineering. The initiative seems to have come from the Board, which first approached the Mechanicals. Having made sure of them, it came to the Institution in May 1921.[23] The Institution was asked to supply three members of a joint Board to run the scheme: that is, to approve or turn down courses submitted by schools and technical colleges, to participate in drawing up syllabuses, and to appoint assessors to review the drafting and marking of examination papers. The Council not only agreed to all this, but to the grant of £100 too, and the final decision was taken in March 1922.[24]

At the heart of the scheme were courses of instruction at two levels: 'Senior' and 'Advanced', leading respectively to the grant of an Ordinary National Certificate and a Higher National Certificate. The courses were clearly intended to train engineers at two levels of qualification, roughly corresponding to 'non-corporate' and 'corporate' membership of the Institution. The Senior courses were intended for starters aiming at both levels. Boys might take them after they had started work, probably as craft apprentices, and passed through a two years' junior part-time course, aiming to go no further than the Ordinary National Certificate, which would not carry them to corporate membership. Boys who had stayed at school to the age of sixteen and were intending to go on to Advanced courses leading to the Higher National Certificate, in order, eventually, to become professional engineers, might also take the ONC courses.[24]

These were boys, mostly from the county secondary schools set up under the Education Act of 1902, or perhaps from public schools, who had passed the School Certificate examination (the predecessor of GCE at O level). 'The majority of the boys who ultimately become Corporate Members of the Institution', said C L Fortescue, Professor of Electrical Engineering at Imperial College and later President of the IEE, in 1937 'come from secondary schools'.[25] They came from a class which had long supplied recruits to the English professions, but in the 1930s it was not, on the whole, a class which had yet acquired the university habit. W E Highfield, a speaker in the discussion on electrical engineering education which Fortescue led, estimated that of 5,000 students intending to become professional engineers there might be 700 at universities.[26] How he arrived at his estimate he did not say, but there is no reason to suppose that it was unduly low. The corresponding figure for solicitors and accountants would have been a good deal lower.

The normal route into engineering and most other professions was by way of apprenticeship, often known at the professional level as 'articles' or 'pupilage', for which a premium would probably be asked, and by part-time study. Even for medicine strong traces of an apprenticeship system remained, and there was no necessity to take a university degree in order to qualify. Part-time study, whether 'senior' or 'advanced', was a serious undertaking. No course would be approved for the award of a certificate unless it was carried on for at least 150 hours in each of two years, and if all the instruction was to be given in evening classes, there should be classes on three evenings a week during the school session. Some employers would allow day release, and in large firms with a long tradition of apprentice training – Siemens, British Thomson-Houston, Metropolitan-Vickers, for example – instruction within the works was elaborately organised. However, whatever method was followed, sustained effort over a period of years was required to reach even the lowest levels of professional qualification.

Above and beyond the part-time courses for the ONC and the HNC, the Board of Education also provided for full-time Diploma courses, again at Senior and Advanced levels. The Senior course, lasting two years and leading to an Ordinary Diploma, was designed for students who had had full-time continous education up to the age of sixteen. Three years were required for the Advanced course, leading to a Higher Diploma, and it was designed for students who had had full-time continuous education up to the age of seventeen or eighteen or who had been for two years in regular employment, taking Senior or Advanced part-time courses. The intention was that there should be no difference in the standard of attainment required for Higher National Diplomas and university degrees, but there was no doubt a difference in prestige, which may be the reason why the HND remained a rare distinction (see Table 6). Probably most of those able to contemplate three years' full-time higher education went to a university instead.

At the level of ONC and HNC the courses approved by the Board of Education and the IEE rapidly became the standard British route, below degree level, to a recognised first qualification in electrical engineering. In 1924, the first complete year for which records are available, seventy-four courses were approved in England and Wales, 282 certificates were awarded at Ordinary level, forty-three at Higher level, and nine Ordinary and fifteen Higher Diplomas were conferred. Fourteen years later, in the last full year before war broke out, there were 226 approved courses, leading to 917 ONCs, 379 HNCs, thirty-three Ordinary Diplomas and nine Higher Diplomas. From 1930 onwards a similar scheme was running in Scotland, and in 1938 there were fifteen approved courses, yielding thirty-five ONCs, fifteen HNCs and eight Higher Diplomas.[27]

Table 6: Electrical Engineering Courses Approved: National Certificates and Diplomas Awarded, 1924–1938

	1924	1925	1926	1927	1928	1929	1930	1931	1932	1933	1934	1935	1936	1937	1938
England & Wales															
Approved courses	74	67	86	95	105	120	128	150	159	180	184	192	202	211	226
Certificates:															
ONC	282	229	245	333	361	433	510	592	732	707	804	737	735	816	917
HNC	43	79	116	147	155	209	230	279	353	347	353	438	374	407	379
Diplomas:															
Ordinary	9	8	8	4	8	10	20	8	15	28	18	15	20	27	33
Higher	5	2	6	1	6	4	4	3	7	12	9	7	15	16	9
Scotland															
Courses							5	5	9	14	14	14	18	16	15
Certificates:															
Ordinary								5	12	13	19	20	28	38	35
Higher						6	3	6	17	16	6	18	18	15	
Diplomas:															
Higher						15	11	9	10	14	17	12	7	8	

Source: Annual Reports of Council, *JIEE*, LXII,324; LXIII,336; LXIV,348; LXV,360; LXVI,372; LXVII,384; LXVIII,396; LXIX,408; LXXI,426; LXXIII,439; LXXV,451; LXXVII,463; LXXIX,475; LXXXI,487; LXXXIII,499; LXXXIV,505.

The Board of Education's scheme was thus an immediate and rapid sucess, with schools and colleges eager to have their courses of instruction approved by the Board of Education and the Institution and students equally eager to take advantage of the courses provided. Of those who entered for the various examinations, it would appear from figures preserved for the years 1929-1931 that in England and Wales about 60 per cent were likely to gain the ONC and about 66 per cent the HNC. During the fourteen years from 1924 to 1938 the total number of certificates and diplomas granted, including the Scottish equivalents, were 8,603 ONCs, 4,014 HNCs, 231 Ordinary Diplomas and 209 Higher Diplomas.

Table 7: Pass Rates in Electrical Engineering Examinations, England and Wales, 1929–1931

Examination	Candidates entered	Pass rate
ONC	2,581	59.5
HNC	1,078	65.9
Post-HNC	21	71.4
Ordinary Diploma	51	74.5
Higher Diploma	18	61.1
Total	3,749	61.6

Source: National Certificates and Diplomas in Electrical Engineering (England & Wales), Report for 1931. Attached to Joint Committee Minutes, 11 Dec. 1931.

For the first time, electrical engineers in Great Britain, in the years between the wars, were being trained to a common standard, surely an indispensable requirement if their profession were ever to stand as high as they wished in public esteem, and just as important also, below the professional level, for the increasing numbers of technicians and skilled workmen. University courses, it is true, were not assessed in the same way as courses in schools and colleges, but in the universities the influence of the IEE was strong, and through such acedemic figures as W H Eccles, E W Marchant, W M Thornton and C L Fortescue it was brought to bear on professional education generally.

National diplomas and certificates were added to the considerable battery of educational qualifications which, together with suitable professional experience, were accepted for admission to corporate membership of the IEE. The Higher National Diploma was accepted alongside university degrees, the Diploma of Faraday House and certain other more specialised qualifications, as exempting its holders from the whole of the Institution's own Associate Membership examination or, as it was known from 1929 to 1939, the Graduateship examination. The Ordinary National Diploma or National Certificate (with credits in two electrical subjects) would exempt candidates from Part I, with certain stipulations, and so would the Higher Grade National Diploma in Mechanical Engineering. Holders of the Higher Grade National Certificate, like those who had passed the final examination in Electrical Engineering Practice of the City and Guilds of London Institute, were exempt from Part II of the Graduateship examination.[28]

What this meant in practice may perhaps be judged from a report to the IEE's Examinations Committee on candidates admitted to the class of Graduates from 30 January to 23 April 1936.[29] They had between them 265 educational qualifications, of which the principal were:

Degrees	73	28%
National Certificates	63	24%
Higher National Diplomas	6	2%
IEE Graduate Examination	64	24%
Faraday House Diplomas	27	10%

City & Guilds with others	19	7%
Others	13	5%
Total	265	100%

Admission to the class of Graduates, as we have seen (page 119) was far from being a guarantee of Associate Membership and might lead merely to disgruntled frustration. Nevertheless, for many electrical engineers it was an essential step along the road to full professional standing, and from the figures quoted above it is evident that National Certificates and Diplomas, by the mid-thirties, were widely used for taking it.

The Graduateship or Associate Membership examination was held twice a year, in April and October, in centres all over the world: in 1927, for instance, in eleven towns in Great Britain and Ireland, and also in the Azores, India, Japan, New Zealand, South Africa and in the battleship HMS *Ramillies*.[30] During the 1930s a conscious effort was made to raise its standard, and in pursuance of that aim, in 1934, 'Engineering Economics' was introduced as an optional paper into Part III, thus somewhat tardily recognising the importance for British engineers of 'business studies'.[31] As Frank Gill observed, in his inaugural address as President in 1922, 'that question of economics is the fundamental problem of the engineer; let him neglect it and, even though brilliant, he becomes something else, a physicist perhaps, a mechanician or a constructor, but not an engineer'.[32]

Frank Gill was one of those who put a great deal of effort into directing the IEE's attention to professional education in the years between the wars. E W Marchant was another. Their outstanding achievement was the success of the Institution's cooperation with the Board of Education. It established a far more comprehensive and coordinated system of engineering education than had ever before been seen in the United Kingdom. Nothing, perhaps, in the Institution's activities between the wars, did more for the standing of the Institution and for the profession of engineering generally.

III 'The exchange of information and ideas'

The Institution between the wars was a very active learned society constituted, in the words of the Charter, 'to facilitate the exchange of information and ideas ... amongst the Members of the Institution'. Whatever reservations the Council might have about other fields of activity, there could be none about that. It was – and is – among the foremost purposes for which the Institution existed and still exists, and its importance, if the Institution wishes to be taken seriously as a qualifying authority, needs no emphasis.

The Institution might be described as, amongst other things, a machine for holding meetings, and its output between the wars was various, numerous and geographically widely dispersed. Without taking account of General

Meetings, Special Meetings of various kinds, Council meetings and the meetings of an ever greater range of committees, the meetings convened purely for 'the exchange of information and ideas' – that is, for the reading and discussion of papers – rose in number from 207 in the session of 1921-1922, when the membership was about 10,000, to 262 in 1930-1931 (14,000 members) and to 320 in 1938-1939, when there were about 19,000 members. By far the greatest number of these meetings – 158 in 1938-1939 – were held at local centres and sub-centres, and in addition in the same year 104 were students' meetings.[33]

From the first meeting of the Society of Telegraph Engineers (page 24) onward the Institution and its forerunner had international ambitions, and by no means all activities took place in the United Kingdom. Between the wars there was a sustained effort to extend overseas, sometimes in cooperation with the Civils and Mechanicals, particularly in countries of the British Empire and other countries, such as Argentina and China, where British influence was strong. Imperialist sentiment in these years was still powerful. 'Progressive' thought had turned against it but it had by no means been discredited in the nation at large. Businessmen in particular saw the Empire, by which they meant chiefly the Dominions and India, as a promising field for British enterprise, and where British business went, British engineers would go too, taking their institutions with them.

At home, nineteen meetings in 1921-1922, thirteen in 1930-1931 and seventeen in 1938-1939 were the traditional Ordinary Meetings which had been held in London, fortnightly or thereabouts during the session, since the STE began. The proceedings were formal, the discussion was largely prearranged, some of the most eminent electrical engineers of the day took part, and it had long been recognised that many members, particularly the younger ones, found the atmosphere intimidating.

In 1919, during Wordingham's presidency, Informal Meetings, known by that title, were set up.[34] They featured short papers briefly reported in the *Journal*, but they were presided over and largely run by members of a committee of the Council, including, *ex officio*, the current President. Promising paper-givers would come early to the Council's notice, thus helping to solve the perennial problem of finding speakers for the Ordinary Meetings. Informal meetings were at first reported to be popular, but the average attendance fell from eighty to a hundred in 1921-1922 to fifty-five to sixty-five in the late thirties. Ten informal meetings were held in 1921-1922, eleven in 1930-1931, sixteen in 1938-1939.

Analysis of the subjects covered by papers read and discussed at Ordinary Meetings shows how dominant power engineers and their interests were in the proceedings of the Institution in the 1920s and 1930s. In volumes of the *Journal* covering sessions in the years 1921-1923, 1926-1927, 1931-1932 and 1937-1938, which may perhaps be taken to provide a sample of the period

Table 8: IEE Meetings Held for the Exchange of Information and Ideas, 1921–1939

	1921–22		1930–31		1938–39	
Ordinary Meetings		19		13		17
Section Meetings						
Wireless		7		7		10
Meter & Instrument				8		10
Transmission						7
Informal Meetings		10		11		16
Local centres	7(a)	66	8(a)	90	8(a)	93
Local sub-centres	5	44	6	45	8	65
Students' sections	7	61	8	88	9	104
Total		207		262		320
IEE Membership		10,275		14,670		19,044

Note: (a) Number of Centres, Sub-centres, Students' Sections

between the wars, the reading and discussion of eighty-two papers are reported. Of these papers nine dealt with some aspect of telephony or telegraphy, four were on miscellaneous subjects, and all the rest – 85 per cent of the total – were concerned with the generation, distribution or use of electric power.

Many papers, particularly those which dealt with more theoretical and mathematical aspects of electrical engineering, were published in the *Journal* but not read at Ordinary Meetings. Those which were read tended to hold scientific theory at a distance and kept strictly to practical matters. Their subjects included 'Telephone Line Work in the United States' (E S Byng, 17 November 1921), 'The Design of City Distribution Systems and the Problem of Standardization' (J R Beard and T G N Haldane, 4 November 1926), 'Large Electric Baking Ovens' (W Ellerd-Styles, 19 January 1928), 'Modern Systems of Multi-Channel Telephony on Cables' (A S Angwin, 15 April 1937), and 'Electrification of the Paris-Orleans and Midi Railways' (A Bachellery, 18 November 1937).[35]

Every year in the Kelvin Lectures, some of the most distinguished British scientists addressed the members of the Institution. 'Electricity and Matter', for instance, was discussed by Sir Ernest Rutherford in 1922, 'Electric Forces and Quanta' by J H Jeans in 1925, 'The Mechanics of the Electric Field' by Sir J J Thomson in 1926, and 'The Architecture of the Solid State' by Professor W L Bragg in 1931.

In spite of the concern which some engineers felt for the neglect of business studies and management in engineering education, virtually no attention seems to have been paid to them, to judge by the titles of papers delivered during the years surveyed. Engineering economics, also a subject of widespread concern, was dealt with in three papers. The use of electricity in private households was spreading rapidly and five papers were addressed to various aspects of it, as well as two on commercial cooking. Neither marketing nor selling, whether of electric power or of electrical appliances, were considered at all, reflecting almost certainly the orthodox engineer's disdain for these matters and his reluctance to admit the 'sales engineer' to membership of the Institution. The use of electricity in farming, very little developed between the wars, was discussed by R Borlase Matthews, an enthusiast, in 1922 and 1927 ('Electric Ploughing') and by J S Pickles in 1937. Among the few non-technical papers read were 'Co-operation between the Architect and the Electrical Engineer' (Francis Hooper and J W Beauchamp, 15 March 1923) and 'Lightning' (Professor B L Goodlet, 7 January 1937).

An examination by Dr Bowers of papers read more than twice at meetings between the wars, which presumably covered subjects of relatively wide interest, shows an unsurprising rise in 'light current' topics, but at the same time interest in 'power' remained constant, though with a shift from power stations and generators towards components. Papers on the household applications of electricity were more frequent in the thirties than earlier, presumably as more and more households were connected to the mains and more electrical gadgets came into use.

In 1923 the Council instituted annual 'Faraday Lectures' on electrical subjects, and the first, 'World-Wide Radio Telegraphy', was given by Professor G W O Howe a year or so later. The lectures, aimed at the general public, were delivered by eminent figures in electrical engineering, including Sebastian de Ferranti ('Electricity in the Service of Man', 1928) and P P Eckersley of the BBC ('Broadcasting by Electric Waves', 1930). They were sent on tour throughout the country, usually to seven or eight provincial towns as well as London, and they soon began attracting large audiences.

Table 9: Subjects of IEE Papers Read Two or More Times, 1920–1939

Note: The following is an analysis by Dr Brian Bowers of the subjects of IEE Papers which were presented more than once in the years 1920 to 1939 inclusive. It is based on the entries in the indexes to the journals. The figures in the table show the number of different papers in each subject category and each span of years. The table includes all papers read more than once.

	1920–24	1925–29	1930–34	1935–39
Non-electrical aspects of power stations	7	4	6	2
Generator design	4	2	2	0
ESI systems: distribution	12	12	11	9
Loads – domestic	2	3	1	6
Loads – non-domestic	11	11	8	9
Components	1	8	5	9
Telegraphy	0	1	1	1
Telephony	2	3	4	3
Radio	1	1	1	5
Television	0	0	0	2
Measurement	0	2	8	10
Other science	0	5	7	5
Management	7	4	3	9
Other topics/unclear	4	1	9	16

Eckersley, speaking in nine centres, was heard by 7,000 people, of whom 5,500 were not members of the IEE.[36] Between the two wars, they represented probably the shrewdest move made by the IEE in the public relations of electrical engineering.

The Ordinary Meeting, as a medium for the exchange of information and ideas, was based on the assumption that electrical engineers shared a wide field of common interests. Since the turn of the century or earlier that assumption had been questionable and by the 1930s it was out of date. 'The Committee', said the General Purposes Committee in 1934, 'believe that the high degree of specialization of many papers given at the full meetings of the Institution tends to make them more or less unintelligible to electrical engineers who are not intimately associated with the subjects treated, and discourages general attendance.'[37]

It did more. It encouraged the formation of specialised societies and associations outside the IEE. The IEE's reaction to the suggestion of a new foundation was invariably hostile. First, in the opinion of its Council it was not necessary, since the Institution could itself cater for every conceivable branch of electrical engineering. In extreme cases specialised sections could be set up after the pattern of the Wireless Section, although that had not prevented the bitterly resented formation, in 1925, of the Institute of Wireless Technology (Chapter 8). Secondly, in the Council's view more would mean worse, since new foundations' standards were bound to be lower than those insisted on by the IEE.[38]

Playing, no doubt, on these sentiments, two groups including many members of the IEE formed associations of their own: the Meter Engineers' Technical Association in the mid-twenties and the Overhead Lines Association in 1927. The ploy – it almost certainly was a ploy – worked, for both associations were absorbed into the IEE and sections were set up to cater for their members' interests, the Meter and Instrument Section in 1928 and the Transmission Section in 1934.[39] A move by Borlase Matthews, however, to get the activities of the Institution extended to cover 'commercial matters' was firmly repulsed for the usual reason: 'commercial matters ... are outside the scope of the Institution as defined by its Charter.'[40]

By the mid-thirties, then, the Institution as a learned society was firmly set on a path towards 'sectionalisation'. Three sections were in existence – Wireless, Meter and Instrument, Transmission – which by 1938-1939 had 1,079, 726 and 1,683 members respectively, and there was little doubt that others would be formed as time went on. Discontent, nevertheless, still remained among junior members and among those who were referred to in 1934, a trifle patronisingly, by Sir Thomas Purves, President in 1929, as 'groups of men who are not qualified for any of the existing classes of membership, but who merit encouragement and assistance in the higher aspects of the work which they have taken up'. These were no doubt technicians, and Sir Thomas recommended admitting them 'to a limited and non-executive form of association ... such new class might be designated "Sectional Associates".' The suggestion was not received with any enthusiasm by the Council, and the problem remained.[41]

The *Journal* nearly doubled in size from 852 pages in the 1921 volume to 1,624 pages in the two volumes issued for 1938. It provided many members, no doubt, with their most substantial link with the Institution. *Science Abstracts*, the Institution's other important regular publication, carried 5,081 abstracts in its Physics volume for 1938 and 3,622 in the volume for Engineering. It was not well supported within the IEE. Only 1,424 members out of nearly 20,000 subscribed to it and the Council, in their Report for 1938-1939, expressed a reproachful 'hope that in view of its exceptional value more members will become subscribers'.

The Council and its committees and the committees of Local Centres worked very hard at planning the Institution's sessional programmes and organising meetings. Members' response was hardly proportionate. We have no complete record of attendance at meetings, but Table 10 indicates the average level of attendance at sectional meetings in 1938-1939, varying from just under 6 per cent at meetings of the Transmission Section to 18 per cent at meetings of the Wireless Section. Attendance at Ordinary Meetings in 1938-1939 was proportionately much lower: 251, or 1.3 per cent of the total membership. In looking at the history of voluntary organisations it is salutary to be reminded, from time to time, that the bulk of the membership is passive. It is unlikely that the members of the IEE in the thirties were unusually idle. It is to be hoped that they read the *Journal* more assiduously than they attended meetings.

In the 1930s the IEE was the largest of the British engineering institutions and it was growing increasingly fast (Appendix 5). It had more than half a century behind it and a newly granted Royal Charter. Those who directed its affairs had a sense of purpose, strong but rather narrow, which the terms of the Charter embodied. Similarly they had a clear but rigid specification for an approved pattern of electrical engineer, from which the radio engineer was an unfortunate but apparently inevitable aberration which they would have to endure.

Table 10: IEE Strength of Sections and Average Attendance at Meetings, 1938–1939

Section	Strength	Attendance	
		Numbers	Percentage
Wireless	1,079	195	18.1
Meter & Instrument	726	114	15.7
Transmission	1,683	98	5.8
Informal Meetings	—	65	—
Ordinary Meetings	19,044	251	1.3

Source: Annual Report of Council 1938–1939, *J.IEE*, LXXXIV

For the profession of electrical engineering their ambitions were high, to be achieved by a steady upward pressure on standards of qualification and therefore on technical education. They had a keen eye for the public status of the engineer and they were not unmindful – the membership would not let them be – of his material rewards, though they were debarred from direct efforts to improve them by 'the scope of the Charter', and their distaste for trade unions and for some professional associations is marked. They ran a flourishing learned society. If the government of the Institution just before the Second World War exuded a slight aroma of self-satisfaction – 'One truth is clear, Whatever is, is right'[42] – is that, in the circumstances, to be wondered at?

References

1   W A J O'Meara: 'The Functions of the Engineer: His Education and Training', *J.IEE*, 1919, **57**, pp.225–257
2   *Electrical Times*, 1933, **84**, p.604
3   *J.IEE*, 1925–1926, **64**, pp.193–237, 879–887
4   Reference 3, p.879
5   Fleet Order: 'Annual Report of Council', *J.IEE*, 1925–1926, **64**, p.66; Civil Service: *Electrical Times*, 1929, **75**, p.579; Winnington Hall: W J Reader: *Imperial Chemical Industries, a History*, Vol.1, 1970, pp.91–92, pp.218–219, Vol.2, pp.70–77; Oral information from Lord Hinton of Bankside
6   *J.IEE*, 1919, **57**, p.246
7   'Memorandum prepared by the Chairman of the Membership Committee on the Admission of Sales Engineers', Ref 163/124, 19 March 1931, IEE Archives II/1.1.1
8   Reference 3, p.885
9   Reference 3, p.879
10 CM, 2 Feb. 1922; Sec. Institute of Naval Architects to Sec. IEE, 1 July 1921, IEE Archives 1/6.6
11 'Report on Work of Engineering Joint Council', Council Doc 441/3, 28 June 1927, p.3, IEE Archives II/1.1.1
12 Reference 11, p.6
13 'Memorandum on the Federation of Engineering Institutions, prepared by Mr Pendred', Council Doc 567, 30 June 1932, IEE Archives II/1.1.1; CM, 11 March and 1 July 1937
14 CM, 8 Feb. 1962
15 CM, 5 Nov. 1936
16 CM, 1 July 1937
17 'Agenda for IEE Council Meeting', 11 Apr. 1939, IEE Archives II/1.1.1
18 CM, 4 July 1939
19 *J.IEE*, 1933, **72**, p.1

20   *J.IEE*, 1919, **57**, pp 225–257
21   Reference 20, p.226
22   Reference 20, p.256
23   CM, 26 May 1921; Technical Education Committee Minutes, 2 July, 20 Oct. 1921
24   'Arrangements and Conditions for the Award of National Certificates and Diplomas in Electrical Engineering' (revised July 1936) IEE Archives II/1.1.1
25   *J.IEE*, 1939, **84**, p.161
26   Reference 25, p.168
27   Figures from Annual Reports of Council 1924/25–1938/39, *J.IEE*, **63–84**
28   'Joint Report ... on the Graduateship Examination Exempting Qualifications', Doc 127/269, IEE Archives II/1.1.1, CM, 13 April 1939
29   Examinations Committee Minutes, 7 May 1936
30   'Annual Report of Council', *J.IEE*, 1927–1928, **66**, p.642
31   Examinations Committee Minutes, 26 March 1931; Joint Examinations and Membership Committees' Minutes, 1 July 1931
32   *J.IEE*, 1922–1923, **61**, p.2
33   Annual Reports of Council 1921/22, 1930/31, 1938/39, *J.IEE*, 1921–1922, **60**, p.535; 1931, **69**, p.858; 1939, **84**, p.588
34   Minutes of Informal Meetings Committee OCM Vol.9, 24 Feb. 1919
35   *J.IEE*, 1921–1922, **60**, p.85; 1926–1927, **65**, p.97; 1927–1928, **66** II, p.569; 1937, **81**, p.573; 1938, **82**, p.233
36   'Annual Report of Council' *J.IEE*, 1930, **68** II, p.755
37   Report of the General Purposes Committee, Doc 587/7, 29 Nov. 1934; CM, 6 Dec. 1934
38   GPCM, 28 Oct., 3 Nov. 1927; Rollo Appleyard: *The History of The Institution of Electrical Engineers (1871–1931)*, 1939, pp.244–245
39   'Annual Reports of Council', *J.IEE*, 1929, **67** II, p.845; *J.IEE*, 1934, **75**, p.810
40   GPCM, 3 Nov. 1927
41   'Report of the General Purposes Committee': (b) Sectionalization, CM, 6 Dec. 1934
42   Alexander Pope: *An Essay on Man*, 1744, Epistle 1, line 294

Chapter 11

The Second World War, 1939–1945

I The Impact of War

It gives us comfort to regard warfare – one of mankind's principal and most enduring occupations – as an aberration, an interruption to a normal state of peace. History, especially the history of the twentieth century, suggests that in truth peace may be an interruption to a normal state of war. Processes of change, social, economic and technological, run uninterrupted, though they may be accelerated, slowed down or deflected, through war and peace, and it may be misleading to draw too rigid a dividing line between the two. In the 1930s changes in electrical science and technology were impending which would have forced change upon the IEE whether war had broken out or not. Nevertheless before moving on to consider those matters it will be convenient to deal with the impact of war upon the Institution.

In 1914 war burst upon the European powers when they had long been preparing for it but at a moment when they did not expect it. In 1939 no European government had been preparing for war, in any serious way, for more than about half-a-dozen years at most, but the outbreak, when it came, took neither governments nor peoples by surprise. Moreover the likely nature of a war between advanced industrial powers was far better understood both by peoples and by governments than in 1914, so that on the one hand the carefree patriotic enthusiasm of 1914 was lacking, and on the other hand the preparations that had been made were far better adapted to their purpose than preparations made before 1914.

In Great Britain the administrative lessons of 1914–1918 had been learned and acted upon. In 1939 there was no pretence of 'business as usual' or of 'muddling through'. Elaborate machinery for control and direction of every aspect of the national life was in readiness. Compulsory military service came into force in the spring. After war was declared and during the years that followed control of imports and industrial production, food rationing, direction of labour and the conscription of women were all brought into existence, relying on an absence of corruption and favouritism which in many countries would have been inconceivable. Before the war ended, Great Britain was organised for war more thoroughly and comprehensively than any other belligerent power (nowhere else, for instance, was there conscription of women), and under a government in which Conservative influence was pre-eminent, a centrally directed economy was devised which might have served – and to some extent was later made to serve – as a model for socialism.

The Institution, at the outbreak of war, had just appointed a new Secretary, W K Brasher. He was a Bristol doctor's son, born in 1897, and he had gone to a public school, Clifton College, and St John's College, Cambridge, but his education had been interrupted by the Great War, in which he served for three years, in France, as an officer of RE Signals. Brasher, unlike any of the earlier secretaries, was a practising electrical engineer and a member of the Institution. After he came down from Cambridge in 1921 he joined Marconi's Wireless Telegraph Company at Chelmsford but within a year or so he moved into Government service overseas. In 1933, after experience in British Guiana and Iraq, he became Engineer-in-Chief to the Palestine Posts and Telegraphs, but by 1939 he and his wife Kitty were looking for a chance to go home. Brasher found it by answering an advertisement for the IEE Secretary's post, and he took up his appointment on 1 September 1939.[1]

By upbringing, education and early experience Brasher belonged to the professional English middle class which sustained the IEE. In character he was upright, patriotic, conservative and autocratic: not an easy man, but a strong one. Wherever he worked, he would be likely to leave his mark. He brought to the IEE the habits of thought and the methods of work formed by nearly twenty years in the public service. As the years went by, he built up a position of unique and lonely influence.

Two days after Brasher took office, Great Britain declared war on Germany. Everyone expected immediate heavy air raids, so shelters had been built at Savoy Place in July. The raids did not come at once, but in September 1939 Brasher put forward proposals for evacuating the building. Two houses were leased in Weybridge for documents and, if necessary, staff.[2] The raiders eventually came but the headquarters staff of the IEE remained in London throughout the war. Conditions were hard and sometimes dangerous, as they were for all who worked in London and other large cities. By September 1941 the IEE building, wrote Brasher, had 'long ago' lost all its windows and in October 1946 it was referred to as 'a scarred veteran of the war, having been damaged, mostly by bomb blast, no fewer than sixteen times'.[3]

Against this drab background, and with the loyal service of its staff, the Institution as a body corporate throve. The membership, between 1939 and 1945, rose by 40 per cent, with rather more than half in non-corporate grades. This was clean contrary to the Institution's experience during the Great War, when membership fell.[4] In both wars there was a great rise in electrical activity, especially in radio and related fields, but during the Second World War far greater care than in the Great War was taken to train prospective electrical engineers and then to keep them away from the armed services (page 148). That probably accounts for the fall in membership during one war and the rise during the other.

The number of meetings held in a year, after an initial check caused by Government regulations, went up from 342 in the session 1939-1940 to 682 in 1944-1945. Many of these were committee meetings – 153 out of 342, for instance, in 1939–1940 – and the titles of some of the committees (National Certificates, Science Abstracts, Ship Electrical Equipment, Wiring Regulations) suggest the long-standing concern of the Institution with education, science and practical matters of technology. By the end of the war committees had been set up, following requests from Government departments, to deal with radio interference, regulations for the electrical equipment of aircraft and radio requirements for civil aircraft. Other committees, such as the Emergency Committee and the National Service Committee, had their origins in the war itself.

The rise in the number of meetings suggests also that in spite of the war the Institution was increasingly active as a learned society, and increasingly concerned with specialised interests. The number of Ordinary Meetings devoted to papers of general technical interest remained constant, between eight and ten a year, but the number of meetings of specialised sections – Wireless, Meter and Instrument, Transmission – rose from fourteen in the session 1939-1940 to 41 in 1944-1945.[5] A new section – Installations – was formed in 1941. The idea behind it, which had come from an Associate Member and attracted a good deal of support just before the war, was that whereas the Transmission Section and the Meter and Instrument Section dealt with the supply and measurement of electric power, there was no section concerned with the installation of plant and the use of the power supplied to drive it. The Council were dubious whether such a section would outlast the initial burst of enthusiasm. The war gave them an excellent reason for waiting to see. The demand persisted, and the Council at length acknowledged that 'notwithstanding the difficulties attending such a step in wartime, circumstances had arisen which indicated that the formation of the Section should no longer be postponed'. It would fill a place, they thought, in the activities of the Institution and it might help with the prosecution of the war and with post-war planning. The scope of the new section seems to have been wide and its terms of reference vague, though there was no doubt that they were linked with power engineering rather than with light current. In the section's first session, 1941-1942, R Grierson read a paper on 'Space Heating by means of Electrically Warmed Floors, as applied to Surface-Type Air-Raid Shelters', and there were informal discussions on 'Solving War-Time Electrical Problems' and 'Electrical Installation Problems in War Factories'.[6]

The membership of all the specialised sections rose from about 3,500 in the first year of the war to 7,400 in the last. The largest section, at the beginning of the war, was the Transmission Section, with about 1,700 members, who would nearly all have been power engineers, but it was overtaken by the Wireless Section ('Radio' after 1944) in 1943-1944. By the time the war ended there were about 2,600 members in the Radio Section against 1,900 in the next largest section, which by then was Installations. All this was symptomatic of the way things were going in the electrical engineering profession and hence in the Institution. So was the subdivision of the *Journal*, in the spring of 1940, into three Parts: Part I, 'General'; Part II, 'Power Engineering'; and Part III, 'Communication Engineering'. The immediate reason for this move was the steep wartime increase in production costs – members were required to pay for Parts II and III if they wanted to receive them – but the divisions that were adopted – 'Power' and 'Communication' – showed how electrical engineers' professional interests were diverging.[7]

When J R Beard, a power engineer, gave his Inaugural Address as President in October 1940, he hinted at the shape of things to come. He mentioned 'the particularly strenuous work undertaken by those [members] engaged in the light-current branches ... responsible for such vital services as communications and broadcasting, and for the design and manufacture of the apparatus for them and of similar apparatus for the rapidly expanding needs of the Royal Navy, the Army and the Royal Air Force. Those engaged upon research and development in the multifarious new applications of wireless deserve special record.'[8]

Attendance at meetings, no doubt sensitive to the severity of bombing, varied, but at Ordinary meetings it was usually over 200, and in the Wireless/ Radio Section and the Meter and Instrument Section (re-named 'Measurement' in 1942) it frequently ran near 10 per cent of the section membership. The Radio Section was exclusively concerned with 'light current' and in the Measurement Section they were beginning to have a strong interest in it. In the power engineers' sections – Transmission and Installations – attendances ran rather lower, about 5 per cent of the section membership in Transmission and from 6 to 8 per cent in Installations.

Many meetings were held away from London, in the Local Centres and Sub-Centres. This was a tendency which the Council wished to encourage, especially in wartime when travel was difficult, slow, uncertain and exhausting. The specialised sections were urged to form 'Groups' in the provinces and the Wireless/Radio Section responded enthusiastically, forming Groups in 1943 in the North-Western and South Midland Centres and in 1944 a Group at Cambridge, where there was no Local Centre to which it could be attached. The setting up of local groups was cited as the principal reason why the Radio Section grew so fast in the latter years of the war. A similar result followed when the Installations Section formed groups in the North-Western and Western Centres in 1944, but up to the end of the war no local groups were formed by either of the other two Sections.[9]

By the Autumn of 1940 there were about 1,285 members of the IEE in the armed forces, and before the end of the war the total rose to 4,463 – perhaps 20 per cent or so of the total membership – of whom 156, or about 3.5 per cent of those who served, lost their lives. Compared with the Great War, more than twice as many members served, but the proportion who lost their lives was less than half as high. Twenty-six of those killed by enemy action were civilians, a figure to which the Great War showed no parallel.[10]

Faced, in the early months of the Great War, with an almost unmanageable rush of volunteers for the Army, the authorities then had failed either to turn away men who could be more usefully employed as civilians or to ensure that they were sent to appropriate arms of the service (see page 89). Mistakes of this kind were made, though less sweepingly, during the Second World War, but far greater care was taken to prevent them, particularly in compiling the lists of 'reserved occupations' from which men could not be called to the armed services and in protecting students reading for scientific and technical degrees.

In spite of these measures, the Secretary's files contain correspondence complaining of the mis-posting of technically trained men. As a lecturer at University College, Nottingham, said in June 1941: 'there is a lot of haphazard use of man power'. Brasher, well-connected in official circles, did his best to put matters right through whatever channels were open to him.[11] He was consulted also about civilian appointments, as, for instance, for 'really good assistants ... a good presence and personality is almost more important than technical ability' in the Ministry of War Production under Beaverbrook, which probably explains the reversed priorities.[12]

Brasher's personal network was supported by an elaborate framework of committees, controls and regulations. Early in 1939 the Ministry of Labour and National Service (itself a creation of the imminence of war) began to compile, with the help of professional organisations, a Central Register of Persons with Specialist Qualifications. Members of the IEE were invited but not, at first, compelled to enrol, and by June 1940, after a certain amount of pressure, nearly all those eligible for enrolment had been enrolled, though the Council doubted whether the authorities were making 'the fullest possible use' of the Register.[13]

After pressure had been applied, through the Engineering Joint Council, by the engineering institutions, the Government agreed in April 1941 to set up an Engineering Advisory Committee under Lord Hankey. Maurice Hankey (1877-1963) could make a confident claim to be the greatest of all committee men, having been Secretary to the Committee of Imperial Defence before the Great War, of the War Cabinet during it, and of the Cabinet from 1919 to 1938. He was also Chairman of the Government's Scientific Advisory Committee which was the model for the Engineering Advisory Committee. Of that Committee's nine members four were drawn from the IEE. Hankey also became Chairman of a Technical Personnel Committee set up by the Ministry of Labour, and he held the post until 1952, although he left the Scientific and Engineering committees after about a year. He became an Honorary Member of the IEE in 1943.

The Central Register was directed at civilian employment, but civilian employment and military requirements were interwoven. There were never enough engineers of any branch of the profession, either trained or in training, and all the institutions, working through committees such as those mentioned above and along with the appropriate government departments, were engaged in a desperate scramble to get more engineers trained at all levels and to ensure the effective deployment of those who were already trained.

In the IEE a National Service Committee under A P M Fleming was set up in 1940. It had a membership identical with the membership of the Electrical Engineering Sub-committee of the Central Register which paid very detailed attention to the placing of individuals. The National Service Committee dealt rather with groups, and in its records plans are preserved for putting bright boys through six-month intensive courses in single subjects at HNC standards, for making sure that boys going to universities to read engineering and kindred subjects were not called up, and even plans for 'enlisting volunteers from the States and overseas parts of the Empire'.

Thus members of the Institution and the Institution itself were swept into the immensely complicated bureaucratic machine which came into existence to run the war (and lingered long after it). At the same time the Institution went on with its normal life, so far as it could. The Council also joined in the widespread national diversion of post-war planning.

II Post-war Planning

War greatly simplifies public life. In national policy, there is only one aim – victory. In laying plans for the future, one confident assumption can be made – that the war will end. It is therefore possible, as it is not possible in peacetime, to split the future into definable periods, of war and peace, which is a great convenience for planners even if, when the time comes, the reality may not be so tidy as the expectation. In both great wars of this century post-war planning has had great attractions. It has allowed the planners and their audiences, for impeccably respectable reasons, to lift their minds away from the grisly, dreary and often intractable present and to contemplate what Churchill in 1940 called 'broader lands and better days'.[14] In Great Britain, once the acute crisis of 1940 had passed, a great deal of attention began to be paid to the remaking of society after the war, helped by the rapidly accumulating folklore, some of it not far from the truth, about the miseries of the 1930s. Sir William Beveridge presided over a committee which in 1942 generated great expectations with its report *Social Insurance and Allied Services*, and in 1944 the Coalition Government passed an Education Act, piloted by R A Butler, which set the national pattern of education for a generation to come.

At a rather lower level, as soon as the war had become something like a matter of routine and as soon as some of the worst problems of production had been solved, post-war planning became very fashionable in large firms and other organisations including professional associations. The idea seems to have been introduced to the IEE by the Civils, who early in 1941 invited J R Beard, the Electricals' President, to serve on a subcommittee which they had set up. The Electricals decided to follow the Civils' example.[15]

The largest and most urgent matter of post-war planning which faced electrical engineers was the future organisation of electricity supply for the country as a whole. It was a problem almost as old as the Institution, and at one time it had been thought that the Institution would provide the natural channel for the expression of professional views on the subject. We have seen in previous chapters, on the contrary, that disagreement between the various interests involved had been so violent as to threaten to pull the Institution to pieces. By the time Lord Weir's committee reported in 1926 the Institution had retired into the safety of silence. Weir's recommendations, however, were directed to generation, and the problem of organising distribution remained. 'The later 1930s', says Professor Hannah, 'were a turbulent time in the history of the electricity supply industry'. He speaks of 'divisive discussion of distribution reorganisation, which threatened the status and independence of the smaller undertakings and their chief engineers.'[16]

The Council in these circumstances, mindful no doubt of previous acerbities, had no option but to steer an unheroic course. In March 1941 the Council considered a recommendation by the General Purposes Committee 'that The Institution should take its part in post war planning in so far as matters appertaining to electrical engineering are concerned', and a Committee for the purpose with distinguished membership and an array of subcommittees and 'panels' was set up. 'It was urged that any question of a political nature must be studiously avoided', and 'the avoidance of any encroachment on political issues' was written into the Post-War Planning Committee's terms of reference.[17] The restriction was linked, inevitably, with the provisions of the Charter. It was recognised, said the Committee's final report, 'that close observance would be required of the restrictions necessarily imposed by the aims and objects of The Institution as laid down in the Royal Charter'.[18]

In this situation the sub-committee under J R Beard, which considered Electricity Supply, Distribution and Installation, observed that electricity supply was 'one of the most popular subjects for post-war planning' and that most of the numerous schemes for reorganising it centred on proposals for ownership and control, 'but there are many questions of a more technical and less controversial kind … on which the guidance of engineers is essential. The Institution … is the natural forum for the discussion of such problems, and it is believed that a considerable measure of agreement exists.'[19] Beard's sub-committee therefore chose to examine three topics: Standardization of Voltage and System, Availability of Supply, and Forms of Tariff. None of these topics was new – all, indeed, were about as old as the electricity supply industry itself – and if the sub-committee's aim was to avoid controversy, they triumphantly achieved it.[20]

In another part of their report, they displayed a less cautious view of their functions. They examined a case for statutory wiring regulations or the compulsory registration of wiring contractors. It had been put forward, before the war, by an alliance of organisations including the Association of Supervising Electrical Engineers, the Electrical Association for Women, the Electrical Power Engineers' Association, the Electrical Trades Union and the Incorporated Municipal Electrical Association. Whether because they disapproved of some of these bodies or for some other reason, the Council of the IEE had never liked the proposals and had refused to serve on the committee which sponsored them.

That committee was unwise enough to base its case on the argument that the risk of electrical accidents, particularly in private houses, was unacceptably high. Beard's sub-committee had no difficulty at all in showing that electricity, far from making home life more risky, in fact made it healthier and safer. 'From this', it was reported, 'the conclusion is drawn that the need for such compulsory arrangements does not exist at present, but that … Basic Safety Regulations could be given the force of law later'. The sub-committee did not rest on the destruction of their opponents' case. They moved on, by official invitation, to offer constructive advice to the Directorate of Post-War Building in the Ministry of Works and Planning. Through a separate report by a specially appointed committee, they dealt in detail with matters of safety and with installation practice generally for post-war council houses and private houses, and for schools, and they promised reports on other kinds of buildings later.[21]

The way in which Beard's sub-committee conducted their investigations and couched their report vindicated the IEE's policy of shunning political controversy, in which the risk of self-inflicted injury was high, and keeping strictly to technical matters on which the Institution could offer professional advice with unrivalled authority. Nevertheless, it seems unfortunate that as the post-war programmes of the political parties were shaped and displayed to the electorate, the Institution had to remain silent. At the supreme moment when the organisation and ownership of the electricity supply industry, after so many years of uncertainty and controversy, was at last being determined, the Institution was precluded from forming any corporate view or offering any corporate advice on the rival proposals, including nationalisation, for the future of the industry in which a high proportion of its members found their livelihood.

The Post-War Planning Committee seem to have had 'political' misgivings about two other matters on which they deliberated. One was Production, Manufacture and Employment. As late as 1946 the report had gone no further than an interim stage, and then the Council rejected a suggestion to send it confidentially to Government Departments because it 'might erroneously be taken to constitute the considered views of The Institution as a whole on matters which were to some extent non-technical and might be regarded as falling outside its professional scope'.[22] Of the report on 'Telecommunication Engineering in the Post-War Period', which was ready for issue early in 1943, the Post-War Planning Committee themselves 'were of opinion that publication ... would not be desirable, as its contents were not suitable for public discussion'.[23] Why, they did not say, and the document itself does not seem to have survived, so that the reason for its suppression remains a mystery.

The Committee's report on the Organization of Post-War Electrical Research, issued in May 1943, was prepared by a sub-committee under Dr Percy Dunsheath, Chief Engineer of W T Henley and previously Research Director. Commenting on the report in the *Journal*, C C Paterson, FRS, Director of Research for GEC, remarked that the Institution had 'come to regard the physicist not merely as a partner but as a member of the family; and we are now hardly concerned to enquire whether a colleague has been trained as an engineer or as a physicist'. Not all physicists who had recently tried to become corporate members of the Institution might have agreed, but his observation is another indication of the way electrical engineering was going. The report itself made a strong plea for cooperation rather than competition in research. 'If post-war industry is expected to be on the same highly competitive basis as heretofore', it said, 'there appears small scope for beneficial reorganization of research.'[24]

Probably it was in dealing with education that the Committee felt most confident, for no one could doubt that it fell within the scope of the Institution's Charter and it was unlikely to embroil the Council in controversy. Certainly the report produced in 1943 by a sub-committee under A P M Fleming, celebrated for his training of apprentices at Metropolitan-Vickers, was the longest and most elaborate of the series. It covered the education not only of professional engineers but of craftsmen and foremen.

The sub-committee, in accord with the spirit of the times and with the doctrine of equality of opportunity underlying R A Butler's Education Act, recommended 'that full-time university courses should be made available to anyone who has the ability to obtain full benefit from them', and it insisted that 'there must be no financial barrier to entry'. University engineering schools, it suggested, should 'cease to treat all students as potential high-grade scientific or technical workers'. Those who were not should be taught economics, law and social science, on the principle that 'it is the duty of the university to equip men for leadership and not merely to impart advanced technical and scientific knowledge. ... All would be better for a broader scientific attitude, less specialization and a good knowledge of the English language'.

Although the traditional path of professional training, by way of apprenticeship and evening classes, was not neglected, it is clear that Fleming and his sub-committee preferred the university route and expected that in the world after the war it would become the normal way in. It is also apparent that they intended the education of an electrical engineer to be designed as a liberal education undertaken in company with students aiming at other professions. 'The association of engineering graduates', said 'E W M' – almost certainly Professor E W Marchant – in the *Journal*, 'with those being trained for the professions of medicine, law, teaching and the arts, is of inestimable value both to them and to the potential members of the other professions.'[25]

Professional engineers who saw no virtue in any system of training but 'going through the mill' were not, in 1943, extinct, but it is evident that in the higher reaches of the Institution they were an endangered species. The profession was changing, change was being accelerated by the technical demands of war, and education for the profession would have to change too. The general direction of change was indicated clearly by a comment in the sub-committee's report that in a typical course for the Ordinary National Certificate 'the attention given to physics is on the whole deficient, while the elementary consideration of electronic devices – now of such importance in most branches of electrical engineering – has not yet penetrated into many courses'.[26]

Percy Dunsheath, in the autumn of 1945, the year before he retired, became President of the Institution, which, he claimed, was 'the largest engineering professional body in the world'.[27] For his Inaugural Address he chose to discuss 'British Electrical Engineers and the Second World War'.

He began with Home Power Supply, which for more than fifty years had been the central concern of the Institution. After revealing, amongst other things, that far more damage had been done to transmission lines by the trailing cables of drifting barrage balloons than by enemy action, he turned to Home Communications, which led him towards radio, overseas communications and broadcasting. Then he turned to radar in various applications, which included the interception of aircraft – 'early in 1939 we were in the throes of installing 20 operational stations' – navigation and gun-laying.

He dealt with the implications of developments in radio and radar for wavelengths (he was old-fashioned enough to speak of 'shorter and shorter wavelengths' rather than 'higher and higher frequencies') and for the design of electronic valves and cathode ray tubes. Towards the end of his address he glanced briefly at Atomic Energy. He sketched, that is to say, the outlines of the professional world into which the Institution would have to advance: a world which differed from the world of the power engineer as much as the power engineer's world, when it began to come into existence in the 1890s, differed from the world of the telegraph engineer which preceded it.

References

1   *Who was Who*, Vol.7, p.91; 'Annual report of Council', *J.IEE*, 1940, **86**, p.575

2   Memorandum of the Proposal to evacuate the Institution Building, 26 Sept. 1939, IEE Archives II/1.1.1; CM, 5 Oct. 1939

3   Sec IEE to Cellon Ltd 19 Sept. 1941; *J.IEE* , 1946, **93**, Pt.1, p.419

4   Appendix 5; 'Annual Report of Council', *J.IEE*, 1946, **93**, Pt. 1, p.218

5   Figures from Annual Reports of Council

6   General Purposes Committee Report of 29 Dec. 1938 attached to CM, 5 Jan. 1939; 'Annual Reports of Council', *J.IEE*, 1939, **84**, p.731; 1940, **86**, p.583; 1942, **89**, Pt.I, p.257

7   'Journal Sectionalization', Report of General Purposes Committee 19 Apr. 1940, with draft circular to Members; Sec. IEE to Sec. RS, CM, 25 Apr. 1940

8   *J.IEE*, 1941, **88**, Pt.1 p.16

9   'Annual Reports of Council', *J.IEE*, 1944, **91**, Pt.1, p.218; *J.IEE*, 1945, **92** Pt.1, p.190

10 'Annual Report of Council' *J.IEE* 1946, **93**, Pt.1 p.206

11 Letter, W K Brasher to A E Laidlaw, 2 Jan. 1941, to H C Lee 29 July 1941, to H J Gillit, 15 Oct. 1941, and correspondence between Willis Jackson and D H Thomas, 8 June and 11 June 1941

12 Letter, G M Nash to W K Brasher, 30 July 1940

13 'Annual Report of Council', *J.IEE*, 1941, **88**, Pt.I, p.216

14 Speech to House of Commons, 20 Aug. 1940

15 GPCM, 28 Feb. 1941

16 L Hannah: *Electricity before Nationalisation*, 1979, p.289

17 CM, 13 March 1941

18 'Post-War Planning – Report of the Post-War Planning Committee', *J.IEE*, 1946, **93**, Pt.I, p.119

19 'Electricity Supply, Distribution and Installation', *J.IEE*, 1944, **91**, Pt.I, p.104

20 Reference 19; 'Post-War Planning in Electricity Supply, Distribution and Installation', *J.IEE*, 1944, **91**, Pt.I, p.97

21 *J.IEE*, 1944, **91**, Pt.I, p.97; see also CM, 3 Dec. 1942 and Doc 2723/122, 23 Nov. 1942, 2723/113 (rev), 12 Dec. 1942; First Draft Report of the

Electrical Installations Committee, PWR/Electrical/50/4, Nov. 1942; 'Annual Report of Council', *J.IEE*, 1943, **90**, Pt.I, p.239

22   Reference 18, p.121
23   CM, 4 March 1943
24   'Research in Industry', *J.IEE*, 1943, **90**, Pt.I p.253; 'The Organization of Post-War Electrical Research', *J.IEE*, 1943, **90**, Pt.I, p.261
25   'Education and Training for Engineers', *J.IEE*, 1943, **90**, Pt.I, pp.223–233, especially para 2.3, p.224; 'The Education of Engineers', *J.IEE*, 1943, **90**, Pt.I, p.211
26   *J.IEE*, 1942, **90**, Pt.I, p.228
27   'Inaugural Address', *J.IEE*, 1946, **93**, Pt.I, pp.17–27

Chapter 12

The World Turned Upside Down

I The Economy: 'never . . . so good'

When Harold Macmillan was Prime Minister, in a moment of uncharacteristic stylistic inelegance, he uttered the lamentable phrase 'never had it so good',[1] and it has remained firmly implanted in the public mind ever since. He was talking of the period of unexampled prosperity – the longest boom in history – which, in contrast with the depression of the 1930s, seemed in the 1950s and 1960s to make economic growth a law of nature. In the countries of the OECD and Japan – the eleven leading industrial countries of the world – production more than doubled between 1948 and 1963 and the value of manufactured exports nearly tripled.[2] One result was that standards of living, even in the more backward parts of the world, rose higher than ever before and there seemed no reason to doubt that they would go on rising indefinitely. Detergent foam floated away from dhobi ghats in India and outboard motors drove dugout canoes on the River Congo.

This was all happening against a background of international tension and instability. The great colonial empires had collapsed or were collapsing, undermining what remained of the nineteenth-century supremacy of the European powers and leaving, like other collapsed empires in the past, a power vacuum which invited conflict. At the head of hostile coalitions the USSR and the USA manoeuvred against each other in what sometimes seemed to be a new version of the religious wars of the sixteenth and seventeenth centuries. Meanwhile, Western Europe, relieved to a large extent of the weight of self-defence, throve in the early, hopeful years of the EEC, founded by the Treaty of Rome in 1957.

In Great Britain in those years, mass unemployment was regarded as a problem solved. Earnings were rising a good deal faster than money was losing its value. Car ownership was spreading downwards from the middle classes, British holiday-makers were crowding to Spanish beaches, television sets were becoming as widely owned as radio sets twenty or thirty years earlier. Economic growth, though not remarkable by comparison with performance in Germany and Japan, was probably as rapid as at any time in the nation's history. 'Sterling crises' gave repeated reminders that the rest of the world regarded the state of the British economy with less respect than in the nineteenth century, but that did little to disturb the general sense of material well-being.

The political and social atmosphere of the day – 'permissive' was the word in vogue – was conducive to experiment of all kinds, and ideas which had long been familiar in the intellectual stratosphere at last entered practical politics. One result was a comprehensive onslaught, often by way of ridicule, on accepted institutions and on conventional mental and moral attitudes of all kinds, from patriotism to the length of skirts, so that by the end of the 'swinging sixties' very little of the traditional British way of life survived undented.

The unprecedented material prosperity of the period was founded on a remarkable flowering, after many years of development in many fields, of science-based technology. Synthetic materials and man-made fibres transformed old crafts and created new industries. New drugs controlled old diseases and 'the pill' began to unsettle immemorial assumptions about the place of women in society. Aircraft, especially after the full development of jet propulsion, shrank the longest journeys to a few hours and immensely cheapened the true cost of travel. Communication, not only oral but visual, became instantaneous. Nor has this technological whirlwind been halted by economic malfunction. It sweeps on, faster than ever, and conditions of life in the 1980s are changing with bewildering, terrifying speed.

Electricity is central. Professor Hannah has calculated that the output capacity of British power stations, in 1980, was nearly six times as great as in 1948. Taking a longer view, he shows that sales per head of the population were nearly ten times as great in 1980 as in 1938, but the price in 1980, in real terms, had dropped to 70 per cent of the 1938 figure for industry and for domestic consumers to 44 per cent. Over the same period the productivity of the supply industry rose enormously, for employment in the industry in 1980 was less than two-thirds greater than in 1938.[2]

These figures are indicative of the rapidly growing use, over thirty years or so, of electrical apparatus of all kinds. Navigational radar has come to be used

Table 11: The Advance of Electricity (United Kingdom), 1938–1980

	Output Capacity at year end (MW)		Sales per head of population (kWh)		Employment (000)		Share of UK energy markets (%)		Prices in real terms (a) Domestic consumers		Industrial consumers	
1938	na		442	100	109	100	8.5	100	4.8	100	2.0	100
1948	11,789	100	797	180	151	138	14.4	169	2.4	50	1.4	70
1963	36,534	310	2,569	581	231	212	28.6	336	1.8	37	1.7	85
1970	56,057	475	3,598	814	208	191	33.3	392	1.6	33	1.6	80
1980	66,541	564	4,137	936	175	161	35.6	419	2.1	44	1.4	70

Note: (a) Average revenue per kWh sold in England and Wales to domestic consumers (1975 retail prices, p) and industrial consumers (1975 wholesale prices, p).

Source: Adapted from figures given in the Statistical Appendix to L Hannah, *Engineers, Managers and Politicians* (Macmillan, 1982), pp. 291–295

in small yachts and fishing boats as well as in intercontinental aircraft and space craft. Private houses large and small, besides being electrically lit, hum with electrical machinery. Farm workers no longer know how to milk cows by hand. Communication goes by way of satellites and fibre optics. Computers, in the 1940s outlandish industrial monsters, have been domesticated by the 1980s into clever fireside pets, capable of the most amazing tricks. Factory employment is becoming as obsolete as the steam engine which created it, and the social strain is severe.

It is against this background that we must consider the latest phases of the history of the IEE. It is the background of a world culturally and politically turned upside down, yet in which the potentialities of engineering technology, especially in electrical engineering, have never been greater. They are in the literal sense infinite. Nuclear engineering deals with particles infinitely small, and space engineering with distances infinitely great. Infinity, stimulating though it may be, is not easy to come to terms with.

II The Institution: Size and Shape.

The IEE, throughout its history, has always served a growing profession, and since the late 1930s the profession has been growing fast and altering rapidly. In war and in peace, in boom and in recession the advance has gone on, and moreover electricity has permeated every branch of engineering, whether heavy or light, civil or mechanical, sophisticated or relatively simple, so that the boundaries of the Institution's field of interest have become more and more indefinite. The opportunity offered to the Institution for extending its influence in the years between the late 1930s and the mid-1980s has thus been very great, but every opportunity carries a challenge, and in the closing pages of this book we must consider both the challenge and the Institution's response.

Let us look at the underlying statistical framework: the size and composition – corporate and non-corporate – of the Institution's membership and at its geographical distribution. The strength of the Institution's influence would not necessarily be proportionate to the number of its members. Nevertheless, a falling membership would be an indication of decline, and in the period with which we are concerned the membership, far from falling, more than quadrupled from fewer than 20,000 in 1940 to 82,288 in 1983 (see Appendix 5).

Growth, in this period of forty-four years, has never been interrupted, but the rate of growth (see Table 12, summarising figures in Appendix 5) has been far from steady and for over thirty years has shown a tendency to slow down. In the first half of the period, between 1940 and 1961, the average annual rate of growth (4.2 per cent) was 68 per cent greater than the comparable figure (2.5 per cent) in the second half, between 1962 and 1983.

The Institution grew fastest during the forties, especially from 1943 to 1949 when the annual rate of growth ran upwards from 3.8 per cent in 1942 to 10.1 per cent in 1944 and then fell back gradually to 3.4 per cent in 1950 (see Appendix 5). After 1948 the rate of growth did not rise to 5 per cent until 1983, and in twenty-two of the thirty-four years from 1950 to 1983 (both inclusive) it was lower than 3 per cent. In 1971 and 1981 it fell below 1 per cent.

Table 12: IEE Membership (Corporate plus Non-Corporate) – Annual Growth Rates, 1940–1983

Under 2 per cent	2–2.9 per cent	3 per cent and upwards
		1940
	1941	
		1942,3,4,5,6,7,8,9,1950
	1951	
1952,3,4		
	1955	
1956		
		1957,8,9,1960
	1961	
		1962
	1963	
		1964,5
	1966,7	
1968		
		1969,1970
1971,2,3,4,5		
	1976	
1977		
		1978
1979		
	1980	
1981		
	1982	
		1983
13 years	10 years	21 years
1940–1961:		
4 years	4 years	14 years
1962–1983:		
9 years	6 years	7 years

Adapted from figures published in Annual Reports of Council; see Appendix 5

The dwindling growth rate was much in the mind of the Council, particularly in the late sixties and early seventies. Reports were called for. Student counsellors were appointed in eighty-four university and college departments providing courses leading to Associate Membership. Forty IEE representatives were appointed in government and industrial establishments in the London area. Much effort was put into various forms of publicity in schools and universities. 'The strength of the Institution', it was observed, 'is in its members, not in money.'[3]

'To the best of my knowledge', wrote Robert Clayton, one of the Institution's most distinguished members, in 1971, 'we have very little knowledge of the reasons why some people join the Institution whilst a large number decide not to join.'[4] None of Clayton's colleagues on the Council seems to have disagreed with him. About students' reasons for joining, therefore, the Council could only speculate, so that their drive for new membership had to be made blindfold. The influence of heads of departments, they knew, might be decisive, but one young man, who later became President, had found in the twenties that a free tea at Savoy Place was an equally powerful inducement. 'There was no obligation', he remarked in 1983, 'to go to the lecture after you'd had the free tea.' Employers also could bring pressure to bear which a young engineer might consider unwise to resist, especially since there has long been a widespread feeling among members, which does not reveal itself in writing, that in the never-ending struggle between 'them' and 'us' the Institution is on 'their' side.

Publicity to schools was not aimed directly at recruitment to the Institution but at recruitment to the engineering profession generally, which the engineering institutions never felt was sufficiently brisk to meet national requirements. In the late forties and early fifties lectures to schoolchildren were arranged in cooperation with the Civils and the Municipals. For the benefit of electrical engineering in particular, the Institution seized an opportunity offered to them in 1953 to play host to a conference run by the Public Schools Appointments Bureau for headmasters and careers masters. That was followed up, in 1955-1956, with a film – *The Inquiring Mind* – and a booklet - *The Chartered Electrical Engineer ... Electrical Engineering as a Professional Career*. The booklet had a run of ten years and was superseded in 1965, after long consideration, by Professor M G Say's *Electrical and Electronic Engineering, a Professional Career*. The title of the book indicates plainly the rising importance of 'light current'.[5]

Within the Institution, between the forties and the eighties, the balance between corporate and non-corporate members has swung to and fro several times. The non-corporate members were in the majority, sometimes by as much as two or three percentage points, from the mid-thirties to 1954, from 1967 to 1973, and from 1979 onwards. For twenty-five of the forty-four years from 1940 to 1983, fewer than half of the Institution's members have been entitled to call themselves 'Chartered Electrical Engineers'.

Among the members, of whatever grade, women in the fifties and sixties remained very scarce indeed. In the fifties, somewhat hesitantly, the Institution began addressing itself to schoolgirls as well as schoolboys, but as late as the mid-sixties Professor Say's book was uncompromisingly masculine in its phraseology. 'It is not really surpising', he says, 'that so many men feel drawn to the engineering career and are happy in it.'[6] The implication is that if a woman had felt drawn to electrical engineering, that would have been very surprising indeed. Among 24,324 corporate members in 1960 seventy-three were women, and the number showed no signs of increase. Nevertheless, some progress was being made. In 1959 two women became Members, the first since Hertha Ayrton was elected in 1899. In 1962 a prize was established for the woman student gaining the best results in the HNC in electrical engineering. It was first awarded to Patricia Bowring in 1963. Between 1871 and 1981, 500 women were admitted to the Institution. In April 1985 the admission of Angela Nash brought the figure to 1,000.[7]

Table 13: IEE Overseas Membership, September 1962

	Corporate Members	Non-corporate Members	Total
Europe	542	443	985
Africa	1,019	531	1,550
Middle East	215	191	406
India, Pakistan, Ceylon	735	1,057	1,792
Far East	272	295	567
Australia	750	476	1,226
New Zealand	590	228	818
Canada	466	373	839
USA	418	286	704
West Indies	64	55	119
South America	65	43	108
Total	5,136 (56%)	3,978 (44%)	9,114 (100%)
Total membership 1962	25,651 (52%)	23,384 (48%)	49,035 (100%)
Overseas members as percentage of total	20	17	19

Source: Overseas Activities Committee; Report of the Activities of the Institution Overseas, December 1962; Document 6820/97. GPC, 13 Feb. 1963

In the early sixties, as Table 13 shows, about 20 per cent of the membership of the IEE were at work overseas. Many, no doubt, would have been expatriates from the United Kingdom, intending sooner or later to return there. Others, without leaving the countries where they were born, would have taken up membership because they sought an internationally respected professional qualification.

Apart from members in Europe and the United States, most of the overseas members were in countries which had belonged to the nineteenth-century British Empire, so that they were heavily concentrated in the Indian subcontinent, in Australasia, in Africa, especially the Republic of South Africa (798 members in 1962), and in Canada. This was a geographical pattern which had been traditional since the earliest days of the Society of Telegraph Engineers, except that in 1962 there appear to have been no Japanese members.

The Institution, with its members thus widely dispersed, had to deal with other engineering institutions throughout the world, and for this purpose it took a leading part in setting up the Commonwealth Engineering Conference in 1946 and the Conference of Engineering Institutions of Western Europe and the USA (EUSEC) in 1948. Neither Conference was limited to associations of electrical engineers and both faced diplomatic problems of considerable delicacy in avoiding conflict between the international institutions, such as the IEE, and national bodies serving the same profession. The leading British institutions all shared the view that the best interests of engineering in any country, especially a developing country, would be served by creating a national society of professional engineers with which outsiders would not compete for members or in any other way.

The general rule of conduct was set out in the constitution of the Commonwealth Engineering Conference: 'No Constituent Institution will initiate any action within the country of another without first informing the Constituent Institution of that country and obtaining its co-operation'.[8]

This principle occasionally came under severe strain. In the mid-fifties there were repeated complaints from Canada that the Engineering Institute of Canada, 'largely ... built on civil engineering', 'was making little, if any, provision to meet the needs of electrical engineers.'[9] The Institution was asked to allow the establishment of an overseas branch, but that would have set off a major inter-institutional incident, and after protracted diplomacy an advisory committee was set up in 1956, apparently as a substitute for a Canadian branch, in Toronto.[10] That did not settle the matter, and after a visit to Canada in 1963 by the President of the IEE and the Secretary, a Canadian branch of the IEE was set up to cooperate and to share activities with the Engineering Institute of Canada.

The exuberant expansionism of the Institute of Electrical and Electronic Engineers, formed by merging the American Institute of Electrical Engineers with the Institute of Radio Engineers, disturbed the IEE on its home ground in the sixties. The new body, despite its membership of EUSEC, proclaimed a 'non-national policy', which meant that it would welcome members and allow them to set up branches in other countries.

The IEE's response, formulated by a committee under Albert Mumford, was a major change in Institution policy. Henceforward, undoubtedly to the gratification of many members overseas, the Council would permit the formation of 'an active unit of the Institution in any locality where a sufficient number of members desire it'. The aim, said the committee, 'would not be to compete with the national engineering societies, but to support them'.[11] The founding of Overseas Branches, by agreement with local bodies, followed in profusion in the later sixties.

Presidents and senior members and officials of the Institution had always travelled widely. With the development of air travel they went further and more frequently, until from the late fifties onward world tours, or something close to them, began to become a routine feature of a President's term of office.[12] In 1968, for instance, Sir Stanley Brown went to Canada, New Zealand, Australia, Hong Kong, Singapore and Kuala Lumpur. In 1969, Professor Meek, immediate Past President, accompanied by the Secretary, attended the 2nd General Assembly of the World Federation of Engineering

Organisations in Paris and then went on to the 7th meeting of the Common-wealth Engineering Conference in India, where they travelled widely. In 1970 the President, David Edmundson, and the Secretary visited Kenya, Uganda, Zambia and South Africa. The Secretary travelled widely on his own. Brasher, for instance, traversed Africa, from south to north, in 1950, and in 1955 he visited Nigeria to advise on technological education. [13] In the late sixties Brasher's successor, G F Gainsborough (page 195) visited India twice, and his second trip, in 1967, took him also to Kuwait, Bahrain and Israel, transacting a variety of Institution business which he reported to the Council when he came back. [14]

From December 1966 onwards, following a revision of the Institution's Charter, corporate members, formerly Members and Associate Members, became Fellows and Members. [15] At the same time Associates and Graduates became Associate Members, but a new class of Associates was created to accommodate 'candidates of at least 26 years of age, of good education, and whose connection with engineering will conduce to the advancement of electrical science and engineering'. Student members who, at the maximum age for students (twenty-eight), were not qualified to become Associate Members, could transfer to the new class. It was also intended for members of other professions interested in the Institution's activities as a learned society, and for technicians. Behind all the changes in classes of membership, as this example indicates, lay considerations arising from the ferment of the times. They included the improved educational and other qualifications to be required for corporate membership, the advance of the technicians, and the relations between the engineering institutions. They are part of the texture of the discussion which follows in later chapters.

The aim of the Institution has always been to come as near as possible to including on its register all those in the United Kingdom who are qualified for membership, whether corporate or non-corporate. How far it has come to achieving that aim no one has ever been able to say with confidence, because in the United Kingdom there is no legal requirement for electrical engineers to be registered in order to practise and therefore no one knows quite how many there are or the precise nature of their qualifications.

In 1971 Robert Clayton, working from figures published by the Depart-ment of Trade and Industry of 'Persons with Qualifications in Engineering, Technology and Science, 1959/1968', calculated that in 1968 'the number of people in the United Kingdom ... qualified to be corporate members of the Institution did not exceed about 60,000 and was probably not more than about 50,000'. On that basis the number of corporate members in that year – 29,819 – represented about 60 per cent of those eligible. He went on to estimate, on even shakier data, that in 1968 the proportion of new Associate Members to new graduates was 86.6 per cent, but that in 1969 it was much lower – 55.8 per cent – though he did not attempt to guess why. [16]

The most, probably, that can be said with any safety is that for many years most electrical engineers, with varying degrees of enthusiasm and for diverse reasons, have seen fit to join the Institution if they are qualified to do so, even though they take no very active part in its corporate life. The Institution therefore probably has on its registers most of the people, including nearly all the most eminent, who have a fair claim to be considered electrical engineers of professional standing.

References
1   Speech at Bedford, 20 July 1957, quoted in Robert Stewart (Ed.): *A Dictionary of Political Quotations*, 1984, p.105

2   Hannah: *Engineers, Managers and Politicians*, 1982, pp.291–295

3   'Membership Advisers', Doc GP(65) 26 (Rev), 21 Aug. 1965; GPCM80, 13 June 1968; CM110 20 June 1968, with Appendix 1 to 'Recommendations of the Membership Committee', Doc C(68)65; 'Report of the Recruitment Panel', Doc C(70) 1, 15 Dec. 1969

4   'Advantages of Institution Membership', GP(71)30, 18 May 1971, with paper by R J Clayton, 'Why Engineers join the IEE', GPCM84, 7 July 1971

5   'Report of the Joint Committee on Lectures to Schools', CM, 5 April 1951; GPCM32, 19 Nov. 1952; 'Headmasters' and Careers Masters' Conference', Doc 5711/1, CM, 6 Nov. 1952; CM, 4 Nov. 1954 (Film: 'Careers in Electical Engineering'); 'Annual Report of Council', *J.IEE*, 1956(n.s.), **2**, p.390; CM, 5 Nov. 1959; copies of booklets mentioned in text

6   M G Say: *Electrical and Electronic Engineering as Professional Careers* (IEE Careers Booklet), 1965, p.11

7   'Annual Reports of Council', *J.IEE* (n.s.), 1957, **3**, p.382; *J.IEE*, (n.s.), 1959, **5**, p.432; *E & P*, 1964, **10**, p.236; *IEE News Release*, May 1985, p.1

8   'Overseas Activities, Policy': Appendix, 'Factors in the Institution's Overseas Relationships', Doc 6800/2, GPCM, 13 Feb. 1963

9   CM, 4 Dec. 1952

10 CM59, 5 Jan. 1956

11 'Report of the ad hoc Committee on the Overseas Relations of the Institution', Doc 6800/19, GPCM, 12 June 1963; See also GPCM, 16 June, 13 Feb. 1963

12 T E Goldup: 'Round the World in 75 Days', *J.IEE* (n.s.), 1958, **4**, p.423; 'A Round of Family Visits', *ibid*, p.424

13 'A Journey in Africa', *Journal IEE*, 1950, p.143; 'A Journey in Africa II', *Journal IEE*, 1950, p.173; 'Nigerian Journey', Doc 6925/1, CM, 21 April 1955

14 CM, 24 April 1967; 'Annual Report of Council', *E & P*, 1968, **14**, p.193

15 'Annual Report of Council', *E & P*, 1967, **13**, p.263

15 'Annual Report of Council', *E & P*, 1967, **13**, p.263
16 'Membership of the Institution', Doc GPFM(71) 3, Appendix 1, General Purposes and Finance Committee, 13 Oct. 1971

Chapter 13

Government and Opposition in the Fifties

I Council and Membership

The last chapter presented a picture of an Institution growing very large between the 1940s and the 1980s, in an environment, both in the world at large and in the profession of engineering, that was changing rapidly and fundamentally. This was a situation bound to raise problems of organisation, definition and communication. How was the Institution to be organised to achieve its purposes, what were its purposes to be, and how was the Council to communicate with the membership?

These problems in themselves were as old as the Institution, which had always been a growing body in a changing world. We have seen the effects, in the 1890s, of the rise of power engineering, and, in the years between the wars, of a changing conception, associated with the grant of the Charter, of the Institution's functions. Although, however, the problems might not be new in nature, they were quite new in scale. No earlier Council had had to deal with so large a membership, and the problems of communication which it raised, nor with so many and such wide-ranging innovations in electrical technology. Nor had Councils in the past conducted the IEE's affairs in the social, political and cultural atmosphere of the 1960s and later.

The principles underlying the government of the Institution have always been democratic, but there have always been difficulties in the way of applying democratic principles to the selection and functioning of the Council, in whose hands by virtue of the Charter the Institution's government lies, largely because of the complex network of interests which the Council has been required to represent. In 1944 they were summarised by T G N Haldane in a *Journal* foreword:

> First there is the representation of the general body of membership – the Ordinary Members of Council and the Officers of the Institution. Secondly there is the geographical representation of the autonomous Local Centres both at home and abroad. Lastly, there is functional representation of the autonomous specialized Sections of Wireless, Measurements, Transmission, and Installations.[1]

This was not a problem which was going to go away as members grew more numerous and electrical engineering more diversified. On the contrary, it was likely to grow more difficult. It carried with it three consequences. First, the Council was always tending to grow too large to be an effective executive body. Second, the range of interests represented on the Council, in this period of rapid change, had to be continually watched. The watchers could only be members of the Council and it was easy for discontented members of the Institution to suspect bias or excessive conservatism. Third, although provision was made, and occasionally used, for nominations to be made from the body of the membership, the selection of new members of Council, apart from Chairmen of Local Centres and of specialised sections, who sat *ex officio*, lay largely in the hands of the existing Council, who alone had a sufficiently wide view of possible candidates. 'All members of Council', said Haldane, '... are expected to be ever on the watch for those whose qualifications and experience will add strength to the Council, and they are reminded each spring to put forward such candidates for nomination by the Council.'

The Council's selection procedure had to allow not only for a proper balance of all interests but for stipulations about previous Council service (which might be a disqualification) and about eligible classes of membership. It required, said Haldane, a division of 'the whole range of electrical engineering interests ... into a number of broad categories, some of which are themselves divided into separate groups', and it culminated in 'a searching series of secret ballots'. The complexities and subtleties arising from these requirements were worthy of Byzantium, and perhaps few but W K Brasher fully understood them. 'During the last few years', wrote Professor E B Moullin in 1946, 'I have been very struck by the ignorance of many of our members about the method of government of our Institution.'[2] It was easy for discontented members to represent the Council as a self-perpetuating oligarchy.

The Council in the 1950s was already a numerous body. By 1956 it had seventy-seven members. The Chairmen of the Local Centres and of the specialised sections were members and the committees of centres and sections were closely associated with it. Altogether at any one time, on the Council, in the Local Centres, in the specialised sections and overseas there may have been nearly 1,000 individuals actively but not professionally engaged in the running of the Institution. It was from this constituency that Presidents would emerge, the succession being settled, more or less, some years in advance. The path to the Presidency lay through committee work, especially on the Finance Committee and the General Purposes Committee, two of the half-dozen committees of the Council itself. It was likely to be in this committee work, rather than his brief year of office, that a President would make a permanent mark on the Institution, but one Past President has said 'I don't think you know the Institution until you're President.' Certainly any really difficult problems which came to a head during a President's year of office would come to him for settlement.

Members of the Council also served, alongside non-members, on numerous other committees. Some idea of the work involved, during the 1950s, may be gathered from the number of committee meetings recorded in the Council's Annual Reports. As time went on, these increased. In 1950-1951 there were 602 Council and committee meetings of all sorts, including ten meetings of the Council itself and eighty-six of its various committees and sub-committees. By 1959-1960 there were 798 Council and committee meetings of all sorts, the Council met thirteen times and its committees and sub-committees 141 times. If meetings even of important committees were sparsely attended, that is scarcely surprising, though it was becoming a matter of concern.[3]

Members of the Council inevitably come to stand apart from the general body of the membership. In the first place, individuals who are willing and able to undertake voluntary service, especially of so arduous a nature, are not numerous in any community, and although several hundred can always be found within the membership of the IEE, that is not a large proportion of the total. Second, however conscientiously the Council may go about its duties of filling vacancies, there must be a tendency to replace like with like, so that the gulf between Council and membership will persist – as it did in the Institution's very early days – and is unlikely to be resented, or much remarked upon, unless something occurs – as it occurred in the 1890s (see Chapter 3, Section III) – to bring on a crisis.

There was such a crisis in the 1950s. To understand it we must look at the other element – the non-elected, professional, 'civil service' element – in the Institution's government. At the head of it was the Secretary, W K Brasher, and a formidable departmental head he was. In 1940 one of his juniors, earning 25 shillings (£1.25) a week, asked for an increase.

> I do not consider, [Brasher replied,] that any permanent increase in your emoluments is justified immediately. Your short period of service has not yet proved that you will make a satisfactory employee of The Institution, although there have recently been indications that the training so far given may not have been wasted ... At any time I am accessible to members of staff, but I do expect firstly that they will call on me at times convenient to me, secondly that they refrain from interrupting me when in consultation and thirdly that an unsportsmanlike effort will not be made collectively to derive personal benefit from a state of pressure due to the national emergency at a time when the future of all we stand for is at stake. Finally, junior members of the staff are not expected *in any organisation* to seek an interview with their Chief without the knowledge of their immediate superior, and I should be glad if you would bear this in mind in future.[4]

Brasher invariably wrote of The Institution with capital letters. No doubt he thought of it in that way, and to the furtherance of its interests, as he saw them, he directed the entire force of his steely personality. His position as a permanent, full-time official gave him unrivalled knowledge of the Institution and its affairs and attendance at Council meetings gave him unrivalled opportunity for pressing his own point of view. He took full advantage of it, so much so that one Past President, who was on the Council in Brasher's time, used to check his oratory by uttering a loud aside which would raise a laugh. Another described him as 'a bit of a rascal – he did like his own way'. Some presidents stood in awe of Brasher. 'He was greedy for power', one Past President has said. 'You had to be extremely firm with him.' He went on to report another Past President as saying that after a session with Brasher he would go back to his room and weep.

Brasher saw himself as the Council's guardian against undesirable intrusions from the membership, and since the greater part of the Institution's business flowed through him, he could act, at his discretion, as a filter, as a channel or as a dam. In 1951 a member of the Mersey and North Wales Centre Committee complained of 'a lack of machinery whereby individual members may express their views on Institution policy or on matters of general interest in electrical engineering' and suggested 'that the Journal might be opened to members for a limited amount of correspondence'. Brasher, wielding Thor's hammer, 'pointed out that he and his staff scrutinized all the minutes of Local Centres and if there was a point which it was felt merited wider discussion, it was considered by the appropriate Committee of Council'. The General Purposes Committee, evidently following his lead, or perhaps browbeaten, unanimously agreed that the member's suggestion about correspondence in the *Journal* 'was out of the question', and asked Brasher to tell the Centre Committee 'that it was considered that the arrangements at present in force were sufficient to ensure that any views put forward by Local Centre members were carefully and adequately discussed'.[5]

The crisis which burst upon the Council of the IEE in 1959 had its roots, as crises of authority so often have, in money. Soon after full Institution activities began again after the end of the Second World War, the effects of inflation began to be felt on costs of all kinds, including, according to a report of the Finance Committee in 1952, 'Paper, Printing and Postal rates, Building and Administrative costs, and the development of activities in the Local Centres, Sub-Centres, and Students' Sections, and overseas'.[6]

To deal with this situation the Institution could cut down its activities and publications or it could put up subscriptions, which in these years provided about four-fifths of its income. Cutting down, at a time when electrical engineering was developing so fast and so variously, was never seriously contemplated, but raising subscriptions was something the Council of the IEE had always been most unwilling to do. Between the wars subscriptions had been reduced to the level of 1913. Perhaps as a consequence of this traditional attitude and also, no doubt, because in the fifties inflation had not yet been accepted as one of the permanent conditions of life, the increases in subscriptions which were put to Special General Meetings between 1948 and 1959 were never large enough. Matters would no doubt have been marginally easier if members had been less tardy with subscription payments. In December 1954 3,599 members (nearly 10 per cent of the total) were one, two or three years in arrears – and this figure was 'lower than in 1951 and in the pre-war years'![7]

There was an increase of 19 per cent in 1948, but that started from a very low base, and although an increase of 15 per cent in 1953 gave some relief it did not last for very long. Three years later the Council sought and gained an increase of 21 per cent in members' subscriptions and of 8 per cent in the subscriptions of students, but within little more than three years again, in April 1959, they were asking for more, presenting for approval an elaborate schedule of increases ranging from 7.7 per cent for students under twenty-three (£1 12s 6d to £1 15s 0d) to 38.1 per cent. (£5 5s 0d to £7 5s 0d) for Associates and Associate Members over forty-five. The subscription proposed for members (all rates quoted are for residents in the United Kingdom) was £9 0s 0d against £7 0s 0d formerly, a rise of 28.5 per cent.[8] These proposals were to come before a Special General Meeting of corporate members on 9 April 1959.

One of the considerations which the Council, and the members, had prominently in mind in considering the proposed increase was the finance of a rebuilding scheme at Savoy Place. With the growth of the Institution and the expansion of its activities, rebuilding was becoming year by year more urgent. Many obstacles had arisen, in the course of ten years or so, to hold it up. The IEE's architect, Charles Holden (1875-1960), was eminent but elderly. There was recurrent uncertainty whether to reconstruct the existing building or put up a new one on the same site or elsewhere. Plans made in June 1955 for partial reconstruction were disallowed by the LCC early in 1956. The Mechanicals, about the same time, rejected a suggestion, which apparently originated with Brasher, for joint development of a site near their building. Their Council, their President said, 'had considered the matter and were not prepared to entertain or discuss the proposal further'. The reason for such asperity is nowhere apparent. The Civils, on the other hand, suggested in 1957 that all three 'senior Institutions' might build jointly on a site near Storey's Gate and Great George Street, and there was a pause while the Electricals decided that they could not bear to give up their separate 'home'. Their decision was conveyed to the Civils by the President with almost overwhelming tact. Throughout the whole tortuous, hesitant ten years' tale the inevitable theme of finance, especially the varying cost of borrowing, is blended with everything else.

Eventually the idea of putting up a new building on a new site was rejected 'because of the links of convenience and sentiment which favoured the present site', and 'rebuilding on the present site was found impracticable on grounds of cost'. By elimination, therefore, the Council decided on 'a major reconstruction of the present building', mainly with a view to improving the accommodation for members and for meetings. 'The accommodation … used for adminstrative purposes', they declared, somewhat unfeelingly, 'though certainly not ideal, was and could remain serviceable.' Accordingly a scheme was drawn up which, broadly speaking, would improve the catering facilities, moving them from the basement to the top storey; which would enlarge the Lecture Theatre; which would improve the Library.[9]

The President laid these ideas, together with certain financial provisions, before a Special General Meeting on 27 June 1957. After discussion, but apparently very little criticism, they were put to the vote. 'I would … remind you', said the President, Sir Gordon Radley, in his summing-up, '… that this proposal … is the culminating point of 10 years' study, … and its attainment must be fitted into The Institution's programmes of meetings and other activities.' The necessary resolutions were carried *nem. con.* and work started in the autumn.[10]

II Membership and Council

When the time came, in April 1959, for holding the Special General Meeting which was to consider the proposed increases in entrance fees and subscription rates, the Council no doubt expected them to go through as easily as the building proposals. None of the earlier increases had been refused: why should this one be? The members, however, or some of them, were not in a mood of complaisance. There had always been a degree of tension between the Local Centres and 'London', and during the 1950s it had not diminished, though the Council always denied that there was any justification for it. Both attitudes were expressed by a Study Committee on Local Centre Organisation in its report to the General Purposes Committee in 1957:

> It is sometimes said that some local members feel that 'London', as such, and the Council as the governing body are remote in their approach and understanding of the part played by the Local Centres in the life of the Institution. Any such attitude is due entirely to misconception.

The Committee went on to suggest 'that the true position should be made more widely known among the general body of Provincial members', but the General Purposes Committee rejected 'a suggestion emanating from one of the Sub-Centres that an article should be published on the subject in the Journal'.[11] Neither the Study Committee nor the GPC, it may be thought, showed much inclination to take provincial complaints as seriously as they might have done.

Besides this general maladjustment there was a specific cause of complaint. The Council's building plans, which were almost certain to come up for discussion, were not universally approved of. In 1956 Dr P A Lindsay, a member of GEC's research staff, had joined with another of the younger members to write a letter to the *Journal* suggesting that, instead of reconstructing the existing building, the Institution would do better to pull it down and replace it with a multi-storey block which would bring in rental income. After a promise of publication, the letter was suppressed by Brasher, who seems to have taken personal offence at criticism of official Institution policy by these two young men. For one of them, Lindsay, the Special General Meeting offered an excellent platform for airing his own sense of grievance, and he found allies. Opinion at the meeting, he thinks, crystallised round his building proposal, though that is not apparent from the report published in the *Journal*.[12]

The meeting on 9 April 1959 was attended by fewer than 100 corporate members, suggesting that grievances were deeply rather than widely felt, and the President – S E Goodall, who was in the chair – received 178 valid proxies. Various proposals for altering by-laws went through easily enough, though not without amendment, but the Council's proposals for raising subscriptions and entrance fees, also presented as alterations to by-laws, met determined opposition. Goodall explained that 'over the past ten years the Building Fund had been milked of £69,000, and that had to stop', that the forecast surplus for 1959 would be less that 1 per cent of revenue, and that the Building Fund would cover only half the cost of the reconstruction.

Goodall was supported by the Chairman of the Finance Committee and by other members of Council, but P W Gatter, from the floor, 'thought it was a case of too much money and too little information'. Dr Lindsay 'criticized the continuous and wasteful changes in *Journal* cover design' and declared that 'the building reconstruction would architecturally be a constant disgrace to The Institution'. F L Coombs, proposing the rejection of the increases, said 'the proper and easy answer was to cut back the activities [of the Institution]'. On a motion proposed by Coombs and seconded by Lindsay the increases were rejected.

This rejection left the Council very short of time if the required increases were to come into force on 1 January 1960, which was essential if the Institution were to have the benefit of a bank overdraft, on very good terms, to finance the rebuilding, which had started. Seeking Privy Council approval for alterations to the by-laws would take far too long. Subscriptions could be increased, within limits, by resolutions of Council confirmed at a Special General Meeting, and that would be both quicker and cheaper than getting the by-laws altered, but it would bring in less money. Nevertheless this was the way the Council felt bound to go, and notice was given of a Special

General Meeting, timed to follow publication of the accounts for 1958, on 25 June 1959.

The President had given an undertaking that, when another Special General Meeting was held, more information would be given about the need for increased subscriptions. With the notice of meeting, accordingly, went a Memorandum on the Proposed Increases in Entrance Fees and Annual Subscriptions. It explained, first, that the cheapest way of raising the £200,000 needed for the rebuilding would be by overdraft, repayable over, say, ten years, and went on to say that £69,000 taken from the Building Fund between 1945 and 1952 ought to be replaced. It then showed how the various post-war subscription increases had never caught up with the falling value of money, and that even with the rates which the meeting was being asked to approve, the subscription income in 1959 would only be worth 63 per cent, in real terms, of the subscription income in 1938. It would be a half of 1 per cent above the expenditure rate: a margin which, combined with other income, would be 'necessary . . . if a further increase in subscription is to be avoided within a reasonable term of years'.

It seems an optimistic hope to hang on such a slender margin, but the members of the Council were assuming that the purchasing power of the pound would remain 'reasonably stable', and even undertook that if their estimates of income and expenditure up to 1967, which were appended to the Memorandum, proved 'unduly pessimistic' they would reduce the annual subscriptions. Old habits, evidently, died hard, and inflation was still seen as a temporary aberration. Instead of increasing subscriptions the Council could save money 'by such devices as curtailment of the number of meetings . . . substantial reductions in our publication of technical papers, and so on'. An Appendix to the Memorandum showed what could be saved by various expedients such as replacing the monthly *Journal* with either a monthly or a bi-monthly bulletin of eight or sixteen pages, reducing Ordinary and Section Meetings to 1948 level, and other 'devices'. The Council did not pretend to like the prospect, and they did not think members would, either. Nevertheless, at the meeting of 25 June 1959, which rather more than 180 members attended (the number of votes cast on a show of hands was 183), there was a demand for some of the economies suggested, and three members demanded a poll on the crucial resolution to increase subscription rates. It was arranged for a fortnight later, 9 July.

While the poll was being held the Council was meeting. Relying on the authority granted by the Special General Meeting of 1957 (see page 171), they signed the contract for the last phase of the rebuilding, costing £200,000, which in the circumstances showed considerable financial confidence, and they discussed the proposals for increased subscriptions. 'It was strongly felt', say the Minutes, 'that a substantial amount of the opposition was due not so much to the increases themselves as to dissatisfaction with the manner in

Table 14: IEE Increase of Entrance Fees Proposed, 25 June 1959

Class of membership	Present Entrance Fee	Proposed Increase in Entrance Fee	Porposed total Entrance Fee
Members	£10 0 0	£5 0 0	£15 0 0
Associate Members	£6 0 0	£3 0 0	£9 0 0
Companions	£10 0 0	£5 0 0	£15 0 0
Associates	£6 0 0	£3 0 0	£9 0 0
Graduates	nil	nil	nil
Students	nil	nil	nil

Provided that a Graduate or Student who as such has paid not less than three consecutive annual subscriptions shall on transfer to the class of Associate Members pay an entrance fee of £6 0s 0d. If he has also paid not less than three consecutive annual subscriptions as a Student over and above such three consecutive annual subscriptions as are referred to in the first sentence of this sub-clause he shall pay an entrance fee of £3 0s 0d in lieu of an entrance fee of £6 0s 0d.

Source: Notice of Special General Meeting, 15 May 1959 – Council, 14 May 1959

which they had been put forward and a feeling that the Council had not shown convincingly that every possible economy had been effected.' After that searching of the collective soul the results of the poll came in; 684 members had voted in person and 478 by proxy, and the resolution had been lost by 423 votes to 739.

There had to be a third Special General Meeting, on 18 August 1959. At least 508 members attended. Acrimony erupted. Lindsay launched a personal attack on the Secretary, holding him responsible for members' lack of adequate information about the affairs of the Institution and for deliberate 'stone-walling'. Lindsay's recollection, though there is nothing in the printed record to support him, is that he called Brasher 'a disgrace to the Institution'. The President asked members to address criticisms to him and not to the Institution staff. One of the members who in June had demanded the poll accused the Council of exceeding their authority in signing the contract for the rebuilding without knowing where the money was to come from. He

Table 15: IEE Increase of Annual Subscriptions Proposed, 25 June 1959

Class of membership	Present Annual Subscription — In Great Britain, Northern Ireland, the Isle of Man and the Channel Islands	Abroad	Proposed increase in Annual Subscription — In Great Britain, Northern Ireland, the Isle of Man and the Channel Islands	Abroad	Proposed total Annual Subscription — In Great Britain, Northern Ireland, the Isle of Man and the Channel Islands	Abroad
Members	£7 0 0	£6 0 0	£2 0 0	£2 0 0	£9 0 0	£8 0 0
Associate Members	£5 5 0	£4 10 0	£1 10 0	£1 10 0	£6 15 0	£6 0 0
Companions	£7 0 0	£6 0 0	£2 0 0	£2 0 0	£9 0 0	£8 0 0
Associates	£5 5 0	£4 10 0	£1 10 0	£1 10 0	£6 15 0	£6 0 0
Graduates 35 and above	£4 15 0	£3 15 0	£1 5 0	£1 5 0	£6 0 0	£5 0 0
Graduates over 28 and under 35	£4 5 0	£3 10 0	£0 17 6	£0 17 6	£5 2 6	£4 7 6
Graduates 26–28	£3 5 0	£3 0 0	£0 12 6	£0 12 6	£3 17 6	£3 12 6
Graduates under 26	£2 7 6	£2 5 0	£0 10 0	£0 10 0	£2 17 6	£2 15 0
Sutdents over 26	£3 5 0	£3 0 0	£0 10 0	£0 10 0	£3 15 0	£3 10 0
Students 23–26	£2 7 6	£2 5 0	£0 5 0	£0 5 0	£2 12 6	£2 10 0
Students under 23	£1 12 6	£1 10 0	£0 2 6	£0 2 6	£1 15 0	£1 12 6

Source: Notice of Special General Meeting, 15 May 1959 – Council, 14 May 1959

went on to say that 'so much false information had been issued by the Council that he asked that the meeting be adjourned so that true information could be circulated'.

Nevertheless, the motion needed by the Council was passed, on a show of hands, by 369 votes to 139. When a poll was demanded and immediately held, the President was able to call up reserves of proxies and the result was at last a victory for the Council by 4,701 votes to 736. T E Goldup, immediate Past President, said he had never enjoyed a meeting so much. Sir Willis Jackson, President-elect, was rather more restrained. His opinion was that the discussions of the last few months though not particularly happy had not been unhealthy. 'It was evident that the Council had not fully succeeded in conveying to some part of the membership the purposes of the policy of The Institution.'

The victory was handsome but scarcely glorious. As Sir Willis Jackson's understatement shows, the Council was deeply disturbed. Communication between Council and membership was at fault and far-reaching changes would be needed, not least in the Secretary's conception of his duties. Although comparatively few members had attended or voted at meetings, many had written letters making suggestions. At the beginning of the August meeting, therefore, the President proposed, with Sir Willis Jackson seconding him, 'to recommend to the Council the setting up of an *ad hoc* committee to study all these ideas and report to the Council the action thought desirable and also to examine means of improving the corporate life of the Institution and the necessary processes of communication'.[13]

III 'A deep-seated malaise'?

During the spring and summer of 1959 about 150 members wrote to the President or the Secretary of the Institution and others wrote to the Chairmen of Local Sections. 'Many hard things were said. The Council recognized that more was involved than the simple question of higher subscriptions; clearly the Council had lost the confidence of a number of members and had engendered doubts in the minds of many more'. Against this background the President, S E Goodall, advised the Council 'to set up a special committee to study the whole problem and to advise it as to how the recurrence of so distressing a situation could be avoided.'[14]

The chairman of the committee was O W Humphreys, a Vice President who became President in 1964. There was another Vice President – G S C Lucas, who became President in 1961 – and twelve other members, including seven who were not at that time on the Council, though two had served on it previously. The members were chosen with an eye to 'the desirability of ensuring representation of members in the Local Centres and of younger

members'. The committee worked hard, holding fourteen day-long meetings as well as studying all the comments and proposals received from
members at meetings and in correspondence. On 22 March 1960 they sent
the newly installed President, Sir Willis Jackson, an 'advanced draft' of a
report to Council, and their definitive report was ready in August.

'There can be no doubt', said the members of the committee in their
'advanced draft', '... that the strong feelings displayed last summer were
symptomatic of a deep-seated malaise. The proposal to increase subscriptions
was merely the trigger that released them.' The 'advanced draft' concentrated
on the machinery of government of the Institution and on the failure of
communication between the Council and the membership, which was
recognised as the central issue. They rejected the suggestion – surely a very
offensive one, especially since it had been publicly made (see page 175) – that
the Council had deliberately given the members misleading information.
Charges of inadequacy and of bias, they said, had more substance, but this
was because over many years 'the members of the Institution have shown
such confidence in their elected Council – *or alternatively* [WJR's italics] *have
taken so little interest in the management of Institution affairs* – that endorsement of
Council's recommendations has been treated largely as a matter of form'.

Having thus neatly turned the critics' weapons against them, the committee, in their recommendations, balanced suggestions for improving the
selection of Council members and for ensuring wide consultation and discussion of matters of policy with a section headed 'Responsibilities of the
Individual Member'. They tartly recommended members 'to take, and to
show that they take, an interest in everything that pertains to the well being of
The Institution': a clear hint that the Council, anxious though it might be
about the Institution's 'deep-seated malaise', had no intention of shouldering
all the blame for it.

The tone of the Special Advisory Committee's definitive report, drafted
no doubt after much consideration and discussion, is far more soothing. It
says nothing of 'so distressing a situation' or 'deep-seated malaise' – indeed,
quite the contrary. 'Whilst it is clear', said the committee in August, 'that
during recent years some members have become restless and a few seriously
dissatisfied with the working of The Institution, our enquiries have satisfied
us that there is nothing basically wrong.'[15] That was not quite what they had
been saying in March.

Before passing to other matters, the report covered similar ground to that
covered by the 'advanced draft', but in greater detail. It paid close attention to
the Local Centres, emphasising their importance in the lines of communication and including the observation that about 40 per cent of the Institution's
United Kingdom members 'live in London and the neighbouring counties,
and have no Local Centre organization'. They recommended the Council to

appoint a panel to study the problem of 'bringing all members living in the United Kingdom within the ambit of the Local Centre organization'.

They looked at the staff of the Institution and decided that its growth, at 27 per cent over ten years, had not kept pace with growth of the Institution's activities which the staff had to administer. 'We are satisfied', they said in response to charges of extravagance, which were freely made, 'that The Institution is maintaining its high level of activity at reasonable cost'.

Members who wanted the Institution to save money aimed also at the *Journal* and *Proceedings*. They suggested, naturally, 'the omission or curtailment of contents which, to them, were unimportant'. The committee considered the costs of both publications 'reasonable' and made only one recommendation, 'that letters dealing with Institution affairs should be accepted for publication in the Journal subject to the overriding discretion of Council'.

Was this a veiled allusion to Brasher's suppression of Lindsay's letter about the Institution's new building (see page 172)? The Secretary and his department, as we have seen, were closely associated with some of the matters about which members were uneasy. In the 'advanced draft' the committee discussed the influence of 'the Secretariat' on the development of policy, saying that inexperienced chairmen and members of committees would 'turn instinctively for advice and guidance to the Secretariat with its extensive and readily available experience. It is in such circumstances that the Secretariat may tend to influence the formation of policy unduly. . . . The Institution owes an immense debt to the Secretary for his devoted service and for his outstanding contributions to its development and wellbeing during the past twenty years. The Council and its Committees need to be on their guard lest by leaning too heavily upon him they expose him and his staff to ill-informed, and undeserved, criticism.' The thrust was delivered with massive anaesthesia, but no doubt it struck home. It was not repeated in the definitive report.

In its final substantive section, the report passed to a matter which, surely, was very near the root of the Institution's troubles. The section is headed: 'The conditions governing the admission of candidates who have not been educated as electrical engineers'. It went on to indicate the nature of the change which was coming over the profession of electrical engineering. The Special Advisory Committee said:

> The frontiers of electrical engineering are continually advancing with the development of new technologies, such as nuclear power and electronic engineering. The educational background of many of those working in these new areas differs from that on which The Institution's membership requirements have, traditionally, been based. This is particularly true of electronic engineers, many of whom graduated in physics. The membership requirements place physicists at an apparent disadvantage as compared with electrical engineers in that the conditions for their election as

Graduates are more onerous.   ... Consequently many electronic engineers feel that
they are not really welcomed in our Institution and that their admission is in the
nature of a concession.

The matter could hardly have been put more succinctly. The committee
was describing a change in electrical engineering which was as fundamental as
the change, sixty or seventy years earlier, from the predominance of telegraph engineering to the predominance of power engineering. In the beginning, the scientist had applied himself to technology, then the technologist
had applied himself to science. Now the scientist was coming to the top
again, and the later change, just like the earlier one, was marked (Chapter 4)
by a rebellion of the membership against the Council.

Stator core and windings for a 660 MW hydrogen water cooled generator in 1976.
(NEI Parsons Ltd)

References
1   'The Government of the Institution', *J.IEE*, 1944, **91**, Pt.I p.207
2   E B Moullin to General Purposes Committee, 5 Feb. 1944, GPC Doc
    2703/1
3   'Annual Report of Council', *J.IEE*, 1951, **98**, Pt.I, pp.254, 255; *J.IEE*,
    1960, **6**, p.421
4   W K Brasher to W D W, 12 June 1940, IEE Document File 2154
5   GPCM, 28 Nov. 1951, Doc 6130/1 and associated Minute
6   'Report on their Review of the Finances', Finance Committee Doc
    1201/14, 27 March 1952
7   Finance Committee Minutes, 12 Oct. 1954; CM, 4 Nov. 1954
8   'Report of the Finance Committee on the proposed increases in Sub-
    scription Rates', Doc 1201/18, 29 Dec. 1958; CM, 8 Jan. 1959
9   Charles Holden, see 'Report of the Joint Building Sub-Committee',
    Doc 2570/38, 6 Feb. 1956, GPCM, 20 Oct. 1954; LCC, see letter,
    Adams Holden & Pearson to W K Brasher, 6 Feb. 1956, Doc 2570/46,
    GPCM, 15 Feb. 1956; IMechE proposal, CM135, 1 March 1956; ICE
    proposal, GPCM, 28 Aug. 1957, GPC Doc 3710/3; 'The Headquarters
    of the Three Institutions', 20 Aug. 1957; see also GPCM50, 22 Jan. 1958,
    15 May 1958
10 'The Special General Meeting in June', *J.IEE* (n.s.), 1957, **8**, pp.637-639
11 'Report of the Study Committee on Local Centre Organization', Doc
    2204/12, GPCM, 13 March 1957
12 'Special General Meetings on the 9 April, 25 June and 18 August 1959',
    J.IEE (n.s.), 1954, **4**, pp.645-649
13 Account of events in 1959 founded on Reference 12; also CM153, 9 July
    1959; 'Revised Rates of Membership Subscriptions and Entrance Fees'
    and 'Special Advisory Committee', both in 'Annual Report of Council'
    J.IEE (n.s.), 1959, **5**, p.407; Interview with Prof Lindsay
14 'Special Advisory Committee of the Council – Advanced Draft Report',
    para 6 Council Doc 2420/41, 22 March 1960
15 'Report to the Council of the Special Advisory Committee', Council
    Document 2420/61, Aug. 1960

Part Three: The Electronics Engineers

The enhanced Manchester University Mark I computer in June 1949. It was capable of 555 additions a second. (Science Museum)

Chapter 14

The Arrival of the Electronics Engineer

I Electronics and Power

The scientists among the Institution's members were represented chiefly by those who held a degree in physics. Most of them stood on the 'light current' side of the line between 'light current' and 'heavy current' which for many years had divided the professional interests of electrical engineers. They were likely to be concerned with radio and television; with radar; increasingly with digital computers and the control mechanisms which governed automation.

The 'light current' engineers were catered for within the Institution by the Radio and Telecommunications Section (renamed Electronics and Communications in 1959) and by the Measurement and Control Section. The other two 'Specialised Sections' – the Supply Section and the Utilisation Section – concerned themselves with the generation, distribution and use of 'heavy current' which was the business of the power engineers who had dominated the affairs of the Institution since the 1890s. On each side of the line a good many members belonged to both of the sections that covered their interests. During the 1950s the numerical balance between the two pairs of sections was almost even. There was a slight bias on the 'heavy current' side, but it was far from overwhelming.

Towards the end of the 1950s the discontent of the 'light current' engineers with their standing within the Institution, long simmering, threatened to boil over. The Electronics and Communications Section, headed by M J L Pulling of the BBC Engineering Division, was the centre of the unrest,

Table 16: Strength of the Specialised Sections, 1950–1960

	1950 (000)	(%)	1955 (000)	(%)	1960 (000)	(%)
Utilisation	3.2		4.1		4.9	
Supply	3.1		4.3		5.6	
Total 'Heavy Current'	6.3	50.0	8.4	53	10.5	52
Radio & Telecommunications (a)	4.5		5.0		6.2	
Measurement & Control	1.8		2.4		3.3	
Total 'Light Current'	6.3	50.0	7.4	47	9.5	48
Total membership	12.6	100.0	15.8	100	20.0	100

Note: (a) Title changed to Electronics & Communications, 5 Feb. 1959
Source: Annual Reports of Council, 1949–50, 1954–55, 1959–60

expressed in 'a desire to provide an easily definable home for electronic engineers'.[1] An essential reform for this purpose, long sought and – it was felt – long denied, was 'to ensure equal facility of entry into The Institution for those who had come into electrical engineering from physics'.[2] Then, if the IEE really was, as it claimed to be, the natural home for electronics engineers, why not make it the Institution of Electrical *and Electronics* Engineers? The suggestion was turned down in 1960 as 'premature, if not undesirable'[3], thus leaving the field clear for the Americans a couple of years later.

Unless electronics engineers could be persuaded to regard the Institution as their professional home, it was widely recognised that many would not join it, others would resign, and yet others would desert to the enemy by joining, as some already had joined, the British Institution of Radio Engineers either in addition to the Institution or, dreadful thought, in preference to it. Alternatively, or as well, the electronics engineers might set up their own professional organisation outside the IEE. They would have the example of the telegraph engineers' departure from the Civils to quote as an early precedent, and the threat of splinter groups had been a bogy to the IEE since its earliest days.

In March 1959, at the same time as the opposition to increased subscriptions was moving to its climax in the Special General Meetings of that year, the General Purposes Committee set up a powerful panel to enquire into the situation. It had fifteen members. Every President from 1959 to 1964 was included, as well as Sir Gordon Radley, President in 1956. Pulling was a member and the Chairman was A H Mumford, who became Engineer-in-Chief at the Post Office (having previously been Deputy Engineer-in-Chief) in 1960. His professional interest, as a radio engineer, was thus firmly on the 'light current' side.[4]

The Panel was asked 'to consider the adequacy of the definitions of the scopes of the four Specialised Sections and, if thought desirable, to review the sectional emphasis of the Institution as a whole'.[5] This was no doubt intended as an invitation to survey the whole field of 'light current' discontents, and the panel certainly took it as such. Consultation of specialised Sections and local centres followed, and the Panel's central suggestion, which they arrived at quite quickly, was floated before them.

The Panel's conclusion was that if the disintegration of the Institution were to be avoided, the duality of its nature – 'two-ness', as it came to be called – would have to be recognised. Their central proposal, set out in numerous documents, was that the four Specialised Sections should be replaced by two Divisions: the Power Division and the Electronics Division. They would be run by elected Divisional Boards and the government of the Institution would 'remain vested wholly in the Council ... but with such representation given from the Boards of the two Divisions as would be consistent with the standing of these Divisions in the activities of The Institution'. This last provision was no doubt intended to meet the long-standing complaint of the 'light current' engineers that the running of the Institution was too much in the hands of the power engineers.

In order to organise the Institution's work as a learned society, particularly in building up balanced programmes and in selecting papers, the Divisional Boards were to set up Technical Committees, 'and their work would be one of the most important aspects of the re-organization'. There were precedents for them both in the panel system of the Electronics and Communications Section and in the special technical committees of the Papers Committee. 'Fresh opportunities would thus be given to keen members to assist … in this important aspect of The Institution's work. But, above all, one of the principal advantages … would be the adaptability of the advancing technical front of the Institution.' In other words, though the Panel did not say so, it was hoped that new developments might be recognised before rather than after they threatened the Institution with shipwreck.[6]

When these proposals, broadly representing large-scale concessions to long-standing grievances on the 'light current' side, came before the Council, they were received with varying degrees of graciousness. T E Houghton, a member of the Panel, but also of the Utilisation Section, 'reported that his Section Committee had reluctantly decided that they must support the proposals but wished … to record an objection to the term "Division" and the titles "Power" and "Electronics"'. Dr J E Mortlock of the Supply Section, also on the Panel, 'said that in general his Section Committee were against the proposals since, in the view of all but two or three dissentients, the case was not proven'. Representatives of the two 'light current' sections, on the other hand, both came out strongly in favour of the Panel's ideas 'as representing', in Pulling's words, 'the logical development of the Institution's structure to meet changed conditions'. Opinion reported from the Local Centres varied from flat opposition in the North-west ('both unsuitable to a Local Centre and detrimental to The Institution as a whole') to qualified support elsewhere. Enthusiasm, except in the 'light current' sections, was nowhere conspicuous.[7]

There was an urgent need, or so it was said in the Electronics and Communications Section, to forestall the formation of a breakaway Institution of Electronic Engineers. Nevertheless, conflicting opinions were so strongly held that discussion of the new scheme went acrimoniously on well into 1961. The principle of "two-ness", the scheme's opponents said, made no provision for subjects of interest to electrical engineers in general but not to 'light current' or 'heavy current' engineers in particular. The view of the Supply Section, put to the General Purposes Committee on 15 February 1961, was that 'the principle of "two-ness" was not acceptable; there should be not less than three Boards, constituted by election and of the same status'.[8]

This view in the end prevailed. The long and rambling controversy was brought suddenly to an end at a meeting of the General Purposes Committee on 19 May 1961. S E Goodall, acting apparently on behalf of Sir Willis Jackson, put forward a suggestion that there should be not two Boards but three. The third Board would handle what were called 'the middle group of Technical Committees' – that is, those which were not exclusively within the field either of 'heavy' or 'light' current – and it would be equal in status, in every way, to the two Boards originally proposed. 'There was considerable support for this arrangement', says the minute, 'and Sir Josiah Eccles [President in 1954] commented that it would remove much of the apprehension which had been caused in some quarters by the proposal for a two-divisional structure.'

The upshot, announced in the Council's Annual Report for 1962-1963, was a major reorganisation of the way the Institution ran its activities as a learned society. On 1 October 1962 three Divisions – Electronics, Power, Science and General – replaced the Specialised Sections, and by the time the Report was published twenty-eight Professional Groups (the name chosen in preference to Technical Committees) had been formed, with the prospect of more to come.

Table 17: IEE Professional Groups, 1962

Electronics Division
E1   Eelectronic measuring instruments and techniques
E2   Computer design
E3   Semiconductor devices
E4   Components, including electronic valves and tubes
E5   Medical electronics
E6   Line and radio communications systems, including circuit theory and communication theory
E7   Electromagnetic wave propagation
E8   Microwave devices and techniques for communication
E9   Sound broadcasting and television, including electro-acoustics
E10   Radio navigation and radio location

Power Division
P1   Rotating electrical machines
P2   Railway traction, including signalling
P3   Road, air and sea transportation
P4   Industrial applications and processes
P5   Non-industrial applications
P6   Rectification and inversion equipment
P7   Transmission and distribution plant
P8   Power cables and overhead lines
P9   Power-system design and operation
P10   Generation: conventional and nuclear

Science and General Division
S1   Novel methods for the generation of electricity
S2   The properties and testing of materials (solids and liquids)
S3   Electrical and magnetic phenomena in ionised gases and in vacua
S4   Generation of coherent radiation from electronic and nuclear energy-transactions
S5   Basic electrical theory, units and standards and advances in methods of measurement
S6   Process and position control, servomechanisms, and associated computers
S7   General applications of computers; data and document handling; recognition systems; combinatorial devices; information theory
S8   Education and training

The electronics engineer had at last established himself, to his own satisfaction, within the Institution. The power engineer had preserved his territory intact. The debatable ground between the two, apparently to everyone's satisfaction, had been handed over to an independent and coequal authority. Never before had the Institution, as a learned society, undergone so fundamental and so comprehensive a reorganisation and renovation, and it was not finished yet. Three of the new Professional Groups – S6 and S7, E2 – were concerned with computers, indicating the rising importance of the control engineers. Before we turn to their demand for recognition, however, we must look once again at relations between the Electricals and the Radio Engineers.

II 'That body': the British Institution of Radio Engineers

Always on the flank of the Institution, in the 1950s, lay a source of intense irritation: the British Institution of Radio Engineers. It was small, having a total membership (6,400) in 1960 scarcely greater than the membership (6,200) of the Electronics & Communications Section of the IEE.[9] The IEE's total membership, by then, was about 46,000. Upon the Radio Engineers' examinations the Institution's Secretariat poured scorn: 'approximately of the order that this Institution would expect that a good Technicians' Association would require of the middle group of its members'.[10] Their technical publications were far fewer, between 1939 and 1953, than those of the IEE's Radio Section.[11] Brasher pointed out that they recruited members, especially students, very heavily in India: looking, perhaps – Brasher did not say this, but he implied it – for an easy route to a technical qualification.[12]

The sheer volume of hostile testimony, painstakingly assembled over many years by the IEE, of which the items listed above are a very small sample, shows how seriously the IEE regarded the threat which the BritIRE presented. It was a threat, frequently mentioned in the discussions leading to the setting up of the new Divisions, to the IEE's claim to be the sole professional home of all British chartered engineers in radio, and it was extending its pretensions to the rapidly expanding field of electronics. The reality of the threat was underlined by those members of the IEE who belonged also to the BritIRE. Some thought it served their professional interests better, being more single-minded.

The animosity between the two Institutions, concentrated in personal hostility between the two Secretaries, Brasher and G D Clifford, strained the patience of observers. 'Surely it is high time', wrote a columnist in the periodical *Control* early in 1959, 'that the BritIRE and the IEE resolved their silent conflict. ... The behaviour of the Councils ... in not publicly recognizing ... each other's existence is, to my mind, childish.' He went on to deplore the fact that although the Radio Engineers took IEE publications into their library, the IEE banned the BritIRE's *Journal* from theirs.[13]

Eventually the BritIRE set out to gain the ultimate British recognition of professional standing: the grant of a Royal Charter. To the existing engineering institutions the move was unwelcome, and to the Electricals especially so. They prepared to oppose it. The BritIRE had a powerful sponsor: Earl Mountbatten of Burma (1900–1979). As a young naval officer after the Great War he had specialised in wireless, and in that branch of his numerous activities his monument is the *Admiralty Handbook of Wireless Telegraphy*. He had become an Associate Member of the IEE in 1927, but by that time he was already irritating the Institution by his support for the Radio Engineers.

At some time during the late fifties it seems clear that Mountbatten decided that the Electricals must be brought on to speaking terms with the Radio Engineers. That, no doubt, was what lay behind his support for the BritIRE's application for a Charter. In their petition, lodged in the summer of 1960, there were eleven petitioners. Six called themselves 'chartered electrical engineers' and must therefore have been corporate members of the IEE. Mountbatten's name led all the rest.

His support for the Charter petition, he must have known, would be a provocative act, and so it was. In July 1960 he entertained Sir Hamish MacLaren, President of the IEE, and Sir Willis Jackson, immediate Past President, to lunch. It must have been a prickly occasion, and afterwards Willis Jackson sent Clifford, the Radio Engineers' Secretary, figures comparing the Electronics and Communications Section of the IEE – favourably, naturally – with the BritIRE. The figures, supplied by Brasher, whom Mountbatten disliked, have disappeared, but Mountbatten's letter in which, to his own satisfaction, he demolished them, has survived. So has the letter in reply, from Sir Willis Jackson, in which, again prompted by Brasher, he demolished the demolition.

This curious episode, in which men of great distinction bandied trivia and bickered over them like schoolboys, is eloquent of the relations between the two institutions. From Mountbatten's letter it is clear that he was determined to bring the IEE into line with his own way of thinking:

> I appreciate, [he wrote,] that these figures were produced to facilitate your discussion with me. In the event they have proved useful to the cause of the BritIRE! I much hope, therefore, that you and the other officers and Council of the IEE may agree that in the wider interests of the two Institutions it will be better to create means of happier association rather than opposition to the development of the BritIRE. In the long run our progress can only be beneficial to the cause of professional engineering as a whole and to the country's interest in general.
>
> I told you that I am prepared to lend my weight toward securing a happier relationship between the two Institutions. I look forward, therefore, to learning whether or not you still intend to oppose the Charter petition of the BritIRE.

To this haughty communication, with its tone of *grand seigneur* and hint of menace, Sir Willis replied that the IEE had not yet decided whether to oppose

the charter petition 'which, so far as we are aware, has not yet been lodged. ...
Please accept my thanks for your kind hospitality.'[14]

Under the guns of the victorious Supreme Allied Commander, South-
East Asia (Mountbatten was not shy of recalling his achievements), the IEE
and the other engineering institutions stopped short of a counter-petition to
the Privy Council. Instead they submitted a lengthy memorandum, drafted
by the Electricals' solicitor, which was intended 'to concentrate on ... two
main arguments ...: firstly that more than one chartered body operating in the
same field was to be deprecated and, secondly, that The Institution covered
this field effectively'.

In support of these two contentions the memorandum put forward an
impressive case with plentiful statistical support, and it hinted strongly that
the proper field of activity for the BritIRE lay among engineering technicians,
not among professional engineers. 'Had the Petitioners laid stress on promoting activities designed to serve the interests of electrical technicians working
in the electronics and communications field, and had the title of the Petitioners' Institution been such as to indicate this service clearly, many of the
observations in this memorandum would no longer be apposite.'[15]

In 1961 the BritIRE received its Charter. A couple of years later it laid
formal claim to the territory it intended to occupy by changing its name to the
Institution of Electronic and Radio Engineers. The IEE remained sceptical:
'although this body has now been granted a Royal Charter, their standards
were still significantly lower than those of this Institution and therefore there
could be no change in attitude towards membership of that body. It was
however recommended that should an opening occur for a discussion on
closer cooperation and even eventual amalgamation it would be desirable to
follow it up.'[16]

Over the succeeding years, still under Mountbatten's watchful eye, the
Institution advanced cautiously towards collaboration with 'that body'. The
Radio Engineers, it may be thought, owed a great deal to Mountbatten in the
success of their petition for a Charter. On the other side, if the Institution of
Electrical Engineers, in the early and mid-twenties, had shown greater tact
and foresight in their dealings with wireless engineers and later, perhaps, in
their attitude towards physics graduates, the question of another chartered
institution for professional electrical engineers might never have arisen.

III 'On the threshold of an era. . .'

'The world', said O W Humphreys in August 1964, in a document written
for the General Purposes Committee, 'is on the threshold of an era of
automation and control which is likely to have fundamental effects over the
whole range of industry and on many aspects of personal life'.[17] What he had
in mind as he wrote was that no sooner had the Institution been drastically

reorganised to accommodate the electronics engineers than the control engineers, of whom there were about 9,000 within the Institution and an unknown number outside, were demanding another reorganisation, the creation of a new Division, to suit themselves, and like other newcomers before them they could make it clear that if the IEE would not look after them there were those – the Mechanicals, perhaps? – who would.

The range of technology in which control engineering was required was sketched in a document prepared by J Caird, of ICI's General Chemicals Division, for the Mersey and North Wales Centre in March 1964. He wrote of 'automatic manufacturing systems used mainly in production lines'; of 'systems for the measurement of process variables and the use of these measurements for the control of the process plant involved'; of 'systems for position control and for remote control of other systems ... used mainly in the aircraft and space flight industries'.[18] He wrote, that is to say, of the most advanced technology of his time.

Electrical engineers took part in it. So did mechanical and production engineers, physicists and, especially in theoretical problems, mathematicians. Some of those working as control and instrumentation technologists, Caird said, might already be members of the Institution but many were not 'because' (a familiar problem) 'they do not qualify under present regulations designed purely for electrical engineers'.

Their pathway into the Institution should, he thought, be made smoother. If that evoked 'the comment that entry to the Institution was being made available to engineers engaged mainly on non-electrical work', then his reply would be 'that the dividing lines between the various branches of engineering are disappearing'. This was the central point: that the nature not only of electrical engineering but of engineering in general was changing so rapidly and so fundamentally that traditional boundaries were being swept away and traditional methods of qualification had become inadequate. It could no longer be assumed that the traditional functions of the professional institutions would meet the demands which would be put upon them, and the institutions, by the mid-sixties, were moving towards much closer collaboration with one another than ever before.

After a debate within the IEE so lengthy – it lasted about two years – as to drive the General Purposes Committee almost to despair and, ironically, after opposition from the newly established Electronics Division, the control engineers got their new division. The Control and Automation Division was established in October 1965 at the expense of the Science and General Division, which was replaced by a Science and Education Joint Board.[19]

Table 18: IEE New Professional Groups, 1965

Control and Automation Division
C1   Control theory
C2   Transducers and measuring devices used for control

C3   Systems engineering (as applied to control)
C4   Control applications
C5   Control equipment
C6   Control aspects of biological and man-machine systems

Joint Professional Groups
J1   Novel processes for energy conservation and storage
J2   The properties and testing of materials (solids and liquids)
J3   Electrical and magnetic phenomena in ionised gases and in vacua
J4   Basic electrical theory, units and standards and advances in methods of measurement
J5   Education and training

The committees of professional groups J1, J2 and J3 were represented on the Power and Electronics Divisional Boards. The committees of J4 and J5 were represented on all three Divisional Boards.

Within about seven years – between, say, 1958 and 1965 – the whole structure of the IEE as a learned society was transformed. In place of four 'Specialised Sections' there was now an array of three Divisions, a 'Joint Board' and about two dozen 'Professional Groups'. Six new groups were set up and allotted to the new Control and Automation Division. Five, known as 'joint professional groups', were formed by transferring work from corresponding groups in the suppressed Science and General Division and it was announced their activities would be 'fostered and co-ordinated by the Science and Education Joint Board'. Thus reorganised, more drastically than at any time in its previous history, the Institution faced the technological future.

References

1   CM, 21 July 1960, 'Specialized Sections', Council Doc 3620/44
2   GPCM 67, 16 March 1960
3   Reference 2
4   GPCM 130, 5 Aug. 1960
5   'A Proposal for the Rearrangement of Specializations within the Institution', Doc. 3620/34, GPCM, 16 March 1960
6   Reference 5
7   CM, 21 July 1960, Council Doc 3620/44
8   GPCM 60, 15 Feb. 1961
9   Appendix 2 to 'Text of proposed Memorandum in the matter of a petition by the BritIRE to the Privy Council', Doc 3785/6 (2nd rev), GPC, 19 Oct. 1960, CM, 3 Nov. 1960
10 'The British Institution of Radio Engineers', 26 June 1954, IEE File 3785
11 'Analysis of BritIRE and Radio Section IEE Papers, 1939-53 inclusive', attached to Reference 10
12 'The British Institution of Radio Engineers', 2 Dec. 1953, IEE File 3785
13 Control, Jan. 1959, p.90
14 Letter, Mountbatten to Jackson, 19 July 1960; 'Notes on Mountbatten's letter of 19 July 1960'; Letter, Jackson to Mountbatten, 25 July 1960, IEE File 3785

15   Reference 9
16   GPCM, 20 Sept. 1961
17   'Control Engineering', Doc GP(64)28, 14 Aug. 1964, GPCM, 14 Oct.
     1960
18   'Provision for Control Engineering in the Learned Society Structure',
     Doc GP(64)12, 6 March 1964 – GPCM, 11 March 1964
19   'Annual Report of Council', *E & P*, 1966, **12**, p.245

Chapter 15

Going into Business

I The Post-war Learned Society

The radical reorganisation of the IEE in the late fifties and early sixties dealt with the Institution in its capacity as a learned society. In that capacity, from 1945 onwards, its activities were being conducted more ambitiously than ever before. It was catering for its own members, as always, by the reading and discussion of papers. It sought more general 'learned' audiences through the long-established Kelvin Lectures and through the Appleton Lectures and the Hunter Lectures more recently instituted, and, from the early sixties onwards, through Annual Lectures presented by the Divisions. For the general public there were the Christmas Holiday Lectures and the Faraday Lectures, which were becoming steadily more elaborate, so that in time only large organisations could afford to present them, and they were reaching ever larger audiences. The Faraday Lecture on Colour Television in 1964-1965, for instance, was given twenty-eight times before audiences totalling 50,000 people.[1]

As well as conducting these traditional activities on a larger scale than ever before, the Institution in the years after 1945 began to arrange large conventions and conferences open (on payment) to all comers. They were often held in collaboration with other bodies; they were often international in scope. They had their origins in the enthusiastic curiosity aroused by the release after the war of a flood of hitherto secret information. The first convention, in 1946, was on Radiolocation, not yet known in Great Britain as Radar. It was addressed by notable speakers, including Sir Robert Watson Watt, and its ten sessions attracted an audience not far short of 8,000.

After this spectacular opening there followed an era of conventions, from the late forties to the early sixties, during which the Institution, largely through the Secretary's Department, developed great skill in organising them. 'I am sure', said the President, Sir John Hacking, in 1952, after attending the centennial celebrations of the American Society of Civil Engineers, alleged to have attracted an attendance of 25,000 (Sir John clearly didn't believe that), 'that in our organization of these functions we have nothing to learn whatever from the Americans'.[2] The Institution used conventions to keep its members, and others, up to date with the onrush of technology, which meant paying particular attention to electronics.

In 1956 there were two five-day conventions, one on Digital Computer Techniques and another on Ferrites, which between them attracted nearly 2,500 paid registrations. During the three or four years that followed, conventions, symposia and discussion meetings ranged over Microwave Valves, New Digital Computer Techniques, Stereophonic Recording and Broadcasting, Transistors and associated semiconductor devices (five-day International Convention, 1959), Reliability and Maintenance of Computer Systems (discussion meetings held in cooperation with the British Computer Society, 1960). In July 1960 a five-day international conference, the third of its kind, was held in association with the International Federation for Medical Electronics. Altogether, between April 1956 and July 1960, the Institution acted as Convenor or Host at fourteen major events, including seven conventions, which attracted 11,050 paid registrations.[3]

There are indications that as early as the mid-fifties the cost of conventions, and no doubt also the elaborateness of the organisation required to run them, began to perturb the Council of the IEE. Members of the GPC, in November 1956, unanimously agreed that any attempt to make a regular feature of conventions was to be deplored, and the Committee set about reviewing the IEE's policy on conventions, looking particularly at their cost.[4] Policy could not be suddenly changed, because it had to be planned years in advance, but between 1966-1967 and 1971-1972 the number of 'conventions' listed in the Annual Reports dwindled almost to vanishing point, while the number of 'conferences' ranged between nine and thirteen a year and the number of 'colloquia' between thirteen and twenty-seven. Conferences were much smaller than conventions. The total attendance at the nine conferences of 1968-1969 was 2,466, and in the same year the International Broadcasting Convention attracted 754 participants: a low figure by convention standards, but nearly twice as great as the highest recorded in that year for a conference (385 at a conference on overhead lines and cables for 220V and above).[5]

From 1966-1967 onward the Institution began to run vacation schools 'to provide tuition in developing fields of interest to the profession'.[6] The first, on microwave techniques, was arranged by the Electronics Division at Leeds University from 10 to 22 July 1966. Two hundred and sixty-two members attended four vacation schools in 1968-1969, and by 1971-1972 the number of schools had risen to seven, but the attendance was not reported.[7] At about the same time as the vacation schools were being developed, and as a complement to them, 'Individual-study Service' was offered 'to provide electrical and electronics engineers who graduated in earlier years with opportunities to study at home subjects which have subsequently become important'. The method was to be by correspondence and the suggested fees for a course of fifteen lessons were £25 for members of the Institution and £30 for non-members. Handbooks to the first two courses, R W King's *Field-effect Transistors* and Professor Cattermole's *Pulse-code Modulation*, came out in

1969-1970. A third, *Digital Instrumentation* by A R Owens, was promised for October 1970.[8]

The activities so far described must be seen as part of a learned-society package, including also the Institution's activities in publishing and data-processing. These, during the years after the reorganisation of the Institution's learned society structure, were being developed on radically new lines, as profit-making enterprises. The idea of making profits was attractive to some of the more commercially minded members of the Council, including the first Lord Nelson of Stafford, Chairman of English Electric, and S E Goodall, but it ran clean contrary to the older traditions of the IEE. 'I am opposed', said a member (P Evans) in 1967, 'to the Institution engaging in a commercial activity for the sake of revenue.'[9]

It may safely be assumed that in the opinion of W K Brasher the traditions of the IEE were in the keeping of the Secretary, and the longer they were allowed to remain there, the better for all. During twenty-three years in office he had devoted himself unwaveringly to the Institution's interests, as he understood them, and to the promotion of the highest standards of professional excellence. His intolerance of other views, however, had played a large part in bringing on the crisis of the late fifties in the Institution's affairs, and in the sixties his general outlook and autocratic methods were out of temper with the spirit of the times. In 1962, when he reached the age of sixty-five, he was firmly required, much to his dismay, to retire.

Dr G F Gainsborough, who at the age of forty-seven succeeded Brasher, had been on the scientific staff of the National Physical Laboratory from 1938 until 1946, when he transferred to the Administrative Class of the Civil Service. Like Brasher, therefore, he had experience of the public service, and like Brasher again he was a member of the Institution. He was also a barrister: a useful qualification for anyone so concerned with legal matters as the Secretary of the IEE must be, and particularly useful if radical changes in the Institution's activities were in prospect. He had a strongly developed commercial instinct.

Gainsborough's account of his appointment is diverting. He replied, he says, on the last permissible day, to an advertisement in the IEE *Journal*. Having done so, he went a couple of days later to a public wine-tasting and afterwards, in his office, fell asleep. He was awakened by a telephone call from Brasher's secretary asking him if he could possibly attend at once for interview at Savoy Place. Without stopping to think, he agreed. The mood of that interview, he says, was 'very relaxed', but not so the mood of one which followed, at which, among other things, Lord Nelson of Stafford made evident a strong dislike of civil servants. Nevertheless, Gainsborough was appointed, becoming the sixth Secretary of the Institution since F H Webb became Secretary of the Society of Telegraph Engineers in 1878.

Any impression of casualness which Gainsborough's story of his interviews might convey would be most misleading. George Gainsborough, a
man of talent, ambition and strong character, soon formed very clear ideas on
the way he wanted the IEE to go in the years of change that lay ahead, and he
was no less aware than his predecessor that as Secretary he was well placed to
make sure that his ideas would prevail. They included plans for profit-
making activities.

II The Business Enterprise

The traditional basis of the Institution's finances was that income from
members' subscriptions should cover running expenses, the cost of learned
society activities, and the building up of capital reserves. Since 1945, with the
increasing scale of conferences and other major events which many non-
members attended, it had become the rule that they should be self-financing,
but in general there was no thought of making a profit, which some
members would certainly have regarded with disapproval, out of any of the
Institution's activities. There was also the Institution's status as a charity,
registered under the Charities Act 1960, to be taken into consideration.
Charitable status carried the privilege of exemption from income tax, but it
restricted the Institution's freedom to engage in business activities.

The Charter contained a provision that 'the Institution shall not carry on
any trade or business or engage in any transaction with a view to the
pecuniary gain or profit of the Members thereof'. That language seems plain
enough, and since the granting of the Charter it had been regarded as an
absolute prohibition. The incoming Secretary, however, held that the
Institution, being a person at law, might engage in any activity lawful for
persons generally. Even more surprising, there were indications that the
Council's attitude towards tax privileges might be altering. In 1961 the
General Purposes Committee recorded a willingness 'to be guided by the
outcome of discussions at present being held at ICE [Institution of Civil
Engineers] on the question of whether it was worth continuing to restrict
activities which ... might affect their [the Institution's] status as a charity'.[10]
Nothing seems to have come of these discussions, but the mere suggestion
that charitable status, and with it tax exemption, might deliberately be put at
risk challenged one of the basic assumptions underlying long-accepted principles governing Institution policy. One can imagine the horror with which
previous General Purposes Committees might have regarded such heresy.

The Institution's traditional financial principles were in any case being
undermined, long before 1961, by post-war inflation. So long as the value of
money remained stable or rose, as it did during the early thirties, subscriptions could be held steady or even reduced and the level of Institution activity
was not threatened. As soon as inflation set in, even at a rate which later came

to be regarded as negligible, the Council was faced repeatedly with a choice between two disagreeable alternatives: an increase in subscriptions or a decrease in activities. The result in the late fifties, as we have seen, was that the Council, like King Charles I and for very similar reasons – expenditure rising faster than income – had to face a rebellion. It escaped with its collective head on its shoulders, but with its financial problem unsolved. The nature of the problem was made clear in estimates prepared in 1962 by the Finance Committee for the years 1963 to 1967.

Gross expenditure since 1945, the Committee said, had been rising, on average, at 7 per cent per year compound, and on that basis, taken with 'a conservatively calculated rise in income', they expected a surplus of £26,000 in 1963 to turn into a deficit of £23,600 in 1967 '*before* making allowance for the reduction of the bank overdraft used to finance the reconstruction of the building'. They recommended 'that strenuous efforts should be made to improve the financial position in future years, both by increasing income if possible (by means other than raising subscriptions) and … by curbing expenditure'.[11]

Income was expected to rise with rising revenue from advertising in the *Journal*. That, as the Finance Committee more than once pointed out, was susceptible to fluctuations in the economy and the Committee was loath to rely on it. During the sixties it was discovered that advertising job vacancies paid better than advertising products. The only other way of getting a larger income, 'assuming that the increase of subscriptions is the last resort', seemed to be to match rising publishing costs with rising prices for publications: 'it is reasonable to charge more for a more bulky volume'.[12]

Notwithstanding these rather gloomy forecasts, it was clear by the mid-sixties that publications, including the *Journal*, were providing the Institution with a substantial and growing business. The *Journal* itself was renamed *Electronics and Power* in 1963 with the aim of making it 'the recognised public forum for the professional electrical and electronics engineer' and of showing more clearly the range of the Institution's activities. It went to all members of the Institution and to some 1,900 subscribers who were not members. Members could also subscribe to *Proceedings*, which was comprehensive, or to collections of papers directly associated with the Divisions, published in 1964 under the three titles *Electronics Record, Power Record,* and *Science & General Record*. Students were catered for in the *Students' Quarterly Journal*.

Alongside these reports of the Institution's own activities, 'a new international periodical', *Electronics Letters*, began to appear in March 1965. For a fee, it refereed and published unsolicited letters of not more than 1,200 words and with not more than two illustrations in Russian, French, German and Italian as well as English, disclosing new discoveries and developments. It attracted contributors by its low fees and by publishing with unheard-of speed – within two to four weeks of receiving a manuscript. As well as periodicals the

Institution issued conference reports and other occasional publications such as the careers booklets already mentioned (page 160). The Institution also had an arrangement with the Cambridge University Press to publish books under a joint imprint. The high standard of these books, the Secretary observed in 1966, 'had not passed unnoticed'. Nor, perhaps, had the possibility of transferring them to the Institution's sole imprint.[13] These were almost all heavyweight publications of a kind recognised since the Institution's earliest days as essential to its standing as a learned society. In January 1964 a novelty appeared: *IEE News*. It was 'a monthly newspaper devoted to the work of the Institution': essentially the Institution's house magazine, directed at the task shown in 1959 to be so necessary – improving communications between the Council and the membership.[14]

Separate from the Institution's publications services but a publication enterprise of considerable magnitude was *Science Abstracts*. Its origins can be traced back to the earliest days of the Society of Telegraph Engineers, and since 1897 it had been run by the Institution in partnership first with the Physical Society and later with the Institute of Physics and the American Institute of Electrical Engineers. *Science Abstracts* circulated throughout the world, contributing handsomely to the Institution's prestige. In 1964 31,000 abstracts were published in Section A (Physics Abstracts) and 16,177 in Section B (Electrical Engineering Abstracts).[15]

By 1965 subscriptions and entrance fees provided about 34 per cent (£273,245) of the Institution's gross income. Of the remaining 66 per cent about £215,000 came from Publications and about £175,000 from *Science Abstracts*, which was an increasingly profitable enterprise. If anyone in the Institution were exploring the possibility of profitable activities, it was fairly evident that he would look first at publications.

At much the same time – the mid-sixties – it was becoming evident that the Institution needed a computer. There were broadly three fields in which the Secretary, in September 1966, foresaw it operating. First, there would be routine office work for the Institution itself and perhaps for kindred societies. Then it could be used for processing information in the fields covered by *Science Abstracts*, and finally it might be possible to set up 'a computational service for electrical and electronics engineers whose employers do not have a computer'.[16] Gainsborough was enthusiastic, and the President, J A Ratcliffe, FRS, urged the Council to take the risk, estimated at £50,000 spread over two or three years. 'This Institution', said Ratcliffe, 'should have the courage to lead in the use of these new techniques and should take the initiative in obtaining a computer.' The installation and running of the computer could be shared, while the load built up to an economic level, with Annan Impey Morrish, a large firm of chartered accountants who, like the Institution, wanted to make a start with a computer but had not immediately enough work to employ it fully.[17]

Behind the proposal to apply a computer to the processing of technical information there arose strong pressure, enveloped in scepticism about the IEE's ability to respond, from one of *Science Abstracts'* most important subscribers, the American Institute of Physics. They made it clear that they expected to take the service over when the IEE failed to operate it in its new form. Members of Gainsborough's staff, however, were looking for greater freedom of action than they had been allowed under his predecessor and one of them, J R Smith, an Assistant Secretary, was given charge of the new system, which he ran with great success. It took shape as INSPEC (Information Service in Physics, Electrotechnology, and Control), and by 1970 it was producing six periodicals in two series: *Science Abstracts*, which in 1969 published 88,440 items, and *Current Papers*. It was also responsible, from 1 January 1970 onwards, for a computer-based information service carrying material published in *Science Abstracts* which found a ready market at home and abroad and attracted Government money for development work.[18] By 1968 INSPEC was the largest single source of the IEE's income, and by 1970 it was producing about 43 per cent of the Institution's income from all sources: more than twice as much as the sum brought in by subscriptions. In its field, it has become the largest English-language information service in the world.

'The engineering profession', observed the Secretary in 1967 while the Institution's computer services were being developed, '... is curiously indifferent to information services. *The Institution could therefore do valuable work ... in developing among its members an awareness of the value of these services.*'[19] However just Gainsborough's observation may have been, and if just at all it casts a none-too-flattering light on British engineers, the Institution was nevertheless enabled, through the installation of a computer, to develop a large and rapidly increasing source of income closely related to the publishing side of its activities.

In the autumn of 1966, while the computer project was being considered, publication services were also being looked at, because as a result of the high standard set by the Institution's periodicals and by its joint arrangement with the Cambridge University Press (see page 198) 'the Secretary has been sounded to ascertain whether the Institution would be prepared to provide publication services for other bodies, on suitable financial terms'. Because the Institution was already a publisher on a considerable scale, with or without the cooperation of the CUP, it could afford to publish for other bodies too small to do the work themselves, on attractive terms.[20]

Since this work would be outside the 'Objects and Purposes' of the Institution's Charter, a form of organisation had to be devised to preserve the Institution's charitable status. The plan eventually adopted, in the summer of 1967, was worked out in consultation with lawyers, with the Inland Revenue authorities, and with the Clerk to the Privy Council. It was presented to the

Council by a Business Advisory Committee set up, in succession to a smaller Business Advisory Panel, on 27 April 1967.[21] The members of the Committee, with Sir Ben Barnett as Chairman, were G S C Lucas and L Drucquer, both recent Past Presidents (1961 and 1965), A N Todd and the Secretary.

The centrepiece of the Committee's plan, as it came into effect after the Council had slightly amended it, was a private company, owned as to 96 per cent by the Institution, called Peter Peregrinus Limited. Peregrinus was a scholar and soldier, born about 1220, whose *Epistola de Magnete* is accepted as 'the first serious work on magnetism'.[22] His name was chosen for the company in default of Faraday's, which had already been taken by a company in America, because the IEE's library holds an illuminated fourteenth-century manuscript of his treatise. The first Chairman of the company was Sir Ben Barnett and the Directors, as well as the members of the Business Advisory Committee, were W G Askew, the Institution's Director of Publishing, and M E Smythe, Director of Computer Services. Askew, Smythe and Gainsborough were executive directors: the rest, non-executive. The company was set up to conduct business in two main fields of activity: publishing and computer services, and its purpose was to deal profitably with customers outside the Institution.[23]

In order to preserve the Institution's exemption from tax a scheme was worked out based on the Institution's status as a charity. It was of a kind which other charities were at the same time adopting, some on the advice of the Board of Trade. Work carried out by Institution staff for Peter Peregrinus, in the computer services department or elsewhere, was charged to Peter Peregrinus at cost, and the profits arose from the contracts made by Peter Peregrinus with its customers in the open market. These profits accrued to Peter Peregrinus and were made over, under deed of covenant, mainly to the Institution and partly to the Institution's Benevolent Fund.[24]

The consequences of these and other arrangements, following on the Council's changed attitude to business activities, were profound. The Institution's income in 1962 was £272,000, of which nearly 90 per cent came from members' subscriptions. By 1971 it had risen to £1,658,000 of which about 72 per cent came from INSPEC (£725,000) and Publications (£460,000). Members' subscriptions produced £298,000 (18 per cent). As well as being a learned society designed for electrical engineers in the latter part of the twentieth century, the Institution had become a business enterprise well able to finance its increasingly expensive learned-society activities.

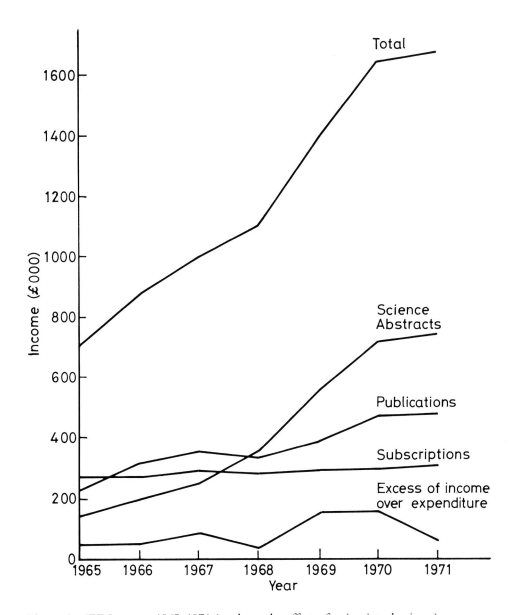

Figure 1   IEE Income, 1965–1971 (to show the effect of going into business)

References:

1   Annual Reports of Council: especially 1964–65, *E & P*, 1965, **11**, p.229; 1958–59, *J.IEE* (n.s.), 1959, **5**, p.438

2   'Sir John Hacking's Observations . . .', Doc 3940/5, CM, 9 Oct. 1952

3   Appendix 4 to 'Text of Proposed Memorandum to the Privy Council . . . in the Matter of a Petition by the British Institution of Radio Engineers', Doc 3785/7, CM, 6 Oct. 1960

4   GPCM, 21 Nov. 1956

5   'Annual Report of Council', *E & P*, 1969, **15**, 169

6   'Annual Report of Council', *E & P*, 1967, **13**, p.264

7   'Annual Report of Council', *E & P*, 1969, **15**, p.169; *E & P*, 1972, **18**, p.180

8   'Continuing Education: Proposed Individual Study Service'; Doc C(69)46, 17 April 1969; CM88, 24 April 1969; Continuing Education: Proposed Individual Study Service; Doc C(69)87, 27 Aug. 1969, CM, 4 Sept. 1969

9   Quoted in 'The Future Role of the Institution', Council Doc C(67)86, 1 Oct. 1967, CM, 14 Sept. 1967

10 GPCM, 17 Feb. 1961

11 Report of the Finance Committee, Doc 1220/202, CM, 10 Jan. 1963

12 Reference 9; see CM115, 26 April 1962 and Report of the Finance Committee, Doc 1200/220, CM, 7 Nov. 1963

13 'Publications Service', Programme and Publications Committee, Doc PP(66)49, 28 Oct. 1966; CM, 3 Nov. 1966

14 'Annual Reports of Council', *E & P*, 1964, **10**, p.237; 1965, **11**, p.231; 1966, **12**, p.248

15 'Annual Report of Council,' *E & P*, 1965, **11**, p.232

16 'The Institution's Requirement for a Computer', Appendix to Council Doc C(66)72, 15 Sept. 1966; CM, 15 Sept. 1966

17 CM125, 15 Sept. 1966

18 'Annual Report of Council', *E & P*, 1970, **16**, p.181

19 'The Future Role of the Institution'; Council Doc C(67)60, 13 May 1967; CM, 14 Sept. 1967

20 Reference 13

21 CM 89.5, 27 April 1967

22 *A Biographical Dictionary of Scientists*, 1974; Article on 'Peregrinus' 23 CM 123, 22 June 1967 contains the definitive resolution to set up the Company, based on the 'Draft Report of the Business Advisory Committee on Arrangements for Undertaking Work for Other Bodies', Council Doc C(67)75, as amended by Council

24 'Publishing and Computer Work for Third Parties', Council Doc C(67)31, 22 Feb. 1967; CM, 22 March 1967

Chapter 16

Coming Together: an Institution of Engineers?

I Forward with Robbins

On 23 October 1963 the 'Robbins Report' was published. This was the report of a committee under Lord Robbins (1898-1984), an economist of great academic and practical distinction. On the grounds that there were vast untapped reserves of intellectual ability in British society, the report recommended expanding existing universities and founding six new ones so as to produce, within ten years, 393,000 places for students in higher education. 'It did not explain', says Professor Medlicott, unfashionably sceptical, 'how the indifference to higher education among large sections of the English working class – the chief reservoir of talent – was to be overcome'.[1] Nevertheless, in the affluent atmosphere of the early sixties the Conservative Government accepted the committee's findings, with their financial consequences, and for several years university education became a growth industry on an unparallelled scale.

For the English professions generally, and for electrical engineering in particular, the implications of the Robbins Report were far-reaching. There had been pressure for many years, as we have seen in previous chapters, towards making a university degree the essential educational requirement for a professional qualification in electrical engineering, but so long as full-time university education remained a scarce commodity most newcomers had to take the part-time route to qualification, by way of apprenticeship, the HNC, and the Institution's own examinations, which for many years were held at numerous centres in the United Kingdom and abroad. One of the Institution's traditional functions, therefore, was to grant qualifications, unconnected with any university but at the highest professional level, which employers and the public at large could rely on.

After Robbins, all that was changed. It became unlikely that anyone with the intellectual ability to become a professional engineer would not, if he chose, be able to go to a university. That was a far more attractive prospect than the hard grind of apprenticeship and part-time study by which so many engineers had clawed their way up the ladder in the past. Moreover, on the other side – the employers' side – if the universities could be relied upon to provide sufficient applicants with appropriate education, the employers themselves could decide, without reference to the Institution, whether they were qualified in other ways.

During the sixties, therefore, those who were responsible for the Institution's affairs became uneasily aware that its position as a qualifying body was being eroded.[2] This was a disturbing thought, especially after all the work which members of the Institution had put into developing the national certificate system before the war and into passing judgment on university courses. Were they worthy to confer exemption from the Institution's own examinations? 'There had been periods', said the President in 1944, 'during which the Council had found it impossible to recognise degrees awarded by the University as exempting qualifications.' He was talking about the University of Cambridge. In the 1940s it was providing about a quarter of the annual crop of engineering graduates but there was no Professor of Electrical Engineering.

The upshot was an undertaking by the Institution to provide funds for five years from 1944 to get a chair established, on the understanding that it would afterwards become the responsibility of the University. When the proposal was discussed in Council Professor C L Fortescue, Professor of Electrical Engineering at Imperial College, demurred. 'Action of this kind', he said, '... should ... be directed towards Universities which had properly played their part in the education of electrical engineers in the past', but he did not press his point. The offer to Cambridge went forward and was accepted. The total cost to the Institution was £7,500 in 3% Savings Bonds 1960-1970 and the first Professor was E B Moullin (1893-1963), President of the Institution in 1949.[3]

A hopeful enquiry from Imperial College, made by Lord Falmouth, in December 1944, for help with setting a Chair of Radio Engineering, was far less graciously received. Brasher put the radio engineers firmly in their place. He 'pointed out the view frequently expressed by the Council, that it was unwise to regard radio engineering as a separate study, but that it should be regarded as a natural branch of electrical engineering'.[4] Scepticism of the overriding value of university education in general long persisted. 'I dislike the limitation of entry to the profession to university graduates,' said one traditionally minded member of Council in 1967.

Linked with the Institution's standing as a qualifying body lay the perennial problem of distinguishing between the Chartered Engineer on the one hand and the engineering technician on the other. With the rapid spread of new technology and the rise in the number of technicians, both matters were becoming more and more urgent, and they faced all the institutions alike, not the Electricals only. So did the awkward fact that new technology would not necessarily fit within the boundaries which the institutions, over many years, had marked out for themselves, and if newcomers could not find a home with one institution they might find it with another, or even set up house for themselves. Surrounding everything there was the perpetual anxiety felt by all engineers – not electrical engineers only – about their standing with the British public.

In other words, it was becoming steadily more apparent that the institutions – not only the traditional three, but all the institutions – had a wide range of interests in common and a wide range of problems to which common solutions would have to be found. One institution for all engineers of every variety was no doubt impracticable even if it was desirable (though from time to time it was discussed) but a stronger bond between the institutions than the long-standing informal cooperation of their presidents was developing which would inevitably limit their independence: again, not an idea universally welcomed. 'It *may* be', said Professor G H Rawcliffe, 'that in a century or so there will in fact be one Institution of Engineers. I think the IEE should do nothing whatever towards accelerating this amalgamation.'[5] We must follow the Institution along the path which Rawcliffe regarded with such suspicion. By the time he spoke, as he was well aware, it had already gone past the point of no return.

II The Professional Engineer and the Engineering Technician

Among its more important duties, an association of all the engineering institutions would have to set a common standard, acceptable throughout the profession, for recognition as a Chartered Engineer. It would also attend to the related question of technician engineers. Could some permanent solution be found, preferably to the technicians' own satisfaction, to the problem of defining their proper station in life *outside* the charmed circle of the Chartered Engineers?

This was a matter which, in one form or another, had engaged the attention of the IEE and the other British engineering institutions for many years, and increasingly from the 1930s onward. It was common, in fact, to engineering institutions throughout the world, and it was raised at various gatherings organised in the late 1940s and the early 1950s by the Commonwealth Engineering Conference and by the Conference of Engineering Societies of Western Europe and USA (EUSEC). For several years after 1945 the members of these bodies sought definitions of the terms 'Professional Engineer' and 'Engineering Technician'. Eventually they arrived at forms of words with which they were satisfied.[6] Whether the technicians also were satisfied nobody seems to have enquired.

The definitions, reproduced at length at the end of this chapter (see page 219), turned on differences in education and training. 'A professional engineer is competent *by virtue of his fundamental education and training* [present author's italics] to apply the scientific method and outlook to the analysis and solution of engineering problems.' 'An engineering technician', on the other hand, 'requires *an education and training* sufficient for him to understand the reasons for and the purposes of the operations for which he is responsible.' From this difference in education and training it followed that a professional engineer 'in due time' would 'be able to give authoritative technical advice, and to assume responsibility for the direction of important tasks in his branch', whereas an engineering technician 'under general professional engineering direction' would be able to carry out a range of tasks which are illustrated by example but not defined in general terms. This failure to generalise illustrates the extreme difficulty of drawing a line, at the top of the technicians' grade, between the functions of the technician and the professional engineer and it exposes a weakness in the concept of a profession which no professional body has so far been able to come to terms with.[7]

The IEE took very seriously its position as gatekeeper to the electrical engineering profession. EUSEC's definitions, it was claimed in November 1953, 'had evolved directly from those adopted by the Education and Training Committee [of the IEE] some six or seven years ago'.[7] The IEE strove, accordingly, to uphold the level of qualification required for professional engineers, which in practice meant steadily raising it. Technical education, as the definitions indicate, lay at the root of the matter and bore closely also on the question of technicians' standing.

During the fifties the IEE and the other two senior institutions engaged in a long and not very rewarding dialogue with successive Ministers of Education. Whether they belonged to Labour or Conservative Governments, Ministers showed a distressing tendency to take advice from bodies appointed by themselves, on which the institutions might or might not be represented and on which they were never predominant. In 1950 the General Purposes Committee of the IEE felt that in certain proposals then being put forward by the National Advisory Council on Education for Industry and Commerce there was 'a very large measure of danger to the future of the three large Engineering Institutions'.[8] Precisely what this danger was is not expressly indicated, but there is little doubt that it lay in the sheer number of engineering technicians. By 1952, it was estimated that there were 100,000 in electrical engineering alone.[9] In the same year the IEE had about 17,757 corporate members, who would be swamped if any considerable number of technicians were allowed to join them.

During the fifties, accordingly, the Council of the IEE regarded technicians with mingled paternalism and unease. On the one hand they had no hesitation in making recommendations for the training and education of engineering technicians, as they did in an elaborate Report on the Education and Training of Electrical Technicians, compiled in 1950.[10] Between 1953 and 1955 the Council convened three conferences on courses for electrical technicians, and the upshot was a scheme of examinations, devised and administered by the City and Guilds of London Institute, leading to Technicians' Certificates endorsed by the IEE.[11]

On the other hand, the Council of the IEE was determined to protect the professional engineers' position. In 1958 they welcomed a report by the National Council for Technological Awards under Lord Hives (1886–1965), ex-Chairman of Rolls-Royce. It recommended the establishment of a Diploma in Technology (Engineering), abbreviated as 'Dip. Tech. (Eng.)'. The diploma was not to be a university award. It was to be granted by the newly established Colleges of Advanced Technology (CATs) according to standards maintained by a Board of Studies on which the Institution was 'strongly represented'.[12] That on the recommendation of Robbins the CATs would before long be raised to university status was not foreseen by Hives.

The Council of the IEE made clear, in its Reports for 1957–1958 and 1958–1959, that establishment of the new Diploma would emphasise the gap between the professional engineer and the technicians working under his direction. It would also make the gap harder to cross. Professional qualification without a degree would still be possible, but it would require either the Dip. Tech. (Eng.) or the Higher National Diploma plus the IEE's Part III examination, each diploma to be gained after a sandwich course: that is, a course which 'sandwiched' full-time technical education between periods spent in practical training. The old part-time route to a professional qualification, by apprenticeship and evening classes, was to all intents and purposes closed. 'This', says the Report for 1957–1958, 'will result in the Higher National Certificate becoming recognized as a Senior Technician qualification with the alternative of a short sandwich course leading to a Technician Diploma.'[13]

The problem of admitting technicians to the Institution remained. The solution, as outlined in 1952 in the interim report of a Study Committee, seemed to be to avoid it altogether by encouraging the formation of associations of technicians.[14] They might be developed from existing bodies: in the utilisation field, the Association of Supervising Electrical Engineers; in the supply industry, the Electrical Power Engineers' Association; in the field of measurement, the Society of Instrument Technology. 'The least encouraging situation' was reported to be in the radio field, where the Study Committee 'thought it possible that discussions might be entered into with an existing body'. The discussions had come to nothing, and it is not difficult to guess the likely identity of the 'existing body'.

The object of all this activity was to give the technicians a permanent institutional home or, more probably, homes – 'no single body could hope to cater for all the technicians working in the electrical engineering field' – which might make them satisfied with the permanency of their subordinate station. The Report said:

> It is the hope of the Committee that there can be fostered in the great body of technicians a pride in their calling and a desire to excel in it, for notwithstanding

views which have been expressed to the contrary, the technician's is not a transitory class, but a stable and essential element of the electrical engineering industry. It follows that an Association should make its appeal as a means by which its members can advance their competence and experience rather than as a means, more often than not illusory, by which they can enhance their personal status.

In other words, the technician belonged not so much to a class as to a caste, from which his chance of rising to join the brahmins – the professionals – was minimal. Yet some members of the associations on which the Committee hoped to build were corporate members of the IEE, which no technician, according to the Committee, could ever hope to become. The Electrical Power Engineers' Association, indeed, had originally been an exclusively professional body (see page 98).

Matters looked even worse when the education and training of technicians was examined again, in 1963, for the basic educational requirements: 'mathematics and science with, desirably, passes at Ordinary or Advanced level in these subjects'[15] was close to the standard required in 1958 for candidates for the Higher National Diploma, a passport to professional status. They needed five GCE passes, including Mathematics and Physics, one of which was to have been passed and the other studied at A Level.[16] The distinction between professional engineers and technicians, at the top of the technician grade, that is to say, was as difficult as ever to define and regulate satisfactorily, and such regulations as there were never stayed the same for long. The way in which the Institution was thus continually raising its requirements for professional standing, though no doubt from one point of view praiseworthy, could hardly be expected to content those who found that they were playing for a prize in a game with ever-changing rules. In spite of an almost continuous process of enquiring and reporting in the early sixties, therefore, there seemed to be no way of satisfying the natural ambitions of those whom the IEE's Panel on Electrical Technicians, in 1963, called 'a substantial proportion of men in the industry whose exclusion from the Institution presented a problem.'[17]

This 'problem', in its various aspects over many years, was consistently, though no doubt unintentionally, discussed in IEE documents in a generally patronising tone, disclosing an attitude of mind which was no doubt detectable on the technicians' side of the Great Divide. It has to be borne in mind also that technicians' representatives, in discussions and negotiations with the IEE, were dealing with representatives of those set in authority over them, on whose good opinion their future security and prosperity might depend. It was hardly a situation conducive to a true meeting of minds.

Eventually, in 1965, the Institution of Electrical and Electronics Technician Engineers was founded. It was the product of patient collaboration between the IEE, the Association of Supervising Electrical Engineers and (a sign of the times) the British Institution of Radio Engineers. Its relations with the IEE were close. Its base was in the IEE building in Savoy Place. Among its Presidents, as time went on, it numbered past Presidents of the IEE. It would perhaps be optimistic to say that the problem of the technicians had been solved, but it had been dealt with.

III Protective Activities

For many years there was a persistent and vocal demand amongst the membership of the IEE that the Institution should take up 'protective activities' for the direct material benefit of its members as individuals. Members, that is to say, were demanding that as well as acting as a learned society and a qualifying body the IEE should also act as a trade union. The example of the British Medical Association was often admired, though without explaining how the IEE could combine the functions of the BMA with functions which, in medicine, were performed by the Royal Colleges.

Engaging in protective activities, like defining a technician engineer, went directly to the heart of the concept of professional conduct and professional standing. No one supposed that a technician compromised his occupational standing by going on strike, but could the same be said for anyone who claimed to be a professional engineer? By extension, could a professional association properly set itself up to conduct protective activities?

The Council of the IEE, like the councils of the other major engineering institutions, always held themselves to be debarred by the terms of the Charter and by the Institution's charitable status from undertaking protective activities. The Charter, with its insistence on 'the general advancement of Electrical Science and Engineering' and its specific prohibition of engaging in 'any transaction with a view to the pecuniary gain or profit of the Members', helped to entrench, at the head of the Institution's affairs, those who abhorred the notion of protective activities. There was nothing in the constitution of the Institution, however, to prevent individual members from joining protective organisations including trade unions if their own principles would allow them to do so. Some members of the IEE Council, as might be expected of middle-class professional men, would have disapproved of the Institution being associated with trade unions even if the Charter had permitted it.[18] Some, on the other hand, were themselves members of unions. The Council in their official capacity were careful not to put any obstacle in the way of individual union membership. About 80 per cent of electrical engineers in the public service and local government service belonged to unions, and union membership might be a condition of employment, but among electrical engineers in private employment, by contrast, only about 22 per cent belonged.

In 1938 the Engineers' Guild had been set up by a group of Civils, Mechanicals and Electricals. Its founders acted as individuals, and they kept the Guild independent of the Institutions because they intended it to carry on the 'protective activities' which the terms of the Royal Charters barred. It was for the benefit of professional engineers and for nearly twenty years, until in 1957 the Chemical Engineers were admitted, it accepted none but corporate members of the three 'senior institutions' to its own membership. It grew slowly, suggesting that the demand for protective activities might not be quite so strong as its more vocal proponents suggested. The Guild attracted 1,000 members by 1948 and 6,000 by 1965: a very low proportion of those eligible for membership.

The IEE's official attitude to the Guild was cautious but never obstructive, and indeed in 1960 it joined the other major institutions in issuing a statement intended to encourage their members to become also members of the Guild. 'The Engineers' Guild', said a draft of the statement, '... can and does properly concern itself with the protection of the interests of members of the profession. Its activities are therefore in a sense complementary to those of The Institution ... and those [members] who wish to support any collective action expressly intended to advance the interests of professional engineers are entirely free to join it.'[19] The Councils of the three major institutions thus indicated as plainly as possible that they were in sympathy with the objects of the Guild, but they could go no further. They could offer no official support, certainly no money.

Among members of the IEE 'protective activities' never lost their attractiveness. In the late sixties the idea that the Institution should in some way give its blessing to the functions of a trade union, in spite of the obvious danger of conflict with professional obligations, was widely accepted. J Williams, an Associate Member, writing to *Electronics & Power* early in 1969, thought many Chartered Engineers felt that it was a mistake for the engineering institutions 'to preclude themselves from being "trade unions"'. He was aware, he said, 'that many professional engineers have come to terms with reality and have turned to trades unionism in order to negotiate effectively with employers both in the public and private spheres'.[20]

Williams was not alone. In late 1968 and early 1969 several letters to *Electronics & Power*, including one signed by seventeen members and another signed by seven, expressed similar sentiments, and in March 1969 Gainsborough told the Council of the IEE: 'for the first time there was pressure for trade union facilities at a professional level'. Opposition to trade unions and their practices also emerged. One member, W Dougharty, attacked concerted action to influence employers – 'the principle behind going slow, working to rule, striking and similar activities' – as 'a principle very difficult to justify on ethical grounds', and M D Morgan thought that the engagement of the engineering institutions in union activities was 'objectionable on both moral and practical grounds'.

That opinions on trade unions and their activities should have been strongly and widely expressed was not surprising. The late sixties, like the latter years of the Great War and the years immediately after it, was a period when trade union power and influence were waxing. In 1969 the Labour Government, in Barbara Castle's document *In Place of Strife*, disclosed some mild proposals aimed at abating the industrial anarchy of the day.[21] The TUC's cry of outrage threatened to bring down the Government, the proposals were withdrawn, and the unions continued on their course of rising militancy.

At much the same time, within the electrical industry, complex diplomacy was bringing about the merger of the country's largest electrical firms: AEI, English Electric and GEC.[22] The nervousness thereby produced among electrical engineers made many of them more anxious than ever for the kind of protection which membership of a powerful trade union might provide. Existing trade unions with members among engineering technicians were quick to seize the opportunity. 'Certain technician unions', wrote A Williams and six other members in January 1969, 'are taking advantage of the present instability in industry, ... caused by large scale mergers, to recruit professional engineers.'[23]

It was the drive for membership by technicians' unions, rather than trade union membership itself, which the Council of the IEE and individual members found disturbing. Not since the latter years of the Great War (page 96) had the IEE been faced with an aggressive campaign by the unions to recruit professional engineers as members.

The Council was permanently uneasy about possible conflict between standard union practices, such as striking and working to rule, and professional ethics, but they were most unwilling to pronounce on these matters publicly. In 1962 the Three Presidents' Committee decided that if members enquired – not otherwise – they should be advised that strike action was unprofessional. Nearly ten years later, in 1971, the IEE issued a Press Release which, with a gesture towards By-law 42 governing professional conduct, made it clear that these matters were left to the consciences of individual members.[24]

The wretched position in which the activities of a technicians' union might place professional engineers, whether employees or employers, was illustrated in 1971. The management of C A Parsons & Company, which included chartered electrical engineers, moved to dismiss thirty-eight members of engineering institutions, including some with as much as thirty-five years' service, for refusing to join the Draughtsmen's and Allied Technicians' Association (the supervisory and technical section of the Amalgamated Union of Engineering Workers) as a condition of continued employment. Members of the IEE – those who issued the threat of dismissal and those who received it – were thus set at odds with each other, and the General Purposes

Committee felt strongly 'that the Council should express its displeasure at the unethical conduct of the chartered electrical engineers who ... had placed a group of other chartered electrical engineers in a position likely to require them to act in an unprofessional way contrary to the requirements of By-law 42'.[25]

One way out of the Council's difficulty had been considered two years before the Parsons case came up. The Institution could petition the Crown for an amendment to the Charter permitting it to provide protective services – that is, to act as a union itself – but that might make matters worse. 'The Council', says a draft letter by the Secretary, intended as a reply to the members' letters quoted above, 'have ample evidence that such a course of action ... would be bitterly controversial.'[26]

The Council of the IEE, in common with the other major engineering institutions, met the problem by discreet support for a negotiating body, the United Kingdom Association of Professional Engineers (UKAPE), set up on the initiative of ten members of the Engineers Guild and registered in 1969 as a trade union.[27] When the President of the IEE, David Edmundson, with some of the Vice Presidents and the Secretary, met the President and Secretary of UKAPE early in 1970 they offered to recommend 'those of our Council who are in a position to do so to consider the recognition of UKAPE in representing their staff'.[28] UKAPE's promoters claimed that it would be 'a body of engineers, organised by engineers for the benefit of engineers, [which] will take full account of and work within the code of ethics of the engineering profession'.[29]

In dealing with problems raised by trade unions, then, the IEE acted in rather the same way as in dealing with profit-making activities. Instead of breaching its Charter obligations or seeking alterations in the Charter, it supported action by an entirely separate body: UKAPE. Similarly the IEE supported the Professional Engineers Insurance Bureau Limited, sponsored by the Civils through their Benevolent Fund in conjunction with the Howden Group of insurance brokers. The Bureau was set up in 1969 and provided with premises in the Mechanicals' building. Each of the three senior institutions provided two of PEIB's directors. Those from the IEE were Sir Ben Barnett and V S Risoe, one of the IEE's Deputy Secretaries.[30] A year or so later, the Council agreed to support the Professional Engineers Association Limited, set up 'to undertake activities directed to the care and welfare of the individual professional engineer', but the General Purposes Committee was careful to make sure that the prospectus made no mention of industrial relations because PEAL 'would not have the protection at law provided by current trade union legislation'.[31]

All in all, the Council in the late sixties found itself obliged to respond to a long-standing demand for services which had never before been offered to the membership. It did so with reluctance, and it took care not to involve the

Institution directly either in trade union activities or in the provision of professional services, which in the event turned out to be unattractively expensive. The members had what some of them had long campaigned for, but scarcely in the form which they had expected.

IV The Council of Engineering Institutions and the All-Graduate Profession

For many years before the events described in Section III of this chapter the major institutions had been in the habit of cooperating informally as the need arose. For thirty years from 1922 there was an Engineering Joint Council, but in 1952 it died of frustration (page 130). More effective, probably because it was smaller, was the Three Presidents' Committee. This was a Committee of the Presidents of the Civils, Mechanicals and Electricals which, continuing a long tradition of cooperation between the Presidents of the major engineering institutions, met three or four times a year from 1940 onwards. Its proceedings were informal and it had no executive power: it was simply a discussion centre. From 1959 to 1964 a buffet lunch for members of the three councils was given once a year by each institution in turn, but after 1964 the custom lapsed.

During 1959 the Presidents began to discuss 'a common desire to give the co-operative machinery a more definite form, without interfering with the autonomy of the separate institutions'. Here at once was a problem: how far were the institutions prepared to go towards the logical end of this road, an all-embracing Institute of Engineering? The Civils, it appeared, 'envisaged eventually complete integration', but the other two demurred. The IEE's President put forward a 'proposal for a minimal overall structure of the simplest possible type, leaving the autonomy of the three Councils undisturbed'.[32]

Whatever the structure of the new organisation, the membership would also have to be decided upon, and as soon as the Presidents' proposals came to be debated beyond the walls of the three institutions' council chambers, the question of membership became a matter of fundamental and lasting importance. The members would be engineering institutions, not individual engineers. Which institutions should be invited to join? How should power over the new organisation's affairs be divided amongst them, and who would pay its bills?

The three senior institutions disliked the proliferation of professional associations, especially those which sought to become qualifying bodies, partly because they distrusted the standards that would be set by newly founded societies hungry for subscription income, and partly because they did not want to lose potential members. Hence the almost unvarying opposition of the IEE to the grant of new charters and their consistent struggle to preserve the title 'institution' for established qualifying bodies. Moreover, the senior institutions knew that the costs of running any new joint organisation would fall heavily on themselves. For all these reasons the instinct of the senior institutions, in framing their proposals for an engineering 'council' or 'congress' (both titles were considered) was to keep the membership select and to ensure that their own voting power was proportionate to their strength and standing in the profession.[33]

Long negotiations, held at first in strict confidence, partly at least because the Electricals did not wish to admit the Radio Engineers, led at last, in 1962, to the formation of the Engineering Institutions Joint Council. There were at first twelve members, amongst whom the Radio Engineers were not included:

The Royal Aeronautical Society
The Institutions of:
      Chemical Engineers
      Civil Engineers
      Electrical Engineers
      Gas Engineers
      Mechanical Engineers
      Mining Engineers
      Mining and Metallurgy
      Municipal Engineers
      Production Engineers
      Structural Engineers
The Institute of Marine Engineers

The President of the Chemical Engineers would previously have been invited to join the Three Presidents if the Civils and the Electricals had had their way. All but one of the twelve members of the new Council – the Production Engineers – had charters, of which six had been granted before the IEE's Charter. It was not likely, therefore, that the three seniors would be granted any special standing within the new Council, and so it proved. Most major decisions, such as increasing the authority of the Joint Council, admitting new members and expelling old ones, and varying the constitution, required the unanimous consent of all members. 'The Joint Council', it was explicitly provided, 'shall have no executive authority over the constituent members.'[34] Above all, voting power was based strictly on the principle 'one Institution, one vote'. The smaller institutions, if they voted together, could block or modify any proposal which came before the Council.

The major institutions' demand for predominant voting power, which they felt to be necessary if the Council were to be expected to take unpopular decisions, was thus blocked from the start. At the same time, although voting power might be equal, paying power was not. The major institutions, as they had forecast, were expected to contribute according to their means. Of the EIJC's initial budget of £55,000 a year the IEE, account being taken of the strength of its membership, was asked to put up £11,000. The IEE's Council suggested forcibly that the budget should be brought down to £25,000 (£5,500 from the IEE) and that any increase 'should depend on the way in which the work of the Joint Council developed'.[35] The budget was reduced.

Early in 1964, before the EIJC's by-laws were settled, Lord Hailsham, Lord President of the Council, intimated that a petition for a Royal Charter would be favourably received by the Government if the new Council offered some prospect of establishing a sound basis of qualification for all branches of the engineering profession. With this encouragement, measures were put in hand to apply for a Royal Charter which, it was hoped, might be granted by the end of the year.

The Council of the IEE then stepped in. The application, some members felt, was premature, and the Council, to the consternation of other institutions, declined to support the petition before the conditions for the grant of the title 'Chartered Engineer' had been agreed upon and defined in the by-laws proposed for the EIJC.[36] 'The establishment of a common title and common high standard of qualification as a means of creating a united engineering profession', wrote George Gainsborough, the IEE's new Secretary, 'would seem to be by far the most important function of the Council', and he reinforced the point by the shameful admission of 'the present unacceptability of Corporate Membership of British Institutions as a qualification to practice in a number of other countries'.[37]

Since 1957 the IEE's educational standard for corporate membership had been set at the level of an ordinary degree, which was higher than some institutions were prepared to aim. The Council of the IEE therefore directed their efforts to getting the by-laws of the proposed chartered institution framed so as to found the title 'Chartered Engineer' not upon corporate membership of an institution but upon a university degree or its equivalent, buttressed by sound evidence of practical training and professional responsibility.

If a degree or its equivalent were to be demanded by the EIJC for 'chartered' status, then as matters stood in 1964 not all the corporate members of the constituent institutions of the new Council could be accepted as Chartered Engineers. There would be no harm in allowing the point to be waived once, at the granting of the Charter, by allowing all who were corporate members on Charter Day to be registered as Chartered Engineers. After that a bitterly contentious question would arise. After what date was the requirement of a degree to be strictly enforced, and for how long were exceptions to be allowed? On the side of strict enforcement stood the IEE: on the other side, the Mechanicals, with the Civils putting forward 'a proposal which would mean in practice that the qualification of Chartered Engineer would not reach the degree standard for some 20–30 years'.[38] The matter had not been finally settled when Charter Day arrived.

On 3 August 1965 the Engineering Institutions Joint Council became the Council of Engineering Institutions and a Royal Charter was granted. By that time two more members had been added to the original twelve. One was the Royal Institution of Naval Architects, which had been consulted very early in the proceedings leading up to the EIJC's foundation. The other had not. It was the Institution of Electronic and Radio Engineers (lately the British Institution of Radio Engineers). On 10 November the Queen, the Duke of Edinburgh and Lord Mountbatten attended a CEI Reception at the Science Museum. For the first time since 1849, when the Mechanicals separated themselves from the Civils, the British engineering profession had a body representative of all its branches: a body from which, in time, a governing authority might be coaxed into emerging.

'The CEI's principal function in practice', says an IEE document of 1970, drafted by George Gainsborough, 'is to control the qualification of Chartered Engineers.'[39] The IEE's intention from the outset, unswervingly pursued, was to see that the CEI's 'control' was exercised to set the level of qualification as high as possible, having regard especially to standards set in other countries of Western Europe. With fourteen 'constituent members' – that is, institutions – which had widely varying conditions of admission to corporate membership but equal voting power, agreement was difficult to arrive at and there was an obvious danger of levelling down, both in the matter of degrees and in the requirements of practical training and responsibility.

Disagreement over the degree requirement, after Charter Day, was long and bitter. The four major institutions – Civils, Mechanicals, Electricals, Chemicals – were not united, and opposition from some of the other institutions was strong. A suggestion by the Electricals that institutions might, if they wished, have their qualifying examinations reviewed to see if they came up to degree standard was at first rejected by the appropriate CEI Panel, which is surely an eloquent comment on some constituent institutions' self-confidence. The IEE nevertheless had its own examination reviewed by the Principal of Chelsea College of Science and Technology, and a voluntary procedure for the review of institutions' examinations was eventually accepted.[40] On the main point, the strict enforcement of academic requirements, the crucial date was eventually set at 31 December 1973. After that day, no one would be accepted as a Chartered Engineer without education up to the standard of a British university degree.[41]

This must be regarded as a considerable victory for the IEE, whose standards in these matters were high. Nevertheless it was the result of a compromise between the IEE and other institutions which would have preferred either to set the date much further into the future or even to have prescribed no requirement for education to degree standard at all. That on so vital a matter as the level of qualification required for recognition as a Chartered Engineer the IEE should have been driven to accept a compromise below the level at which it had been aiming shows how the establishment of the CEI, which the IEE and the other senior institutions had done so much to bring about, imposed severe constraints on their autonomy. 'CEI', says a Council document of December 1969, 'is now firmly established as the focus of authority for professional engineers in this country.'[42]

The CEI's power over qualifying standards, as the same document recognises, came from the authority vested in it to keep a register of Chartered Engineers, each of whom was to be nominated by one of the constituent members of the CEI. For acceptance, each nominee, being at least twenty-five years old and a corporate member of the nominating institution, would need to have passed either an examination set by a Board acting for the CEI or 'such other examinations or academic test as may be accepted by the Board'. He would also be required to have undergone professional training and to have gained at least two years' professional experience, both at a standard which would in practice be set by the nominating institution. The effect of these regulations was that although the fourteen 'Constituent Members' of the CEI could still set their own terms for admitting their own corporate members, they could no longer grant them the right to recognition as Chartered Engineers, except in their own branch of the profession. All membership examinations set by the constituent members, including the IEE, were superseded by the CEI's examination, and in 1969 the IEE's examination, first set in 1914, was held for the last time.[43]

The IEE, as one of the authorities responsible for setting the CEI's examination, kept a high degree of control over its general standard, particularly in the papers dealing directly with electrical engineering. In other matters pertaining to qualification as a Chartered Engineer, however, there was plenty of room for bargaining. One effect, before a degree or its equivalent was made indispensable, was that 'the range of degree subjects admissible ... [was] widened to include just about each and every degree in science and engineering'. The IEE's Education and Training Committee, having made this observation, pointed out a curious consequence: 'that an applicant for admission to *corporate* membership of the Institution of Electrical Engineers should possess some knowledge of "electrical science and engineering" is no longer an essential formal requirement.'

The Committee was more worried by the implications of the requirements for professional training and experience, which remained within the control of the constituent members. It would clearly be undesirable if the conditions set by the various institutions made it easier for some engineers than for others to gain 'chartered' status, and since some institutions badly needed members' subscriptions, 'it may well be that the final answer may be an agreement to accept something nearer the lowest rather than the highest level for one, or both, of the non-academic requirements of training and responsible experience.' There was already what the committee called 'a groundswell of opinion among the general membership of the Institution' that there ought to be 'some liberalisation' of the IEE's requirement of 'responsible experience' and that might 'influence the more ready acceptance of the pressures' towards lower standards.[44]

In the matter of professional qualifications, in the year of its centenary the IEE stood uneasily. It had for many years been recognised as the central qualifying body in its own branch of the engineering profession, and during the years when it was working with the other 'senior institutions' to establish a central governing body for engineering generally, which finally took shape as the CEI, its paramount objective had been to set the level of professional qualification as high as possible. When the CEI was formed, it found itself in the position, by no means comfortable, of fighting for standards higher than some of the other constituent members were prepared to accept. Since the voting power of all members was equal, compromise had to be the result, and compromise inevitably threatened the standards which the IEE wished to uphold for its own membership. Having ceded a great deal of its autonomy to the CEI, which it had worked hard to set up, the IEE now found its powers as a qualifying body, which it set great store by, gravely diminished. It was an uncomfortable situation for all concerned. Could it last?

Recommendations and Resolutions adopted at the Third Meeting of EUSEC held in Paris, 7 – 11 September 1953. Extract from Council Minutes, No 9, Document 3970/33

Resolution 53/1: Definitions of the terms 'Professional Engineer' and 'Engineering Technician'

The Conference, referring to the Recommendation 51/1 and to the report of the Working Party, decided to adopt for the purposes of Conference discussion the definitions of the terms 'Professional Engineer' and 'Engineering Technician' as follows:

Professional Engineer: A professional engineer is competent by virtue of his fundamental education and training to apply the scientific method and outlook to the analysis and solution of engineering problems. He is able to assume personal responsibility for the development and application of engineering science and knowledge, notably in research, designing, construction, manufacturing, superintending, managing and in the education of the engineer. His work is predominantly intellectual and varied, and not of a routine mental or physical character. It requires the exercise of original thought and judgement and the ability to supervise the technical and administrative work of others.

His education will have been such as to make him capable of closely and continuously following progress in his branch of engineering science by consulting newly published work on a world-wide basis, assimilating such information and applying it independently. He is thus placed in a position to make contributions to the development of engineering science or its applications.

His education and training will have been such that he will have acquired a broad and general appreciation of the engineering sciences as well as a thorough insight into the special features of his own branch. In due time he will be able to give authoritative technical advice, and to assume responsibility for the direction of important tasks in his branch.

Engineering Technician: An engineering technician is one who can apply in a responsible manner proven techniques which are commonly understood by those who are expert in a branch of engineering, or those techniques specially prescribed by professional engineers.

Under general professional engineering direction, or following established engineering techniques, he is capable of carrying out duties which may be found among the list of examples set out below.

In carrying out many of these duties, competent supervision of the work of skilled craftsmen will be necessary. The techniques employed demand acquired experience and knowledge of a particular branch of engineering, combined with the ability to work out the details of a task in the light of well-established practice.

An engineering technician requires an education and training sufficient to enable him to understand the reasons for and the purposes of the operations for which he is responsible.

The following duties are typical of those carried out by engineering technicians: Working on design and development of engineering plant and structures; erecting and commissioning of engineering equipment and structures; engineering drawing; estimating, inspecting and testing engineering construction and equipment; use of surveying instruments; operating, maintaining and repairing engineering machinery, plant and engineering services and locating defects therein; activities connected with research and development, testing of materials and components and sales engineering, servicing equipment, and advising consumers.

References:

1 Report of the Committee . . . under the Chairmanship of Lord Robbins 1961–63, Cmd 2154, 1963; W N Medlicott: *Contemporary England 1914– 1964*, 1967, p.567

2 'The Future Role of the Institution', Council Doc C(67)60, 31 May 1967, CM, 22 June 1967; 'The Future Role of the Institution,' Council Doc C(67)86, 1 Sept. 1967; CM, 14 Sept. 1967

3 GPCM 68, 19 April 1944; CM 118, 27 April 1944; 'Institution Notes,' *J.IEE*, 1944, **91**, Pt.I, p.250; 'Annual Report of Council,' *J.IEE*, 1945, **92**, Pt.I, p.195

4 GPCM, 38, 6 Dec. 1944

5 Council Doc C(67)86, p.9; CM, 14 Sept. 1967

6 CM, 3 Dec. 1953, Doc 3970/33 Resolution 53/1

7 GPCM, 18 Nov. 1953

8 CM 44(5), 12 Jan. 1950

9 'Interim Report of the Study Committee on Association for Technicians,' March 1952, Doc 3720/36, Sec 3.19, CM, 18 Sept. 1952; Dip Tech (Eng), *J.IEE* (n.s.), 1958, **4**, p.67

10 Joint Committee on Practical Training in the Electrical Industry: 'Report on the Education and Training of Electrical Technicians', Doc 5540/25, CM, 22 May 1950

11 'Annual Reports of Council', *J.IEE* (n.s.), 1955, **1**, p.432;1956, **2**, p.393

12 'Dip Tech (Eng)', *J.IEE* (n.s.), 1958, **4**, p.67

13 *J.IEE* (n.s.), 1958, **4**, p.367

14 Reference 9

15 'The Education and Training of Electrical Technician Engineers (Report of the Committee of Practical Training in the Electrical Engineering Industry)', sec 4.1; CM 109, 4 April 1963

16 'Annual Report of Council' *J.IEE* (n.s.), 1958, **4**, p.368

17 'Report of the Panel on Electrical Technicians', Doc 3720/63, GPC, 6 July 1960

18 CM 80, 23 April 1970

19 *J.IEE* (n.s.), 1961, **7**, p.270

20 Appendix A to 'The Organisation of Professional Services for the Individual Engineer' (Report from General Purposes Committee) CM, 25 Feb. 1969

21 Henry Pelling: *A History of British Trade Unionism*, 1972, pp.275–278

22 Robert Jones and Oliver Marriott: *Anatomy of a Merger*, 1970, chapters 15 and 16

23 Reference 20

24 'The Impact of Trade Union Membership on the Members of the Institution', Council Doc C(71)22; CM, 17 Feb. 1971, and associated Press Release

25 *IEE News*, 6 Sept. 1971, p.1; CM141, 9 Sept. 1971

26 Reference 20, Appendix B (draft letter by the Secretary)

27 Letter, J A McSparron to *E & P*, 9 Feb. 1969 in Reference 20, Appendix A; GPCM, 17 July 1969

28 CM 80, 23 April 1970

29 Reference 27

30 'Insurance Services for Members', Doc C(69)7, 1 June 1969, CM, 9 Jan. 1969

31 GPCM 51, 18 March 1970

32 GPCM 68, 16 March 1960

33 Documents on the formation of the EIJC include: 'The Co-operation of the Three Engineering Institutions', GPC, 16 March 1960; Sir Willis Jackson, 'An Institute of Engineers,' Doc PM300, 2 March 1960; GPCM, 12 April, 7 June, 18 Oct. 1961; CM, 2 Nov. 1961, 8 Feb. 1962 (includes Address by Sir Kenneth Hague to a gathering of Presidents and Secretaries of 12 Institutions and notes of the discussion which followed); 'The Engineering Institutions Joint Council, Draft Construction', GPC, 12 June 1962; 'The Engineering Institutions Joint Council, Aims and Objects' (two separate papers), GPC, 16 Oct. 1963; 'The Engineering Institutions Joint Council, Comments on Aims and Objects', GPC, 16 Oct. 1963

34 'The Engineering Institutions Joint Council', Doc EIJC 1/62, GPC, 13 Jan. 1962

35 GPCM 10, 16 Oct. 1963; CM, 7 Nov. 1963

36 GPCM 75, 28 Feb. 1964; CM, 5 March 1964

37 'Functions of the Engineering Institutions Joint Council', General Purposes Committee Doc GP(64)11, 9 March 1964, IEE Archives I/4.11; GPCM, 11 March 1964

38 GPCM 125, 15 Sept. 1965

39 'Provisions for Qualification and for Learned Activities', Council Doc C(70)85; CM, 5 Nov. 1970

40 CM, 5 Jan. 1967; 'The Institution and the CEI', Council Doc C(67)48 22 April 1967; CM 102, 27 April 1967

41 CM, 4 Nov. 1965

42 'The Future Role of the Institution: the Significance of the Qualifying Function' Council Doc C(70)4, 19 Dec 1969

43 Annual Report of Council, *E & P* 1971, **17**, p.185

44 Reference 39, sections 1, 2, 4

Chapter 17

Full Circle?

On 17 May 1971 the Institution of Electrical Engineers, under the presidency of Lord Nelson of Stafford, marked the centenary of its foundation – as the Society of Telegraph Engineers – with a Service of Thanksgiving at Westminster Abbey. Then, in the Royal Festival Hall, congratulatory addresses were delivered by the Secretary of State for Trade and Industry, the President of the Royal Society, the President of the IEEE, and the Chairman of the CEI. After that a centenary congress, on the theme 'Electrical Science and Engineering in the Service of Man' opened with an address by the Lord Chancellor, Lord Hailsham. During the next two days scientists and engineers of international distinction delivered a series of seven lectures. The President rounded off the proceedings with a survey of the general theme of the Congress.

Successive evenings glittered with a reception, a banquet and a *conversazione* held in the presence of the Queen and the Duke of Edinburgh. Relations between the IEE and the IERE, on the surface at least, had been amicable for some years and Earl Mountbatten of Burma also attended, having become an Honorary FIEE in 1965. An exhibition at the Science Museum concentrated on the future of electrical engineering, rather than its history, but at the opening that did not prevent the President, Lord Nelson, from swapping reminiscences of crystal sets with one of his contemporaries.

In local centres and overseas the centenary was celebrated with 'lectures, symposia, exhibitions and social activities', and on 21 May members of the Graduate and Student Sections were addressed, at a dinner in the House of Commons, by the Rt. Hon. Anthony Wedgwood Benn, MP, not yet Tony Benn, well known in 1971 for his enthusiasm for technology and for his part in the merger which three years earlier had produced GEC, of which the President of the IEE was Chairman.[1]

From these celebrations no symbol of the IEE's standing in the national life was missing. Royalty, the established church, Government and Opposition, the law, the City of London, the learned societies, all took part. It was a demonstration to the world, in the English style, of the position which the Institution had gained for itself after its first hundred years. The Institution at the beginning of the 1970s stood far more prominently in Great Britain than the Society of Telegraph Engineers had stood in 1871 and for many years thereafter.

Great Britain, on the other hand, ranked far less impressively among the industrial powers in general and in the world's electrical industries in particular. In 1871 the British were foremost in what was still the main commercial use of electricity, the telegraph, especially the long-distance submarine telegraph, and there was no reason to suppose that they would not take a leading position in the development of electric light and power which was just beginning to become a commercial possibility. The Japanese, shrewd observers of the Western world and determined to take advantage of the best that each Western nation had to offer, not only modelled their navy on the Royal Navy but appointed two Englishmen, W E Ayrton and John Perry, both electrical engineers, to be professors in their newly founded Imperial College of Engineering, and among the foreign members of the Institution in 1891 the Japanese, after the Americans and the French, were the most numerous national group.[2]

A hundred years later, in the 1970s, it was difficult to point to any major form of industrial enterprise, except the production of Scotch whisky, in which the British could claim leadership. With the onset of the 'oil crisis' of 1973 and the world-wide recession which followed, British industry entered a period of what may politely be called 'major structural reorganisation' but which looks perilously like collapse, accompanied by figures of unemployment, apparently irreversible, which less than ten years earlier no one would have believed possible. As for the electrical industries, especially those founded on the latest advances in technology, it was only too obvious by the 1970s, that whatever the British and other Western nations had been able to teach, the Japanese had learnt embarrassingly thoroughly, adding their own peculiar skills and temperament as well.

There were, nevertheless, some shafts of light in the prevailing gloom. The BBC had led the world towards television in 1936, and its continuing technical mastery was demonstrated in the 1960s by the development of 'standards convertors' for adapting television pictures from one standard to another: for instance, from 525 lines, 60 fields per second to 625 lines, 50 fields per second, or the other way round. In the 1970s the BBC and the IBA, with CEEFAX and ORACLE, pioneered the development of teletext, and more recently the European Broadcasting Union has developed a vision signal coding standard for direct satellite broadcasting (the C-MAC System) from a proposal by the IBA. At the heavy end of electrical engineering, British manufacturers since the end of the Second World War have come to hold a strong position – second only, but significantly, to Japan, and ahead of manufacturers in West Germany, USA, France and Italy – in the world market for turbogenerators, especially sets above 400MW.

It is too early, at the time of writing this book, to take a long view of the 1970s – even more so, of the 1980s. The economic clouds hanging over Great Britain may have a silver lining, but if so it is effectively concealed. The background to the latest years of the IEE's history appears to be depressing, and it is the background against which the opulent solidity of the Institution's centenary celebrations must be seen to stand.

In recent years, amid the onrush of new technology, the century-old Institution of Electrical Engineers has kept its hold on its branch of the engineering profession. Between the centenary year 1971 and 1984 total membership rose by 32 per cent, to 82,000, and such calculations as the secretariat of the Institution has felt able to make (available data are not very reliable) suggest that a large majority, probably between 60 and 80 per cent, of electrical engineers entering employment in the United Kingdom have in recent years been joining the Institution.[3]

The Institution, moreover, is attracting those who practise the new technologies. In 1984, 17,000 Fellows, Members and Associate Members – 40 per cent of the total UK active membership – were in electronics, telecommunications, computer control and software engineering, or closely related fields. At the same time the number of power engineers, falling as the number of 'new technology' engineers rose, amounted only to 6,200, 15 per cent of the total. Of the membership 45 per cent were in fields as various as university teaching and research, electrical services and the armed forces. It is a fair guess, though it can be no more, that the majority were chiefly concerned with 'new technology'.[4]

In the build-up of its membership, therefore, and in the distribution of members between various fields of activity, the Institution since its centenary has evidently been keeping up with the development of the profession: a matter which was in some doubt in the late fifties. The wholesale reform of its activities as a learned society, undertaken in the early sixties, appears to have been both timely and well designed. The formation of professional groups, in particular, has enabled specialists to concentrate on their own interests without cutting them out of the general field of electrical engineering.

As a learned society the Institution is greatly strengthened by its activities in publishing, remodelled and extended in the sixties, and in data-processing, first undertaken at the same time. These activities are profitable both intellectually and financially, and the financial benefit is two-fold. The wealth of the Institution supports both its work as a learned society and its independence as a professional association.

As a professional association, the Institution is deeply concerned with the standard of professional qualifications and therefore with professional education and training. These are favourite targets for critics in the inquest which goes on and on into the causes of British industrial decline, and the Institution has not been backward in self-questioning. In 1976 the President and Council of the IEE appointed a Working Party under J H H Merriman, President in 1974, 'to consider the education and training requirements of the Institution for Chartered Electrical Engineers, and to make recommendations'.[5] The

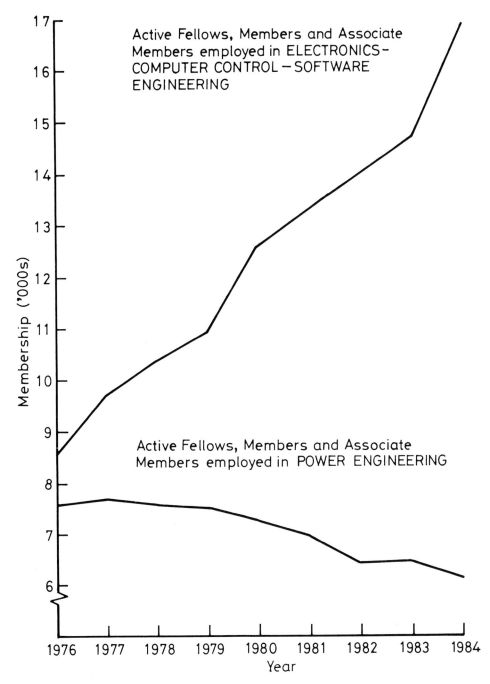

Figure 2: IEE Members based in the United Kingdom, 1976–1984 (*Source*: IEE Salary Surveys)

Working Party, that is to say, was to investigate one of the central functions –
some might have said *the* central function – of the Institution: its role as a
qualifying body.

The main reason for setting up the Working Party, which had been
emerging since the recommendations of the Robbins Report were accepted
and which has been glanced at in previous chapters, went to the root of the
whole matter:

> We were set up ... because of growing evidence that the Institution's qualifications
> had ceased to have a distinctive role.... Nearly all entrants to the profession are now
> graduates and the possession of a degree is widely regarded, albeit erroneously, as a
> qualification equivalent to corporate membership of the Institution. This confusion
> is compounded by the fact that large numbers of present-day graduates are
> recruited, and will remain, as technician engineers... in addition, it was clear that
> our qualification levels were not recognised as sufficient by authorities in other
> countries.[6]

This gloomy assessment of the situation was confirmed when the Working
Party made enquiries among employers. Only in electricity generation and
supply, consultancy, and some smaller industrial organisations was importance attached to the Institution's qualifications – that is, grades of membership and the title Chartered Electrical Engineer – either in recruitment or at
later stages of an engineer's career. Generation and supply, now in decline as a
source of employment for electrical engineers, was probably the last major
stronghold of those who relied on traditional methods of training, in which
university degrees did not figure very prominently.

'Most employers,' said the Working Party, 'pay little attention to the
qualification, Chartered Electrical Engineer', and they went on to observe:
'The general impression that a graduate electrical engineer is equivalent to a
corporate member of the Institution, coupled with the fact that large numbers
of graduates are now employed as technician engineers, has both obscured
the significance of corporate membership and depressed its standing as a
professional qualification.' Many foreign authorities, they said, found it
difficult to relate British professional engineering qualifications to their own
and some regarded them as inferior. 'We are convinced ... that the present
qualification of Chartered Electrical Engineer has ceased to be of distinctive
significance.'[7]

Foreign authorities were not alone in their confusion. As far back as 1928 a
lawyer had vainly pointed out that the Institution had not helped people to
understand its system of qualifications by setting up so many grades of
membership.[8] Some were 'corporate', others not, and most of the designa-
tory letters, as the Privy Council had complained in 1962, meant nothing to
outsiders.[9] The fog of incomprehension was not dissipated by throwing over
some grades of membership (but not all) the blanket of the title 'Chartered

Engineer'. No doubt, however, the matter ran deeper than this, and after all the effort which over a long period of years the IEE had put into raising and refining standards of qualification, both its own and those of the CEI, the Merriman Committee's findings were devastating.

As an immediate measure, almost an emergency measure, the Working Party recommended making a second-class honours degree 'the main educational qualification for corporate membership', and that was done in 1982. Beyond that, they hoped to impose still more ambitious academic qualifications – 'enhanced degree courses' – and, as well as that, post-degree training leading up to 'a rigorous test of professional attributes … some years after graduation'.[10]

The Merriman Report, as it has come to be known, is clear-sighted, plain-spoken and courageous. Its main thrust is a demonstration that the traditional qualifying function of the IEE and the other engineering institutions, in so far as it is based on their own examinations, has become obsolete. The IEE, along with the other institutions, resigned its autonomy as a qualifying body in the late sixties to the forerunner of the CEI, and although the career of the EIJC and the CEI was inglorious and short, the institutions have not resumed their authority. It has passed to the CEI's successor, the Engineering Council, chartered in 1981.

In the late seventies the perennial problem of the condition of the engineering profession in Great Britain, and especially its low standing in public esteem, was investigated by a Committee of Inquiry with Sir Monty Finniston as Chairman. They directed much of their attention, inevitably and rightly, to what they rather curiously termed 'the formation of engineers'. The elaborate proposals which they put forward for education, training and qualification at several different professional and sub-professional levels tended in the same direction as the Merriman Report. The Institution's submission of evidence to the Committee made no bones about the changes which had come over the qualifying role of the engineering institutions.[11]

The Committee's proposals, besides relying heavily on the universities, required a central qualifying body for the engineering profession as a whole, and with no great superfluity of tact the Committee said they would 'free the Professional Institutions of their responsibilities as qualifying bodies'.[12] In other words, the Committee found no place for the institutions because concentration on an academic pathway to qualification was intended to kill off the last remnants of the traditional English system of professional education and training in which the institutions had a central part to play.

This system, which we examined in some detail in Chapter 1, was based on apprenticeship combined with book learning. It had historical roots running well back into the Middle Ages, and it existed independently of the universities. It was in this system, as earlier chapters of this book have shown, that the IEE and other engineering institutions found their place, first as learned societies and then, as faith in written examinations built up, as qualifying bodies.[13]

To some extent, then, the institutions developed because Oxford and Cambridge, and later other universities in Victorian England did not regard professional education, especially in engineering, as their proper concern. To regard this, however, as the only reason for the institutions' development, and to suggest, as Finniston appears to do, that with university education in its post-Robbins phase the institutions should retire, with what grace they can muster, into the dust-bin of history, is to take far too narrow a view of the institutions' place in professional life. They have, in the first place, a part to play in maintaining the pride of professional people in their work and in upholding the decencies of professional conduct which, whatever cynics may say, is not purely a matter of preserving restrictive practices. They are also, or they should be, the chief authorities on the professions which they represent, and this is crucial to the qualifying process. 'This Institution', says the IEE's submission to the Finniston Committee, 'is the most authoritative repository of knowledge of the diverse activities embraced by the profession of electrical and electronic engineering and of industrial requirements in this area. It must therefore continue to play a major part in determining the qualifications by which Chartered Electrical Engineers are identified.'[14]

That 'major part' has two aspects. First, the Institution is better placed than any other body to assess the levels of practical training and professional experience which are required for qualification as an electrical engineer. This is part of the Institution's traditional role as a qualifying body. It has always insisted that adequate training – only to be acquired by some form of apprenticeship – and experience, gained in a substantive appointment, areas important as the professional education which the universities nowadays provide. Secondly, in the matter of university education, the Institution and the universities nowadays so interpenetrate each other that they may almost be taken as two parts of the same whole. The Institution is consulted when the content of courses is being determined, and at the same time it remains sufficiently detached to be capable of assessing courses and deciding whether they provide the education which is required.

The setting up of the CEI and its successor, the Engineering Council, has made two differences to the Institution's role as a qualifying body. First, since only the Engineering Council can create Chartered Engineers, the Institution only acts independently in determining the standard at which it will accept its own corporate members. It still, however, keeps the gate, for the Engineering Council will only accept corporate members of engineering institutions for registration as Chartered Engineers. Secondly, it has accepted responsibility, jointly with other institutions, for setting 'a suitable common standard for chartered engineers of all disciplines'.[15] This 'common standard' at present is not so high as the standard required by the IEE for corporate membership.

Taking the long view, then, it appears that although the qualifying function of the Institution – and of all the institutions – has changed, becoming less direct and more interdependent, yet it has not diminished. The Institution, in these matters, is still powerful and influential. Whether it will remain so in the future will depend on how it responds to the challenge of the times. Another crisis like the crises of 1895 and 1959, mishandled, might be disastrous.

Again, taking the long view, it may be argued that the Institution of Electrical Engineers of the 1980s, with its elaborate organisation of professional groups, its flourishing publishing and computer-based information services, its close links with the universities, is above all a learned society. So was the Society of Telegraph Engineers in the 1870s, before the qualifying function in its modern form had begun to evolve. In a sense, after more than a hundred years, the wheel has come full circle.

The Apricot Xen multiuser computer in 1986. Capable of over 6 million additions a second, it was designed for computer networking. (Apricot Computers plc)

References

1   'Annual Report of Council', *E&P*, 1972, **18**, p.173; see also *IEE Centenary Lectures 1871-1971*, IEE 1971
2   Figures extracted from membership list in *J.IEE*, 1891, **20**
3   'Evidence to House of Lords Select Committee on Science and Technology: Sub-Committee II – New Technologies' 1984, paras 3.1 3.9, Appendix C to Council Doc C(84)40, CM, 6 June 1984
4   Reference 3, paras 3.3 3.4
5   *Qualifying as a Chartered Engineer: the Merriman Report*, 1978, preface, 1st para
6   Reference 5, preface, 2nd para
7   Reference 5, paras 15-19
8   'Counsel's Opinion of proposed Alterations of Membership Qualifications', 1 Nov. 1928, Ref 499/2. In IEE Archives II/1.1.1. Secretary's marked copy of Council documents
9   CM, 5 June 1962
10 Reference 5, p.1 (Main Recommendations), paras 21-42
11 *IEE Submission to the Committee of Inquiry into the Engineering Profession, IEE News*, Feb. 1978, pp.13–15
12 *Engineering our Future*, 1980, p.150
13 Lord Hailsham: 'Opening Address', *IEE Centenary Lectures 1871-1971*, 1971, p.16
14 Reference 11, para 38
15 Reference 14

Appendices

Appendix 1

Select Chronology, 1871–1971

1871 (17 May) Foundation of the Society of Telegraph Engineers

1872 (28 Feb.) First Ordinary Meeting

1875 Ronalds Library presented to the Society under Trust Deed

1881 Change of name to The Society of Telegraph Engineers and of Electricians

1882 Issue of *Rules and Regulations for the Prevention of Fire Risks arising from Electric Lighting*

1883 The Society of Telegraph Engineers and Electricians registered with the Board of Trade under the Companies Act 1867

1889 Change of name to The Institution of Electrical Engineers

1897 Decision by IEE and the Physical Society to publish jointly *Abstracts of Physical Papers*

1898 Publication of *Science Abstracts* commenced

1899 Formation of the first Local Sections, in Dublin, Glasgow, Newcastle and Cape Town
Mrs Hertha Ayrton admitted to Membership: no more women admitted to full membership until 1958

1900 The Northern Society of Electrical Engineers amalgamated with the IEE, and became the Manchester District Local Section.

1908 Purchase of the lease of the Medical Examination Hall, Victoria Embankment, London, which became the Savoy Place headquarters of the IEE
First Kelvin Lecture, by Silvanus Thompson: 'The Life and Work of Lord Kelvin'

1912 Articles of Association revised and an Associate Membership Examination instituted

1914 First examination for Associate Membership held

1918 IEE set up an Employment Register to assist members of HM Forces to find employment on demobilisation.

1919 Reorganisation of seven Local Sections into seven Centres and five Sub-centres
Wireless Section formed
Publication of *Regulations for the Electrical Equipment of Ships*, and their adoption by Lloyd's Registry of Shipping

1921 Grant of the Royal Charter
The Institution returned from 1 Albemarle Street, London, W1, to Savoy Place, which had been occupied by HM Office of Works since 1917

1922 Bylaws for the Chartered Institution approved
First award of the Faraday Medal

1923 Faraday Lectures instituted
Rooms in Savoy Hill let to the BBC

1924 Approval by the Privy Council of By-law sanctioning the use of the designation 'Chartered Electrical Engineer' by corporate members of the Institution

National Certificates and Diplomas in Electrical Engineering instituted by a Joint Standing Committee representing the Board of Education and the IEE

1928   Special Joint Meeting between the IEE, London, and the American Institute of Electrical Engineers, New York, by transatlantic wireless telegraphy
Formation of the Meter and Instrument Section

1930   Inauguration of the *Students' Quarterly Journal*

1931   Celebrations to mark the centenary of Faraday's discovery of electromagnetic induction

1932   First annual meeting of Honorary Secretaries of Students' Sections

1934   Formation of the Transmission Section
Tenth edition of the *Regulations for the Electrical Equipment of Buildings*

1939   Publication of *The History of the Institution of Electrical Engineers 1871–1931* by Rollo Appleyard
The IEE collaborated with the Ministry of Labour in the compilation of a Central Register of those with professional qualifications in electrical engineering, and advised on the proper use of professional electrical engineers in wartime

1940   IEE engaged in intensive technical education for HM Forces and for civilians

1941   Post-war Planning Committees on various aspects of electrical engineering began work
Formation of the Installations Section

1944   Research Committee established
Chair of Electrical Engineering at Cambridge endowed for five years by the IEE

1945   Advisory Committee on Education and Training established
Physics graduates with an honours degree and four years' work in electrical engineering (two in a 'responsible position') to be eligible for Associate Membership
Gift by C W Speirs of 'The Chesters' estate, to establish Benevolent Fund homes

1946   Common Preliminary Examination for Students (21 or over), conducted by Engineering Joint Examination Board
Convention on Radiolocation, the first of the post-war conventions held to discuss wartime technical developments

1947   First District Meeting, a 'pub and bike meeting' at Kettering

1948   First rise in subscriptions since 1913
Grant of Arms by the Earl Marshal

1950   Bylaws on requirements for Associate Membership: Education, training and responsible experience

1953   Measures taken by the IEE to stimulate recruitment to the profession

1954   Technical Publications Panel established an 'Institution Series' of textbooks.

1955   *The Chartered Electrical Engineer* (a careers booklet) published (see 1964)

1956   Faraday Lecture on 'Nuclear Energy in the Service of Man'

1957   Proposals for major alterations to the Savoy Place building approved

1958   Two women admitted to full membership (equivalent to later Fellowship): the first since Mrs Ayrton (1899)

1959   Introduction of Training Regulations

1960   Honours graduates in Physics allowed complete exemption from IEE examination

1961   Savoy Place reconstruction completed

IEE established an Advertising Department
Joint committee with Brit.IRE set up
1962   Membership of IEE reaches 50,000
New Divisional structure, comprising three Divisions and twenty-eight Professional Groups
London District Committee set up
Engineering Institutions Joint Council set up
1963   IEE registered as a charity
1964   Name of the Institution Journal changed to *Electronics and Power*
Launch of *IEE News*
Control and Automation Division established
Faraday Lecture on 'Colour television'
Institution Prize for Women endowed
Electrical and Electronic Engineering – A professional career by Prof M G Say published, to replace *The Chartered Electrical Engineer* (1955)
1965   *Current Papers* and *Electronics Letters* launched
Institution of Electrical and Electronics Technician Engineers founded
1965   Appointment of Membership Advisers in Centres and Sub-centres
Entrance fees and subscriptions little more than one-third of IEE income
Charter granted to the Council of Engineering Institutions, giving authority to lay down the conditions for registration as a Chartered Engineer
1966   New classes of membership (see Appendix 5)
First Summer School
IEE acquired a computer
1967   Publishing Department moved to Stevenage
Establishment of INSPEC
Peter Peregrinus Limited set up to undertake publication and computer service work on a commercial basis for third parties
First IEE Monograph
Overhaul of Council procedure
1968   Student Counsellors appointed in universities
1969   Institution examinations discontinued and replaced by CEI examinations
Metric Supplement to the Wiring Regulations issued
Science Abstracts and *Current Papers* produced by computer-based method
IEE computer to handle office work for Civils and Mechanicals
1970   Individual advanced courses in specialised subjects introduced for home study by correspondence
Science, Education and Management Division formed
No candidate to be admitted to corporate membership unless eligible for registration by CEI as a Chartered Engineer
1971   Move of Computer Department and INSPEC to Hitchin
PPL took over the publication of IEE Monographs from Cambridge University Press.
New machinery of government for the IEE
(17–19 May) Celebrations to mark the Centenary of the Institution

Appendix 2

Royal Charter and Bylaws as amended up to 21 December 1983

To The King's Most Excellent Majesty in Council

The Petition of
LLEWELYN BIRCHALL ATKINSON, Electrical Engineer, of Sardinia House, Sardinia Street, Kingsway, in the County of London; WILLIAM ASH-COMBE CHAMEN, Electrical Engineer, of Royal Chambers, Queen Street, Cardiff, in the County of Glamorgan; WILLIAM HENRY ECCLES, D.Sc., F.R.S., Electrical Engineer, of The Finsbury Technical College, Leonard Street, Finsbury in the said County of London; JOHN SOMERVILLE HIGHFIELD, Electrical Engineer, of 36 Victoria Street, Westminster, in the said County of London; ALAN ARCHIBALD CAMPBELL SWINTON, F.R.S., Electrical Engineer, of 66 Victoria Street, Westminster in the said County of London; and Sir JAMES LYNE DEVONSHIRE, K.B.E., Electrical Engineer, of Electric Railway House, Broadway, Westminster, in the said County of London.

Most Humbly Showeth:
1. That in the year 1871 a voluntary association was formed under the name of The Society of Telegraph Engineers having for its objects the general advancement of electrical and telegraphic science.
2. That in view of the fact that the qualification for membership of the society was not confined to telegraph engineers the name of the society was in the year 1880 changed to The Society of Telegraph Engineers and Electricians with the object of indicating more clearly its scope and the eligibility of persons engaged in all or any branches of electrical science for membership of the society.
3. That in the year 1883 The Society of Telegraph Engineers and Electricians was incorporated under the Companies Acts 1862 and 1867 with the object (*inter alia*) of succeeding to and taking over the property rights and obligations of the society the name of the society being changed in the year 1888 [sic] to The Institution of Electrical Engineers in consequence of the great development which took place about that time in the application of electricity to lighting and heavy engineering the term 'electrical engineer' being substituted as embracing all classes or members of the Institution.
4. That the Institution is composed of corporate members (namely Honorary Members Members and Associate Members) and noncorporate members (namely Associates Graduates and Students) to the total number at the present time of about 9400.
5. That the property and affairs of the Institution are under the direction and management of a Council consisting of the President and Past-Presidents four Vice-Presidents the Honorary Treasurer 18 Ordinary Members of Council all of whom are elected by the corporate members and Associates of the Institution and the Chairman and a Past-Chairman of each local Section of the Institution which the Council may create in any district.

6. That the name of a candidate for admission to corporate membership of the Institution cannot be submitted for ballot unless with the approval of the Council who before giving such approval satisfy themselves as to the professional status and qualifications of the candidate and that corporate membership of the Institution is universally recognised as implying the possession of high professional qualifications for the practice of the profession of electrical engineering.

7. That the Institution is not constituted for gain and that its members have not received and cannot under the terms of its constitution receive any remuneration or other personal financial advantage from their membership.

8. That in pursuance of the objects for which the Institution was established its efforts have been particularly directed to the promotion of the general advancement of electrical science and its applications and the facilitating of the exchange of information and ideas on subjects connected with that science among the members of the Institution and otherwise.

9. That the incorporation in 1883 of the Institution under its then name of The Society of Telegraph Engineers and Electricians was approximately contemporaneous with the commencement of the vast and rapid development of electrical science and discovery and of modes of application of electricity which has taken place within the last generation.

10. That the Institution includes and has for many years past included among its members all the leading British electrical engineers of the time and has become an increasingly important body representative of the profession of electrical engineering.

11. That members of the Institution have either originated or been intimately concerned with all the principal developments of electrical science which have taken place since the establishment of the Institution.

12. That the development and improvement through the instrumentality of the Institution and its members of the modes of application of electricity to many and varied purposes have proved highly beneficial to human life and health and have played an important part in the growth of the trade and commerce of the world.

13. That your petitioners believe that the incorporation of the Institution by Your Majesty's Royal Charter and the recognition thereby of its status as the body representative of the profession of electrical engineering will be the means of enabling the Institution more fully to achieve the objects which it has in view and will tend towards the further development of electrical science and the maintenance of a high standard of professional conduct among its members and thus serve the best interests of the community.

14. That your petitioners Llewelyn Birchall Atkinson, who is President of the Institution, William Ashcombe Chamen, William Henry Eccles, John Somerville Highfield, and Alan Archibald Campbell Swinton, who are Vice-Presidents of the Institution and Sir James Lyne Devonshire, who is Honorary Treasurer of the Institution, have been duly authorised by the Council of the Institution to present this petition, and that such presentation has been approved by a resolution passed at a Special General Meeting of the Institution.

For these and other reasons your petitioners on behalf of themselves and the other members of The Institution of Electrical Engineers most humbly pray that Your Majesty will be graciously pleased to grant a Royal Charter for incorporating under the title of 'The Institution of Electrical Engineers' or under such other title as to Your Majesty may seem fit and with all such powers and privileges as may be necessary or proper the petitioners and the several persons who are now members of the present Institution and other parties who may hereafter become members of the said Institution to be incorporated in pursuance of the regulations thereof and that in terms of the draft Charter herewith submitted or in such other terms as to Your Majesty may seem proper.

And your petitioners will ever pray, etc.

SIGNED at London this twenty-ninth day
   of June One thousand nine hundred
   and twenty-one

LLEWELYN B. ATKINSON
W. A. CHAMEN
W. H. ECCLES
J. S. HIGHFIELD
A. A. C. SWINTON
JAMES LYNE DEVONSHIRE

Royal Charter

Granted on the 15th day of August 1921. Amended by resolutions dated 30 June 1966 (amendment allowed 11 November 1966), 14 October 1971 (amendment allowed 22 March 1972) and 26 May 1983 (amendment allowed 21 December 1983).

Copies of the original Charter, and of the Supplemental Charters of 1946 and 1956 of which the provisions are now deleted, may be inspected at the headquarters of the Institution.

George the Fifth, by the Grace of God of the United Kingdom of Great Britain and
   Ireland and of the British Dominions beyond the seas King, Defender of the Faith:
   to all to whom these presents shall come, greeting:

Whereas the Association or Institution incorporated under the Companies Acts, 1862 and 1867, and known as The Institution of Electrical Engineers hath petitioned Us for a Charter of Incorporation such as is in and by these Presents granted:
And Whereas we are minded to comply with the prayer of such Petition:

Now, therefore, We, by virtue of Our Royal Prerogative in the behalf, and of all other powers enabling Us so to do, of Our Special Grace certain knowledge and mere motion do hereby, for Us, Our Heirs and Successors, will, grant, direct, appoint, and declare to the said Association or Institution as follows:
1. The persons now members of the said Association or Institution known as The Institution of Electrical Engineers, and all such persons as may hereafter become members of the body corporate hereby constituted pursuant to or by virtue of the powers granted by these Presents, and their Successors, shall for ever hereafter (so long as they shall continue to be such members) be by virtue of these Presents one body corporate and politic by the name of 'The Institution of Electrical Engineers' and by the same name shall have perpetual succession and a Common Seal, with power to break, alter, and make anew the said seal from time to time at their will and pleasure, and by the same name shall and may implead, and be impleaded in all Courts, and in all manner of actions and suits, and shall have power to do all other matters and things incidental or appertaining to a body corporate.
2. We do also hereby, for Us, Our Heirs, and Successors, license, authorise and for ever hereafter enable The Institution of Electrical Engineers hereby incorporated, or any person or persons on its behalf, to acquire for the purposes of the Institution any

lands, tenements or hereditaments or any interest in any lands, tenements or hereditaments whatsoever within Our United Kingdom of Great Britain and Northern Ireland, and to hold the same in perpetuity or otherwise and from time to time (subject to all such consents as are by law required) to grant, demise, alienate, or otherwise dispose of the same or any part thereof.

3. (Deleted).

4. The objects and purposes for which The Institution of Electrical Engineers (hereinafter call 'the Institution') is hereby constituted are to promote the general advancement of electrical science and engineering and their applications and to facilitate the exchange of information and ideas on these subjects amongst the members of the Institution and otherwise and for that purpose—

(a) To hold meetings of the Institution for reading and discussing communications bearing upon electrical science or engineering, or the applications thereof, or upon subjects relating thereto.

(b) To hold or promote exhibitions of instruments, apparatus, machinery or other appliances connected with electrical science or engineering, or their applications.

(c) To print, publish, sell, lend or distribute the proceedings or reports of the Institution, or any papers, communications, works or treatises on electrical science or engineering or their applications, or subjects connected therewith, in the English or any foreign tongue, or any abstracts thereof, or extracts therefrom.

(d) To take charge of the books, pamphlets, publications and manuscripts known as the Ronalds Library, which are the subject of a deed of trust dated 24 June 1875, and to observe and perform the trusts of the said deed, and to add to the said Ronalds Library, and form, acquire, receive, hold and take charge of any supplemental or additional library of books, works or manuscripts on electrical science or engineering, or the applications thereof, or other subjects allied thereto.

(e) To make grants of money, books, apparatus, or otherwise for the purpose of promoting invention and research in electrical science or engineering, or their applications, or in subjects connected therewith.

(f) To do all other things incidental or conducive to the attainment of the said objects and purposes.

5. The Institution shall not engage in any trade or business or transaction with a view to the pecuniary gain or profit of the members thereof. No member shall have any personal claim on any property of the Institution and no part of the income or property of the Institution shall be paid or transferred directly or indirectly by way of dividend or bonus or otherwise howsoever by way of profit to the members of the Institution except in the case of and as a salaried officer of the Institution.

Provided that nothing herein or elsewhere contained shall prevent

(a) the payment by the Institution in good faith of reasonable and proper remuneration to any member of the Institution as an officer or servant of the Institution or to any such member in return for any services rendered to the Institution;

(b) the payment by the Institution of interest at a rate not exceeding 5 per centum per annum on money lent to the Institution by any such member or reasonable and proper rent for premises demised or let by any such member to the Institution; or

(c) the giving by the Institution to any such member of prizes whether in cash or otherwise and scholarships and exhibitions;

and the Institution shall have power to make all such payments and gifts as aforesaid.

6. There shall be a Council of the Institution consisting of such number of members, with such qualifications, and to be elected or constituted as such members of Council in such manner, and to hold office for such period, and on such terms as to re-election and otherwise, as the by-laws for the time being of the Institution shall direct.

7. Of the members of the said Council of the Institution one shall be the President, two shall be the Deputy-Presidents and two or more shall be the Vice-Presidents of the Institution. The said President, Deputy-Presidents and Vice-Presidents shall be elected in such manner, and shall hold office for such period, and on such terms as to re-election and otherwise, as the by-laws for the time being of the Institution shall direct.

8. The first President of the Institution shall be Llewelyn Birchall Atkinson and the first Vice-Presidents shall be William Ashcombe Chamen, William Henry Eccles, D.Sc., F.R.S., John Somerville Highfield and Alan Archibald Campbell Swinton, F.R.S.

The first Honorary Treasurer of the Institution shall be Sir James Lyne Devonshire, K.B.E.

The first members of the Council shall be the said President, Vice-Presidents and Honorary Treasurer the following Past-Presidents of the said Voluntary Association or Institution, namely: Alexander Siemens, Colonel Rookes Evelyn Bell Crompton, C.B., Sir Henry Christopher Mance, C.I.E., LL.D., James Swinburne, F.R.S., Sir John Gavey, C.B., Sir Richard Tetley Glazebrook, K.C.B., D.Sc., F.R.S., William Morris Mordey, Gisbert Kapp, M.Sc., Sebastian Ziani de Ferranti, D.Sc., Sir John Francis Cleverton Snell, Charles Pratt Sparks, C.B.E., Charles Henry Wordingham, C.B.E., and Roger Thomas Smith; the following Ordinary Members of Council, namely: Percy Ruskin Allen, O.B.E., Henry James Cash, Henry William Clothier, John Robert Cowie, Daniel Nicol Dunlop, Samuel Edgar Fedden, Ernest Arthur Gatehouse, Frank Gill, O.B.E., Philip Vassar Hunter, C.B.E., Edgar Walford Marchant, D.Sc., Albert Henry Weaver Marshall, Sir William Noble, Clifford Copland Paterson, O.B.E., Alexander Russell, D.Sc., Josiah Sayers, O.B.E., Philip Debell Tuckett, Charles Vernier and Burkewood Welbourn, and the following Chairmen and Past-Chairmen of local Sections of the said existing Association or Institution, namely: James Robert Beard, Albert George Bruty, William Cross, Arthur Ellis, Frank Forrest, Julius Frith, Charles Cornfield Garrard, Frank Graham, William Benison Hird, Charles James Jewell, William Cranswick Laidler, John Willoughby Meares, Arthur Joseph Newman, James Archibald Robertson, James Edmund Sayers, William Morrish Selvey and Richard Tanham. The said President, Vice-Presidents, Honorary Treasurer and members of the Council shall respectively hold office as such until the due election and coming into office of their successors in accordance with the bylaws of the Institution, but shall be respectively eligible, subject to such bylaws, for re-election if otherwise qualified.

9. The Institution shall have such officers, with such functions, tenure and terms of office, as the bylaws of the Institution may prescribe, and such other officers and servants as the Council of the Institution may from time to time appoint. The first Secretary of the Institution shall be Percy Fitz-Patrick Rowell.

10. The government and control of the Institution and its affairs shall be vested in the Council subject to the provisions of these Presents and to the bylaws of the Institution. The business of the Council shall be conducted in such a manner as the Council may from time to time prescribe.

11. Unless and until the bylaws of the Institution shall otherwise provide there shall be seven classes of members of the Institution termed respectively Honorary Fellows, Fellows, Members, Companions, Associate Members, Associates and Students of whom the Honorary Fellows, who when elected Honorary Fellows were already Fellows or Members or who prior to 1 December 1966 were already Members or Associate Members, Fellows and Members shall be known as Corporate members and all others shall be known as noncorporate members.

The members of the said existing Association or Institution known as The Institution of Electrical Engineers, who by virtue of these Presents become members of the Institution, shall be deemed to have entered the Institution as members of the same class as that to which they belonged in the said existing Association or Institution.

12. The qualifications, method and terms of admission, privileges and obligations, including liability to expulsion or suspension of members of each of the said seven classes respectively, shall be such as the bylaws for the time being of the Institution shall direct.

13. The Council shall alone have power to decide conclusively respecting each person proposed for or seeking admission to any class of membership of the Institution whether he has or has not fulfilled such conditions as are applicable to his case.

14. An Honorary Fellow shall be entitled to the exclusive use after his name of the designation 'Hon.F.I.E.E.'; a Fellow of the designation 'F.I.E.E.'; a Member of the designation 'M.I.E.E.'; a Companion of the designation 'Companion I.E.E.'; and an Associate Member to whom bylaw 14(a)(i) applies the designation 'A.M.I.E.E.'.

15. Every person being at any time a corporate member of the Institution may so long as he shall be a corporate member take and use the name or title of or describe himself as a Chartered Electrical Engineer.

16. The meetings of the Institution shall be of such classes and shall be held for such purposes as may from time to time be prescribed by the bylaws of the Institution, and the rights of the several classes of members of the Institution of attending and voting at the said meeting shall be such or subject to such restrictions as may be so prescribed.

17. The corporate members or the majority of such members present in person or by proxy and voting at any duly convened Special General Meeting of corporate members with respect to which notice has been given of the matters to be taken into consideration thereat, shall have power from time to time to make such bylaws of the Institution as to them shall seem requisite and convenient for the regulation, government and advantage of the Institution, its members and property, and for the furtherance of the objects and purposes of the Institution, and from time to time to revoke, alter or amend any bylaw or bylaws theretofore made so that the same be not repugnant to these Presents or to the Laws and Statutes of this Our Realm; Provided that no such bylaw, revocation, alteration or amendment shall take effect until the same has been allowed by the Lords of Our Privy Council of which allowance a Certificate under the hand of the Clerk of Our Privy Council shall be conclusive evidence.

18. The first bylaws to be made under these Presents shall be made by the corporate members of the Institution within the period of six months from the date of these Presents, unless the Lords of Our Privy Council shall see fit to extend such period, of which extension the Certificate of the Clerk of Our Privy Council shall be conclusive evidence.

19. Pending the making and approval of the bylaws to be made under these Presents but no longer, the Articles of Association of the said existing Association or Institution known as The Institution of Electrical Engineers shall be the bylaws of the Institution, and shall have effect as though the Institution, its officers and members had therein been referred to throughout in lieu of the said existing Association or Institution, its officers and members.

20. The property and moneys of the said existing Association or Institution known as The Institution of Electrical Engineers (including any property and moneys held by them as trustees) shall from 15 August 1921 become and be deemed to be the property and moneys of the Institution.

21. The Council of the Institution may by a resolution in that behalf passed at any meeting of such Council by a majority of not less than two thirds of the members of such Council present and voting (being an absolute majority of the whole number of the members of such Council entitled to vote at meetings thereof) and confirmed at a Special General Meeting of corporate members of the Institution held not less than one month nor more than four months afterwards by a majority of not less than two thirds of the corporate members present in person or by proxy and voting amend or add to this Our Charter and any such amendment or addition shall when allowed by Us, Our Heirs or Successors in Council become effectual so that this Our Charter shall thenceforward continue and operate as though it had been originally granted and made accordingly. This provision shall apply to this Our Charter as amended or added to in manner aforesaid.

22. We do hereby revoke the provisions of the Supplemental Charters of the Institution of 1946 and 1956.

23. And We do hereby, for Us, Our Heirs, and Successors, grant and declare that these Our Letters Patent, or the enrolment or exemplification thereof, shall be in all things good, firm, valid, and effectual, according to the true intent and meaning of the same, and shall be taken, construed and adjudged in all Our Courts or elsewhere in the most favourable and beneficial sense and for the best advantage of the said Institution, any misrecital, nonrecital, omission, defect, imperfection, matter or thing whatsoever notwithstanding.

In Witness whereof We have caused these Our letters to be made patent.

Witness Ourself at Westminster, the fifteenth day of August in the year of our Lord One thousand nine hundred and twenty-one and in the twelfth year of Our Reign.

Warrent under the King's Sign Manual.

SCHUSTER

Bylaws of The Institution of Electrical Engineers

Adopted by resolution dated 23 March 1922, and allowed by the Lords of His Majesty's Most Honourable Privy Council on the 1st day of June 1922. Amended by resolutions dated 28 February 1924 (amendment allowed 20 March 1924), 9 May 1929 (amendment allowed, 2 August 1929), 23 November 1944 (amendment allowed 16 February 1945), 5 June 1947 (amendment allowed 10 September 1947), 19 October 1950 (amendment allowed 12 December 1950), 15 May 1952 (amendment allowed 26 August 1952), 22 March 1956 (amendment allowed 3 August 1956), 9 April 1959 (amendment allowed 2 September 1959), 2 November 1961 (amendment allowed 12 February 1962), 30 June 1966 (amendment allowed 11 November with effect from 1 December 1966), 14 October 1971 (amendment allowed 26 April with effect from 1 October 1972), 14 December 1972 (amendment allowed 30 July 1973), 22 May 1975 (amendment allowed 15 October 1975), 18 May 1978 (amendment allowed 20 November 1978), 22 May 1980 (amendment allowed 22 July 1980), 21 May 1981 (amendment allowed 2 July 1981), 26 May 1983 (amendment allowed 21 December 1983).

Definitions and special provisions

1. In these bylaws except where the context forbids words importing males are intended to include females and words implying the singular number are intended to include the plural number, and vice versa.

'the Institution' means The Institution of Electrical Engineers incorporated by Royal Charter dated 15 August 1921.

'the predecessors of the Institution' means The Institution of Electrical Engineers incorporated under the Companies Acts, 1862 and 1867.

'the Charter' means the Royal Charter of the Institution dated 15 August 1921, and any amendments or additions thereto and any Supplemental or other Charter of the Institution for the time being in force.

'abroad' means outside Great Britain, Northern Ireland, the Isle of Man, and the Channel Islands.

'the examination regulations' means the regulations made by the Council pursuant to bylaw 67(b)(i).

'the training regulations' means the regulations made by the Council pursuant to bylaw 67(b)(ii).

'the Institution examination' means the examination bearing the name which is prescribed in the examination regulations.

2. For the purposes of bylaws 45, 46, 47 and 48, any period of service as President, Vice-President, or ordinary member of the Council of the predecessors of the Institution shall be deemed to be service in a similar capacity with the Institution.

Membership

3. The Institution shall consist of:

Honorary Fellows
Fellows
Members
Companions
Associate Members
Associates
Students

Of the above

(a) Honorary Fellows who, when elected Honorary Fellows, were already Fellows or Members, or who, prior to 1 December 1966, were already Members or Associate Members

(b) Fellows, and

(c) Members

shall be known as corporate members, and all others shall be known as non-corporate members.

4. The members of the several classes referred to in the Charter, and such other persons as shall be admitted in accordance with these bylaws, and none others, shall be members of the Institution (either as Honorary Fellows, Fellows, Members, Companions, Associate Members, Associates or Students, as the case may be), and be entered on the register as such. A member of any class who changes his name shall thereupon inform the Secretary in writing of that fact, stating his new name.

5. The rights and privileges of every member of any class shall be personal to himself, and shall not be transferable or transmissible by his own act, or by operation of law.

6. No Honorary Fellow, Fellow, Member, Companion, Associate Member, Associate or Student shall, by reason of being a member of the Institution, be entitled

to any rights or privileges other than those which, by these bylaws, attach to the specific class of members of the Institution to which he belongs, and wherever the term 'Fellow' is herein used without qualification, it shall (except where otherwise expressly mentioned) be taken to include such Honorary Fellows as are corporate members, but to exclude such Honorary Fellows as are not corporate members, Members, Companions, Associate Members, Associates and Students; and wherever the term 'Member' is herein used without qualification, it shall (except where otherwise expressly mentioned) be taken to exclude Honorary Fellows, Fellows, Companions, Associate Members, Associates and Students.

7. The Institution may admit such other persons as may be hereafter qualified and elected in that behalf as Fellows, Members, Companions, Associate Members, Associates and Students, respectively, and such persons shall sign the form A in that behalf contained in the schedule hereto, or such form to the like effect as may from time to time be authorised by the Council.

Abbreviated titles and description of membership

8. (a) An Honorary Fellow shall be entitled to the exclusive use after his name of the designation 'Hon. F.I.E.E.'; a Fellow of the designation 'F.I.E.E.'; a Member of the designation 'M.I.E.E.'; a Companion of the designation 'Companion I.E.E.'; and an Associate Member to whom bylaw 14(a)(i) applies the designation 'A.M.I.E.E'.

(b) Every corporate member is entitled to the use of the style or title of Chartered Electrical Engineer for so long as he shall be a corporate member. In using that description after his name he may associate with it the designation of the class in the Institution to which he belongs, stated in accordance with the following abbreviated forms, namely Hon.F.I.E.E., F.I.E.E., or M.I.E.E. as the case may be.

(c) A corporate member practising

 (i) under the title of, or as an officer or employee of, a limited company authorised to carry on the business of an electrical engineer in all or any of its branches, or

 (ii) in partnership with any person who is not a corporate member of the Institution under the title of a firm

shall not use or permit to be used after the title of any such company or firm the designation 'Chartered Electrical Engineer' or 'Chartered Electrical Engineers' or describe or permit the description of such company or firm in any way as 'Chartered Electrical Engineer' or 'Chartered Electrical Engineers'.

(d) No person shall adopt or describe himself by any other description or abbreviation to indicate the class to which he belongs than is provided in this bylaw for such class.

Diplomas and certificates

9. Subject to such regulations and on payment of such fees as the Council may from time to time prescribe, the Council may issue to any Honorary Fellow, corporate member or Companion a diploma under seal, and to any Associate Member a certificate, showing the class to which he belongs. Every such diploma or certificate shall remain the property of, and shall on demand be returned to, the Institution.

Honorary Fellows

10. An Honorary Fellow shall be:

(a) A person who is distinguished by his work in electrical science or engineering, or

(b) A distinguished person whom the Institution desires to honour for services rendered to the Institution or whose association therewith is of benefit to the Institution.

Honorary Fellows shall be elected by the Council, and every such election shall be announced at the next ordinary meeting of the Institution. Not more than two Honorary Fellows shall be elected in any one year except that there may be elected not more frequently than once in each period of three successive years, dating from 1 January 1966, an additional Honorary Fellow who is not at the time of election a member of any class of the Institution. The number of Honorary Fellows coming under paragraph (b) above shall not at any time exceed a total of five.

Fellows

11. Every candidate for election or transfer to the class of Fellows shall satisfy the Council that he

(a) has been in the class of Members of the Institution for a period of at least three years or such shorter period as the Council may in any particular case or class of cases decide, provided that, in the case of a candidate who possesses the qualifications for election to the class of Members, the Council may waive the stipulation as to his having been in the class of Members, and

(b) has had experience involving superior responsibility for at least five years in the field of electrical science and engineering and their applications

and he is, disregarding temporary unemployment, engaged in or associated with any branch of engineering.

Members

12. Every candidate for election or transfer to the class of Members shall satisfy the Council that he

(a) is at least 25 years of age, and

(b) has attained a standard of general education and has received further education as an electrical engineer or otherwise which satisfy the requirements of the examination regulations, and

(c) has undergone training which satisfies the requirements of the training regulations, and

(d) has had not less than two years' experience in a responsible position in the field of electrical science and engineering and their applications in addition to any such experience which may have been accepted in satisfaction of (c) above;

and the aggregate of his engineering education, training and responsible experience is not less than seven years; and he is, disregarding temporary unemployment, engaged in or associated with any branch of engineering.

Companions

13. Every candidate for election to the class of Companions shall be a person who, not being eligible for election as a Fellow, satisfies the Council that he has rendered important services to electrical science or engineering or their applications or is so connected therewith that his admission as a Companion would conduce to the interests of the Institution.

Associate Members

14.(a) Every candidate for election or transfer to the class of Associate Members shall satisfy the Council either

   (i) that he has attained a standard of general education and has received further education which satisfy the requirements of the examination regulations, or

   (ii) that he was, prior to 1 December 1966, a member of the class of Associates.

(b) Until the end of the calendar year in which he attains the age of 30 years an

Associate Member shall be entitled to the same privileges as a Student, and thereafter to such privileges and for such period as the Council may prescribe.

Associates
15. Every candidate for election or transfer to the class of Associates shall satisfy the Council
(a) that his is at least 21 years of age, and
(b) that he is of good education, and
(c) that, by his connection with engineering, the sciences or arts or otherwise, his association with the Institution will conduce to the general advancement of electrical science or engineering or their applications.

Students
16. Every candidate for election to the class of Students shall have attained the age of 17 years, but not the age of 28 years, and shall satisfy the Council
(a) that he is undergoing a regular course of further education approved by the Council for the purposes of this bylaw, and
(b) that he intends to satisfy the requirements for admission to the class of Associate Members.
17. (revoked)
18. Every Student who satisfies the requirements for admission to the class of Associate Members shall be transferred by the Council to that class unless he satisfies the Council that he is qualified for election to the class of Members. At the end of the calendar year in which a Student attains the age of 28 years, he shall, unless the Council have decided otherwise, cease to be a Student.

Election
19. The election of candidates for membership of the Institution in any class shall be by the Council.
20. Candidates for election shall be proposed and supported as provided hereunder, from personal knowledge and in writing, according to a form approved by the Council:
(a) Any person desirous of election as a Fellow or Companion shall be proposed by two Fellows and supported by three corporate members other than the proposing Fellows.
(b) Any person desirous of election as a Member shall be proposed by two corporate members and supported by two Chartered Engineers other than the proposing corporate members.
(c) Any person desirous of election as an Associate Member or as an Associate or as a Student shall be proposed by one corporate member who shall in the case of a person desirous of election as a Student sign a declaration that he has personal knowledge of the means by which the person to whom such proposal relates proposes to satisfy the requirements for admission to the class of Associate Members.
For the purposes of this bylaw all members of the Council shall be deemed to be Fellows.
Provided that
(d) any person desirous of election as a Fellow or as a Companion who resides abroad may be proposed by two corporate members and supported by three Chartered Engineers or persons in a class of membership of a national engineering society or body established in the country in which the candidate works or resides and for the time being approved by the Council for the purposes of this bylaw

(e) any person desirous of election as a Member who resides abroad may be proposed by two corporate members and supported by two Chartered Engineers or persons in a class of membership of a national engineering society or body established in the country in which the candidate works or resides and for the time being approved by the Council for the purposes of this bylaw.

21. Proposals for election shall be delivered to the Secretary, who shall lay before the Council such as are duly completed. The Council shall cause the full names of candidates for election as Fellow, Member or Companion to be published with an intimation that they are candidates for election, stating to which class, and that after the expiration of one month from the date of publication their applications for election will be considered by the Council in the light of any information that may have come to their knowledge. The Council may, without assigning any reason, withhold their approval from any candidate.

The Council may require any candidate to attend an interview conducted on their behalf in order that he may the better satisfy them that he possesses the requisite qualifications for admission, and shall fix the fees (if any) to be paid or deposited by candidates for interview.

22. A candidate elected shall be admitted a Fellow, Member, Companion, Associate Member, Associate or Student as the case may be on payment of such entrance fee and annual subscription as the bylaws may prescribe. Until admitted a candidate shall not be entitled to any of the rights or privileges of membership.

23. Unless the Council decide otherwise any member of any class who is the subject of a country or state at war with Her Majesty or her successors shall *ipso facto* cease to be a member of the Institution and shall not be eligible for re-election to membership of the Institution so long as the aforesaid state of war shall continue and for such further period thereafter as the Council may determine.

Transfer from one class to another

24. The transfer of a member from one class to another shall be by the Council. Subject to bylaw 18, every candidate for transfer from one class to another class shall be proposed and supported in the manner prescribed in bylaw 20 for election to the class to which he is desirous of being transferred.

25. Subject to bylaw 18, bylaws 21 and 22 shall *mutatis mutandis* apply to the transfer of a member from one class to another in like manner as they apply to election to membership.

Entrance fees, annual subscriptions and life compositions

26. Fellows and Members shall on election as such and non-corporate members shall on transfer pay an entrance fee equal to the annual subscription payable under bylaw 27 by the class to which they are elected or transferred at the date of their election or transfer as the case may be.

The Council shall have power at any time to prescribe that the respective entrance fees for any of them shall be less than those prescribed above.

27. Subject to the right of compounding hereinafter referred to, the following annual subscriptions shall be payable by the members of the Institution.

The change in the rate of subscription consequent upon the attainment of the ages specified above shall take effect from the 1st day of January next following the day on which the specified age is attained.

Provided that the Council shall have power at any time to prescribe that the respective annual subscriptions or any of them shall be less than those set out over.

	Age	UK and Abroad £
Fellows, Companions and Members	45 and over	29.00
Fellows, Companions and Members under 45: Associate Members, Associates and Students	Over 40	21.00
	35–40	18.50
	29–34	16.00
	26–28	12.50
	23–25	8.50
	21–22	6.00
	Under 21★	3.00

★ and full-time students preparing to satisfy the Institution's examination requirements.

Provided also that notwithstanding anything hereinbefore in this bylaw contained the Council may from time to time by a resolution in the behalf passed at any meeting of the Council and confirmed at a special general meeting of corporate members of the Institution held not less than one month nor more than four months afterwards by a majority of the corporate members present and voting increase all or any of the annual subscriptions set out above by such sums (not being more in the case of any annual subscription than one half of the amount thereof) as may be specified in the resolution of the Council.

Note: The powers conferred in bylaw 27 to reduce and to increase all or any of the annual subscriptions were exercised in 1981, 1982 and 1983.

From 1 January 1985, the fees payable are as follows:

	Age	UK and Abroad £
Fellows, Companions and Members	45 and over	37.00
Fellows, Companions and Members under 45: Associate Members, Associates and Students	Over 40	28.00
	35–40	26.00
	29–34	22.00
	26–28	17.00
	23–25	12.00
	21–22	8.00
	Under 21★	4.00

★ and full-time students preparing to satisfy the Institution's examination requirements.

28. Every member of any class not being an Honorary Fellow who has not compounded, and whose place of residence is abroad, shall pay the annual subscription shown in the second column of bylaw 27 for the class to which he belongs, in respect of each complete calendar year of such residence abroad, provided that his address in the address register of the Institution is one which is abroad.

29. The annual subscriptions shall be due on the 1st day of January in each year for the year commencing on that day.

30. Members of any class elected before the 1st day of July in any year shall pay the annual subscription for that calendar year, and those elected on or after the 1st day of July in any year shall for that calendar year pay half such annual subscription.

Provided that in the case of any Fellow, Member, Companion, Associate Member, Associate and Student elected in the last two months of any calendar year who shall elect to pay his first subscription at the full rate, such first subscription shall cover both the remainder of the year of his election and the next succeeding year.

31. Every member of any class residing abroad shall be liable to pay, in addition to his annual subscription, a sum to be fixed by the Council from time to time to defray the expense of posting the publications of the Institution to him.

32. Any member of any class (except Associate Members and Students) may compound for his annual subscription by the payment to the Institution in one sum of a composition calculated in such manner as the Council may from time to time determine.

33. Subject to bylaw 34, when any member of any class who has previously compounded is transferred from the one class to another class, he shall pay either such additional composition as the Council may determine or in place of such additional composition an annual subscription equal to the difference between the annual subscription of the class to which he is transferred and the annual subscription on which the previously paid composition was based.

34. Any Fellow, Member, Companion or Associate Member who compounded with the predecessors of the Institution before the 31st day of December 1912 by the payment of forty-two pounds shall not be required to pay any further composition or annual subscription.

35. Any member of any class who has compounded by payment to the predecessors of the Institution shall have the same rights and privileges as if he had compounded by payment to the Institution.

36. Any member of any class whose annual subscription remains unpaid after the 31st day of March shall not be entitled, before he has paid his subscription in full, to exercise or benefit from any of the rights or privileges of membership.

37. Any member of any class whose annual subscription remains unpaid after 30 June in any year may by resolution of the Council be excluded from the Institution, and he shall thereupon cease to be a member and his name shall be removed from the Register; but such removal shall not relieve him from his liability for the payment of the arrears of subscriptions due from him calculated up to the 31st day of December in the year of his exclusion.

38. Any member of any class may retire from the Institution by sending his resignation in writing to the Secretary, after payment of all the subscriptions due from him, including that for the current year.

39. The Council may readmit to membership in the appropriate class any person whose membership has terminated from any cause provided that he satisfies the Council that his is worthy of readmission and pays such amounts in respect of entrance fee and arrears of subscriptions as the Council may determine.

In the event of the Council deciding to refuse readmission in any particular case, they may do so without assigning any reason.

40. Where in their opinion it is desirable to do so, the Council may in any particular case or class of case, including those arising under reciprocal arrangements entered into with kindred bodies, reduce or remit any entrance fee, annual subscription or life composition, or arrears of annual subscriptions.

Expulsion and other disciplinary action

41.(a) For the purposes of this bylaw 'improper conduct' shall mean:
  (i) the making of any false representation in applying for election or transfer to any class of membership of the Institution, or

(ii) any breach of these bylaws or of any regulation or rule or direction made or given thereunder, or

(iii) any conduct injurious to the Institution.

(b) In case any member of any class shall be adjudicated bankrupt or convicted of any criminal offence which in the opinion of the Council makes him unfit to be a member, the Council may decide that his name shall be removed from the register of the Institution, and the Secretary shall communicate such decision to such member according to the form B in the schedule.

(c) Any allegation of improper conduct which may be brought before the Council properly vouched for and suported by evidence shall be investigated and dealt with by the Council or by a committee or committees appointed by the Council for the purpose pursuant to bylaw 41(d). If a member of any class shall be found by the Council or a committee so appointed to have been guilty of improper conduct, the Council or the said committee may order him to be expelled from the Institution, or that his membership be suspended for any period, or that he be reprimanded or admonished. If the Council or the said committee shall order that such member be expelled, the Secretary shall communicate any such decision to such member according to the form C in the schedule. Such member shall have the right of appeal therefrom to a Committee consisting of three past Presidents of the Institution nominated for the purpose by the President for the time being of the Institution. Notice in writing of such appeal shall be given within fourteen days from the date of the said decision to the Secretary of the Institution. The decision of the Committee of appeal shall be final and conclusive. The Council shall have power to extend the time within which notice of appeal may be given.

(d) The Council may make, vary and rescind regulations for the purpose of:

  (i) setting up a committee or committees to investigate and adjudicate upon any complaint or allegation of improper conduct on the part of a member of any class;

  (ii) determining the constitution and membership and regulating the procedure of any such committee; and

  (iii) dealing with any other matters which may be relevant to any such committee or its functions.

The said regulations shall be designed to secure that any complaint or allegation of improper conduct shall be properly investigated and adjudicated by an impartial tribunal consisting either wholly or partly of members of the Council; that before being called on to deal with any complaint or allegation of improper conduct on his own part a member shall know what is the complaint or allegation; that before being found guilty of such conduct the member shall be given a full and fair opportunity of being heard and of calling witnesses and cross-examining any other witness testifying before the tribunal; that in all other respects the investigation shall be made and the proceedings conducted and the decision reached in accordance with natural justice; and that any decision shall be made known to members of the Institution and others so far as may appear to be necessary or desirable with a view to the furtherance of the objects of the Institution. No such regulation, variation or rescission shall be in any way repugnant to the Charter or bylaws or take effect until the same has been approved at a special general meeting of corporate members.

Professional conduct

42.(a) Every corporate member shall at all times so order conduct as to uphold the dignity and reputation of his profession, and so safeguard the public interest in matters of safety and health and otherwise. He shall exercise his professional skill and judgement to the best of his ability and discharge his professional responsibilities with integrity.

(b) Every member of any class shall at all times so order his conduct as to uphold the dignity and reputation of the Institution, and act with fairness and integrity towards all persons with whom his work is connected and towards other members.
(c) For the purpose of ensuring the fulfilment of the requirements of paragraphs (a) and (b) of this bylaw, but without prejudice to their generality, the Council may make, vary and rescind rules to be observed by members of all classes with regard to their conduct in any respect which may be relevant to their positions or intended positions as members of the Institution, and may publish directions or pronouncements as to specific conduct which is to be regarded as proper or as improper as the case may be. No such rule, variation or rescission shall be in any way repugnant to the Charter or bylaws or take effect until the same has been approved at a special general meeting of corporate members.

Officers
43. There shall be a President, two Deputy-Presidents, six Vice-Presidents, an Honorary Treasurer and a Secretary of the Institution.

Constitution and election of the Council
44. The Council shall consist of:
The President
the Deputy-Presidents
the five past Presidents who have most recently held the office of President and who are available to serve
the Vice-Presidents
the Honorary Treasurer
not less then 43 and not more than 50 ordinary members of Council as determined by the Council from time to time
three representatives of each Centre having, on 1 March prior to the date on which such representatives are to take office, a membership of over 3000, two representatives of each Centre having on the date aforesaid a membership not less than 1250 and not more than 3000, and one representative of each Centre having on the date aforesaid a membership below 1250, such representatives being corporate members chosen annually by the committee of each Centre to hold office from 1 October next following, except that no such representative shall serve on the Council for more than three years in succession
the Chairman and the Deputy-Chairman and the immediate past Chairman of each Division, or in place of the immediate past Chairman any other past Chairman chosen by the board of the Division, except that no Chairman or Deputy-Chairman or past Chairman of a Division shall serve on the Council in any or all of those capacities for more than three years in succession
the Chairman of each board other than the board of a Division set up under the provisions of bylaw 93, who shall not serve in that capacity on the Council for more then three years in succession
all of whose offices shall be honorary and without remuneration
provided that any member of Council who shall have been elected for a term of three years' service to a committee of the Council appointed under the provisions of bylaw 60 and designated by the Council for the purposes of this bylaw shall continue his membership of the Council until the expiry of his term of service on the committee so designated.
Any cases of doubt or difficulty as to eligibility for or retirement from office shall be decided by the Council.

The President

45. The President shall be chosen by the Council from those who are or have been Deputy-Presidents, failing whom from those corporate members who are or have been Vice-Presidents. He shall retire each year on the 30th day of September and no person shall hold the office of President for more than three years in succession.

The Deputy-Presidents

45A. Each Deputy-President shall be a Fellow; the period of office of a Deputy-President shall be two years and he shall be eligible for re-election, but no person shall hold the office of Deputy-President for more than four years in all.

The Vice-Presidents

46. The Vice-Presidents shall be Honorary Fellows, Fellows or Companions. The period of office of a Vice-President shall be three years, and he shall be eligible for re-election but no person shall hold the office of Vice-President for more than three years in succession and six years in all.

The Honorary Treasurer

47. The Honorary Treasurer shall be an Honorary Fellow, a Fellow or a Companion, and he shall be chosen from those who are or have been ordinary members of Council. He shall retire each year on the 30th day of September, and no person shall hold the office of Honorary Treasurer for more than three years in succession.

Ordinary members of Council

48. Subject always to bylaw 44 and until the Council otherwise decide, of the ordinary members of Council, 24 shall be chosen from the class of Fellows, 12 from the class of Members, one from the class of Companions and six from the class of Associate Members.

The period of office of an ordinary member of Council shall be three years, and no person shall hold that office for more than three years in succession; and no person who has previously held office as a member of the Council in any capacity shall hold office as an ordinary member of Council unless at least one year shall have elapsed since his last period of office.

Nominations for election to the Council

49. (a) Not later than the 21st day of May in each year the Council shall send in respect of vacancies about to occur on the 30th day of September next following

  (i) to each corporate member and Associate Member to whom bylaw 14(a)(ii) applies a list of duly qualified persons whom they nominate as candidates for election to fill the vacancies about to occur in the membership of the Council which may be filled by Honorary Fellows, corporate members or Companions

  (ii) to each Associate Member a list of duly qualified persons whom they nominate as candidates for election to fill the vacancies about to occur in the office of ordinary member of Council to be filled from the class of Associate Members

  (iii) to each Companion the name of each duly qualified person whom they nominate as a candidate for election to fill any vacancy about to occur in the office of ordinary member of Council to be filled from the class of Companions.

(b) The number of persons nominated by the Council as candidates for election to fill vacancies in the office of ordinary member of Council from each of the several classes of Fellows, Members and Associate Members shall exceed the number of vacancies reserved by bylaw 48 to be filled from each of these classes.

(c) In the list of persons nominated by the Council as candidates for election to fill the vacancies in the office of ordinary members of Council, not less than half of the names shall be those of persons who have not previously served on the Council in any capacity, but a person who has only served in one or more of the offices of Chairman of a Centre and as a corporate member chosen pursuant to bylaw 44 or of Chairman, past Chairman and Deputy-Chairman of a Division or of any other board, or Chairman and past Chairman of a former specialised Section for a total period of not more than three years shall for the purposes of this bylaw be deemed to be a person who has not previously served on the Council.

50. Not later than 21 days after the issue of the Council's list any ten corporate members (but no more than ten) may nominate any other duly qualified person as a candidate for election to fill any vacancy other than that in the office of President or in the office of ordinary member of Council to be filled by an Associate Member, and any ten corporate members or Companions (but no more than ten) may nominate any qualified Companion as a candidate for election to fill a vacancy as ordinary member of Council, and any ten Associate Members (but no more than ten) may nominate any qualified Associate Member as a candidate for election to fill a vacancy as ordinary member of Council, by delivering such nomination in writing to the Secretary together with the written consent of such person to accept office if elected, but each such nominator shall be debarred from nominating any other person for the same election.

Ballot for election to the Council

51. Not later than the 1st day of July in each year or such later date as the Council may approve, the Council shall send to each corporate member and Associate Member to whom bylaw 14(a)(ii) applies a ballot paper containing the names of all persons duly nominated to fill the vacancies which may be filled by Honorary Fellows, corporate members or Companions and to each Associate Member a ballot paper containing the names of all persons in the class of Associate Members duly nominated in the like manner and to each Companion a ballot paper containing the names of all persons in the class of Companions duly nominated in the like manner stating which persons are nominated by the Council, giving the names of the Fellows or Members or Associate Members or Companions by whom every other person (if any) is nominated and being in other respects in such form as the Council shall prescribe. Provided that if the candidates nominated for any class of vacancy are not more in number than the vacancies of that class the persons so nominated shall be deemed to be duly elected and there shall be no ballot with respect to that class of vacancy.

The Council may make, vary and rescind regulations governing the conduct of the ballot subject always to the provisions of the Charter and bylaws. No such regulation, variation or rescission shall take effect until the same has been approved at a special general meeting of corporate members. The persons elected pursuant to the regulations shall take office on the 1st day of October next following.

51A. In the event of the death after the close of nominations and before the next following 1st day of October of a candidate for election to the office of Deputy-President, Vice-President or Honorary Treasurer or of the member elected to fill any of those offices the ballot for that office shall be void, and the Council shall appoint a duly qualified member to fill the office, and the person so appointed shall take office as if he had been duly elected by ballot.

In the event of the death after the close of nominations and before the last day for the return of ballot papers of a candidate for election as an ordinary member of Council the deceased candidate shall be deemed not to have been nominated. If in that event there shall not remain as candidates as many Fellows, Members, Companions and Associate Members as are to be elected, or in the event of the death after election and before the next following 1st day of October of a member elected an ordinary member of Council, the Council shall appoint such number of members of the appropriate class as may be required to fill the vacancies, and the member or members so appointed shall take office as if he or they had been duly elected by ballot.

Vacancies

52. The members of Council whose terms of office would otherwise expire on the 30th day of September in any year shall in all cases continue in office until others are elected in their place.

53. The office of a member of the Council shall *ipso facto* be vacated

(a) if he become bankrupt or of unsound mind, or

(b) if by notice in writing to the Institution he resigns his office, or

(c) if he ceases to be a member of any class of the Institution, or

(d) if without leave of the Council he absent himself from more than half the meetings of the Council held in any session, and the Council resolve that his office be vacated, or

(e) if a resolution that he vacate his office be passed at a special general meeting of corporate members and Associate Members to whom bylaw 14(a)(ii) applies by a majority of not less than two-thirds of the corporate members and Associate Members to whom bylaw 14(a)(ii) applies present and voting.

54. Vacancies in the offices of President, Deputy-President, Vice-President, Honorary Treasurer, and ordinary member of Council, other than those arising under bylaws 45, 46, 47 and 48, may be filled by the Council, and the name of each person selected shall be announced at the next ordinary meeting of the Insititution. The Council shall determine the period for which the person so chosen shall hold office provided that such period shall not be longer than the vacating member of Council would in the ordinary course have retained office, and any period of office so served shall not be taken into account in computing the period of office under the provisions of bylaws 45, 46, 47 and 48.

55. The Council shall direct and manage the property and affairs of the Institution in accordance with the Charter and the bylaws of the Institution and may exercise all such powers of the Institution as may be exercised by the Institution, and which are not hereby or by the Charter required to be exercised by the Institution in general meeting.

56. The Institution building held on lease from the Duchy of Lancaster shall not be sold or disposed of except with the sanction of a special general meeting of corporate members and of Associate Members to whom bylaw 14(a)(ii) applies.

57. The Council shall meet as often as the business of the Institution may require and may act notwithstanding any vacancy in their body. At every meeting of the Council seven corporate members shall constitute a quorum. The President or the Deputy-Presidents or any two Vice-Presidents or any three members of the Council may, and the Secretary shall, on the request of such officer or officers or members, convene a meeting of the Council.

58. At any meeting of the Council, each member of Council present shall have one vote and if there be an equality of votes the Chairman shall have a second, or casting

vote. Provided that, at any meeting of the Council at which more than one representative of a Centre chosen by the committee of that Centre under the provisions of bylaw 44 shall be present, only one of such members shall be competent to vote. The Chairman my direct, or any two members present may demand, that the voting shall be by a secret ballot.

59. On the demand of any five members of Council present at any meeting of the Council, any resolution of the Council passed at such meeting shall be adjourned to the next meeting for further consideration, and in such a case the resolution shall not become effective unless it be confirmed by a majority at such next meeting. Provided always that the consideration of such resolution shall not be further adjourned at such next meeting except by a resolution of the Council.

60. The Council may appoint committees chosen from their own body and where special circumstances prevail may include therein one or more members of the Institution who have been members of the Council. Committees so appointed may be designated committeess of the Council. The Council may also appoint committees for special purposes consisting of members of Council and others. The Council may delegate to committees appointed under this bylaw such powers as they may prescribe.

61. The Council shall cause to be kept proper and sufficient accounts of the capital, funds, receipts and expenditure of the Institution, so that the true financial state and condition of the Institution may be at all times exhibited by such accounts.

62. The financial year of the Institution shall end on the 31st day of December in each year; and the accounts of the Institution shall be made up each year to that date, and, after having been approved by the Council and examined and found correct by an auditor or auditors, shall be laid before the annual general meeting next following.

63. The appointment, powers and duties of the auditor or auditors shall be regulated as nearly as may be and with the necessary modifications in accordance with the provisions of Sections 159 to 162 inclusive of the Companies Act, 1948, as amended by Sections 13 and 14 of the Companies Act, 1967 or with any statutory modification thereof for the time being in force, as if the Institution were a company registered under those Acts.

64. The Council shall pay to the Secretary and to all persons employed under him such salaries, wages, or remuneration as the Council shall from time to time think proper, and the Council shall make provision for and grant such pensions to them after their retirement from the service of the Institution as the Council may think proper.

65. The Council shall arrange for the publication, in any manner which they may deem advisable, of such papers, documents, and publications as may be considered by the Council to be likely to advance electrical knowledge and the objects of the Institution.

66. The Council shall prescribe such rules and regulations in reference to the Ronalds Library, and the inspection thereof, as to them may seem reasonable, and generally they shall do everything and execute all such instruments as may be necessary in the judgment of the Council for giving full and complete effect to the trust deed affecting the Ronalds Library.

67.(a) The Council may at any time cause examinations to be held for the purpose of testing the qualifications of candidates for election or transfer to any class of membership and shall from time to time define the subjects to be comprised in such examinations and shall fix the fees to be paid or deposited by candidates for examination.

(b) The Council may make, vary and rescind regulations for all or any of the following purposes, subject always to the provisions of the Charter and bylaws for the time being in force:
  (i) to establish by examination or otherwise the educational requirements to be satisfied by candidates for election, or transfer, to any class of membership
  (ii) to establish the training requirements to be satisfied by candidates for election, or transfer, to any class of membership.

68. (revoked)

69. The Council may at any time cause examinations to be held for the purpose of testing the proficiency and knowledge of persons in the applications of electricity. The Council may grant certificates on the results of such examinations, and shall fix the fees to be paid or deposited in respect thereof.

70. The Council may, upon receipt of a request to that effect from any society with objects kindred to those of the Institution, arrange for the union, alliance, or incorporation of such society with the Institution; and may also if they think fit remit or reduce the entrance fees of the members of such society at the time of union, alliance, or incorporation; provided that no such union, alliance, or incorporation shall be effective unless it is sanctioned by a special general meeting of corporate members and of Associate Members to whom bylaw 14(a)(ii) applies.

The Secretary

71. Subject to the provisions of the Charter the Secretary of the Institution shall be appointed by the Council. Subject to the direction of the Council, it shall be the duty of the Secretary to conduct the correspondence of the Institution; to attend all meetings of the Institution, and of the Council, and of committees; to take minutes of the proceedings of such meetings; to read all minutes and communications that may be ordered to be read; to superintend the publication of such papers and publications as the Council may direct; to have charge of the library; to direct the collection of the subscriptions and other amounts due to the Institution and the preparation of the account of the expenditure of the funds, and to present all accounts to the Council for inspection and approval. He shall also engage, subject to the approval of the Council, and be responsible for all persons employed under him, and shall generally conduct the ordinary business of the Institution under the direction of the Council.

Sessions and meetings

72. The annual sessions of the Institution shall begin on the 1st day of October of each year. The meetings of the Institution shall be held at such places and at such times as the Council may appoint.

73. The meetings of the Institution shall be as follows:
(a) Ordinary meetings for the reading and discussion of papers on electrical and allied subjects, and for lectures and discussions on those subjects
(b) The annual general meeting
(c) Special general meetings of corporate members and Associate Members to whom bylaw 14(a)(ii) applies
(d) Special general meetings of corporate members
  (i) for the purpose of confirming any resolution duly passed by the Council for amending or adding to the Charter
  (ii) for the purpose of revoking, or amending any bylaws of the Institution
  (iii) for the purpose of confirming any resolution duly passed by the Council for altering the entrance fees or any of them

(iv) for the purpose of confirming any resolution duly passed by the Council for increasing the annual subscriptions or any of them or

(v) for the purpose of confirming any resolution duly passed by the Council for making, varying or rescinding any regulation concerning the conduct of the ballot for the election to the Council of officers and ordinary members of the Council.

The corporate members and Associate Members to whom bylaw 14(a)(ii) applies shall alone be competent to vote at the meetings specified in paragraphs (a), (b), and (c) of the bylaw, and the corporate members alone at the meetings specified in paragraph (d). Subject to bylaw 36, each person voting shall have one vote. For the purposes of this bylaw all members of the Council shall be deemed to be corporate members.

74. In addition to the ordinary meetings specified in bylaw 73, the Council may at their discretion arrange for other meetings to be held for the dissemination of electrical knowledge by means of lectures or for the discussion of electrical and allied subjects and the reading and discussion of papers thereon; and the Council shall determine the conditions of admission to such meetings, and the manner in which they shall be conducted.

75. The ordinary meetings of the Institution shall be conducted as prescribed by the Council from time to time; and the Council shall determine the conditions of admission to such meetings.

76. Every member of any class shall have the privilege of introducing one visitor at each ordinary meeting of the Institution, by writing his name in a book provided for that purpose, or supplying him with an admission ticket to be obtained from the Secretary.

77. No question shall be discussed, or motion be made, at the ordinary meetings relating to the direction and management of the Institution.

78. The annual general meeting shall be held in the month of May. The business of the annual general meeting shall be to receive and consider the report of the Council and the accounts of the Institution for the past year; to elect auditors; and (with the approval of the Council) to transact any other business of which notice in writing shall have been given to the Secretary at least seven days before such meeting.

79. A special general meeting constituted as provided by paragraph (c) of bylaw 73 may be called at any time by the Council for any specific purpose relating to the direction and management of the affairs of the Institution except for any of the purposes specified in paragraph (d) of bylaw 73, and the Council shall at all times call such a meeting on a requisition, in writing, of ten corporate members or Associate Members to whom bylaw 14(a)(ii) applies, specifying the general nature of the business to be transacted.

80. A special general meeting for any of the purposes specified in paragraph (d) of bylaw 73 may be called at any time by the Council. The Council shall at all times call a special general meeting of corporate members for the purpose numbered (ii) in such paragraph (d) on a requisition in writing of ten corporate members specifying the alterations, revocations, and the amendments of the bylaws suggested by them.

Proceedings at meetings

81. Votes may be given at any annual or special general meeting either personally or by proxy. On a show of hands every member of any class present in person and entitled to vote at such meeting shall have one vote. In case of a poll every member of any class present in person or by proxy and entitled to vote at such a meeting shall have one vote.

82. No person shall be appointed a proxy to vote at any meeting who is not entitled in his own right to vote at such meeting.

83. The instrument appointing a proxy shall be in writing under the hand of the appointor or his attorney, and shall as nearly as circumstances will admit be in the form or to the effect following:

The Institution of Electrical Engineers
of
being (a corporate member *or* an Associate Member to whom bylaw 14(a)(ii) applies as the case may be) of the above Institution hereby appoint

of   or failing him   of
as my proxy at the (annual general meeting, special general meeting of corporate members and Associate members to whom bylaw 14(a)(ii) applies *or* special general meeting of corporate members as the case may be) of the Institution to be held on the

day of   19   and at any poll held

in connection therewith.

As witness my hand this   day of   19

Signature . . . .

Class of membership in I.E.E. . . . .

84. The instrument appointing a proxy and the power of attorney (if any) under which it is signed shall be deposited at the office of the Institution not less than 48 hours before the time for holding the meeting at which the person named in the proxy proposes to vote, but no instrument appointing a proxy shall be valid after the expiration of six calendar months from its date except on a poll demanded at a meeting in cases where the meeting was originally held within six calendar months of such date.
85. A vote given in accordance with the terms of an instrument appointing a proxy shall be valid notwithstanding the previous death of the principal or revocation of the proxy unless previous intimation in writing of the death or revocation shall have been received at the office of the Institution.
86. A poll may be demanded by the Chairman of any annual or special general meeting or by any three presons personally present and entitled to vote thereat and if so demanded shall be taken in such manner and at such time within 28 days next after the meeting and at such place as the Chairman of the meeting directs and either immediately or after an interval or at an adjourned meeting, and the result of the poll shall be deemed to be the resolution of the meeting at which the poll was demanded. The fact that a poll has been demanded shall not prevent the continuance of the meeting for the transaction of any business other than the question on which a poll has been demanded. A demand for a poll may be withdrawn. No notice need be given of a poll not taken immediately.
87. In the case of an equality of votes the Chairman of the meeting shall both on a show of hands and at a poll have a casting vote in addition to his personal vote.
88. The quorum at any annual or special general meeting shall be 12 of those persons entitled to be present and vote thereat and no business shall be transacted at any such

meeting unless the quorum be present at the commencement of the business. If a quorum be not present within a quarter of an hour from the time appointed for holding the meeting the meeting shall be dissolved.

89. Fourteen days' notice at the least shall be given of all annual and special general meetings. The notice shall specify the general nature of the business to be transacted, and no other business shall be transacted at these meetings except such business (if any) at an annual general meeting of which notice shall have been given as provided in bylaw 78.

The accidental omission to give notice of a meeting to any member of any class shall not invalidate the meeting.

90. The President shall preside at all meetings of the Council and ordinary and general meetings of the Institution at which he is present; in the absence of the President, a past President, a Deputy-President, a Vice-President, or, if none be present, another member of Council present shall preside.

91. No report of the proceedings at any meeting of the Institution or of the Centres or of the Divisions or of the Boards or of the Groups established pursuant to bylaw 93 shall be taken or published except with the consent of the Council previously obtained.

Centres

92. The Council may, at their discretion, upon receipt of a request to that effect from a sufficient number of corporate members, resident in any district, create a Centre of the Institution in such district for the holding of regular meetings for the reading of papers and for discussions on electrical subjects, and the Council shall have the power to dissolve such Centre at any time after it has been formed. Each Centre shall be constituted, and its affairs shall be carried on, in accordance with rules and regulations to be laid down from time to time by the Council, and it shall elect annually for its Chairman a Fellow of the Institution.

Divisions

93. The Council may, at their discretion, create one or more Divisions of the Institution, for the fostering of such branches of electrical science and engineering as they shall specify, by the holding of meetings for the reading of papers and for discussions on technical subjects and by such other means as to the Council shall seem fit and the Council shall have power to dissolve any Division at any time. Each Division shall be constituted, and its affairs shall be carried on, in accordance with rules and regulations to be laid down from time to time by the Council, which may make provision for the establishment of Groups within the Division, and it shall elect annually for its Chairman a Fellow of the Institution.

The Council may also appoint committees to be known as boards to foster and co-ordinate in like manner such branches of electrical science and engineering as subserve the interests of more than one Division, and the Council shall have power to dissolve any such board at any time. Each such board shall be constituted, and its affairs carried on, in accordance with rules and regulations to be laid down from time to time by the Council. The Chairman of each such board shall be a Fellow of the Institution.

Investments

94. All the moneys of the Institution not required to meet the current expenditure of the Institution shall be invested in any mode in which trustees are or shall be by law, in absence of special direction, authorised to invest trust moneys under their control, or in any public stocks or funds or government securities of Great Britain or of any

British Dominion, or in freehold or leasehold securities in Great Britain, or in stocks, shares or securities the capital whereof or a minimum rate of interest or dividend thereon is guaranteed by the British Government or by the Government of any British Dominion, or in stocks, bonds, mortgages or securities of any municipal or local body or authority situated in Great Britain, or in the stocks, shares or securities, being fully paid stocks, shares or securities quoted on the Stock Exchange, London, of any company incorporated with limited liability in Great Britain or in any British Dominion having an issued capital of not less than one million pounds sterling or the equivalent thereof if in other currency, which shall either

(a) during or in respect of each of the five years next before the date of investment have paid dividends or interest at a rate of not less than 5 per cent. per annum upon stocks, shares, or securities of the nominal value of at least £500,000 (or the equivalent thereof in other currency) ranking for dividend or interest behind the investment taken, or

(b) during or in respect of the ten years next before the date of investment have paid dividends upon its ordinary capital at an average rate of not less than 4 per cent. per annum.

or in the purchase of freehold or leasehold land in the United Kingdom, the latter having 60 years or more unexpired at the time of purchase.

Provided always that no investment shall be made in the securities of any such company as aforesaid if the value of the investments to which this bylaw relates in investments authorised by the general law for the investment of trust funds shall then be or would thereby become less than two thirds of the value for the time being of all the investments of the Institution to which this bylaw relates.

And provided further that for the purposes of this bylaw the value of any investment or investments may be taken to be the amount shown by any valuation made at the request of the Institution by a member of the London Stock Exchange within the preceding six calendar months as to which a letter purporting to be signed by any such member shall be conclusive evidence.

And provided further that the Institution may accept and retain in their existing state of investment for such period as the Council may think fit any securities, obligations, stock, or shares of whatsoever nature or denomination not otherwise authorised under this bylaw which have been or may be transferred to the Institution as part of any benefaction however such benefaction be created.

Copyright

95. Every paper presented to the Institution, and accepted for reading, or for publication in full or in abstract, and every paper read at a meeting of the Institution or any part thereof, and the copyright therein, shall be the property of the Institution. The Council, in such cases as they may think fit, shall have power to release or surrender the rights of the Institution in respect of any such paper or the copyright therein. The right of publishing all such papers and the reports of the proceedings and discussions at meetings of the Institution or any part thereof shall be reserved to the Council who may, as they think fit, give their consent to publication in approved cases.

Indemnity

96. Each number of the Council and each member of the Institution in his capacity as a member of any council, board, committee, panel or other body appointed pursuant to these bylaws or otherwise by or with the approval of the Council for the purposes of the Institution shall be accountable in respect of his own acts only, and

shall not be accountable for any acts done or authorised by which he shall not have expressly assented. And no member of any such body shall incur any personal liability in respect of any loss or damage incurred through any act, matter, or thing done, authorised, or suffered by him, being done in good faith for the benefit of the Institution, although in excess of his legal power.

97. Each member of the Institution referred to in bylaw 96 and the Secretary shall be indemnified out of the funds and property of the Institution from and against all costs, charges, damages and expenses whatsoever which they or any of them shall sustain by reason of their respectively accepting office or acting in execution of the duties or power imposed upon or given to them by the Charter or the bylaws of the Institution.

Common seal

98. The Council shall provide a common seal of the Institution, and make rules for the safe custody and the use thereof, and it shall never be used except by the authority of the Council previously given, and in the presence of two members of the Council at the least who shall sign every instrument to which the seal is affixed, and every such instrument shall be countersigned by the Secretary, or some other person appointed by the Council.

Notices

99. Any notice may be served or any communication may be sent by the Council or by the Secretary of the Institution upon or to any member of any class either personally or by sending it prepaid through the post addressed to such person at his address as registered in the books of the Institution.

100. Any notice or communication. if served or sent by post, shall be deemed to have been served or delivered on the third day following that on which the same is posted; and in proving such service or sending it shall be sufficient to prove that the notice or communication was properly addressed and posted.

101. No member of any class, whose registered address is abroad, shall be entitled to any notice; and all proceedings may be had and taken without notice to such person in the same manner as if he had due notice.

The schedule above referred to

FORM A

I, the undersigned, agree that, in the event of my election to membership of any class in the Institution of Electrical Engineers, I will be governed by the Charter and bylaws of the Institution as they now are, or as they may hereafter be altered; and that I will advance the objects of the Institution as far as shall be in my power; provided that, whenever I shall signify in writing to the Secretary that I am desirous of withdrawing from the Institution I shall after the payment of any arrears which may be due by me at that period be free from this obligation.

Witness my hand, this . . . . day of . . . . 19 . . . .

FORM B

Sir,

I am directed to inform you that, at a meeting held on the. . . . day of. . . . 19. . . . ,
the Council decided that you name should be removed from the register of The
Institution of Electrical Engineers, in pursuance of bylaw 41(b).

I am, Sir,

Yours faithfully,

Secretary

FORM C

Sir,

I am directed to inform you that, at a meeting held on the. . . . day of. . . . 19. . . . ,
the Council★ ordered that you be expelled from the Institution of Electrical Engineers, in pursuance of bylaw 41(c).

I am, Sir,

Yours faithfully,

Secretary

★ or the Disciplinary Board appointed by the Council as the case may be.

Disciplinary regulations
*Made by the Council pursuant by bylaw 41(d) and approved at a special general meeting of
corporate members of the Institution held on 14 December 1972.*

1. In these regulations, unless the contrary intention appears, 'member' means a
member of any class referred to in bylaw 3; and 'improper conduct' has the meaning
assigned to it in bylaw 41(a).
2. The Council shall appoint two bodies for the investigation of and the adjudication
on allegations of improper conduct on the part of any member or members. One
such body shall be known as the investigating panel and the other as the disciplinary
board.
3. The members of the investigating panel and the disciplinary board shall hold office
for such period as the Council shall determine and may be reappointed. Unless
otherwise determined, one fifth of the members for the time being, or if their
number is not a multiple of five then the number nearest to one fifth, shall retire from
office on the thirtieth day of September; the members to retire in each year shall be
those who have been longest in office since their last appointment, and as between
those who became members on the same day those to retire shall (unless they
otherwise agree among themselves) be selected by lot. Nevertheless a retiring
member who shall have entered on the investigation or hearing of a particular case of
alleged improper conduct and shall not be reappointed shall be deemed to continue as
a member for the purpose of that particular case until the same shall have been finally
disposed of.
4. Subject to the bylaws and these regulations each of the said bodies shall have power
to regulate its own practice and procedure.
5. The Council shall appoint a Chairman and Vice-Chairman of the investigating
panel and (subject to regulation 13) of the disciplinary board. If the Chairman of

either body shall be unable to carry out his functions under these regulations, those functions shall be carried out by the Vice-Chairman of that body. Should both the Chairman and Vice-Chairman be unable to carry out the said functions, the President may appoint a member of the appropriate body to act as Chairman until the Chairman or Vice-Chairman is again available and able to carry out his functions. Subject as aforesaid any meeting of one of the said bodies may choose its own Chairman. The Council shall cause two persons, who may be members of the Institution staff, to be appointed by the Secretary to act as clerks to the investigating panel and to the disciplinary board respectively.

6. Any act done by a Vice-Chairman or by a person whom the President or the relevant body has purported to appoint under the preceding regulation to act as Chairman shall be valid and effectual and shall not be questioned on the ground that no occasion had arisen for a person to be so appointed or for the Vice-Chairman (or a person so appointed) to act in place of the Chairman.

7. The investigating panel shall consist of nine corporate members of the Institution including the Chairman and Vice-Chairman. Three members of the investigating panel shall be a quorum. The Chairman of the investigating panel may at any time appoint any three or more members of the panel (who may, but need not, include the Chairman himself or the Vice-Chairman) to deal with any particular complaint or allegation, and all acts, proceedings and decisions of the members so appointed shall be deemed to be the acts, proceedings and decisions of the investigating panel.

8. If any allegation of improper conduct on the part of a member shall be received from any source, the same shall in the first instance be referred to the investigating panel, which may also (if it thinks fit) initiate an enquiry where it has reason to suppose that a member may have been guilty of improper conduct.

9. If any allegation does not appear to the investigating panel to disclose any prima facie case of improper conduct the investigating panel may dismiss the case without informing the member concerned and without hearing the person making the allegation.

10. In all other cases the investigating panel shall send written notice to the member of the nature and particulars of the allegation and invite him to put forward his observations in writing to the investigating panel. The member shall at the same time be informed that he is under no obligation to make any observations to the investigating panel but that, if he does not do so (or if the panel does not regard any explanations of his as satisfactory), the matter will be referred to the disciplinary board, which will then give him a full opportunity of presenting his case.

11. On receiving a member's observations the investigating panel may dismiss the case if satisfied that the allegation is unfounded or does not disclose a prima facie case. It may also dismiss the case if it considers that the alleged improper conduct is of such a trivial nature that it calls for no action. In all other cases the investigating panel shall, after investigation, refer allegations of improper conduct to the disciplinary board.

12. As soon as practicable after an allegation has been referred by the investigating panel to the disciplinary board, the investigating panel shall arrange that
(a) notice shall be given to the member concerned that the allegation has been referred to the disciplinary board;
(b) the member shall be informed of the date of the meeting of the disciplinary board at which (subject to any observations of the member with regard to the date) the allegation will be dealt with; and
(c) information shall be given to the member as to the practice of the disciplinary board in relation to the hearing of allegations and the manner in which he may be represented before that board.

13. The disciplinary board shall consist of fifteen corporate members, including the Chairman and Vice-Chairman, none of whom shall for the time being be members of the investigating panel. The Chairman of the disciplinary board shall be either the President for the time being (if he is a member of the disciplinary board) or a past President.

14. Any allegation referred to the disciplinary board shall be dealt with by five or more members of the board to be nominated for the purpose by the Chairman. The disciplinary board may appoint a practising barrister or solicitor of at least seven years' standing to sit with it for the purpose of advising it as to the manner in which it should exercise its functions.

15. On the hearing of any allegation the investigating panel shall place before the disciplinary board such information as is available to it in relation to the allegation and may, if it thinks fit, employ solicitors or counsel for the purpose or may nominate one of its members to conduct the case. The accused member shall be given a full and fair opportunity of being heard and of calling witnesses and cross-examining any other witness testifying before the board. He shall be allowed to conduct his own case or, if he prefers, to be represented by solicitors or counsel or by another member of his own choice but not by any other person.

16. The disciplinary board may take into consideration and act on such information as may be available to it whether such information would or would not be admissible as evidence in a Court of Law.

17. Any notice directed to be given under these regulations shall be deemed to be properly served if sent by registered first-class post to the last known address of the member concerned. If no reply shall be received from him within twenty-eight days after the time when such letter might be expected to have been delivered to him and a reply received from him in the ordinary course of post, the investigating panel or the disciplinary board may proceed in default. For the purposes of this regulation air mail shall be deemed to be first class post, and delivery by air mail shall be deemed to be delivery by first class post, where the member is overseas and air mail can conveniently be used. Provided that if the member shall, either before or after the allegation has been disposed of, satisfy the relevant body that any notice to him was not in fact delivered or was delivered later than delivery might have been expected in the ordinary course of post and that in consequence he was ignorant, or ignorant until too late, of the proceedings being taken against him, the relevant body shall at his request re-open the proceedings notwithstanding that they may have been concluded.

18. The disciplinary board may in any case where it appears just or expedient to do so extend the time for doing anything or may dispense with service of any notice and may adjourn any hearing from time to time.

19. In case the disciplinary board decides that a member has been guilty of improper conduct, it shall, unless it sees special reason to the contrary, cause the fact and particulars of its order to be posted in the Institution and published in the journal. It may, and at the request of the accused member shall, similarly publish the fact that any complaint has been dismissed.

Rules of conduct
Made by the Council pursuant to bylaw 42(c) and approved at a special general meeting of corporate members of the Institution held on 14 December 1972.
A code of professional conduct designed to cover all eventualities must necessarily be written in general terms expressing broad ethical principles. Almost every case of

doubt as to the proper course of action required to conform to the code of professional conduct arises from a conflict between a member's personal interest and his duty to others. Rules issued by the Council to interpret the code indicate the manner in which members are required to conduct themselves in a number of situations that are frequently encountered. In other situations, members are required to order their conduct in accordance with the principle that, in any conflict between a member's personal interest and fair and honest dealing with other members of the community, his duty to the community must prevail.

In these rules 'member' means a member of any class referred to in bylaw 3, and 'employer' includes 'client'.

1. A member shall at all times take care to ensure that his work and the products of his work constitute no avoidable danger of death or injury or ill health to any person.

2. A member shall take all reasonable steps to avoid waste of natural resources, damage of the environment, and wasteful damage or destruction of the products of human skill and industry.

3. A member shall take all reasonable steps to maintain and develop his professional competence by attention to new developments in science and engineering relevant to his field of professional activity and shall encourage persons working under his supervision to do so.

4. A member shall not undertake responsibility as an electrical engineer which he does not believe himself competent to discharge.

5. A member shall accept personal responsibility for all work done by him or under his supervision or direction, and shall take all reasonable steps to ensure that persons working under his authority are competent to carry out the tasks assigned to them and that they accept personal responsibility for work done under the authority delegated to them.

6. A member called upon to give an opinion in his professional capacity shall, to the best of his ability, give an opinion that is objective and reliable.

7. A member whose professional advice is not accepted shall take all responsible steps to ensure that the person overruling or neglecting his advice is aware of any danger which the member believes may result from such overruling or neglect.

8. A member shall not make any public statement in his capacity as an electrical engineer without ensuring that his qualification to make such a statement and any association he may have with any party which may benefit from his statement are made known to the person or persons to whom it is directed.

9. A member shall not, in self-laudatory language or in any manner derogatory to the dignity of the profession of electrical engineers, advertise or write articles for publication, nor shall he authorise any such advertisement or article to be written or published by any other person.

10. A member shall not recklessly or maliciously injure or attempt to injure, whether directly or indirectly, the professional reputation, prospects or business of another.

11. A member shall inform his employer in writing of any conflict between his personal interest and faithful service to his employer.

12. A member shall not improperly disclose any information concerning the business of his employer or of any past employer.

13. A member shall not accept remuneration in connection with professional services rendered to his employer other than from his employer or with his employer's consent; nor shall he receive directly or indirectly any royalty, gratuity or commission on any article or process used in or for the purposes of the work in respect of which he is employed unless or until such royalty, gratuity or commission has been authorised in writing by his employer.

14. A member shall not improperly solicit work as an independent adviser or consultant, either directly or by an agent, nor shall he improperly pay any person, by commission or otherwise, for the introduction of such work; provided that, if a member shall be working in a country where there are recognised standards of professional conduct, laid down in that country by a competent authority recognised by the Council, which are in conflict with the previous provisions of this rule, he may order his conduct according to such standards.

15. A member acting as an independent adviser or consultant shall not be the medium of payment made on his employer's behalf unless so requested by his employer; nor shall he place contracts or orders in connection with work on which he is employed, except with the authority of and on behalf of his employer.

Appendix 3

The Presidents and Secretaries of the Institution 1872–1986

Biographical notes and photographs of the Presidents from 1872 to 1938 appear in *The History of the Institution of Electrical Engineers 1871–1931* by Rollo Appleyard, and only their names and dates, and titles in their final form, are listed here. Of the Presidents from 1939 to 1986, the name and title of each is given as at the time when he assumed office as President, and brief biographical notes appear, to the extent that information is available. The titles of awards and the names of awarding organisations are given, as far as possible, as they were when an award was made.

Abbreviations used

AB	Bachelor of Arts
ADC	Aide-de-Camp
AEI	Associated Electrical Industries
AHQ	Allied Headquarters
AM	Master of Arts
ASEE	Association of Supervisory and Executive Engineers, which up to 1969 was called the Association of Supervising Electrical Engineers
BBC	British Broadcasting Corporation
BEAMA	British Electrotechnical and Allied Manufacturers' Association
BEARA	British Electrical and Allied Industries Research Association
BICC	British Insulated Callenders Cables
Bn	Battalion
BS	Bachelor of Science (USA)
BSc	Bachelor of Science
BSI	British Standards Institution
Bt	Baronet
BTH	British Thomson-Houston Company
CB	Companion, Order of the Bath
CBE	Commander, Order of the British Empire
CEGB	Central Electricity Generating Board
CH	Companion of Honour
CIE	Companion, Order of the Indian Empire
CMG	Companion, Order of St Michael and St George
DCL	Doctor of Civil Law
DEng	Doctor of Engineering
DFC	Distinguished Flying Cross
DPhil	Doctor of Philosophy
DrEng	Doctor of Engineering
DSc	Doctor of Science
DSC	Distinguished Service Cross
DSIR	Department of Scientific and Industrial Research

DSO	Companion, Distinguished Service Order
DTech	Doctor of Technology
FCGI	Fellow of the City and Guilds of London Institute
FCS	Fellow of the Chemical Society
FEng	Fellow of Engineering
FHWC	Fellow of Heriot-Watt College
FIC	Fellow of the Institute of Chemistry
FIEE	Fellow of the Institution of Electrical Engineers
FIEEE	Fellow of the Institute of Electrical and Electronics Engineers
FIMechE	Fellow of the Institution of Mechanical Engineers
FInstP	Fellow of the Institute of Physics
FKC	Fellow of King's College, London
FRAeS	Fellow of the Royal Aeronautical Society
FRAS	Fellow of the Royal Astronomical Society
FRS	Fellow of the Royal Society
FRSC	Fellow of the Royal Society of Chemistry
FRSE	Fellow of the Royal Society of Edinburgh
GB	Great Britain
GBE	Knight Grand Cross, Order of the British Empire
GCB	Knight Grand Cross, Order of the Bath
GCMG	Knight Grand Cross, Order of St Michael and St George
GCSI	Knight Grand Commander, Order of the Star of India
GCVO	Knight Grand Cross, Royal Victorian Order
GEC	General Electric Company
GE Co	General Electric Company of America
GPO	General Post Office
HonFIEE	Honorary Fellow of the IEE (awarded since 1966)
HonMIEE	Honorary Member of the IEE (awarded up to 1966)
IEETE	Institution of Electrical and Electronics Technician Engineers (now the Institution of Electrical and Electronics Incorporated Engineers)
IERE	Institution of Electronic and Radio Engineers
IMechE	Institution of Mechanical Engineers
JP	Justice of the Peace
KBE	Knight Commander, Order of the British Empire
KCB	Knight Commander, Order of the Bath
KCMG	Knight Commander, Order of St Michael and St George
KCSI	Knight Commander, Order of the Star of India
KCVO	Knight Commander, Royal Victorian Order
KG	Knight of the Garter
KT	Knight, Order of the Thistle
LAMA	Locomotive and Allied Manufacturers Association
LLD	Doctor of Laws
MA	Master of Arts
MC	Military Cross
MEng	Master of Engineering
MIEE	Member of the Institution of Electrical Engineers
MRCS	Member of the Royal College of Surgeons
MS	Master of Science
MSc	Master of Science
MVO	Member, Royal Victorian Order

NE	North East
OBE	Officer, Order of the British Empire
OM	Order of Merit
PC	Privy Counsellor
PhD	Doctor of Philosophy
PO	Post Office
QC	Queen's Counsel
RA	Royal Artillery
RAF	Royal Air Force
RE	Royal Engineers
RN	Royal Navy
RNAS	Royal Naval Air Service
RNVR	Royal Naval Volunteer Reserve
RSA	Royal Society of Arts
SBAC	Society of British Aircraft Constructors
ScD	Doctor of Science
SRC	Science Research Council
TA	Territorial Army
TD	Territorial Decoration
UCL	University College, London
UGC	University Grants Committee
UK	United Kingdom
UKAEA	United Kingdom Atomic Energy Authority
UMIST	University of Manchester Institute of Science and Technology

Presidents, 1872–1938

Elected

1872 } 1878 } Charles William Siemens, DCL, FRS (1823–1883)

1873 Frank Ives Scudamore, CB (1823–1884)

1874 } 1889 } 1907 } The Rt. Hon. Lord Kelvin, OM, GCVO, FRS (1824–1907)

1875 Latimer Clark, FRS (1822–1898)

1876 Charles V Walker, FRS (1812–1882)

1877 Sir Frederick Abel, Bt, FRS (1827–1902)

1879 Lt. Col. Sir John U Bateman-Champain, RE (1835–1887)

1880 } 1893 } Sir William Henry Preece, KCB, FRS (1834–1913)

1881 Prof. George Carey Foster, LLD, DSc, FRS (1835–1919)

1882 Maj. Gen. Charles E Webber, CB, RE (1838–1904)

1883 Willoughby Smith (1828–1891)

1884 Prof. W Grylls Adams, FRS (1836–1915)

1885 Charles Ernest Spagnoletti (1832–1915)

1886 David Edward Hughes, FRS (1831–1908)

1887 Sir Charles Tilston Bright (1832–1888)

1888 Edward Graves (1834–1892)

1890 } 1896 } John Hopkinson, DSc, FRS (1849–1898)

1891	Sir William Crookes, OM, FRS (1832–1919)
1892	Prof. William Edward Ayrton, FRS (1847–1908)
1894 } 1904 }	Alexander Siemens (1847–1928)
1895 } 1908 }	Col. Rookes Evelyn B Crompton CB, FRS (1845–1940)
1897	Sir Henry Mance, LLD, CIE (1840–1926)
1898	Sir Joseph Wilson Swan, DSc, FRS (1828–1914)
1899	Prof. Silvanus Phillips Thompson, DSc, FRS (1851–1916)
1900	Prof. John Perry, LLD, DSc, FRS (1850–1920)
1901	William Edward Langdon (1832–1905)
1902	Sir James Swinburne, Bt, FRS (1858–1958)
1903	Robert Kaye Gray (1851–1914)
1905	Sir John Gavey, CB (1842–1923)
1906	Sir Richard Tetley Glazebrook, KCB, KCVO, DSc, FRS (1854–1935)
1908	William Morris Mordey (1856–1938)
1909	Gisbert Kapp, DrEng (1852–1922)
1910 } 1911 }	Sebastian Ziani de Ferranti, DSc, FRS (1864–1930)
1912 } 1913 }	William Duddell, CBE, FRS (1872–1917)
1914	Sir John Francis Cleverton Snell, GBE (1869–1938)
1915 } 1916 }	Charles P Sparks CBE (1866–1940)
1917 } 1918 }	Charles Henry Wordingham (1866–1925)
1919	Roger Thomas Smith, BSc (1863–1940)
1920	Llewelyn B Atkinson (1863–1939)
1921	John Somerville Highfield (1871–1945)
1922	Sir Frank Gill, KCMG, OBE (1866–1950)
1923	Alexander Russell, MA, DSc, LLD, FRS (1861–1943)
1924	William Bradley Woodhouse (1873–1940)
1925	Richard Alexander Chattock (1865–1936)
1926	William Henry Eccles, DSc, FRS (1875–1966)
1927	Sir Archibald Page (1875–1949)
1928	The Rt. Hon. The Earl of Mount Edgcumbe, TD (1873–1965)
1929	Col. Sir Thomas F Purves, OBE (1871–1950)
1930	Sir Clifford Copland Paterson, OBE, DSc, FRS (1879–1948)
1931	John Muir Donaldson, MC (1877–1963)
1932	Prof. Edgar Walford Marchant, DSc (1876–1962)
1933	Philip Vassar Hunter, CBE (1883–1956)
1934	Prof. William Mundell Thornton, OBE, DSc, DEng (1870–1944)
1935	Sir John Macfarlane Kennedy, OBE (1879–1954)
1936	Henry Thomas Young (1888–1968)
1937	Sir George Lee, OBE, MC (1879–1967)
1938	Sir Arthur Percy M Fleming, CBE, DEng, LLD (1881–1960)

Johnstone Wright
(later Sir Johnstone Wright)

James Robert Beard

Sir Noel Ashbridge

Prof Cecil Lewis Fortescue OBE

Presidents, 1939–1986

1939 **Johnstone Wright** (later Sir Johnstone Wright) (1883–1953) Born in Perthshire. Educated at Perth Academy and the Royal Technical College, Glasgow. Joined British Electrical Power Plant Co, Alloa, in 1903. Moved in 1905 into electricity supply. 1906–1919 With the Cleveland and Durham Electric Power Co, involved in rapid expansion of industrial supplies in the NE, including the development of waste-heat power stations. 1919–1922 Deputy Chief Engineer, Bradford Corporation Electricity Dept. 1922–1927 Chief Electrical Engineer, Belfast Corporation Electricity Dept, constructing the Harbour power station and preparing a comprehensive scheme for electricity throughout N Ireland. Deputy Chief Engineer, Central Electricity Board, 1927–1933; Chief Engineer 1933–1944; General Manager 1944–1947; Chairman 1947–1948. He was much concerned with the planning and operation of the National Grid and, in the war years, with the efficient production of cables. Member of the Fuel Research Board 1944–1947. Institution Premium (with C W Marshall) for paper on the National Grid 1929. Knighted 1943.

1940 **James Robert Beard, CBE** (1885–1962) Born in Manchester. Educated at Manchester Grammar School and the University of Manchester; MSc. Briefly with the NE Electric Supply Co and the Cleveland and Durham Electric Power Co before joining Merz and McLellan in 1907. Worked on the distribution of electric power, particularly the standardisation of frequency and voltage in Great Britain and the planning and construction of the National Grid. Involved in Scottish hydroelectric schemes and other power supply and traction schemes in GB, S Africa, India and elsewhere. Partner 1930; Senior Partner 1940, on Merz's death in an air raid. Retired 1961. Member of Engineering Advisory Committee of the War Cabinet 1941–1945. Chairman (appointed by Minister of Works) of Council for Codes of Practice for Buildings, Construction and Engineering Services 1947–1949. Twice awarded the Institution Premium. Had a great gift for creating friendships. Hon MIEE 1955.

1941 **Sir Noel Ashbridge** (1889–1975) Born in Wanstead. Educated at King's College, London; BSc. Engineering training with Yarrow & Co Ltd and with BTH Co Ltd. Served in Royal Fusiliers and Royal Engineers 1914–1919. After six years with Marconi's at the Writtle Experimental Station, joined BBC in 1926 as Assistant Chief Engineer. Promoted to Controller of Engineering and directed the BBC's engineering developments during the subsequent 26 years. Became Deputy Director-General 1943. Director of Technical Services 1948–1952. Chairman of Radio Research Board 1952–1957. Member of Television Committee 1934 and 1943, and of Television Advisory Committee 1935. Knighted 1935. Knight of Royal Order of Dannebrog (Denmark). Hon MIEE 1957.

1942 **Professor Cecil Lewis Fortescue, OBE** (1881–1949) Born in Northants. Educated at Oundle and Christ's College, Cambridge; (Natural Science Scholar) 1st class Mechanical Sciences Tripos 1903. Post-graduate apprenticeship at Siemens Dynamo Works, Stafford. Appointed to HMS *Vernon*, Portsmouth, as Instructor of Officers at the Torpedo and Gunnery Schools. In 1911 became Professor of Physics at Royal Naval College, Greenwich. During 1914–1918 was posted to HM Signal School, Portsmouth, for wireless telegraphy duties and awarded OBE. 1922 Appointed Professor of Electrical Engineering at Imperial College, University of London, where he remained until his retirement in 1946. Dean of the City and Guilds College for two periods, including during the 1939–1945 war. An enthusiastic teacher and keenly interested in the well-being of students. Contributed much to discussions on professional education for electrical engineers. Enjoyed rowing, sailing and gardening.

Col Arthur Stanley Angwin
(later Col Sir Arthur Stanley Angwin)

Sir Harry Railing

Dr Percy Dunsheath OBE

Vincent Ziani de Ferranti MC
(later Sir Vincent de Ferranti)

1943 **Colonel Sir Stanley Angwin**, KCMG, KBE, DSO, MC, TD (1883–1959) Born in Cornwall. Educated at St John's School, Chatham, and at East London College (now Queen Mary College). Pupil with Yarrow & Co, engineers and shipbuilders. 1906 Joined Post Office Engineering Dept as assistant engineer. Stationed in Glasgow, where he raised the Lowland Division Telegraph Company of the Territorial Army, recruited from Post Office staff. The unit was mobilised in 1914 as 52nd Divisional Signal Company, and Angwin served with it in Gallipoli, Egypt and France. Awarded DSO and MC. After the war he commanded 44th Divisional Signals; later became Deputy Chief Signal Officer (Supplementary Reserve). On return to Post Office worked on construction of Rugby radio station, becoming henceforward primarily a radio engineer. Member of Television Committee 1934 and 1943, and Chairman of Radio Research Board 1947–1952. 1939–1946 Engineer-in-Chief of the Post Office. 1946–1951 Chairman of Cable and Wireless Ltd.1951–1956 Chairman of Commonwealth Telecommunications Board. Knighted 1941; KBE 1945; KCMG 1957. Fellow of Queen Mary College 1946. Faraday Medallist 1953. HonMIEE 1956. DSc (London).

1944 **Sir Harry Railing** (1878–1963) Born in Munich. Educated at University of Munich; DEng 1901. Practical experience in Germany and USA. 1905 Joined General Electric Co as head of Test Department in the newly established Witton works. Transferred to London as technical assistant to Hugo Hirst (later Lord Hirst). 1911 Director of GEC, with responsibility for the Witton group of works. 1933 Moved to London. 1941 Joint General Manager of GEC. 1942 Vice-Chairman of the company. 1943–1957 Chairman. Member of various Government committees and councils. Knighted 1944. President BEAMA 1952. HonMIEE 1953. A skilled engineering administrator, but also a friendly and approachable man, of wide interests.

1945 **Dr Percy Dunsheath, CBE** (1886–1979) Born in Sheffield; educated at the Universities of Sheffield, London and Cambridge. 1908 Joined Engineer-in-Chief's office of the General Post Office. In 1914–1918 war was commissioned, twice mentioned in dispatches and appointed OBE. 1919 Appointed director of research, W T Henley's. 1929 Chief Engineer. 1936–1959 Director of the company. 1946 Consulting engineer. Pioneer of undersea pipeline, Pluto. 1956–1963 Chairman, Cambridge Instrument Co. 1955–1958 President of International Electrotechnical Commission. 1946–1967 Member of Senate, University of London. CBE 1946. Faraday Lecturer 1947. HonMIEE 1964. HonDEng, Sheffield; HonLLD London; Hon Fellow, University College, London 1967. Author of a number of books, as well as papers and articles on scientific, technical and educational subjects.

1946 **Vincent Ziani de Ferranti** (later Sir Vincent de Ferranti) (1893–1980) Educated Repton. Served in European War 1914–1919, in Royal Engineers; Captain, MC. Chairman of Ferranti Ltd, 1930–1963. 1939–1940 Was Major Commanding Field Company, Royal Engineers, France. 1940–1944, Lt. Col. Commanding 63rd County of Lancs Bn Home Guard. Hon Colonel 123 Field Engineer Regiment RE, TA 1948–1957. Chairman International Executive Council and British National Committee, World Power Conference, 1950–1962. Chairman of BEAMA 1938–1939, Vice-President 1946–1957, President 1957–1959. President of British Electrical Power Convention 1949–1950. President of Television Society 1954–1957. Knighted 1948. HonLLD; HonDEng; HonFIEE 1971.

Percy Good CBE

Thomas Graeme N Haldane

Prof Eric Bailleul Moullin

Sir Archibald Gill

1947 **Percy Good, CBE, FCGI** (1880–1950) Born in London. Educated Ongar Grammar School, City of London School, and Central Technical College. Diploma 1900. Practical training with Thames Ironworks, Shipbuilding and Engineering Co. 1902 Joined Electrical Standardizing, Testing and Training Institution (Faraday House). 1905–1906 Superintendent of Testing Dept. Started businesses for the manufacture of insulating materials and of electric fires and other equipment. 1914 Part-time member of staff of Engineering Standards Committee. By 1918 this body had become the British Engineering Standards Association, and Good was full-time Assistant Secretary. In 1931 the name changed again, to the British Standards Institution, with Good as Deputy Director. He rose to Director in 1942. Chairman of the Joint Lighting Committee, set up by the Illumination Engineering Society and the Ministry of Home Security; this led to the award of the CBE in 1945. Much work at home and internationally on standardisation. Member of Council of the International Electrotechnical Commission from 1922 until his death. Fellow of City and Guilds of London Institute 1938. Hon Fellow of Imperial College 1945. Yachtsman, farmer and enthusiastic Londoner.

1948 **Thomas Graeme Nelson Haldane** (1897–1981) Born in Edinburgh. Educated at Edinburgh Academy and Royal Naval Colleges, Osborne and Dartmouth. After First World War (commissioned in RN) went to Trinity College, Cambridge (Hons Physics). 1925 Joined Merz & McLellan, consulting engineers. Partner 1941. Retired 1957 but remained consultant with the firm until 1972. Involved with the design, construction and application of power supply systems throughout the world. 1929 Kelvin Premium. 1973 ScD Cambridge. 1950–1952 President of Association of Supervising Electrical Engineers. 1954 Chairman of Association of Consulting Engineers.

1949 **Professor Eric Bailleul Moullin** (1893–1963) Born in Dorset. Educated privately and at Downing College, Cambridge (Mathematical Scholar). MA 1919; ScD 1939. University Lecturer in Engineering at Cambridge and Assistant Lecturer at King's College until 1929. Donald Pollock Reader in Engineering Science at Oxford 1930–1945. Fellow of Magdalen College, Oxford 1932–1945. Served as temporary Senior Experimental Officer at Admiralty Signals Establishment, Portsmouth 1940–1942. Member of Senior Research Staff of Metropolitan-Vickers Electrical Co Ltd, Manchester, 1942–1944. Professor of Electrical Engineering, Cambridge, and Fellow of King's College 1945–1960. Member of Radio Research Board of Ministry of Scientific and Industrial Research 1934–1942. Involved in wartime development of radio and radar devices. Associated with work on the vibration of ships. Inventor of Moullin torsionmeter, voltmeter and various electrical measuring instruments. Numerous scientific papers, and also antiquarian papers on Guernsey. Chairman of Council of Guernsey Society and Seigneur du Fief des Eperons. HonLLD Glasgow 1958; HonMIEE 1963.

1950 **Sir Archibald Gill** (1889–1976) Educated at Regent Street Polytechnic, Paisley Technical College, Glasgow Technical College. BSc(Eng), London University. Pupil of Yarrow & Co, engineers and shipbuilders. Draughtsman with British Thomson-Houston Co, Rugby. Entered PO Engineering Dept 1913. Staff Engineer, radio branch, 1932. Assistant Engineer-in-Chief 1938. Deputy Engineer-in-Chief 1944. Engineer-in-Chief 1947–1951. In wartime, planned deep-level tunnels to safeguard communications from central London. Was involved in the laying of the Pluto pipeline. Responsible for the design of several GPO cableships. A bold and imaginative leader of GPO radio engineering teams. Knighted 1949.

Sir John Hacking

Col Bruce Hamer Leeson OBE TD

Harold Bishop CBE
(later Sir Harold Bishop)

Josiah Eccles CBE MM
(later Sir Josiah Eccles)

1951 **Sir John Hacking** (1888–1969) Born in Lancashire. Educated at Burnley Grammar School, Leeds Technical Institute and Leeds University. 1908–1913 Newcastle upon Tyne Electric Supply Co. Various engineering posts with Merz and McLellan, Consulting Engineers, in Newcastle 1913–1915; in Buenos Aires 1915–1923; in London, S Africa and Bombay 1923–1933. Central Electricity Board, Deputy Chief Engineer 1934–1944, Chief Engineer 1944–1947. On passage of the Electricity Act 1947, became Deputy Chairman (Operations) of the British Electricity Authority, engaged largely on the engineering problems arising from grave plant shortages, and on the planning of the 275kV transmission system. On retirement from electricity supply in 1953 he rejoined Merz and McLellan as a consultant, 1954–1966, making overseas tours for them to Australia and S Africa. Knighted 1949; HonMIEE 1962.

1952 **Colonel Bruce Hamer Leeson, CBE, TD** (1890–1979) Born in Sutton. Educated at Battersea Polytechnic. Premium pupil with Prestwich & Burt of Kingston. Joined Siemens Dynamo Works Ltd to work on high-voltage switchgear development. Joined Territorial Army on its formation in 1908. Served with the Royal Naval Division in Gallipoli (mentioned in dispatches) and with the Royal Engineers on the Western Front. In 1919 joined A Reyrolle & Co and set up a technical and research department for the company. In 1929 established the first short-circuit testing station in GB, and later became chairman of Association of Short-Circuit Testing Authorities. Continued active in TA and from 1939 commanded Tyne Electrical Engineers RE, with responsibility for anti-aircraft defences, retiring with hon. rank of colonel. 1945 Managing Director of A Reyrolle & Co. 1946–1959 Director of BEAMA. President of British National Committee of International Electrotechnical Commission 1948–1959. Last Chairman of Governors of Faraday House Engineering College, disbanding the establishment in 1967. CBE 1953; HonMIEE 1960.

1953 **Harold Bishop, CBE** (later Sir Harold Bishop) (1900–1983) Educated at Alleyn's School, Dulwich, and City and Guilds College; BSc(Eng). 1920 Engineer with HM Office of Works. 1922 Engineer, Marconi's Wireless Telegraph Co Ltd. 1923 BBC Senior Superintendent. 1929 BBC Assistant Chief Engineer. 1943 Chief Engineer. He managed the post-war expansion of television and the introduction of FM radio. 1952–1963 Director of Engineering. 1963–1968 Consultant BICC Group. 1956–1958 President of Association of Supervising Electrical Engineers. 1965–1969 President of Institution of Electrical and Electronic Technician Engineers. 1960–1962 President of Royal Television Society. Fellow of Imperial College. HonFIEE 1966; CBE 1938; knighted 1955.

1954 **Josiah Eccles, CBE, MM** (later Sir Josiah Eccles) (1897–1967) Educated at Queen's University, Belfast; BSc(Eng); DSc 1956. Served in European War 1914–1918. 1922–1928 Metropolitan-Vickers Electrical Co Ltd. 1928–1944 Edinburgh Corporation Electricity Undertaking (Engineer and Manager 1940–1944). 1944–1948 City Electrical Engineer and City Lighting Engineer, Liverpool. 1948–1954 Chairman, Merseyside and N Wales Electricity Board. 1954–1957 Deputy Chairman, British Electricity Authority. Electricity Council 1957–1961. Member of Organising Committee of British Electricity Authority 1947. President of Incorporated Municipal Electrical Association 1947–1948. Chairman of Council, British Electrical Development Association 1948–1949. President, British Electrical Power Convention 1957. CBE 1950; knighted 1957; HonFIEE 1967.

Sir George Nelson Bt
(later first Lord Nelson of Stafford)

Sir William Gordon Radley KCB CBE

Thomas Edward Goldup CBE

Sidney Edward Goodall

1955 **Sir George Nelson, Bt** (later first Lord Nelson of Stafford) (1887–1962) Born in London. Educated at City and Guilds College. Premium pupil of Brush Electrical Engineering Co, Loughborough. 1911 Joined British Westinghouse Co, Trafford Park. 1920 Manager of Sheffield Works of Metropolitan-Vickers Electrical Co. 1930–1956 Managing Director of English Electric Co. Chairman 1933–1962. President of Federation of British Industry 1943–1945. President of BEAMA 1950–1953. President of BEARA 1952. President of British Electrical Power Convention 1957–1958. Chairman or member of many public committees. President of IMechE 1957–1958. Prime Warden of Worshipful Company of Goldsmiths 1960. Hon Fellow, Queen Mary College 1947; Hon Fellow, Imperial College 1955. Hon LLD, Manchester 1957; knighted 1943; baronet, 1955; peerage 1960; HonMIEE 1961.

1956 **Sir William Gordon Radley, KCB, CBE** (1898–1970) Educated at Leeds Modern School and Faraday House Engineering College. BSc(Eng) London, PhD London. Served in 1914–1918 war in Royal Engineers. Apprentice with Bruce Peebles Ltd, Edinburgh. 1920 Entered GPO Engineering Dept. Pioneer work on ocean-spanning submarine-cable communication systems. 1944–1949 Controller of Research, GPO. 1949–1951 Deputy Engineer-in-Chief. 1951–1954 Engineer-in-Chief. 1955–1960 Director General. 1960 Retired and entered industry as Director of English Electric Co, becoming Chairman of English Electric Computers and Chairman of Marconi International Marine. Chairman of various public committees. President of BEARA 1957. Various international awards. Faraday Medal IEE 1958. HonFIERE 1964. Voluntary work for the Abbeyfield Society and the British Council of Churches. CBE 1946; knighted 1954; KCB 1956; HonFIEE 1969.

1957 **Thomas Edward Goldup, CBE** (1894–1959) Born in London. Educated at Royal Naval College, Greenwich. 1914 Joined research staff of Admiralty Signal School, Portsmouth, as lieutenant. 1919 Civilian senior research officer at the Signal School, responsible for development of valves. 1923 Joined Mullard Co, Balham, with responsibility for valve manufacture. 1928 Transferred to head office to set up a technical service department. 1938 Director of Radio Transmission Equipment Ltd. 1940 Director of Mullard Radio Valve Co. 1951 Director of Mullard Ltd. CBE 1954. Fellow of American Institute of Radio Engineers 'for his pioneering achievements in the design and development of thermionic tubes'. Much involved with the education and training of young engineers.

1958 **Sidney Edward Goodall, CBE** (1903–1986) Graduated at Queen Mary College, London 1924; MSc(Eng) 1927. After three years on telephone development with Siemens Bros. joined the research department of Metropolitan-Vickers at Manchester. During the war responsible for aerial development. In 1945 joined W T Henley's as Assistant Chief Engineer; Chief Engineer 1950. After takeover by Associated Electrical Industries Ltd, appointed Engineering Director of AEI Woolwich Ltd and of the Telephone Cable Co. President of the International Electro-Technical Commission 1970–1973.

Sir Willis Jackson FRS
(later Lord Jackson of Burnley)

Sir Hamish MacLaren KBE CB

George Sail C Lucas OBE

Cecil Thomas Melling CBE

1959 **Sir Willis Jackson, FRS** (later Lord Jackson of Burnley) (1904–1970) Born in Burnley. Educated at Burnley Grammar School and at Victoria University of Manchester. 1926–1929 Lecturer at Bradford Technical College. 1929–1930 College Apprentice with Metropolitan-Vickers. 1930–1933 Lecturer at Manchester College of Technology. 1933–1936 Lecturer in Engineering Science at Oxford. 1936–1938 Research Engineer with Metropolitan-Vickers. 1938-1946 Professor of Electrotechnics, Victoria University of Manchester. 1946–1953 Professor of Electrical Engineering at Imperial College of Science and Technology. 1953–1961 Director of Research and Education, Associated Electrical Industries (Manchester). 1961–1967 Professor of Electrical Engineering at Imperial College, becoming Pro-Rector in 1967. President of Association of Supervising Electrical Engineers 1961–1963. President of British Association for the Advancement of Science 1966–1967. President of Electrical Research Association 1969. Chairman or member of many public bodies concerned with education or research. Holder of many honorary doctorates. HonFCGI; HonFIEE 1968; FRS 1953. Research on the applications of solid-state physics to electrical and electronic engineering. Involved in the promotion of higher education overseas, particularly the establishment of the Indian Institute of Technology, Delhi. Knighted 1958; Life Peer 1967.

1960 **Sir Hamish MacLaren, KBE, CB** (1898–   ) Educated Fordyce Academy, Banffshire, and Edinburgh University (BSc 1921). Served in European War 1914–1918 in RNVR, RNAS and RAF (DFC and Bar, French Croix de Guerre with Palm). 1921 Joined British Thomson-Houston Co as student apprentice. 1923–1924 BTH Fellowship to spend a year with the GE Co of Schenectady. 1924–1926 On staff of BTH, Rugby. 1926 Joined Admiralty Service as Assistant Electrical Engineer. Served at HM Dockyards at Chatham and at Devonport, in Ceylon and in the Admiralty. 1937–1940 Superintending Electrical Engineer, HM Naval Base, Singapore. 1940–1945 Assistant Director, Electrical Engineering Dept, Admiralty. 1945–1960 Director of Electrical Engineering, Admiralty. HonLLD St Andrews 1954; Hon DSc Bath 1970; CB 1946; KBE 1951; HonFIEE 1970.

1961 **George Sail Campbell Lucas, OBE** (1901–1986) Entered British Thomson-Houston Co as an apprentice instrument maker. As a result of works training courses, was awarded a BEAMA scholarship to Imperial College London. After graduating, returned to the BTH Co. Early work on radio and sound equipment for the cinema, then on radar equipment during the war. Appointed Director and Chief Engineer of the BTH Co in 1953, and in 1963 was appointed Group General Manager of the AEI Electronics Group. Retired in 1966 after 51 years with the Company. OBE; HonDTech; FCGI; HonFIEE 1972.

1962 **Cecil Thomas Melling, CBE** (1899–   ) Born in Wigan. Educated at Manchester Central High School and Manchester College of Technology. MScTech. 1918 2nd Lt., RE. 1920–1934 with Metropolitan-Vickers Electrical Co Ltd. 1934–1935 Yorkshire Electric Power Co. 1935–1943 Edmundson's Electricity Corporation Ltd. 1943–1948 Borough Electrical Engineer, Luton. 1948–1957 Chairman, Eastern Electricity Board. 1952–1953 and 1957 Member of British Electricity Authority. 1957–1961 Full-time member of the Electricity Council. Chairman of BEARA 1953–1955. President of Association of Supervising Electrical Engineers 1952–1954. Deputy Chairman, Electricity Council 1961–1965. Chairman, British National Committee for Electro-Heat 1958–1968. President, International Union for Electro-Heat 1968–1972. Chairman, Electricity Supply Industry Training Board 1965–1968. Chairman (1964–1973) and President (1973–1984) of British Electrotechnical Approvals Board. Vice President, Union of International Engineering Organisations 1969–1975. CBE 1955; HonFIEE 1978.

Sir Albert Mumford KBE

Oliver William Humphreys CBE
(later Sir Oliver Humphreys)

Leonard Drucquer
(later Sir Leonard Drucquer)

John Ashworth Ratcliffe CB CBE FRS

1963 **Sir Albert Mumford, KBE** (1903–) Educated at Bancroft's School and Queen Mary College, London; BSc(Eng) 1st class Hons 1923. 1924 Entered GPO Engineering Dept. 1938 Staff Engineer (Radio Branch). 1948 Imperial Defence College. 1951 Assistant Engineer-in-Chief GPO. 1954 Deputy Engineer-in-Chief GPO. 1960-1965 Engineer-in-Chief GPO. 1964–1966 President of Association of Supervising Electrical Engineers. Fellow of Queen Mary College 1962. Hon Treasurer IEEIE 1967– ; Hon Fellow IEEIE 1978. Hon Member of City and Guilds of London Institute. Hon Fellow, Polytechnic of the South Bank 1982. OBE 1946; KBE 1963; HonFIEE 1980.

1964 **Olliver William Humphreys, CBE** (later Sir Olliver Humphreys) (1902–) Educated at Caterham School and University College London. 1925 Joined Staff of GEC Research Laboratories. Director 1949–1961 and Chairman GEC Research Ltd 1961–1967. Director GEC Ltd 1953 and Vice-Chairman with special interest in electronics and telecommunications subsidiaries 1963–1967. President of Institute of Physics 1956–1958. IEE Faraday Lecturer 1953–1954. Member of Council of BSI 1953–1956 and of Executive Committee 1953–1960. Chairman of International Special Committee on Radio Interference 1953–1961. Chairman, Electrical Research Association 1958–1961. Chairman, DSIR Radio Research Board 1954–1962. President, Electronic Engineering Association 1962–1964. Founder Chairman of Conference of Electronics Industry 1963–1967. Fellow UCL 1963; CBE 1957; knighted 1968.

1965 **Leonard Drucquer** (later Sir Leonard Drucquer) (1902–1975) Educated at Haberdasher's Aske's School and at Regent Street Polytechnic, London. Joined BTH Ltd 1920. 1945 Manager Switchgear Sales. 1950 Manager Home Sales (Plant and Apparatus). 1956 Director Home Sales. 1958 Director and General Manager AEI Heavy Plant Division. Consultant to Industrial Group AEI 1966–1968. Chairman of Council of Engineering Institutions 1967–1969, having earlier been Chairman of the CEI overseas relations committee and of the finance subcommittee. Knighted 1968.

1966 **John Ashworth Ratcliffe, CB, CBE, FEng, FRS** (1902–) Born in Rawtenstall, Lancashire. Educated at Giggleswick School and Sidney Sussex College, Cambridge; MA. Taught Physics at Cambridge 1924–1960 and did research into radio-wave propagation. War service with Telecomumunications Research Establishment, Malvern. Reader in Physics, Cambridge, 1947–1960. Fellow of Sidney Sussex College 1927–1960; Hon Fellow 1962. 1960–1966 Director of Radio and Space Research Station, Slough. President Physical Society 1959–1960. President Section A of British Association 1964. Faraday Medal IEE 1966. Royal Medal of Royal Society 1966. Guthrie Medal of Institute of Physics 1971. HonFInstP; HonFIEE 1977; OBE 1947; CBE 1959; CB 1965.

Sir Stanley Brown CBE

Prof John Millar Meek CBE

David Edmundson

Second Lord Nelson of Stafford

1967 **Sir Stanley Brown, CBE, FEng** (1910–) Educated at King Edward's School, Birmingham, and Birmingham University; BSc. 1932–1946 Corporation of Birmingham Electric Supply Dept. 1946–1947 West Midlands Joint Electricity Authority. 1947–1948 Liverpool Corporation Electricity Supply Department. 1948 Joined Merseyside and N Wales Division of British Electricity Authority, becoming Chief Generation Engineer (Construction) 1949–1951. 1951 Appointed Deputy Generation Design Engineer of British Electricity Authority, becoming Chief Engineer of Central Electricity Authority 1957. 1959 Deputy Chairman of CEGB; Chairman 1965–1972. Hon DSc Aston 1971 and Salford 1972; CBE 1959; knighted 1967.

1968 **Professor John Millar Meek, CBE, FEng** (1912–) Born in Wallasey. Educated at Monkton Combe School and University of Liverpool. DEng. 1934–36 College Apprentice, Metropolitan–Vickers Electrical Co. 1936–1938 Research Engineer, Metrovick. 1938–1940 Commonwealth Fund Research Fellow, Physics Dept, University of California, Berkeley. 1940–1946 Research Engineer, Metrovick. 1946–1978 David Jardine Professor of Electrical Engineering, University of Liverpool. Books and numerous papers on high-voltage laboratory technique and on electrical discharges in gases. HonDSc Salford 1971. Hon Member, Institute of Electrical Engineers of Japan, 1970. Faraday Medal IEE 1975; CBE 1975.

1969 **David Edmundson** (1909–1979) Born in Gateshead, into a family closely connected with electrical engineering. Engineering apprentice with BTH Co, Rugby, and part-time study at Rugby College of Technology and Arts; BSc(Eng). 1933 Design engineer with AC machines dept of BTH. 1940 In charge of measurement laboratory, involved in development work for microwave radar and instrumentation for the first jet engines. After the war became superintendent of the test department. 1959 Appointed general manager of the Rugby works. 1962 Manufacturing manager of AEI electronic apparatus division at Leicester, later becoming chief executive of the electronics group. 1967 Director of GEC-AEI (Electronics) Ltd. Silvanus P Thompson Premium 1954. Keen mountaineer.

1970 **Henry George Nelson, second Lord Nelson of Stafford, FEng** (1917–) Born in Manchester. Educated at Oundle and King's College, Cambridge (Exhibitioner); Mechanical Sciences Tripos 1937. 1937–1939 Practical experience in England, France and Switzerland. 1939 Joined English Electric Co and became superintendent of the Preston works. 1941 Deputy works manager, Preston. 1942–1949 Managing Director, D Napier & Son Ltd. 1946–1958 Executive Director, Marconi Co Ltd. 1946 Deputy Managing Director, English Electric Co Ltd. 1956 Managing Director. 1962 Chairman and Chief Executive. 1968–1983 Chairman, General Electric Co Ltd. 1961– Director, Bank of England. Member of many Government and other public committees. President SBAC 1961–1962. President LAMA 1964–1966. President BEAMA 1966. President British Electrical Power Convention 1965–1967. President Orgaline 1968–1970. Chairman, British National Committee, World Energy Conference 1971–1974. Chairman, National Defence Industries Council 1971–1977. Numerous honorary doctorates. Fellow of Imperial College 1969. Benjamin Franklin Medal, RSA, 1959. HonFIMechE; HonFIEE 1983.

Prof John Flavell Coales OBE FRS

Sir Eric Eastwood CBE FRS

Archibald George Milne

James Henry H Merriman CB OBE

1971 **Professor John Flavell Coales, CBE, FEng, FRS** (1907–) Educated at Berkhamsted School and Sidney Sussex College, Cambridge; MA. Emeritus Fellow, Clare Hall, Cambridge; Hon Fellow, Hatfield Polytechnic. 1929–1946 Admiralty Department of Scientific Research. 1946 Research Director of Elliott Bros (London) Ltd. 1953 Assistant Director of Research in the Engineering Dept. Cambridge University. 1956 Lecturer. 1958 Reader in Engineering. 1965–1974 Professor of Engineering. Later Emeritus Professor. 1963 Mackay Visiting Professor of Electrical Engineering at University of California, Berkeley. 1955–1962 Executive Director of Tube Investments Technological Centre. 1967–1973 Part-time member of Eastern Electricity Board. 1963 President of International Federation of Automatic Control. 1963–1966 Chairman of UK Automation Council. 1958 President of Society of Instrument Technology; Hon Fellow 1971. Chairman, Council of Engineering Institutions 1975. Chairman, Commonwealth Board for Engineering Education and Training 1975–1979. Papers on radar, information theory, automatic control and technical education. OBE 1945; CBE 1974; HonDSc City 1970; HonDTech, Loughborough 1977. HonDEng, Sheffield 1978. Harold Hartley Medal 1971; Giorgio Quazza Medal 1981; Honda Prize 1982. Foreign Member of Serbian Academy of Sciences 1981. HonFIEE 1985.

1973 **Archibald George Milne** (1910–1980) Born in India. Educated at Faraday House Electrical Engineering College. Apprentice with C A Parsons & Co. 1934 Junior charge engineer with the County of London Electric Supply Co. 1935 Yorkshire Electric Power Co. 1937 Deputy Assistant Works Manager with T Firth & J Brown Ltd, Sheffield. 1946 Senior Technical Assistant with the Yorkshire Electric Power Co. 1947 Technical Superintendent, Blackburn Corporation electricity dept. 1948–1961 Various appointments with the SW Electricity Board in Bath and Bristol. 1961–1966 Chief Engineer, London Electricity Board. 1966 Deputy Chairman SEEB. 1974 Chairman, SE Electricity Board. Keen golfer. Talented sculptor and painter. Founded Milne Museum of electrical antiques, now run by the SE Electricity Board at Tonbridge, and made many gifts to it, including historic collection of telephones.

1972 **Sir Eric Eastwood, CBE, FRS** (1910–1981) Educated at Oldham High School and Manchester University (State and Open Scholar); BSc (first class Hons Physics). Research Assistant in spectroscopy. 1933 Research student at Christ's College, Cambridge; 1935 PhD. Taught physics at Collegiate School, Liverpool, and then joined the RAF, becoming a squadron leader and working on technical problems in the use of radar by the fighter defences. After war, joined Nelson Research Laboratory of English Electric Co, transferring later to the Marconi Research Laboratory, Great Baddow. Became Director of Research of General Electric Co and Chief Scientist of the Marconi Co, until his retirement in 1973. Wakefield Gold Medal of Royal Aeronautical Society 1961; Glazebrook Medal of Institute of Physics 1970. Honorary doctorates from Exeter, Loughborough and Cranfield. Hon Fellow of UMIST. CBE 1962; knighted 1972; HonFIEE 1979.

1974 **James Henry Herbert Merriman, CB, OBE, FEng** (1915–) Born in Pembroke. Educated at King's College School, Wimbledon, and at King's College, London; BSc (Hons Physics) 1935; MSc 1936. Entered GPO Engineering Dept (Research Station, Dollis Hill). During war and until 1948 was in charge of communications research laboratory at Castleton, Mon, then worked in London GPO Headquarters on HF, VHF and microwave systems. 1954 Imperial Defence College. 1955–1959 Deputy Director, Organisation and Methods, HM Treasury. 1963 Assistant Engineer-in-Chief, GPO, with oversight of all transmission including space systems. 1965 Deputy Engineer-in-Chief. 1967 Senior Director of Engineering, becoming, a few months later, Senior Director, Development. On creation of Post Office Corporation, became Board Member for Technology 1969–1976. 1977–1983 Chairman, National Computing Centre. 1977–1983 Member NEDC Electronics Committee; Chairman NEDC Sector Working Party on Information Technology. Chairman, Independent Review of Radio Spectrum 1983. Member, the Honourable Society of Cymmrodorion 1975– 1969–1979 Visiting Professor of Electronic Science and Telecommunications, Strathclyde University. Faraday Lecturer 1969–1970. Fellow of King's College 1972. HonDSc Strathclyde 1974; OBE 1961; CB 1969; HonFIEE 1981.

Robert James Clayton CBE
(later Sir Robert Clayton)

Eric Stuart Booth CBE FEng FRS

John McIntyre Ferguson CBE

James Redmond FEng
(later Sir James Redmond)

1975 **Robert James Clayton, CBE, FEng** (later Sir Robert Clayton) (1915–) Born in London. Educated at Christ's College, Cambridge (Major Scholar, and later Honorary Fellow). Read Natural Sciences (Physics). 1937 Joined GEC Research Laboratories, working on television, radar and telecommunications, particularly in microwave field. 1955 Manager, GEC Applied Electronics Labs. 1960 Deputy Director, Hirst Research Centre. 1963 Managing Director, GEC (Electronics). 1966 Managing Director, GEC (Research). 1968 Technical Director, GEC. 1971–1977 Visiting Professor, Imperial College. 1976–1980 Member of Advisory Council on Applied Reseach and Development; Chairman of Groups on Applications of Semiconductors, Computer Aided Design and Manufacture, and Information Technology. 1981– Member, British Library Board. 1982–1984 Chairman, Ordnance Survey Advisory Board. 1982– Member, UGC. 1983– Member, Monopolies and Mergers Commission. 1982 President, Institute of Physics. 1980–1982 Vice-President, Fellowship of Engineering. Faraday Lecturer IEE. Hon doctorates from Aston, Salford and City universities. Hon FIEE 1982; OBE 1960; CBE 1970; knighted 1980.

1976 **Eric Stuart Booth, CBE, FEng, FRS** (1914–) Born in Yorkshire. Educated at Batley Grammar School and Liverpool University; MEng. Apprentice with Metropolitan-Vickers Electrical Co Ltd. 1938–1946 Technical Engineer with Yorkshire Electric Power Co. 1947 City Electrical Engineer and Manager, Salford. 1948–1957 Various posts associated with the construction of power stations with the British (later the Central) Electricity Authority. 1958 Chief Design and Construction Engineer, CEGB. Board Member of the CEGB for Engineering 1959–1971, responsible for the design and construction of all new conventional and nuclear power stations and of the Transmission System including the Supergrid. Part-time member of UKAEA 1965–1972. Chairman of Yorkshire Electricity Board 1972–1979. HonDTech Bradford 1980; CBE 1971.

1977 **John McIntyre Ferguson, CBE, FEng** (1915–) Educated at Armstrong College, Durham University; BSc(Eng). 1936 Joined research department of English Electric Co, Stafford. 1953 Became Chief Engineer. 1965 Director of Engineering, Heavy Electric Products. 1969 Director of Engineering, GEC Power Engineering Co. 1973 Engineering consultant. Member of Metrication Board 1969–1976. Member of Science Research Council 1972–1976. Chairman of the Engineering Board of SRC 1972–1976. Member of UGC 1977–1982. President of IEETE 1979–1981. CBE 1976; FEng 1978; HonDSc Birmingham 1983.

1978 **James Redmond, FEng** (later Sir James Redmond) (1918–) Educated at Graeme Muir School, Falkirk, Caledonian Wireless College, Heriot Watt College, Edinburgh. 1937–1938 Junior sound engineer, BBC Edinburgh. 1938–1939 Junior television engineer, BBC Alexandra Palace. 1939–1945 Radio officer, Merchant Navy. Returned to BBC in 1945 to help re-start the world's first television service. Became a planning engineer, engaged in spreading the BBC Television Service throughout the United Kingdom. Was particularly active in developing television recording and colour television. 1968–1978 BBC Director of Engineering. 1970–1975 President, Society of Electronic and Radio Technicians. 1970–1978 Member of European Broadcasting Union Technical Bureau. 1974–1978 Vice President Engineering, Commonwealth Broadcasting Association. 1982– Hon Treasurer, National Electronics Council. 1983– Member of Board, Services Sound and Vision Corporation. 1983– Hon Secretary Electrical, Fellowship of Engineering. FEng 1978; knighted 1979.

Prof John Brown

Air Marshal Sir Herbert
Durkin KBE CB

Sir Francis Tombs FEng

John Banks

1979 **Professor John Brown, CBE, FEng** (1923–) Born at Auchterderran, Fife. Educated at Edinburgh University. 1944–1951 On the research staff of the Radar Research and Development Establishment, Malvern. 1951 Lecturer in electrical engineering, Imperial College, London. 1954 Lecturer at University College, London; 1956 Promoted to Reader; 1964 Professor. 1962–1965 Seconded to Indian Institute of Technology, Delhi, as Visiting Professor. 1967–1981 Professor of Electrical Engineering, Imperial College (Head of Dept 1967–1979). 1981 Technical Director, Marconi Electronic Devices Ltd. Chairman of Engineering Board of Science Research Council 1977–1981. President of IEEIE 1981. DSc(Eng). Author of a number of books and many papers on radio waves, telecommunications, etc. CBE 1982.

1980 **Air Marshal Sir Herbert Durkin, KBE, CB** (1922–) Born in Burnley, Lancs. Educated at Burnley Grammar School and Emmanuel College, Cambridge; MA. Commissioned into Technical Branch, RAF Oct 1941. 1945–1947 Served in India, becoming ADC to the Air Officer Commanding-in-Chief, India. 1947–1950 At Central Bomber Establishment, rising to Squadron Leader. 1950–1952 At Atomic Weapons Research Establishment. 1953 RAF Staff College. 1954–1956 Chief Signals Officer, AHQ Iraq. 1956–1958 Wing Commander, Chief Instructor of Signals Division of RAF Technical College. 1958–1960 Air Ministry. 1964 Senior Technical Staff Officer, HQ Signals Command. 1967 Air Commodore, Director of Engineering (Policy), Ministry of Defence. 1973 Director-General Engineering and Supply Management. 1976–1978 Controller of Engineering and Supply (RAF), CB 1973; KBE 1976.

1981 **Sir Francis Tombs, FEng** (1924–) Educated at Elmore Green School, Walsall, and Birmingham College of Technology; BSc(Econ). 1939–1945 With GEC. 1946–1947 With Birmingham Corporation. 1947–1957 British Electricity Authority, Midlands, then Central Electricity Authority, Merseyside and N Wales. 1957–1965 GEC Erith. 1965–1968 C A Parsons, Erith. 1968–1969 James Howden & Godfrey Ltd. 1969–1977 South of Scotland Electricity Board, as Director of Engineering, then Deputy Chairman, then Chairman. 1977–1980 Chairman, Electricity Council. 1981–1983 Chairman of the Weir Group. 1982 Chairman of Turner & Newall, and Director of other public companies. 1981 Vice-President of YHA. 1982 Chairman of Association of British Orchestras. Hon doctorates from Strathclyde; Loughborough; Aston; Lodz, Poland. Knighted 1978.

1982 **John Banks, FEng** (1920–) Educated at University of Liverpool. 1st class Hons Electrical Engineering, and later MEng. 1941 Joined BICC Ltd, Prescot, at first developing communication cables for radar. 1949 Moved into technical management, eventually becoming chief engineer of BICC power-cable operations. 1968 Director of Supertension Cables Division of BICC, Erith. 1975 Executive Director of BICC Research and Engineering. 1978 Chairman of BICC Research and Engineering Ltd and Technical Director of BICC plc.

Maldwyn Noel John FEng

Prof John Clifford West CBE FEng

Admiral Sir Lindsay Sutherland
Bryson KCB FEng

Dr Geoffrey Thomas Shepherd CBE

1983 **Maldwyn Noel John, FEng** (1929–) Educated at University College, Cardiff. 1st class Hons Electrical Engineering, and University Page Medal. Postgraduate training at Metropolitan-Vickers Electrical Co, Manchester, followed by an appointment in the power systems engineering dept. 1959 Group leader on analogue computation with UKAEA, Winfrith, Dorset. 1962 Returned to AEI Ltd, Manchester, as assistant chief engineer, power systems. 1965 Chief Engineer of systems engineering dept. 1966–1968 Divisional Chief Engineer of AEI Transformer Division, and then Manager of AC Transmission Division, GEC Switchgear Ltd. 1969 Chief Electrical Engineer of Kennedy and Donkin, consulting engineers, becoming a partner in 1972. He has been responsible for much work overseas, particularly in Iran, Iraq and Jordan. FEng 1979; FIEEE 1985.

1984 **Professor John Clifford West, CBE, FEng** (1922–) Educated at Hindley and Abram Grammar School, and at Victoria University of Manchester. DSc 1957. 1943 Electrical Lieutenant, RNVR. 1946 Lecturer, University of Manchester. 1958–1965 Professor of Electrical Engineering, Queen's University, Belfast. 1965–1978 Professor of Electrical and Control Engineering, University of Sussex, and Founder Dean of the School of Applied Sciences, 1965–1973. Pro-Vice Chancellor 1967–1971. 1979 Appointed Vice-Chancellor and Principal of University of Bradford. Director ACE Machinery Ltd 1966–1979. Chairman of Technology Committee of UGC 1973–1978. Chairman or member of a number of public committees. Author of a number of textbooks and scientific papers. Hon Fellow of Institute of Measurement and Control 1984 and Hartley Medallist 1979. Keen philatelist. CBE 1977.

1985 **Admiral Sir Lindsay Bryson, KCB, FEng, FRSE** (1925–) Born in Glasgow. Educated at Allan Glen's School, Glasgow. Engineering Cadet 1942. Electrical Mechanic RN 1944. Midshipman 1946. In 1947 posted to Telecommunications Research Establishment, Malvern, to work on airborne radar. 1948 London BSc(Eng) (External) with 1st Class Hons. 1949–1954 Fleet Air Arm. 1954–1956 Service in frigates and destroyers. 1956–1958 Working on control systems at Department of Electrical Engineering, Bath. 1958–1969 Service at sea, at Naval Aircraft Department, London, and at Royal Military College of Science, Shrivenham. 1970 Took command of Royal Naval Air Station, Lee-on-Solent, HMS *Daedalus*. 1973 Director, Naval Guided Weapons Systems. 1975 Director, Surface Weapons Systems. 1977 Promoted Rear Admiral and appointed Director General Weapons (Naval). 1979 Chief Naval Engineer Officer. Promoted Vice Admiral. 1981 Controller of the Navy. Had responsibilities over the years for the introduction into service of new airborne radars, new aircraft, new ships and new weapons systems. 1983 Promoted Admiral, the first Weapons Electrical Engineer to achieve this rank. Retired 1984. FRAeS 1971. Faraday Lecturer IEE 1976. KCB 1981; FEng 1982; FRSE 1984.

1986 **Dr Geoffrey Thomas Shepherd, CBE** (1922–) Born at Moseley, Birmingham. Educated at King Edward's School, Birmingham and Birmingham Central Technical College. BSc(Eng), Hons. 1938–1946 Apprentice and Design Draughtsman at GEC Witton. 1946–1952 Several positions in power stations. 1952–1954 Deputy Superintendent, Skelton Grange Power Station. 1955–1958 Member of original team inaugurating civil nuclear power in UK. 1958–1961 CEGB Nuclear Operations Engineer, becoming Regional Director of the CEGB Western Division in 1962. 1965 South of Scotland Electricity Board, becoming Director of Engineering 1968–1969. 1969–1972 Deputy Chairman of the London Electricity Board. 1972–1982 Chairman, the Midlands Electricity Board. 1977–1984 Part-time member of the CEGB. 1982 Management and Engineering Consultant. President of the Combined Heat and Power Association. 1986 Awarded Honorary DSc from University of Aston.

Secretaries

1878 Francis Hughes Webb (1824–1908) Educated University College School, London and Ecole Normale, Brussels. Spent two years in Germany in training with the engineer to the British Nassau Iron Co. Returned to England to become clerk of the Audit Office of the London, Brighton and South Coast Railway. 1844 Appointed Librarian of the Royal Institute of British Architects. 1850 Joined the Electric Telegraph Co as Resident Engineer. 1865–1878 Secretary to various railway and harbour companies in Nova Scotia, Malta and Montevideo. 1878 Appointed Secretary of the Society of Telegraph Engineers, at first part-time, but full-time from 1885. Retired in 1898 at the age of 73. Associate IEE.

1898 Walter George McMillan, FIC, FCS (1861–1904) Educated at King's College School and King's College, London. Awarded Daniell Scholarship 1880 for research on the effect of an electric spark on mixtures of oxygen and nitrogen. Spent one year in the office of an accountant. Returned to scientific work, joining King's College staff as Demonstrator in Metallurgy. 1888–1893 In India as Chemist and Metallurgist to Cossipore Ordnance Factories, near Calcutta. 1893 Lecturer in Metallurgy, Mason's College, Birmingham, writing textbooks, articles and abstracts on electro-metallurgy and electro-chemistry. 1897 Appointed Secretary of the Institution and Editor of the Journal, and elected an Associate of the Institution. Died suddenly in 1904 at the age of 43.

1904 George Christopher Lloyd (1861–1942) Born in Lincolnshire. Educated at the Moravian School, Königsfeld, Baden. Five-year apprenticeship with Robert Stephenson & Co, Newcastle upon Tyne. Marine engineer, sailing to Central and South America, East Indies and China. 1891–1900 with various engineering companies in London and Glasgow. 1900 Joined staff of Iron and Steel Institute. 1904–1909 Secretary of the IEE. 1909 Returned to Iron and Steel Institute as Secretary, remaining until his retirement in 1933. Member of Council of Chartered Institute of Secretaries. Vice-President of International Association for Testing Materials. Légion d'Honneur; Swedish Order of the North Star.

1909 Percy Fitz-Patrick Rowell (1874–1940) Born in London. Educated at Royal College of Mauritius and King's College, London (Maths and Physics). Spent several years in engineering firms, including BTH Co. Joined IEE staff in 1901. Appointed Assistant Secretary in 1904 and Secretary in 1909. Took a considerable personal interest in wireless developments, constructing many sets himself. Spoke French and Italian. Keen chess player. Associate IEE 1913; Companion IEE 1929; Chevalier de la Légion d'Honneur 1936.

William Kenneth Brasher CBE   Dr George Fotheringham
                                               Gainsborough CBE

Dr Howard Harold W Losty FEng

1932 William Morris Mordey
1933 Llewelyn B Atkinson
1934 René Thury
1935 The Rt. Hon. Lord Hirst of Witton
1936 Sir John Francis Cleverton Snell, GBE
1937 Alexander Russell, MA, DSc, LLD, FRS
1938 Sir Frank Gill, KCMG, OBE
1939 Sir Archibald Page
1940 Roger Thomas Smith, BSc
1941 The Rt. Hon. Sir Andrew Rae Duncan, GBE, MA, LLD
1942 Gen. the Hon. A G L McNaughton, CB, CMG, CH, DSO, MSc, LLD, DCL
1942 The Rt. Hon. Lord Hankey, PC, GCB, GCMG, GCVO, FRS
1944 Sir Ernest Thomas Fisk
1945 John Somerville Highfield
1946 The Rt. Hon. the Earl of Mount Edgcumbe, TD
1947 Sir John Macfarlane Kennedy, OBE
1948 Col. Sir Thomas F Purves, OBE
     Admiral of the Fleet Sir John H D Cunningham, GCB, MVO
1949 John Muir Donaldson, MC
1950 Sir Edgar Walford Marchant, DSc
1951 Philip Vassar Hunter, CBE
1952 Sir Edward V Appleton, GBE, KCB, MA, DSc, LLD, FRS
     Sir Arthur Percy M Fleming, CBE, DEng, LLD
1953 Sir Harry Railing, DEng
1954 Ernest Leete
1955 HRH The Prince Philip, The Duke of Edinburgh, KG, PC, KT, GBE, FRS
     James Robert Beard, CBE, MSc
1956 Col. Sir Stanley Angwin, KCMG, KBE, DSO, MC, TD, DSc(Eng)
1957 Sir Noel Ashbridge, BSc(Eng)
     Brig. Gen. Sir Harold Hartley, GCVO, CBE, MC, MA, FRS
1958 Henry Thomas Young
1959 Charles William Spiers, FCGI, JP
1960 Richard Lankaster Hearn, BA Sc, DEng, LLD
     Col. Bruce Hamer Leeson, CBE, TD
1961 The Rt. Hon. Lord Nelson of Stafford, DSc(Eng)
1962 Sir John Hacking
1963 The Rt. Hon. Lord Fleck of Saltcoats, KBE, DSc, LLD, FRS
     Prof. Eric Bailleul Moullin, MA, ScD, LLD
1964 Percy Dunsheath, CBE, MA, DSc(Eng), LLD
1965 Admiral of the Fleet the Rt. Hon. Earl Mountbatten of Burma, KG, PC, GCB,
     OM, GCSI, GCVO, DSO, LLD, DCL, DSc, FRS
1966 Sir Harold Bishop, CBE, BSc(Eng), FCGI
1967 Sir Josiah Eccles, CBE, DSc
     Prof. Sir Bernard Lovell, OBE, FRS
1968 The Rt. Hon. Lord Jackson of Burnley, DSc, DSC, DEng, LLD, FRS
1969 Sir William Gordon Radley, KCB, CBE, PhD
1970 Sir Hamish Duncan MacLaren, KBE, CB, DFC (and bar), LLD, DSc
1971 Sir Vincent Ziani de Ferranti, MC
     The Rt. Hon. Lord Hinton of Bankside, KBE, MA, DSc, FRS
1972 George Sail C Lucas, OBE, Hon. DTech, FCGI

The Rt. Hon. Lord Hailsham of St Marylebone, QC
1973 Sir Ben Lewis Barnett, KBE, CB, MC, MA
1974 Wilfred Bennett Lewis, CC, CBE, FRSC, PhD, FRS
The Rt. Hon. Lord Penney of East Hendred, OM, KBE, MA, PhD, DSc, FRS
1975 Prof. H B G Casimir, PhD
Sir Brian Flowers, FRS
Sir Arnold Hall, FRS
1976 HRH the Duke of Kent, GCMG, GCVO, ADC
Pierre R R Aigrain
1977 John Ashworth Ratcliffe, CB, CBE, MA, FRS
Prof. John Samuel Forrest, DSc, MA, FRS
1978 C Lester Hogan, BS, MS, MA, PhD, DSc, DEng
Cecil Thomas Melling, CBE, MScTech
Prof. Gordon Hindle Rawcliffe, MA, DSc, DTech, FRS
1979 Sir Eric Eastwood, CBE, DSc(Hon), PhD, FRS
Prof. Sir Hermann Bondi, KCB, FRAS, FRS
1980 Sir Albert Mumford, KBE, BSc(Eng), FQMC
Prof. Maurice George Say, PhD, MSc, FRSE
1981 HRH the Prince of Wales, KG, KT, GCB
James Henry H Merriman, CB, OBE, MSc, FKC, DSc, FEng
Sir John Hill, BSc, PhD
1982 Sir Robert Clayton, CBE, MA, DSc(Eng), FEng
Geoffrey F Kennedy, MA
1983 The Rt. Hon. Lord Nelson of Stafford, MA, Hon. DSc, Hon. LLD, FEng
Fredric Harald Flurscheim, MA, FEng
1984 The Rt. Hon. the Viscount Caldecote, DSc, MA, FEng
Sir James Lighthill, FRS
Sir Duncan McDonald, CBE, DSc, BSc, FHWC, FEng, FRSE
1985 Prof. John Flavell Coales, FEng, CBE, DEng, FRS
Sir Kenneth Corfield, FEng

Faraday Medallists

1922 Oliver Heaivside, FRS
1923 The Hon. Sir Charles Algernon Parsons, OM, KCB, FRS
1924 Sebastian Ziani de Ferranti, DSc, FRS
1925 Sir Joseph John Thomson, OM, MA, FRS
1926 Col. Rookes Evelyn B Crompton, CB, FRS
1927 Elihu Thomson, DSc
1928 Prof. Sir John Ambrose Fleming, MA, DSc, FRS
1929 Guido Semenza
1930 The Rt. Hon. Lord Rutherford of Nelson, OM, FRS
1931 Charles H Merz, DSc
1932 Sir Oliver Lodge, DSc, FRS
1933 No award
1934 Sir Frank E Smith, GCB, GBE, DSc, FRS
1935 Frank Baldwin Jewett, PhD
1936 Sir William H Bragg, OM, KBE, MA, DSc, FRS

1937 Prof. André Blondel
1938 Sir John F C Snell, GBE
1939 William David Coolidge, BSc, PhD
1940 Alexander Russell, MA, DSc, LLD, FRS
1941 Sir Arthur P M Fleming, CB, DEng, LLD
1942 Dr Peter Kapitza, FRS
1943 Sir Archibald Page
1944 Irving Langmuir, LLD, PhD, DSc
1945 Sir Clifford C Paterson, OBE, DSc, FRS
1946 Sir Edward Victor Appleton, GBE, KCB, MA, DSc, LLD, FRS
1947 Sir Leonard Pearce, CBE, DSc
1948 Prof. Marcus L E Oliphant, FRS
1949 Charles Samuel Franklin, CBE
1950 Sir James Chadwick, MSc, PhD, FRS
1951 Thomas Lydwell Eckersley, BA, BSc, PhD, FRS
1952 Prof. Ernest Orlando Lawrence, AM, PhD
1953 Col. Sir Stanley Angwin, KBE, DSO, MC, TD, DSc(Eng)
1954 Sir Isaac Shoenberg
1955 Sir John Douglas Cockcroft, KCB, CBE, MA, MScTech, PhD, FRS
1956 Prof. George William Osborne Howe, DSc, LLD
1957 Dr Waldemar Borgquist
1958 Sir William Gordon Radley, KCB, CBE, PhD
1959 Luigi Emanuely
1960 Sir George Paget Thomson, DSc, FRS
1961 Julius A Stratton, ScD, LLD
1962 Sir Basil F J Schonland, CBE, MA, PhD, FRS
1963 Pierre Marie J Ailleret, Commandeur de la Légion d'Honneur
1964 Joseph Ronald Mortlock, BSc(Eng), PhD
1965 Vladimir K Zworykin, EE, PhD, DSc
1966 John Ashworth Ratcliffe, CB, CBE, MA, FRS
1967 Prof. Harold Everard M Barlow, PhD, DEng, DSc, FRS
1968 Leslie Herbert Bedford, CBE, BSc(Eng), MA
1969 Dr Philip Sporn, EE
1970 Prof. Sir Charles William Oatley, OBE, DSc, FRS
1971 Prof. Sir Martin Ryle, MA, FRS
1972 Prof. Frederic Calland Williams, CBE, DSc, DPhil, Hon. DSc, Hon. DEng,
        FRS
1973 Prof. Sir Nevill Mott, MA, FRS
1974 George Millington, MA, BSc
1975 Prof. John Millar Meek, CBE, DEng, DSc
1976 Thomas Otten Paine, AB, MS, PhD
1977 John Bertram Adams, CMG, MA, DSc, FRS
1978 Erich Friedlander, DrIng
1979 Dr Robert N Noyce
1980 Prof. Eric Albert Ash, PhD, DSc
1981 Prof. Maurice V Wilkes, MA, PhD, FRS
1982 Prof. Brian David Josephson, MA, PhD, FRS
1983 Prof. William Alexander Gambling, DSc, PhD, FEng
1984 Prof. Alexander Lamb Cullen, OBE, DSc(Eng), FEng, FRS
1985 Prof. Charles Antony Richard Hoare, MA, Hon. DSc, FRS

Appendix 5

Statistics of Membership

Classes of Membership, with the years in which they were established

1871	1899	1912	1929	1966
Honorary Members	Honorary Members	Honorary Members	Honorary Members	Honorary Fellows
Members	Members	Members	Members	Fellows
Associates	Associate Members	Associate Members	Associate Members	Members
Foreign Members	Associates	Associates	Companions	Companions
Students	Foreign Members	Graduates	Associates	Associate Members
	Students	Students	Graduates	Associates
			Students	Students

Corporate Members, as established by the Articles of Association in 1912, are those in the first three classes of membership in each case, except that only those Honorary Members or Honorary Fellows who on election were already Corporate Members are included in this category.

On the grant of the Royal Charter in 1921 Corporate Members obtained the right to use the designation 'Chartered Electrical Engineer'.

The title 'Chartered Engineer' (CEng) is derived from powers originally granted to the CEI under their Charter of 1965 and transferred in 1983 to the Engineering Council.

Membership Numbers, 1871–1985

Year	Corporate Members (a)	Total Members	Increase	Increase (%)	Year	Corporate Members (a)	Total Members	Increase	Increase (%)
1871		110			1888		1465	123	9.2
1872		353	243	220.9	1889		1491	26	1.8
1873		522	169	47.9	1890		1760	269	18.0
1874		648	126	24.1	1891		1976	216	12.3
1875		763	115	17.7	1892		2152	176	8.9
1876		751	−12	−1.6	1893		2316	164	7.6
1877		958	207	27.6	1894		2448	132	5.7
1878		974	16	1.7	1895		2604	156	6.4
1879		1019	45	4.6	1896		2674	70	2.7
1880		980	−39	−3.8	1897		2753	79	2.9
1881		981	1	0.1	1898		2930	177	6.4
1882		991	10	1.0	1899		3254	324	11.1
1883		1126	135	13.6	1900		3660	406	12.5
1884		1187	61	5.4	1901		4018	358	9.8
1885		1257	70	5.9	1902		4406	388	9.6
1886		1342	85	6.7	1903		4818	412	9.3
1887		1342	0	0.0	1904		5410	592	12.2

Year	Corporate Members (a)	Total Members	Increase	Increase (%)	Year	Corporate Members (a)	Total Members	Increase	Increase (%)
1905		5670	260	4.8	1946	13447	29158	2493	9.3
1906		5803	133	2.3	1947	14501	31260	2102	7.2
1907		5945	142	2.4	1948	15206	32907	1647	5.3
1908		6068	123	2.1	1949	16027	34371	1464	4.4
1909		6117	49	0.8	1950	16648	35548	1177	3.4
1910		6210	93	1.5	1951	17146	36558	1010	2.8
1911		6327	117	1.9	1952	17757	37253	695	1.9
1912		6600	273	4.3	1953	18510	37782	529	1.4
1913	5091	7084	484	7.3	1954	19552	38496	714	1.9
1914	5111	7045	−39	−0.5	1955	20355	39298	802	2.1
1915	5016	6817	−228	−3.2	1956	21089	40038	740	1.9
1916	4973	6676	−141	−2.0	1957	22097	41522	1484	3.7
1917	5019	6613	−63	−0.9	1958	22879	43228	1706	4.1
1918	5041	6667	54	0.8	1959	23708	44544	1316	3.0
1919	5365	7023	356	5.3	1960	24324	46222	1678	3.8
1920	5768	8146	1123	16.0	1961	25007	47422	1200	2.6
1921	6293	9449	1303	16.0	1962	25651	49035	1613	3.4
1922	6471	10275	826	8.7	1963	26084	50384	1349	2.8
1923	6594	10911	636	6.2	1964	26646	52125	1741	3.5
1924	6605	11415	504	4.6	1965	27316	54150	2025	3.9
1925	6589	11743	328	2.9	1966	27768	55578	1428	2.6
1926	6623	12142	399	3.4	1967	28132	57071	1493	2.7
1927	6829	12647	505	4.2	1968		58137	1066	1.9
1928	7080	13043	396	3.1	1969		60420	2283	3.9
1929	7328	13561	518	4.0	1970	30030	63387	2967	4.9
1930	7501	14200	639	4.7	1971	30830	63731	344	0.5
1931	7646	14670	470	3.3	1972	31827	65690	1959	3.1
1932	7804	14884	214	1.5	1973	33918	65950	260	0.4
1933	7937	15149	265	1.8	1974	34846	67771	1821	2.8
1934	8142	15619	470	3.1	1975	35398	69163	1392	2.1
1935	8317	16150	531	3.4	1976	36034	70350	1187	1.7
1936	8569	16788	638	3.9	1977	36690	72034	1684	2.4
1937	8842	17399	611	3.6	1978	37164	74254	2220	3.1
1938	9110	18252	853	4.9	1979	37338	75135	881	1.2
1939	9462	19044	792	4.3	1980	37620	77063	1928	2.6
1940	9838	19872	828	4.3	1981	37905	78426	1363	1.8
1941	10121	20273	401	2.0	1982	38465	79553	1127	1.4
1942	10483	21050	777	3.8	1983	38695	80762	1209	1.5
1943	11097	22315	1265	6.0	1984	39122	82839	2077	2.6
1944	11924	24558	2243	10.1	1985	39529	86848	4009	4.8
1945	12574	26665	2107	8.6					

Note: (a)
This term is first used in the Articles of Association which came into operation on 1 July 1912.

IEE Members' Employment, 1881–1911

	1881 M		1881 A		1891 M		1891 A		1901 M		1901 AM		1901 A		1911 M	
	n	%	n	%	n	%	n	%	n	%	n	%	n	%	n	%
Educational bodies	6	1.9	3	1.0	10	3.9	14	3.0	25	8.6	14	5.8	36	6.9	58	13.5
Electric lighting & supply	1	0.3	1	0.3	16	6.2	31	6.6	48	16.4	91	36.8	90	17.34	100	23.2
Electric tramways	—	—	—	—	—	—	—	—	7	2.3	13	5.3	14	2.7	16	3.7
Railways	23	7.2	9	3.0	17	6.6	26	5.5	24	8.2	8	3.2	21	4.0	36	8.4
Electrical manufacturers	13	4.0	19	6.5	39	15.2	95	20.3	60	20.5	64	25.9	122	23.5	72	16.7
Government (UK):																
Army	36	11.2	4	1.4	33	12.8	34	7.3	25	8.6	8	3.2	32	6.2	22	5.1
Navy	3	0.9	1	0.4	3	1.2	4	0.9	1	0.3	—	—	3	0.6	6	1.4
GPO	12	3.7	66	22.5	9	3.6	50	10.7	7	2.4	6	2.4	28	5.4	7	1.6
Miscellaneous	5	1.6	5	1.7	1	0.4	6	1.3	1	0.3	—	—	3	0.6	4	0.9
Government (foreign)	10	3.1	1	0.4	6	2.4	5	1.1	18	6.2	6	2.4	19	3.7	18	4.2
Industry	1	0.3	1	0.4	2	0.8	7	1.5	2	0.6	9	3.6	18	3.5	24	5.6
Telegraphs	199	61.8	181	78.7	100	39.1	154	33.0	54	18.4	11	4.6	95	18.3	35	8.1
Telephones	9	2.8	—	—	11	4.2	21	4.5	11	3.8	9	3.6	21	4.0	18	4.2
Miscellaneous & unidentified	4	1.2	2	0.7	9	3.6	20	4.3	10	3.4	8	3.2	17	3.3	15	3.6
Total in sample	322		293		256		467		293		247		519		431	
Total in Membership class	339		475		535		1079		832		774		1712		1331	

The information for this chart has been extracted from the membership lists, relying on the professional addresses and other information given by the members concerned. It can only be regarded as an approximation to the facts. To extract similar information from later lists is impracticable.

Note: M = Member
      AM = Associate Member
      A = Associate
      n = number

IEE Members' Employment, 1986

Figures taken from IEE Salary Survey 1986, as published in *IEE NEWS* March 1986.

1986 Membership: Corporate (Hon Fellows, Fellows and Members)   39728
                  Non-Corporate   48378

                                       TOTAL   88106

Class of Employment	Fellows and Members		Associate Members	
	(Numbers)	(%)	(Numbers)	(%)
University	141	3.7	84	2.5
Polytechnic, Technical College (or other Educational Establishment)	174	4.5	84	2.5
Postgraduate student (not on full pay from employer)	3	0.1	62	1.9
Nationalised industry or Public Corporation*	727	18.9	565	17.0
Industrial or commercial company	1832	47.7	2075	62.4
Government:				
(i) Armed forces	103	2.7	75	2.3
(ii) Central Government	181	4.7	82	2.5
(iii) Local Authority (excluding Educational Establishments)	54	1.4	21	0.6
(iv) Health Authority	34	0.9	16	0.5
UKAEA and associated companies	40	1.0	39	1.2
Consulting practice	142	3.7	58	1.7
Self Employed	182	4.7	76	2.3
Retired or working part-time	136	3.5	12	0.4
Unemployed and seeking re-employment	21	0.5	30	0.9
Other	72	1.9	47	1.4
Number of replies from random sample	3842		3326	

* Presumably includes Railways, Post Office, Telephones, CEGB and Area Boards.

Financial Statistics

Decennial summary of IEE finances, 1872–1981 (pounds sterling)

	1872 (2 yrs a/cs)	1881	1891	1901	1911	1921	1931	1941	1951	1961	1971	1981
Income												
Subscriptions	312	1466	2851	6191	11880	30000	40000	52000	112000	244000	298000	1246000
Other	205	180	314	328	4519	6000	16000	18000	82000	150000	1361000	8586000
TOTAL	517	1646	3165	6519	16399	36000	56000	70000	194000	394000	1659000	9832000
Expenditure												
Members services	476	1279	2274	5861	13496	32000	46000	52000	159000	332000	620000	2663000
Others					1629	3500	9000	7000	44000	49000	988000	5724000
Surplus/(deficit)	41	367	891	758	1274	500	1000	11000	(6000)	13000	50000	1445000
TOTAL	517	1646	3165	6519	16399	36000	56000	70000	194000	394000	1659000	9832000

Source: D. Hunter 9 April 1985

Appendix 7

Sections and Divisions

Chairmen of the Sections of the IEE, 1919–1961

	Wireless	*Meter & Instrument*	*Transmission*	*Installations*
1919	W H Eccles			
1920	W H Eccles			
1921	Prof. G W O Howe			
1922	Prof. G W O Howe			
1923	E H Shaughnessy			
1924	E H Shaughnessy			
1925	Major B Binyon			
1926	Prof. C L Fortescue			
1927	Lt. Col. A G Lee	G D Malcolm		
1928	Commander J A Slee	E W Hill		
1929	Captain C E Kennedy-Purvis			
1930	C E Rickard	E Fawssett		
1931	Col. A S Angwin	F C Knowles		
1932	L B Turner	R S J Spilsbury		
1933	G Shearing	W Lawson		
1934	S R Mullard	Prof. J T MacGregor-Morris	R Borlase Matthews	H T Young
1935	P A Watson-Watt	O Howarth	W Fennell	
1936	E Mallett	G F Shotter	P Dunsheath	
1937	T Wadsworth	H Cobden Turner	J L Eve	
1938	A J Gill	Captain B S Cohen	S R Siviour	
1939	E B Moullin	F E J Ockenden	F W Purse	
1940	W J Picken	C W Marshall	H J Allcock	
1941	H Bishop	W Phillips	S W Melson	
		Measurements	*Supply*	
1942	R L Smith-Rose	E H Miller	P E Rycroft	R Grierson
1943	T E Goldup	E W Moss	T R Scott	A G Ramsey

	Radio	Measurements (cont.)	Supply (cont.)	Installations (cont.)
1944	H L Kirke	W S Radley	H W Grimmitt	G O Watson
1945	A H Mumford	S H Richards	E T Norris	Forbes Jackson
1946	Prof. Willis Jackson	L J Matthews	J Andrew Lee	J F Shipley
1947	C E Strong	D C Gall	Prof. W J John	R H Rawll
				Utilisation
1948	F Smith	S Whitehead	C O Boyse	R O Ackerley
1949	R T B Wynn	Prof. J Greig	J W Leach	C T Melling
1950	Captain C F Booth	G A V Sowter	S E Goodall	A N Irens
1951	D C Espley	F J Lane	R Davies	A H Young
1952	E C S Megaw	L Hartshorn	C M Cock	J W T Walsh
1953	J A Smale	J F Coales	L G Brazier	B L Metcalf
1954	C W Oatley	M Whitehead	J D Peattie	J I Bernard
		Measurement & Control		
1955	H Stanesby	W Bamford	L Drucquer	D B Hogg
	Radio & Telecommunication			
1956	R C G Williams	D Taylor	P J Ryle	H J Gibson
1957	J S McPetrie	H S Petch	Prof. M G Say	J Vaughan Harries
1958	G Millington	J K Webb	D P Sayers	R A Marryat
1959	M J L Pulling	Prof. A Tustin	J R Mortlock	T E Houghton
	Electronics & Communications			
1960	T B D Terroni	C G Garton	J E L Robinson	J M Ferguson
1961	R J Halsey	W S Elliott	J S Forrest	H G Taylor

Chairmen of the Divisions of the IEE 1962–1985

	Electronics	Power	Science & General
1962	J A Ratcliffe	D B Irving	D Taylor
1963	R C G Williams	C D Wilkinson	J R Mortlock
1964	G G Gouriet	C H Flurscheim	Prof. M W Humphrey Davies

Year	*Electronics (cont.)*	*Power (cont.)*	*Science, Education & Management*	*Control & Automation*
1965	Prof. A I Cullen	D T Hollingsworth		Prof. J F Coales
1966	P A T Bevan	E S Booth		S S Carlisle
1967	J H H Merriman	E C Rippon		E Eastwood
1968	R J Clayton	F J Lane		Prof. J H Westcott
1969	J A Saxton	C F Freeman		P L Taylor
1970	Prof. J Brown	A G Milne	R W Sillars	Prof. J C West
1971	P E Trier	Prof. E R Laithwaite	L A Thomas	R H Barker
1972	J Redmond	J M Ferguson	T Mayer	D S Hiorns
1973	J R Pollard	J Banks	E R L Lewis	J F Roth
1974	Prof. E A Ash	W J Outram	B C Lindley	I R Young
1975	I L Davies	M N John	J R Thompson	Prof. J L Douce
1976	D M Leakey	R W Flux	A E Bailey	G A Montgomerie
1977	C A May	D J Miller	Prof. F A Benson	F D Boardman
1978	Prof. P J P Clarricoats	F W T Davenport	P C McNeill	Prof. H A Barker

Year	*Electronics*	*Power*	*Science, Education & Technology*	*Computing & Control*	*Management & Design*
1979	C P Sandbank	Prof. B M Bird	Prof. J H Calderwood	P H Hammond	
1980	F H Steele	D A Jones	R C Hills	R W Sutton	D M Leakey
1981	Prof. D E N Davies	P C Hoare	K F Raby	M W Sage	T B McCrirrick
1982	B W Manley	G R C McDowell	C W Davidson	Prof. H A Prime	H Tomlinson
1983	C A P Foxell	J D McColl	D T Swift-Hook	M H Westbrook	R N G Burbridge
1984	A W Rudge	B S Townsend	Prof. E M Freeman	M G Shortland	Prof. L Finkelstein
1985	Prof. J H Collins	Prof. P J Lawrenson	Prof. R W Burns	R J Scott-Kerr	D H O Allen

Appendix 8

Local Centres and Overseas Activities

Development of Centres and Sub-Centres

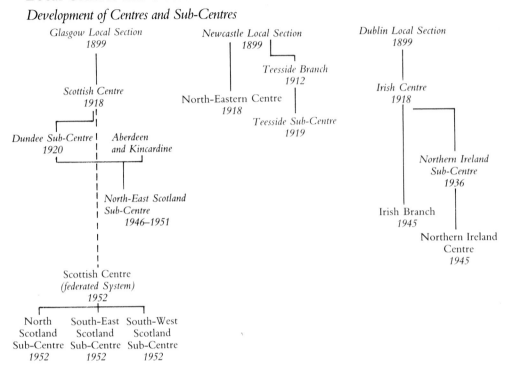

Centres which still exist are marked thus: Scottish Centre

(cont.)

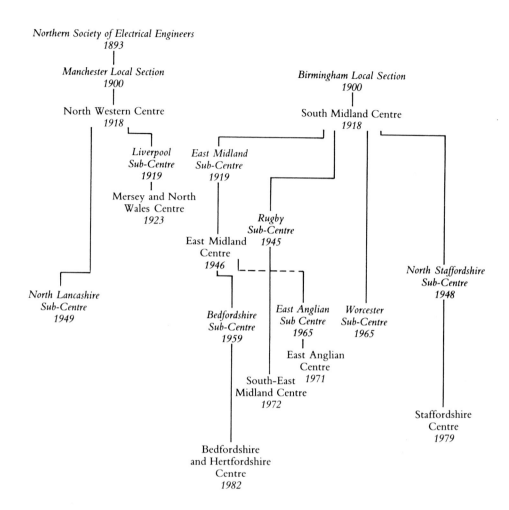

Development of Centres and Sub-Centres (cont.)

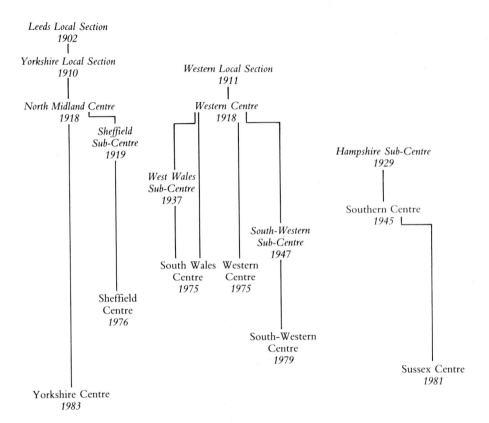

Leeds Local Section
1902

Yorkshire Local Section
1910

North Midland Centre
1918

Sheffield
Sub-Centre
1919

Western Local Section
1911

Western Centre
1918

West Wales
Sub-Centre
1937

Hampshire Sub-Centre
1929

Southern Centre
1945

South-Western
Sub-Centre
1947

South Wales   Western
Centre   Centre
1975   1975

Sheffield
Centre
1976

South-Western
Centre
1979

Sussex Centre
1981

Yorkshire Centre
1983

South Eastern Centre   1982

Surrey Centre   1982

Thames Valley Centre   1982

Development of Centres and Sub-Centres

The Centres 1984

Scottish Centres
1   N Scotland Sub-Centre
2   S W Scotland Sub-Centre
3   S E Scotland Sub-Centre

N Eastern Centre
4   N Eastern
5   Teesside Sub-Centre

N Western Centre
6   N Lancashire Sub-Centre
7   N Western

8   Yorkshire Centre
9   Sheffield Centre
10 E Midlands Centre
11 Staffordshire Centre
12 Mersey & N Wales Centre

E Anglian Centre
13 Norwich Area
14 Cambridge Area
15 Ipswich Area

S E Midland Centre
16 Rugby Area
17 Coventry Area

S Midland Centre
18 S Midland
19 Worcester Sub-Centre

S Wales Centre
20 E Wales Area
21 W Wales Area

Western Centre
22 Gloucester &
    Cheltenham Area
23 Bristol Area
24 Bath &
    Chippenham Area
25 Swindon Area

Thames Valley Centre
26 Oxford Area
27 S Bucks Area
28 Reading Area

Beds & Herts Centre
29 Beds Area
30 Herts Area

S East Centre
31 Essex Area
32 London Area
33 Kent Area

34 Surrey Centre
35 Sussex Centre

Southern Centre
36 Solent Area
37 Wessex Area

38 S Western Centre
39 N Ireland Centre

Overseas Activities

During the history of the Institution there have been centres of Institution activity in:

Aden	Ireland
Argentina	Israel
Australia	Jamaica
Bahamas	Malawi
Barbados	Malaya
Bermuda	Malta
Brazil	Middle East
British Guiana	New Zealand
Canada	Pakistan
Channel Islands	Singapore
China	South Africa
Cyprus	Sri Lanka
East Africa	Thailand
Ghana	Trinidad and Tobago
Gibraltar	United States of America
Hong Kong	West Africa
India	

The exact form has varied between Overseas Centre, Overseas Branch, Overseas Committee, and Joint Group or Professional Group with other Institutions.

In certain of the above countries there have also been Local Honorary Secretaries abroad, later known as Overseas Representatives of the Council, and similar appointments have been held at various periods in:

Burma	Norway
France	Palestine
Holland	Rhodesia
Italy	Spain
Japan	Switzerland
Near East	Zambia
Nigeria	Zimbabwe

A special class of Foreign Members existed from the start of the STE in 1871 until 1912.

Appendix 9

List of Sources

Unpublished Sources

I Sources at the IEE

Council Minutes (CM), 1871–1922: Old Series vols 1–12
Council Minutes (CM), and Documents 1922 onwards: New Series vols 1–31
Minutes of Ordinary (OGM), Annual (AGM) and Extraordinary General Meetings, 1872–1954: vols 1–9
Finance Committee Minutes, 1875 onwards
Occasional Committee Minutes (OCM), 1879–1942: 13 vols
Committee Minutes and Documents 1920 onwards, including General Purposes Committee (GPCM), General Purposes and Finance Committee (GPFM): vols 1–56
IEE Archives material, particularly
       Special collections, Mss 5, 42, 66 and 76
       OFS file 3785
       Files I/6.2 Early Activities
              I/6.5 Early Correspondence, 1877–1904
              II/1.1.1 Secretary's files

II Other sources

Science Museum, Crompton Historical Collection

III List of persons interviewed

Sir Harold Bishop, CBE	Prof. P A Lindsay
Mrs W K Brasher	Mr G S C Lucas, OBE
Prof. John Brown, CBE	Mr John Lyons
Sir Robert Clayton, CBE	Mr J H H Merriman, CB
Sir Monty Finniston, FRS	Sir Albert Mumford, KBE
Mr R H Franklin	Sir Charles Oatley, FRS
Dr G F Gainsborough, CBE	Mr Jervis Smith
Mr S E Goodall, CBE	Major P A Worsnop

Published Sources

I Publications of the STE, STEE and IEE

Journal of The Society of Telegraph Engineers (J.STE), 1872–1880
Journal of The Society of Telegraph Engineers and Electricians (J.STEE), 1881–1888
Journal of The Institution of Electrical Engineers (J.IEE), 1889–1948
Proceedings of The Institution of Electrical Engineers (Proc.IEE), 1949 onwards
Journal of The Institution of Electrical Engineers (Journal IEE), 1949–1954
Journal of The Institution of Electrical Engineers (New Series) *J.IEE (n.s.)*, 1955–1963
Electronics & Power (E&P), 1964 onwards
IEE News, 1964 onwards (incorporated in *Electronics & Power*, 1973–1975)
Memorandum and Articles of Association, 1892 and 1899
Royal Charter, 1921
Rollo Appleyard: *The History of The Institution of Electrical Engineers (1871–1931)* (IEE 1939)
Lawrence H A Carr: *The History of the North Western Centre of the IEE* (IEE, 1950)
M G Say: *Electrical and Electronic Engineering, as Professional Careers* (IEE Careers Booklet) (IEE, 1965)
IEE Centenary Lectures 1871–1971 (IEE, 1971)
Qualifying as a Chartered Engineer: The Merriman Report (IEE, 1978)

II Parliamentary Papers

Matthew Arnold, 'Report on Secondary Education' in Schools Inquiry Commission – *General Reports of Assistant Commissioners*, Vol 4 (HMSO, 1868)
Report of the Select Committee on Lighting by Electricity, 1879
Report of the Departmental Committee appointed by the Board of Trade to consider the Position of the Electrical Trades after the War. Cmd, 9072/1918, BPP (1918) Vol.13
Interim Report on Electric Power Supply in Great Britain, Cmd 8880/1917, BPP (1917–1918) Vol.18
Report of the Committee appointed by the Board of Trade to consider the Question of Electric Power Supply. Cmd. 9602/1918, BPP (1918) Vol.8
Report of the Committee on Higher Education under the Chairmanship of Lord Robbins, 1961–1936. Cmd. 2154/1963 (HM Stationery Office, 1963)
Engineering our Future, Report of the Committee of Inquiry into the Engineering Profession. Cmd. 7794/1980 (HM Stationery Office, 1980)

III Published Works Cited in the Text

E C Baker: *Sir William Preece FRS, Victorian Engineer Extraordinary* (Hutchinson, 1976)
Bernard H Becker: *Scientific London* (King, 1874)
Brian Bowers: *A History of Electric Light and Power* (Peter Peregrinus, 1982)
Asa Briggs: *The Birth of Broadcasting* (Oxford University Press, 1961)
Charles Bright: *The Life Story of Sir Charles Tilston Bright, Civil Engineer* (Constable, 1908)
British Almanac and Companion (Knight, 1843), (Stationers' Co. 1871, 1872, 1894)
The British Economy – Key Statistics 1900–1966, published for the London and Cambridge Economic Service by Times Newspapers Ltd.

W S Churchill: *The World Crisis 1911–1918*, (Odhams, 1938, new edn.) 2 vols

R E Crompton: *Reminiscences* (Constable, 1928)

T L Dennis (Ed): *Engineering Societies in the Life of a Country* (Institution of Civil Engineers, 1968)

Dictionary of National Biography and Supplements (DNB) (Oxford University Press)

P Dunsheath: *A History of Electrical Engineering* (Faber & Faber, 1962)

T H S Escott: *England: its People, Policy and Pursuits* (Chapman & Hall, 1885 revised edn.)

Bernard S Finn: *Submarine Telegraphy – the Grand Victorian Technology* (HM Stationery Office, 1973)

A Rupert Hall: *Science for Industry* (Imperial College, London 1982)

L Hannah: *Electricity Before Nationalisation* (Macmillan, 1979)

L Hannah: *Engineers, Managers and Politicians* (Macmillan, 1982)

L Hannah: *Entrepreneurs and the Social Sciences* (London School of Economics, 1983)

Robert Jones and Oliver Marriott: *Anatomy of a Merger* (Cape, 1970)

Peter Mathias: *The First Industrial Nation* (Methuen, 1983 2nd edn.)

W N Medlicott: *Contemporary England 1914–1964* (Longman, 1967)

Geoffrey Millerson: *The Qualifying Associations* (Routledge & Kegan Paul, 1964)

Jack Morrell and Arnold Thackray: *Gentlemen of Science* (Oxford University Press (Clarendon), 1981) and (Royal Historical Society, University College, London, 1984)

H Osborne O'Hagan: *Leaves from my Life* Vol.1 (Bodley Head, 1929)

Alexander Pope: *An Essay on Man*, 1744

Peter Pagnamenta and Richard Overy: *All our working Lives* (BBC, 1984)

Henry Pelling: *A History of British Trade Unionism* (Macmillan, 1972, 2nd edn.)

W J Reader: *Professional Men* (Weidenfeld & Nicolson, 1966)

W J Reader: *A House in the City* (Batsford, 1979)

W J Reader: *Imperial Chemical Industries, a History* (Oxford University Press) Vol.1, 1970; Vol.2, 1975

The Record of the Royal Society of London for the Promotion of Natural Knowledge (printed for the Royal Society, 1940)

Sir John Rennie: *Autobiography of Sir John Rennie FRS* (Spon, 1875)

H W Richardson: *Economic Recovery in Britain 1932–1939* (Weidenfeld & Nicolson, 1967)

L T C Rolt: *The Mechanicals* (David & Charles, 1967)

J D Scott: *Siemens Brothers 1858–1958* (Weidenfeld & Nicolson, 1958)

J R Seeley: *The Expansion of England. Two Courses of Lectures* (Macmillan, 1909)

Robert Stewart (Ed): *A Dictionary of Political Quotations* (Europa Publications, 1984)

F M L Thompson: *The Chartered Surveyors: The Growth of a Profession* (Routledge & Kegan Paul, 1968)

H Byerley Thomson: *The Choice of a Profession* (Chapman & Hall, 1857)

D G Tucker: *Gisbert Kapp 1852–1922* (University of Birmingham Press, 1973)

A Twentieth Century Professional Institution: Story of the IERE since 1925 (IERE, 1960)

Paul Vaughan: *Doctors' Commons* (Heinemann, 1959)

Who Was Who (A & C Black)

Martin Wiener: *English Culture and the Decline of the Industrial Spirit, 1850–1980* (Cambridge University Press, 1981)

Trevor I Williams (Ed.): *A Biographical Dictionary of Scientists* (A & C Black, 1974, 2nd edn.)

IV Periodicals Cited in the Text

Control
Daily Chronicle
Economic History Review
Electrical Review
Electrical Times
The Electrician
The Engineer
Engineering
Fortnightly Review
Journal of the Institute of Wireless Technology, (J.Inst. W. Tel.)
The Times Engineering Supplement
The Times Law Reports

Index